DATE			
DEC 18 1984			
DEC 14 1987			
		*	

MENTAL RETARDATION

MENTAL RETARDATION

REHABILITATION AND COUNSELING

By

PHILIP L. BROWNING, Ph.D.

University of Oregon
Eugene, Oregon

With a Foreword by

Rick Heber, Ph.D.

University of Wisconsin
Madison, Wisconsin

CHARLES C THOMAS · PUBLISHER
Springfield · Illinois · USA

Published and Distributed Throughout the World by
CHARLES C THOMAS • PUBLISHER
Bannerstone House
301-327 East Lawrence Avenue, Springfield, Illinois, U.S.A.

© *1974, by* CHARLES C THOMAS • PUBLISHER
ISBN 0-398-03006-5
Library of Congress Catalog Card Number: 73-14979

*With THOMAS BOOKS careful attention is given to all details of
manufacturing and design. It is the Publisher's desire to present books that are
satisfactory as to their physical qualities and artistic possibilities and
appropriate for their particular use. THOMAS BOOKS will be true to those
laws of quality that assure a good name and good will.*

Printed in the United States of America
C-1

Library of Congress Cataloging in Publication Data

Browning, Philip L.
    Mental retardation; rehabilitation and counseling.

    Bibliography: p.
    1. Mentally handicapped—Rehabilitation—Addresses,
essays, lectures. 2. Mentally handicapped—Addresses,
essays, lectures, 3. Rehabilitation counseling—
Addresses, essays, lectures. I. Title. [DNLM:
1. Counseling. 2. Mental retardation—Rehabilitation.
WM300 B885m 1974]
HV3005.B73   362.3   73-14979
ISBN 0-398-03006-5

PRINCIPAL CONTRIBUTORS

GEORGE E. AYERS, Ed.D.

Vice President
Minnesota Metropolitan State College
Former Professor and Director
Rehabilitation Counselor Education Training Program
Mankato State College
Mankato, Minnesota

PHILIP L. BROWNING, Ph.D.

Associate Director
Rehabilitation Research and Training Center in Mental Retardation
Associate Professor
Departments of Special Education and Counseling Psychology
University of Oregon
Eugene, Oregon

ALFRED J. BUTLER, Ph.D.

Professor
Rehabilitation Counselor Education Training Program
Department of Studies in Behavioral Disabilities
University of Wisconsin
Madison, Wisconsin

JAMES E. CROSSON, Ed.D.

Director
Regional Resource Center, Center on Human Development
Associate Professor
Department of Special Education
University of Oregon
Former Director of Research
Rehabilitation Research and Training Center in Mental Retardation
University of Oregon
Eugene, Oregon

v

R. WILLIAM ENGLISH, Ph.D.

Associate Professor
Rehabilitation Counselor Education Training Program
Division of Special Education and Rehabilitation
Syracuse University
Syracuse, New York

PATRICK J. FLANIGAN, Ph.D.

Associate Director
Rehabilitation Research and Training Center in Mental Retardation
Professor, Department of Studies in Behavioral Disabilities
University of Wisconsin
Madison, Wisconsin

GILBERT FOSS, M.A.

Doctoral Fellow
Rehabilitation Research and Training Center in Mental Retardation
University of Oregon
Former Rehabilitation Counselor
Oregon Division of Vocational Rehabilitation

WILLIAM I. GARDNER, Ph.D.

Associate Director of Research
Rehabilitation Research and Training Center in Mental Retardation
Professor, Department of Studies in Behavioral Disabilities
University of Wisconsin
Madison, Wisconsin

ANDREW S. HALPERN, Ph.D.

Director
Rehabilitation Research and Training Center in Mental Retardation
Associate Professor
Department of Special Education
University of Oregon
Eugene, Oregon

RICK F. HEBER, Ph.D.

Director
Rehabilitation Research and Training Center in Mental Retardation
Director
Waisman Center on Mental Retardation and Human Development
Professor
Department of Studies in Behavioral Disabilities
University of Wisconsin
Madison, Wisconsin

HERBERT J. PREHM, Ph.D.

Professor and Chairman
Department of Special Education
University of Oregon
Former Director
Rehabilitation Research and Training Center in Mental Retardation
University of Oregon
Eugene, Oregon

JOHN M. STAMM, Ph.D.

Assistant Professor
Department of Special Education
University of Oregon
Former staff member
Rehabilitation Research and Training Center in Mental Retardation
University of Oregon
Eugene, Oregon

OWEN R. WHITE, Ph.D.

Research Director
Regional Resource Center
Center on Human Development
University of Oregon
Former staff member
Rehabilitation Research and Training Center in Mental Retardation
University of Oregon
Eugene, Oregon

FOREWORD

THIS MANUSCRIPT presents in a very clear positive fashion a compilation of knowledge obtained from both research and training endeavors which were undertaken by professional individuals representing a number of scientific disciplines, i.e., counseling, rehabilitation, research, etc., the major outcomes of which have as their primary focus the contribution of knowledge and information relating to a better understanding of the complex phenomenon of mental retardation.

The manuscript for this publication was developed through the Rehabilitation Research and Training Center in Mental Retardation which is one of the three categorically focused centers of this type in the country. The interdisciplinary nature of these centers provides a unique opportunity for the development of manuscripts such as, "Mental Retardation: Rehabilitation and Counseling," edited by Dr. Philip L. Browning. It represents another attempt of the Research and Training Centers' programs which are coordinated at the Federal level by Dr. Joseph Fenton, Chief, Special Centers, Department of Health, Education and Welfare, as well as the regional and state rehabilitation offices to bring about the integration and organization of new knowledge which has already been acquired from the field of mental retardation and related fields. Of paramount importance in this total thrust is the dissemination of this new knowledge in a practical and understandable manner to all professional practitioners who deal with the developmental rehabilitation process. This manuscript bridges the previously well-documented gap between the development of and dissemination of knowledge where it has the most value; that is, in the programs which serve the retarded and their families.

In the field of rehabilitation it has been rare that a group of scientists representing primarily the behavioral or programmatic research thrusts has been afforded the opportunity to bring the work of divergent fields into focus in a single volume. This extraordinary manuscript promises to contribute substantially to the advancement of our knowledge of the developmental rehabilitation process with the mentally retarded. It should serve as a stimulus to individuals involved in training of professionals to increase their capabilities to provide more adequate programs and services for the mentally retarded and their families. It should also serve to augment and enrich programs currently in operation whose major purpose is to assist the mentally retarded in making adequate vocational and/or social adjustments.

As in many projects of this nature, a number of indirect benefits will accrue which cannot be predicted at this time and will not necessarily be measurable. Of primary importance in this regard may be the dissemination of new specialized knowledge such as that represented in this manuscript through its distribution to libraries and other rehabilitation related programs which provide these types of services. It should also serve to stimulate discussion of tools and techniques as reflected in the manuscript in both a formal and informal training environment. Ideally it should become an invaluable aid to the practicing professional in these areas.

In the past decade there has been a reawakening of society's conscience concerning mental retardation. During this period, both research and training endeavors have increased significantly. Manuscripts such as this reflect the final staging in this process. That is, the transference of necessarily acquired information into practical, usable programmatic skills and techniques. This manuscript provides those of us who have had the privilege of working in these areas with an opportunity to assess and reflect upon the progress made in the field of mental retardation with which we as a society are confronted.

Rick Heber, Ph.D., Director
Rehabilitation Research and Training
    Center in Mental Retardation
Harry A. Waisman Center on Mental
    Retardation and Human Development
University of Wisconsin, Madison, Wisconsin

PREFACE

THIS BOOK is an attempt to update and upgrade the literature in the areas of rehabilitation and counseling as they relate to the field of mental retardation. In order to facilitate this effort, several guidelines were closely followed during the preparation of the manuscript. The criterion of *comprehensiveness* was utilized with respect to both breadth and depth. The chosen topics were wide-ranged in scope and viewed as fairly representative of major content areas. Some chapters were written primarily for the practitioner or researcher whereas others were designed for both audiences. In addition, the material contained within was intended to serve as a training resource for professional personnel in a field setting as well as undergraduate and graduate students in a university.

As for comprehensiveness in depth, an effort was made to gather a sufficient body of knowledge with the objective of integrating and synthesizing previously published literature related to mental retardation and respective topics in the areas of rehabilitation and counseling. A number of chapters could be characterized as "critical" reviews which summarize past and current thoughts and findings. Finally, special attention was given to documentation in order that the manuscript would serve as an extensive resource handbook.

The second criterion was *newness*. Even though none of the chapters cover totally new and novel material related to these areas, a definite attempt was made to give emphasis and visibility to areas which the editor felt were especially important, yet had received only scant attention in prior literature.

This product represents the diligent effort of many persons. First, however, it should be recognized that the book would not have occurred without the Division of Rehabilitation Research and Training Centers in the Social and Rehabilitation Service branch of the U. S. Department of Health, Education, and Welfare. This is best evidenced by the fact that the major portion of the manuscript reflects the professional efforts of staff affiliated with the Universities of Oregon and Wisconsin Rehabilitation Research and Training Centers in Mental Retardation.

Appreciation is also extended to the contributors of the chapters and the individuals responsible for the preparation of the manuscript: the typist, Anita Chavan, whose excellence makes the work enjoyable; Janet Clark and Jennifer Lovejoy, assistant editors, whose skills in writing add to the pleasure of reading; Arden Munkres, the communications designer, whose expertise is pictorially visible; and Sharon Babic and Kathy Rybloom, the secretaries, whose laborious task of proofreading was most needed and welcomed.

PHILIP L. BROWNING

ACKNOWLEDGMENTS

for professional *awakening*
  Robert P. Anderson, Ph.D.

for professional *direction*
  Alfred J. Butler, Ph.D.

for professional *incentive*
  Patrick J. Flanigan, Ph.D.

for professional *opportunity*
  Herbert J. Prehm, Ph.D.

CONTENTS

xv

MENTAL RETARDATION

MENTAL RETARDATION:
A FRAME OF REFERENCE

How we perceive or how we conceptualize the field of mental retardation has a significant bearing upon our behavior, whether we happen to be a physician, teacher, psychologist, social worker, researcher [rehabilitationist], or parent. Perceptions of mental retardation range from the shadows of despair to the sunlight of unwarranted optimism. Our goal should be to strive to perceive mental retardation realistically in the light of available scientific knowledge.

Gardner, W. I., and Nisonger, H. W.: A manual on program development in mental retardation. *American Journal of Mental Deficiency*. (Monograph Supplement), January, 1962, p. 30.

OVERVIEW

THIS BOOK IS ABOUT a group of persons commonly thought of as the "less intelligent" and often referred to by such names as idiot, feebleminded, mentally deficient, mentally retarded and slow learner. In a society like ours, which places a high premium on man's cognitive and intellectual domain, these words have repeatedly rung a sharp note of public rejection. Viewed by many as "deviants," they have been considered often unfit to join our educated and cultured community of thinkers and achievers. This disparity has resulted in their being enduring victims of prejudice, discrimination and neglect.

Only within recent years have these de-humanizing effects of stigmatization toward the retarded been seriously recognized and challenged. Impetus was especially mounted through the leadership of John F. Kennedy and his task force on mental retardation. This was a historical period in that a comprehensive nationwide attack upon the problem was set in motion. One visible impact has been a proliferation of parental, civil, legal, professional, and governmental advocates. These combined forces have helped lead to an era of "normalization," a time in which the major aim is for the retarded to enter the mainstream of society as much as possible.

Also set in motion during this period was a surge of research activities from the medical-biological and behavioral-social sciences. In spite of their significant advances in better understanding the condition of mental retardation, there continue to exist, in the minds of many, perceptions like "incurable," "psychologically unstable," "criminally prone," "sexually dangerous," "incapacitated." In addition, these and similar characteristics are often seen as merely "symptoms" of a "disease" called mental retardation. Such misconceptions, which are still prevalent in both the lay and professional community, are one of the main obstacles to be overcome if we are to truly achieve the goal of normalization with this group.

The chapters in this section are intended to lessen these misunderstandings among persons within the rehabilitation and counseling profession. This compilation of up-dated knowledge about what mental retardation is also lays the foundation for the remainder of the book. In essence, it serves as a "framework" for the incorporation of the rehabilitation and counseling materials in the second and third sections.

Chapter 1 is based on the premise that mental retardation is not a disease but a concept. A concept is simply an idea contrived by man and given verbal expression through labels and terms, e.g. mental retardation. Thus, there have been many and varying "definitions" offered in an attempt to understand this condition, some of the more traditional ones discussed and critically compared in this chapter. Most attention is directed to the current and popularly accepted definition and classification system which is endorsed by the American Association on Mental Deficiency. One of its more important features pertains to the emphasis placed upon adaptive behavior. In addition to subnormal intelligence, a criterion long acknowledged and over-emphasized in this country, one must also demonstrate sufficient maladaptive behaviors before joining the group of persons labeled retarded. In short, *we* decide the membership requirements for this group. The distressing note is that most people, including professionals, have their own "private" definitions which determine, at least for them, who should wear the stigmatizing label.

One of the major advances to appear recently in the behavioral sciences is a technology of learning. This noninferential, functional and empirical approach to human behavior has had a significant influence in increasing our understanding of persons with "retarded" behavior. First, mental retardation has been associated historically with physical conditions, e.g. disease, brain damage, organic impairment, dysfunction of the central nervous system and genetic defect. The truth is that these medical considerations apply only to a small portion of this population, mainly those who are severely and profoundly impaired. Also, they are practically nonfunctional in the amelioration of maladaptive behavior. The application of this behavioral technology affords us a method for achieving such goals, as well as representing a substantive base for shift toward a behavioral emphasis. Second, learning is central to the condition of retardation, and the demonstration of this new science is rapidly discarding the stereotypes of "incurable" and "unable." Retarded behavior *is* subject to change and significant learning *can* occur. Third, the technology is based upon the principle that behavior is a function of one's environment. This puts society clearly in the center of responsibility. Chapter 2 presents a behavioral perspective we must consider if our goal is to prevent, treat and habilitate persons with mental retardation.

Of course, the psycho-social nature and dynamics of persons with retardation seldom goes unnoticed when one attempts to describe, explain, and understand who they are. Unfortunately, like other disability groups, they have had a myriad of stereotypic personality profiles attached to them, e.g. poor self-concept, low frustration tolerance, rigidity, impulsivity, and perseveration. Chapter 3, a critical review of research on personality characteristics with the retarded, clearly refutes the position that they represent such "clinically" distinct types. Also presented is evidence to counter the too often held assumption of an unusually high incidence of emotional problems and psychopathology among this group.

Not many years ago mental retardation was a subject no one knew much about. However, recent interests have led the way to an accumulation of new knowledge, such as that exemplified in these three chapters. Realizing this to be a very limited version of what is now known, we have provided additional bibliographic resources for the convenience of the reader who is interested in further pursuing the area, i.e. twenty-five basic readings on mental retardation (Appendix A), and a description of eleven films on the subject (Appendix C).

Chapter 1

MENTAL RETARDATION: DEFINITION, CLASSIFICATION AND PREVALENCE

Herbert J. Prehm

IN ORDER TO PROVIDE A FRAME of reference for the remaining papers within this volume, this chapter briefly explores three aspects of mental retardation: (1) concepts basic to defining the retarded, including several basic definitions with emphasis on the one most currently accepted; (2) the classification of the retarded according to intellectual level, adaptive behavior, and etiology; and (3) data indicating the prevalence of retardation. Treatment of controversial issues associated with these topics is beyond the scope of this paper. For detailed explications of such issues, the reader is referred to other sources (e.g., Bartel and Guskin, 1971; Clausen, 1972; Jones, 1972; Mercer, 1972).

DEFINITION OF MENTAL RETARDATION

Definitions are theoretical, abstract attempts to identify the essence of whatever it is that one is speaking about. They attempt to reduce a complex phenomenon to the smallest number of attributes that are both necessary and sufficient to make that phenomenon whatever it is that it is. Definitions are also attempts to provide precision in terminology so that communication is facilitated. Reducing the phenomenon of mental retardation to its identifying components has been no easy task. There are many definitions of mental retardation, and in addition to the "public" definitions, most persons have their own "private" ones as well.

Conceptual Base for Defining the Retarded

Historically, five concepts have been used in most definitions of mental retardation, three major and two minor. Almost all

8

definitions concerning this disability group have stressed one or more of these concepts.

General agreement exists about the first of the major concepts: Mental retardation is a condition that *originates during the developmental period.* Although a precise age for the termination of the developmental period cannot be determined, most workers in the area of mental retardation use the age of eighteen as their cut off. Mental retardation, then, is usually considered to be a condition that begins prior to an individual's eighteenth birthday.

The second major concept used to define this condition is the criterion of *mental subnormality.* This concept has been used primarily by American workers in mental retardation. It specifies that an intelligence quotient that is below a given IQ score—usually seventy or seventy-five—is indicative of mental retardation. Historically, this concept has been frequently used as the sole defining characteristic of mental retardation.

When used alone, the concept of mental subnormality is subject to criticism. One problem in using IQ as the sole indicator of mental retardation is that some persons with IQ's below seventy-five function within the limits of normal behavior while other persons with IQ's above the cut off are unable to function normally within a group.

A second problem is that the IQ does not have exactly the same meaning from one test to another. A large number of tests are used to measure intelligence. Because of differences in both standardization samples and the skills or behaviors evaluated, most tests of intelligence do not yield comparable scores. For example, Test A may have a standard deviation (a statistical measure of the dispersion of a set of scores around their average) of thirty points; Test B, twenty points; Test C, sixteen points; and Test D, fifteen points. A child who obtains a score exactly one standard deviation below the mean on each test would have reported IQ scores of seventy, eighty, eighty-four, and eighty-five. This variation in score makes the IQ alone meaningless unless reference is made to both the specific test used and the reference population upon which the test was standardized.

Because of these problems, the IQ alone is no longer considered to be definitive of mental retardation.

The third criterion which has been used to define the mentally retarded is *social inadequacy*. This criterion reflects European usage and suggests that a person who is unable to meet the demands of society is mentally retarded. By itself, this criterion provides an inadequate basis for defining mental retardation. As indicated earlier, some persons, with low IQ's, function adequately while other persons, with high IQ's, are not able to function adequately within society. A second problem with social inadequacy as a concept is that the criterion of socially inadequate behavior varies from culture to culture and from setting to setting within a culture. An individual may be able to cope with the natural and social demands of a rural environment but when placed in an urban environment he may not be able to cope at all. Would this person, then, be retarded in one setting and normal in another? The concept of social inadequacy presents the worker in mental retardation with problems because the definition of social inadequacy is nebulous.

The fourth concept that has been used to define mental retardation is the hypothesis that it has an *organic cause*. This concept, although important historically, can be considered minor. Some professionals in the area maintain the organic cause hypothesis because they believe there is some central nervous system (CNS) pathology present in all cases of mental retardation. Other professionals take the position that this concept cannot be considered to be definitive because it is impossible to demonstrate CNS pathology in 75 to 80 percent of all the mentally retarded. Whatever the reason, the inability to demonstrate CNS pathology argues strongly against including this concept as a major criterion until refined observations can be made. A further argument against including organic cause as a major definitional concept is provided by Zigler's (1967) division of the population of retarded into the two groups, organic and non-organic.

The fifth criterion—*incurability*—is conceptually related to the fourth. It has been assumed that CNS tissue cannot be regenerated once it is destroyed. Therefore, if all retardation has an organic cause, it must be incurable. This concept stresses that once a person is identified as retarded, he is always retarded. This concept is threatened both by failure to demonstrate CNS pathology in most cases of retardation and by the fact that an individual's status may change over a long time period. A child may be diagnosed as mentally retarded at, for example, age ten. He may have an IQ of seventy, be a "trouble maker" in school, and be functioning academically at the first grade level. Fifteen years later he may be married, attending church, working steadily, buying a modest home, keeping out of trouble with the law and, in general, being a "good" citizen. The status of many retarded individuals does change, as described, over long spans of time. What is important for any individual is how he is functioning at a given point in time. Because of these changes, the concept of incurability is both questionable and superfluous.

Common Definitions

Many attempts to define the mentally retarded have been made. Most definitions are based on one of the major concepts discussed above. Included among the more common definitions are those of

Edgar A. Doll (1941)

The mentally deficient person is (1) socially incompetent, that is, socially inadequate and occupationally incompetent and unable to manage his own affairs; (2) mentally subnormal; (3) retarded intellectually from birth or early age; (4) retarded at maturity; (5) due to heredity or disease, and (6) essentially incurable (p. 214).

Seymour B. Sarason (1965)

1. Mental retardation refers to individuals who, for temporary or long standing reasons, function intellectually below the average of their peer groups but whose social adequacy is not in question or, if it is in question, there is the likelihood that the individual can learn to function independently and adequately in the community.

2. Mental deficiency refers to individuals who are socially inadequate as a result of an intellectual defect which is a reflection of an impairment of the CNS which is essentially incurable (pp. 440-442).

A. F. Tredgold (1952)

Mental defectiveness means a condition of arrested or incomplete development of mind existing before the age of eighteen years, whether arising from inherent causes or induced by disease or injury (p. 6).

The American Association on Mental Deficiency

Mental retardation refers to subaverage intellectual functioning which originates during the developmental period, and is associated with impairment in adaptive behavior (1961, p. 3).

Mental retardation refers to significantly subaverage general intellectual functioning existing concurrently with deficits in adaptive behavior, and manifested during the developmental period (1973, p. 11).

These definitions are examples of the major attempts to concisely define the term "mental retardation." Each stresses one or more of the concepts previously discussed. Table 1-I illustrates the position each definition takes on each of the concepts as well as the differences between definitions. The 1973 AAMD definition receives an equivocal rating on organic cause because "for medical purposes, mental retardation is regarded as a manifestation of some underlying disease process or medical condition" (Grossman, 1973, p. 8).

TABLE 1-I

THE POSITION OF MAJOR DEFINITIONS WITH REGARD TO
CONCEPTS TRADITIONALLY USED IN DEFINITIONS OF
MENTAL RETARDATION

Criterion	Doll	Sarason 1	Sarason 2	Tredgold	AAMD 1961	AAMD 1973
Onset prior to age 18	Yes	Yes	Yes	Yes	Yes	Yes
Intellectual subnormality	Yes	Yes	Yes	No	Yes	Yes
Social inadequacy	Yes	No	Yes	Yes	Yes	Yes
Organic cause	Yes	No	Yes	No	No	Equivocal
Incurable	Yes	No	Yes	Yes	No	No

The AAMD Definition

Both the original and most recent definitions proposed by the American Association on Mental Deficiency (AAMD) were formulated after a thorough study of the current (then) status of definitions of retardation. This AAMD approach stresses that mental retardation is a complex condition involving both intellectual subnormality and impairment in adaptive behavior. Unless both conditions—subaverage intellectual functioning and impaired adaptive behavior—are present, the person cannot be labeled mentally retarded. Thus, if a person has a low IQ and is socially adequate he is not, by definition, mentally retarded. Neither can he be so labeled if he is socially inadequate and has a high IQ.

The term "adaptive behavior" refers to a person's ability to meet those standards of "social responsibility" and "personal independence" appropriate for his "age and cultural group" (Grossman, 1973, p. 11). This term is currently divided into seven subareas. Deficits in four of the subareas (sensory motor skills development, communication skills, self-help skills, socialization) are observed mainly in infancy and early childhood. Deficits in the remaining three areas (application of eight basic academic skills in daily life activities, application of appropriate reasoning and judgment in mastery of the environment, and social skills) are observed mainly during childhood and early adolescence. It is this impairment in adaptive behavior that calls attention to an individual. If, after thorough diagnosis, it turns out that the impairment in adaptive behavior is associated with subnormal intelligence, then the person is labeled "mentally retarded."

The AAMD requirement that a person demonstrate both low intelligence and impaired adaptive behavior suggests that at least mild retardation is "curable." This does not mean that we can raise the retarded person's IQ, nor that a permanent change in status can occur, but it does mean that we can remove the label "retarded" from a person by bringing his adaptive behavior within the limits of normalcy. Rehabilitation, special education, and the other helping professions are in the business of changing adaptive behavior. If we do a good job, then we can change a person's status under the terms of the definition.

CLASSIFICATION OF MENTAL RETARDATION

Many systems for classifying the mentally retarded have been proposed. The *legal-administrative* classification system is one that is found in the laws of most states. This system regulates who is eligible for services for the mentally retarded. An *educational* classification system divides the retarded into three groups: The educable, the trainable, and the custodial (or totally dependent). A familiar system is the *psychiatric* classification system, which divides the retarded into groups called morons, imbeciles, and idiots. Today, these terms are rarely used at all.

The most extensive and elaborate system for classifying this group has been developed by the AAMD. This system is, primarily, a scientific one, based on the individual's current level of functioning and emphasizes that classification is an on-going, continual process. The AAMD classifies the retarded according to (1) intelligence, (2) adaptive behavior, and (3) etiology.

Classification According to Intellectual Level

The 1961 AAMD system divided the population of retarded into five levels of retardation on the dimension of intelligence. The current system eliminates borderline retardation and uses only four levels of retardation. Instead of using IQ scores, the AAMD uses standard deviation units as the basis for classification. This has the advantage of increasing the comparability of IQ scores obtained from different tests. Table 1-II presents the levels of retardation used by the AAMD. Also included in the table are the IQ ranges from the Stanford-Binet Test of Intelligence and the Wechsler Intelligence Scale for Children.

Classification According to Adaptive Behavior

Adaptive behavior, like intelligence, is classified according to levels of impairment. Because the instruments used to measure adaptive behavior (e.g. Vineland Social Maturity Scale, Doll, 1936; Adaptive Behavior Scales, Nihira, Fosters, Shedhaas, and Leland, 1969) are less precise than most individual intelligence tests, AAMD recommends against using a score derived from these tests to specify a person's adaptive behavior level. The

TABLE 1-II

CLASSIFICATION OF MENTAL RETARDATION
ACCORDING TO LEVEL OF INTELLECTUAL FUNCTIONING

1961[a] Standard Deviation Units	Level	Stanford-Binet	Wechsler Scales	1973[b] Level	1973[b] Standard Deviation Units
-1.01 to -2.00	Borderline retardation	83-69	84-70		
-2.01 to -3.00	Mild retardation	68-52	69-55	Mild	-2.01 to -3.00
-3.01 to -4.00	Moderate retardation	51-36	54-40	Moderate	-4.01 to -5.00
-4.01 to -5.00	Severe retardation	35-20	39-25[c]	Severe	-4.00 to -5.00
-5.01 +	Profound retardation	20-20	24[c]	Profound	-5.01 +

[a] Adapted from Heber, R.: A manual on terminology and classification in mental retardation. *American Journal of Mental Deficiency Monograph Supplement.* (Second Edition), April, 1961.
[b] Adapted from Grossman, H. J.: *Manual on Terminology and Classification in Mental Retardation.* Washington, D. C., American Association on Mental Deficiency/Special Publication Series No. 2, 1973.
[c] Extrapolated.

1973 manual provides general descriptions of the highest level "8 [score] performance routinely found for a particular dimension . . . for a given (adaptive behavior) level at a specified age" (Grossman, 1973, p. 23). Clinicians are required to compare samples of a person's behavior with the examples provided in the manual in order to make a judgment about that person's adaptive behavior level.

There is a positive relationship between adaptive behavior and intelligence. This relationship is depicted in Figure 1-1. As this figure shows, the higher the level of intelligence, the greater the number of persons within the population at that IQ level who

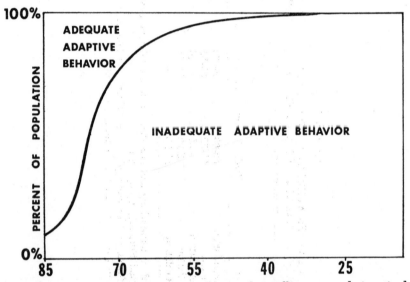

Figure 1-1. Relationship between measured intelligence and impaired adaptive behavior. From: Heber, R. F. (Ed.): *Special Problems in the Vocational Rehabilitation of the Mentally Retarded.* U. S. Department of Health, Education and Welfare, Rehabilitation Service Series No. 65-16, 1965, p. 13.

have adequate adaptive behavior. No percentage figures between zero and 100 percent are given because we do not know the exact percentage of persons with given IQ's who exhibit impaired or adequate adaptive behavior.

As can be seen from Figure 1-2, most of the population of the

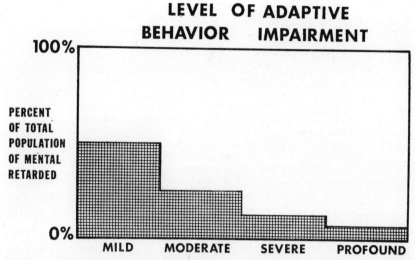

Figure 1-2. Proportion of total population of mentally retarded at each level of adaptive behavior. Adapted from: Heber, R. F. (Ed.): *Special Problems in the Vocational Rehabilitation of the Mentally Retarded*. U. S. Department of Health, Education and Welfare, Rehabilitation Service Series No. 65-16, 1965.

mentally retarded exhibit mild impairment in adaptive behavior. As in the last illustration, exact percentages are not given because they are not known.

Classification According to Etiology

The third dimension in which the retarded can be classified is one dealing with the cause of the retardation. The ten categories within which the many causes of mental retardation are organized are presented in Table 1-III. Within the first seven categories are those retarded most often termed "clinical types." Persons classified in these first seven categories frequently have IQ's below fifty-five. The 1973 AAMD manual also provides seven additional categories of medical information that can be used with the medical classification. Included in these supplementary categories are: genetic component, secondary cranial anomalies, impairment of special senses, disorders of perception and expres-

TABLE 1-III

CLASSIFICATION ACCORDING TO ETIOLOGY

Category Name
Mental Retardation Due to Infections and Intoxications
Mental Retardation Due to Trauma or Physical Agent
Mental Retardation Due to Metabolism or Nutrition
Mental Retardation Due to Gross Brain Disease (Postnatal)
Mental Retardation Due to Unknown Prenatal Influence
Mental Retardation Due to Chromosomal Abnormality
Mental Retardation Due to Gestational Disorders
Mental Retardation Following Psychiatric Disorder
Mental Retardation Due to Environmental Influences
Mental Retardation Due to Other Conditions

sion, convulsive disorders, psychiatric impairment, and motor dysfunction. Subdivision of these categories is used in conjunction with the medical causes to provide a more precise medical description of the retardates.

PREVALENCE

The most common figure used to specify the number of mentally retarded persons within a given population at a given point in time is 3 percent. However, this figure is based on expert opinion rather than hard data. The percentage of a given population identified as being mentally retarded is a function of (1) the criteria used to identify the retarded; (2) the socioeconomic level of the community; and (3) the age range sampled.

Of course, when a very broad definition (e.g. all children *suspected* of being mentally retarded) of retardation is used, the

TABLE 1-IV

ESTIMATED RATE PER 1000 SCHOOL-AGE CHILDREN

SES Level of Community	*Totally Dependent*	*Trainable*	*Educable*	*Slow Learner*
Low	1	4	50	300
Middle	1	4	25	170
High	1	4	10	50

Source: Kirk, S. A.: *Educating Exceptional Children,* Boston, Houghton-Mifflin Company, 1963, p. 92.

prevalence estimate is much higher than when a narrow one is used. Prevalence estimates also vary with the socioeconomic (SES) level of the community. Kirk (1962) has proposed the prevalence estimates presented in Table 1-IV. The table illustrates that the prevalence of trainable and totally dependent (organically impaired) does not vary as a function of SES, but the prevalence of borderline and mild levels of retardation does.

Table 1-V illustrates how prevalence varies as a function of age. As can be seen, the prevalence of mental retardation increases markedly during the school age period. This is probably due to (1) the fact that the limits of tolerance for developmental deviations is broader for both pre- and post-school age persons than it is for school age persons and (2) referral and diagnostic services are more readily available for the school age group.

TABLE 1-V

REPRESENTATIVE EPIDEMIOLOGICAL STUDIES

Age	England and Wales*	Baltimore†	Onondaga County‡
0-4	0.1	0.1	0.5
5-9	1.6	1.2	3.9
10-14	2.6	4.4	7.8
15-19	1.1	3.0	4.5
20-24	1.0	0.7	—

* Lewis, 1929.
† Lemkau, Tietze, & Cooper, 1942.
‡ 1953.

SUMMARY

Although there are many varying definitions of mental retardation, the AAMD has isolated subnormal intelligence and impaired adaptive behavior as the major conditions of retardation. The possibility of changing a retarded individual's status depends, in part, on the definition used, as does the percentage of retarded persons given for any population. The selection of the definition and classification system to be employed with the retarded is critical in that it influences our approach to their identification and treatment.

REFERENCES

Bartel, N. R., and Guskin, S. L.: A handicap as a social phenomenon. In Cruickshank, W. M. (Ed.): *Psychology of Exceptional Children and Youth.* Englewood Cliffs, N. J., Prentice Hall, 1972, pp. 75-114.

Clausen, J.: Quo Vadis, AAMD? *Journal of Special Education,* 6:51-60, 1972.

Doll, E. A.: *The Vineland Social Maturity Scale: Revised Condensed Manual of Directions.* Vineland, N. J., Training School, 1936.

Doll, E. A.: The essentials of an inclusive concept of mental deficiency. *American Journal of Mental Deficiency,* 46:214-219, 1941.

Grossman, H. J.: *Manual on Terminology and Classification in Mental Retardation.* Washington, D. C., American Association on Mental Deficiency—Special Publication Series No. 2, 1973.

Heber, R. F. (Ed.): *Special Problems in Vocational Rehabilitation of the Mentally Retarded.* U. S. Department of Health, Education and Welfare, Rehabilitation Service Series No. 65-16, 1965.

Jones, R. L.: Labels and stigma in special education. *Exceptional Children,* 38:553-564, 1972.

Kirk, S. A.: *Educating Exceptional Children.* Boston, Houghton Mifflin, 1962.

Lemkau, P.; Tietze, C.; and Cooper, M.: Mental hygiene problems in an urban district. *Mental Hygiene,* 25:624-646, 1941, 1942; BF, 110-119, 275-288.

Lewis, E. O.: *Report on an Investigation into the Incidence of Mental Deficiency in Six Areas,* 1925-1927. (Part IV of Report of the Mental Deficiency Committee, being a Joint Committee of the Board of Education and Board of Control.) London, H. M. Stationery Office, 1929.

Mercer, J. R.: The lethal label. *Psychology Today,* 6:44-47, 95-97, 1972.

New York State Department of Mental Hygiene, Mental Health Research Unit: A special census of suspected referred mental retardation, Onondaga County, New York. Int.: *Technical Report of the Mental Health Research Unit.* Syracuse, Syracuse University Press, 1955.

Nihira, K.; Foster, R.; Shellhaas, M.; and Leland, N.: *Adaptive Behavior Scales.* Washington, D. C., American Association on Mental Deficiency, 1969.

Sarason, S. B.: Mentally retarded and mentally defective children: Major psycho-social problems. In Cruickshank, W. (Ed.): *Psychology of Exceptional Children and Youth.* New York, Prentice Hall, 1955, pp. 438-474.

Tredgold, A. F.: *A Textbook on Mental Deficiency,* 8th ed. London, Bailliere, Lindal, and Cox, 1952.

Zigler, E.: Familial mental retardation: A continuing dilemma. *Science,* 155:292-298, 1967.

Chapter 2

MENTAL RETARDATION:
A BEHAVIORAL PERSPECTIVE

Owen R. White

Efforts to understand and treat the mentally retarded have been impaired by a plethora of models and labels all attempting to explain the same conditions. In order to review the behavioral alternative to these many and often unwieldly systems of definition-diagnosis and etiology-classification, the following will be presented: (1) the generalizable, logical implications of causation and classification with specific reference to mental retardation; (2) the basics of the behavioral system; and (3) selected interpretations of the development of retarded behavior from the standpoint of behavioral learning principles.

ETIOLOGICAL CLASSIFICATION

An etiological classification is one which assigns cause or origin. Knowledge of the cause or origin of mental retardation is only of use, however, if it (1) provides specific suggestion for effective remediation or treatment of the problem once it exists, (2) provides specific direction for effective prevention of the continued occurrence of the problem, or (3) provides specific direction for further research leading eventually to one of the above. Classification types *appearing* to meet one or more of these criteria are frequent. In order to more closely examine those appearances, a brief introduction into the logical foundations of causative statements is necessary.

Circumstances *A* are said to "cause" circumstances *B* if the occurrence of *A* in some way leads to the occurrence of *B*. However, such relationships are rarely perfect and in most cases *A* will not always be followed by *B*, nor will *B* always be preceded by *A*. Usually one or more qualifying conditions must be considered.

21

First, it may be that A will lead to B *if and only if* other variables do not intervene. For example, the statement, "rain always wets the ground if and only if the ground is not protected by a cover," does not deny that rain may cause the ground to be wet—rather, it specifies that whenever rain falls, we can be certain of the outcome only if we are aware of the other intervening variables and their effect.

Second, whereas A may lead to B, B may also result from a third variable C. Rain may cause the ground to be wet, but the ground may also become wet as a result of flooding, heavy dew, or artificial means, such as lawn watering.

Third, *both* A and B may be caused by still another variable. Knowledge that wet grounds follow or are caused by rain really does not aid us in averting wet ground or in correcting that condition once it occurs. However, knowledge that the probability of rain is governed by the amount of moisture in the air, the temperature, barometric pressure, proximity of large bodies of water, the prevailing winds, and the topography of the region in question (just to name a few of the variables) *does* begin to offer possibility of human intervention. In fact, many of those same variables which control the probability of rain, *also* control the probability of heavy dews and flooding, two other "causes" of wet ground.

Causation, then, is no simple matter. It is complicated and all too often elusive. What may appear logical may also lead to a "dead end" with no scientific usefulness. Great care must be exercised in the application or acceptance may govern the lives of many people who need a great deal more than a pat "reason" for their conditions. Therefore, each of the several forms of etiological classification which follow should be judged in the light of criteria presented above. Furthermore, no single classification is likely to exhaust all possible variables or conditions which may prevail in even the smallest segment of the retarded population.

Bio-Medical Etiological Classification

A bio-medical statement of causation, correctly phrased, might read: *One* of the causes of severe mental retardation is cretinism, which can result from faulty development of the thyroid gland, which can be due to an iodine deficiency in the mother during pregnancy, which can be caused by improper diet. The social scientist is likely to add that diet can be determined by the geographic region, which can be determined by level of income, which can be determined by family background, which can be determined by national origin. At each of these levels of "causation" there would be many other variables which, in the interest of brevity, have been omitted.

Such a statement of classification, delineated as it is, does meet the criteria of usefulness. It offers very specific suggestions for prevention and perhaps even for amelioration after the onset of the condition. The greater proportion of bio-medical classifications share this quality of usefulness. Unfortunately, only 20 to 25 percent of the mentally retarded population can be so precisely classified (Robinson and Robinson, 1965). Excluded from that count, of course, are those described as having "minimal brain dysfunction" or "undifferentiated minimal brain damage," classifications with little or no usefulness, despite their camouflage of neuro-medical phraseology. Perhaps some day the medical profession will complete its work in mental retardation and reduce our concern about it to that presently felt for such highly improbable diseases (in the U. S., anyway) as the Black Plague. However, until that time, there remains some 75 to 80 percent of the population of mentally retarded persons for which we must account. Also, a bio-medical classification, which may eventually lead to the prevention of a disorder, by no means exonerates us from our task with those who presently suffer from the condition.

Psycho-Social Etiological Classification

In virtually all areas of mental retardation that have not been adequately classified under the bio-medical system, psychological causation has been hypothesized at one time or another. "Intellectual deficit," "cultural deprivation," and "emotional disturbance" are but a few of the terms used to explain these remaining conditions. However, the advisability of using these labels as etiological classifications is doubtful (Stuart, 1970; Turner and Cumming, 1967; McConnell, 1968).

First among the problems in using psychological labels is the fact that they usually amount to little more than loose categories describing groups of people whose backgrounds and behaviors correlate crudely at best (Zigler and Philips, 1961; Stuart, 1970). A "culturally deprived" child may be one raised in a ghetto by parents that do not read or write, or a child raised in a mansion with well-educated but all-too-often absent parents. Certainly there are similarities between the two situations, but the discrepancies are at least as numerous, if not more so. Given that it is difficult to *identify* all the variables in such a classification, it would be nearly impossible to deal with them as a group from a research or treatment point of view. Without further delineation, such classifications are simply not discrete enough to meet the criterion of a valid and useful etiological category.

Second, the majority of psychological categories refer to hypothetical constructs which are not directly observable. "Intellect," for example, must be inferred from the behaviors of the subject during a standard testing situation. Although for predictive purposes, classifying groups of individuals has proved useful, IQ is too often treated as a label to describe a specific and unique class of individuals which at best is a gross over-simplification (Bijou, 1966). Further, although IQ classification has predictive value for differentiation of large groups, the value of applying that statistic to the prediction of individual abilities has proved to be extremely tenuous (Kirk, 1962). Such use of gross and inferential classifying terms only limits more detailed investigation and transcription of the observable phenomenon (behavior) and cannot help in the treatment or remediation of the problem in the individual (Bijou, 1966).

Third, more frequently than not, the onset of the specific psychological anomaly and the associated retardation occur in such close temporal proximity (usually during infancy) that it is virtually impossible to determine which occurred first. Did the retardation result from the emotional disturbance, or did the child become emotionally disturbed because of the pressures of being retarded? In fact, both conditions may have been caused by a third!

A BEHAVIORAL FRAME OF REFERENCE

An alternative system for viewing the development of retarded behavior is a *behavioral* frame of reference. Numerous studies (e.g. Friedlander et al., 1967; Barrett and Lindsley, 1962; Baumeister, 1967; Ferguson, 1967; Foxx and Azrin, 1973; and O'Brian et al., 1972) have demonstrated that behaviors often labeled "retarded" can be created, shaped, controlled, or eliminated through analysis and programming under a behavioral system (Skinner, 1953, 1964).

System

In a behavioral paradigm, the individual is considered a set of responses and response systems. The individual may affect the environment as a responder to physical manipulation or as a source of stimulation (Skinner, 1964).

The environment is defined as the set of effective (noticeable) stimuli from social and physical events outside the body and from biological events within the body itself. Psychological development is considered the progressive change in the form of the interaction between the individual and the environment (Bijou, 1966).

This behavioral system applies to the analysis of normal as well as retarded development (Bijou and Baer, 1961 and 1965). By general definition, a "normal" individual is one for whom the type and nature of environmental interaction has led to the development of "acceptable" behaviors; in contrast, a "retarded" individual is one whose history of interaction has led to the development of a noticeably *limited* repertoire of effective and/or acceptable behaviors.

The types of behavior most relevant to the distinction between normal and retarded individuals are called *operants,* so termed because they are the most responsible for the manner in which an organism manipulates his environment (White, 1972). Operants derive their form and frequency of occurrence from their effectiveness in procuring for the organism "desirable" changes in the environment. An operant then, is any behavior which is controlled by its consequences or by events which occur subsequent to its emission.

Events which strengthen the form of an operant or increase the frequency of its emission are called "reinforcers" (White, 1972). In the absence of reinforcement, an operant will weaken, change in form, and eventually fail to be emitted by the organism.

Because the specific form of an operant is determined through its interaction with the environment, we speak of "responses" and "behaviors," the latter generally being used to describe relatively large classes or chains of more discrete responses.

Events which occur prior to the emission of a response to "cue" the organism as to which response will be effective in procuring reinforcement, are called "discriminative stimuli" (White, 1972). These antecedent events gain the power to control the emission of a response only through repeated association with the reinforcing events occurring *after* the emission of the response. Because of the necessity of this association, stimulus "control" does not violate the basic tenet that operants are actually controlled by their subsequents.

Due to changes in psychological and environmental variables, responses vary slightly in form with each new emission; consequently, it is possible to reinforce and institute into the repertoire of the organism only those variations which successively approximate a new, previously unemitted response.

The information in this brief introduction to the behavioral system may be augmented by an exploration of the many introductory texts in the field (e.g. Millenson, 1968; Ferster and Perrott, 1968). Here, however, in the examples which follow, some additional detail is provided in order to explain how behavioral principles may be used (or misused) to shape retarded behavior.

Response Deficiency

Retardation may be a function of response deficiency. If an organism is incapable of responding in a manner which produces reinforcement from the environment, then, by definition, the organism goes unreinforced. Since operant behavior is generated and maintained by reinforcement, it follows that an un-reinforced individual would exhibit an extremely low level of operant activity. Not that the subject would necessarily cease *all* activity (although this may be the case, as in the catatonic schizophrenic), but his activities would probably be limited to self-stimulation (e.g. masturbation, rocking) or behaviors that are drastic enough to *force* some interaction with the environment (e.g. tantrums, screaming, head-banging). The expected results of nonreinforcement, i.e. low levels of operant behavior or high levels of self-stimulation or disruptive behavior, correlate well with the observed phenomena (Bijou, 1966; Lindsley, 1964; Bostow and Bailey, 1969; Lovaas and Simmons, 1969).

Two basic situations may impair an individual's necessary repertoire of responses: first, birth defect or later trauma, which make the responses physically impossible; second, a lack of opportunity to develop the responses at a reasonable pace with adequate reinforcement for all successive approximations. We can only expect "retarded" (if any) development where: (1) an individual is forced into a situation in which a completely new set of behaviors is required to obtain reinforcement; and (2) he is expected to emit those behaviors fully intact without a period in which successive approximations are reinforced.

Children who are sick during the period when most basic athletic skills are formed will probably never develop them; children raised in a ghetto where academics are frowned upon will probably never be scholars. Not that they cannot develop these skills, but by the time the opportunity is made available, they are too far behind to gain reinforcement for the initial steps in the natural progression of events. In this regard, Lindsley (1964) stated:

> Children are not retarded, it's only that their behavior is sometimes retarded in certain environments; or, our ability to train a child appropriately is retarded (p. 62).

The obvious steps for the remediation of response deficiencies are the analysis of the person's present repertoire and the programming of the environment to reinforce successive approximations to desirable behaviors, thus enabling him to procure reinforcement in a more natural manner. In cases of severe retardation or physical disability, this approach might include permanent prosthetic alterations within the environment to compensate for the response losses.

Reinforcement History

In addition to effecting response deficiency, nonreinforcement or inappropriate use of reinforcement can result in retarded behavior in other ways. First, regardless of the response repertoire, it may be that reinforcement is not delivered. For example, a child's physical unattractiveness may produce such an aversion in peers and adults that they avoid him and consequently, do not reinforce him. The responses are intact and the reinforcers available, but the reinforcing agent is too infrequently present. The same condition might occur when a child is left to his own devices while the parents work; when a child is deliberately removed from the normal environment, for instance, institutionalized in an undermanned facility; or when a child is involved in the rare but dramatic "attic" cases. Another possibility is the removal of the prime reinforcing agent, for instance, through death or separation of a parent or close friend from whom the majority of reinforcement was received. In any of these cases, we would expect deterioration of previously acquired behaviors and the failure of new, appropriate, behaviors to develop (Lindsley, 1964; Terrace, 1966).

Second, it is possible that even though reinforcement is adequate and appropriately delivered during the initial stages of the developing behavior, the reinforcement may be leaned-out too rapidly. A previously attentive parent might return to work after the child is five or six years old but still in a stage of rapid development and, therefore, in need of large amounts of reinforcement; or a parent impatient for a behavior to be fully instated might terminate reinforcement for it as soon as it reached a minimally acceptable level, thereby placing it on extinction, eventually leading to its deterioration. Deterioration might lead to further impatience, punishment and other aversive controls, less positive reinforcement, etc.

Third, it may be possible that reinforcement is delivered frequently but in a noncontingent manner. For example, when a child has become the object of sympathy due to sickness or physical anomaly, his family may "over-react" to the situation by comforting and praising any and *all* behaviors indiscriminately. Because no particular behavior receives more reinforcement than any other, we could not expect any single behavior to predominate in strength or frequency. The result could be the child's failure to form specific and useful skills. Lindsley (1964) noted that many retarded individuals live in this type of environment; but, when reinforcement is made contingent upon the development of specific skills in a programmed manner, but without an increase or decrease in the actual amount of reinforcement, then adequate development begins. Hernstein (1966) observed the same results in more controlled studies at the infrahuman level.

Fourth, it is possible that reinforcement is actually made contingent upon aversive, "retarded" behaviors. As was mentioned before, in the absence of reinforcement an organism may attempt behaviors so drastic that they *force* interaction with the environment. For example, a mother may ignore her child until the child cries. When crying reaches a particularly annoying state, the mother is likely to pick the child up in an attempt to terminate the behavior. The mother is reinforced for picking the child up by the cessation of crying, and child is reinforced for the crying (Bijou and Baer, 1961 and 1965). Tantrums, head-banging and other particularly disruptive behaviors are often reinforced in this manner (Sidman, 1966). If this is the only manner in which the child is assured of reinforcement, the deviant behavior may become so strong as to dominate the child's entire repertoire. In such a case, the result would be retarded development (Bijou, 1966; Ferster and Perrott, 1968).

Fifth, it may be the case that reinforcement is delivered frequently and is made contingent upon the development of specific and useful behaviors but is too delayed to be effective. Generally speaking, reinforcement reinforces whatever event just preceded it, whether or not there is any causal relationship (contingency). Consequently, in order for reinforcement to be maximally effective, it must be delivered soon after the desired behavior is emitted. Although this is not always possible, the gap between the behavior and the ultimate reinforcer may be bridged by what is called a "conditioned" reinforcer. Conditioned reinforcers gain effectiveness in controlling behavior when they are paired (presented simultaneously) with previously experienced primary reinforcers. Once this association is formed, the delivery of the primary reinforcer may be delayed for long intervals of time without ill effects on the generation or maintenance of the behaviors followed by the conditioned reinforcer. Conditioned reinforcers may include social praise, money, the simple occurrence of an event such as a light flashing or a bell ringing, or even the response itself, if reinforcement has been consistently paired with that response in the past. Conditioned reinforcers can be created from any noticeable environmental event.

Without conditioned reinforcers an individual could not be expected to make the association between his behavior and the subsequent, delayed delivery of the primary reinforcer. That is, a situation similar to that discussed above under "noncontingent" reinforcement would result and responding would occur but in a random or unpredictable fashion (Ferster and Skinner, 1957). Lindsley (1964) observed this phenomenon in a study of delayed reinforcement with retarded children. There, remediation of the problem followed a restructuring of the environment which provided consistent pairing of primary reinforcement with more natural stimulus events (praise, task completion, etc.) until the chosen events gained reinforcing properties. The process of developing "natural" conditioned reinforcers requires a high degree of consistency, but, even with the severely retarded, may take only a few days after which response is controlled by the same events controlling the behavior of "normal" persons (e.g. Hopkins, 1968; Schumaker and Sherman, 1970).

Finally, retarded behavior might be a function of excessive punishment or aversive stimulation. Whereas punishment has been demonstrated to be effective in the reduction of undesired behavior, further studies (e.g. Azrin and Holz, 1966; Lovaas and

Simmons, 1969) indicate that if the punishing stimulus is not extremely severe, the behavior has a high probability of returning. In addition to being of questionable stability, punishment may generate avoidance behaviors, behaviors which remove the organism from the punishing environment. If the punishing agent, e.g. the parent, is paired too frequently with the aversive situation, the child will try to avoid or escape his presence. Such a situation leads to loss of control altogether. If the parent represents the child's primary source of behavioral education, or if the aversive qualities of the parent have generalized to the class of all adults, then the child will be essentially in a state of non-reinforcement, the effects of which have been discussed above. In cases of extreme punishment, the child might become neurotic or psychotic (e.g. autistic, catatonic). Cases demonstrating these points have been cited by Bijou (1966), Azrin and Holz (1966), and Lindsley (1964).

Not that punishment should never be used or is never effective, but it should not be used exclusively (i.e. in an environment where no positive reinforcers are available) or indiscriminately.

Effective, contingent and frequent reinforcement is the basis of all operant behavior. Retarded development should first be viewed with respect to this parameter of environmental interaction. A detailed and careful analysis should lead to the appropriate remedial program for eliminating or minimizing the behaviors which result in the label "retardation" (Bijou, 1966). Do not assume, however, that reinforcers are equally effective with all persons. Some reinforcers work with a large number of persons, some with only a single individual. When an attempt is made to manipulate assumed reinforcers without the collection of frequent and precise data regarding the results, the behavior frequently will *worsen* rather than improve; without a data-based means of analyzing this situation, a great deal of harm may result (e.g. Herbert et al., 1973).

Stimulus Deficiencies

Even when the response is intact and reinforcement is available, the organism may not be able to determine *when* to emit a response for reinforcement. In addition, although an organism knows that a response is required, he may not be able to determine *which* of a number of behaviors is appropriate. Deficiencies of this nature arise from the *stimulus* component of the behavioral equation (Bijou, 1966).

Environmental events which allow the organism to determine when to emit a response are called "discriminative stimuli" which are formally defined as stimuli in the presence of which a specified operant, class of operants, or chain of operants eventually will be emitted (by positive or aversive contingencies), and in the absence of which the possibility of emission is indeterminable (White, 1972). The presence of an effective discriminative stimulus, i.e. one to which the subject responds in a discriminating manner, produces highly predictable rates or probabilities of response. In the absence of a discriminative stimulus, response is erratic or less predictable but does not necessarily *cease*. Stimuli gain discriminative properties through consistent and prolonged pairing with specific reinforcement contingencies.

If, due to physical limitations such as blindness or confinement to bed, a child is not exposed to these stimuli, or if they are not consistently paired with the same reinforcement contingency, then two patterns of behavior may develop: first, the child may behave in a random, unpredictable manner in an attempt to find that behavior which procures reinforcement; or, second, his behavior may "perseverate" in a form which *was* once effective, but is no longer.

Lindsley (1964) demonstrated with a group of retarded children that perseveration may, in fact, be due to a lack of stimulus control, and that the subjects might have the appropriate response in their behavioral repertoires but simply be unable to determine when a change in the environment requires a change in response. Specific training ameliorated this deficit in all of Lindsley's subjects and completely eliminated it in some. Following training, the majority of subjects were able to learn visual discriminations *faster* than normals of the same MA or CA (Lindsley, 1964; Barrett and Lindsley, 1962). Stimulus deficiencies are not irreversible but only require specific and consistent

training (Baumeister, 1967; Lunzer and Hulme, 1967) and experiences with a variety of stimulus situations (Terrace, 1966).
In one case (Stolz and Wolf, 1969), a sixteen-year-old boy diagnosed as *blind* was trained by operant procedures to respond effectively to a wide range of visual stimuli. Obviously, the original diagnosis was incorrect, but the stimulus deficiency must
have been great, to say the least.

The importance of stimulus control to the formation of social and concept-formation skills (Skinner, 1953) cannot be
over-emphasized. If an organism cannot determine what to do
or when, then development can only be "retarded."

Critical Timing

The notion that timing is critical in a learning situation has
been held for a number of years (Harlow, 1961, 1963; Bowlby,
1952; Lorenz, 1937). The same idea was touched upon earlier in
this chapter in the sections on response and reinforcement deficiencies. In the past, the feeling has been that there are periods
during which specific types of training, education, or rehabilitation must take place to be effective (Bowlby, 1952; Lorenz,
1937). More recent investigations indicate that behaviors learned
during these "critical periods" are *not* irreversible (Moltz, 1960)
but may certainly be strong and persistent (Hess, 1959).

A theory that behaviors developed during critical periods
could owe their strength to unusual reinforcement conditions
was first proposed and tested by Gerwirtz (1961). Later, Scott
(1969) performed studies at the infra-human level which im-
plicated the role of restricted stimulus conditions as well. In addition to these studies, a number of analytical projections may
be drawn from the system with which we are working.

First, it is known (Terrace, 1966) that an organism raised in
an environment devoid of specific types of stimuli exhibits
marked deficiencies in the use of these stimuli for discriminative
purposes later in life. However, careful training and experience
can ameliorate these deficiencies (Terrace, 1966).

Furthermore, if an organism is raised in one environment and
then placed in another with little or no similarity to the first, all

stimulus conditions previously associated with reinforcement will be lacking. In such a situation, one could expect only a general lowering of activity level and the emission of escape behaviors. These behaviors have been observed to persist (Scott, 1969), but to be reversible if appropriate shaping techniques are utilized.

Seemingly fixed behaviors may also be determined by shaping or programming which remains at one level of development for a longer than necessary period of time. Such a program would reinforce behaviors for *not* changing when they should. Therefore, before the behavior may be altered, the previous history of reinforcement for that behavior must be overcome, e.g. through extinction.

Since the degree to which a reinforcement contingency controls behavior is dependent, in part, upon the proportion of the total history of reinforcement that it represents, it follows that all other things being equal, the later a contingency change is instituted, the longer it must be in effect before it reaches equivalent proportions to previous contingencies in the history and, subsequently, begins to control the behavior of the organism. Consequently, it would seem that behaviors are most easily shaped in the early stages of development, and they *may* be shaped later in a proportionately equal length of time.

On the basis of these analytical projections, one might conclude that the rigidity of behavior formed in the "critical periods" of life may be alleviated or avoided by careful programming which minimizes the possibility that any one stimulus setting, reinforcer, or reinforcing agent predominates the majority of the subject's developing history. The balance between consistency and flexibility which seems paradoxical *is* possible. Let there be no illusion, though, that data on the subject of critical periods are complete and that all the answers are known. Relatively speaking, very little is known, from a behavioral standpoint, regarding this subject.

SUMMARY

Utilizing the behavioral model to deal with developmental retardation as an observable, functionally-determined phenomenon, subject to objective analytical techniques, probable and demonstrable conditions through which retardation may develop have been discussed. However, demonstrating how retarded behavior *can* be created does not necessarily pinpoint how retarded behavior *was* created in any given individual. The preceding discussions of potential behavioral etiologies should be viewed as a basis for experimentation and analysis with individual children, not as an *a priori* answer. Indeed, it is only through the manipulation of the individual's environment (i.e. stimuli and potential reinforcers/punishers) and the objective measurement of the behavioral result in the subject that the practitioner eventually may determine which of the several environmental deficiencies probably resulted in or contributed to retardation. The problem must be ameliorated or resolved before the specific etiology of it may be determined.

Still, however, knowledge of possible environmental conditions serves as a starting point. Several clues were discussed which may narrow the field of initial therapeutic attempts. Similarly, close familiarity with the behavioral principles discussed provides the parent or practitioner with several possibilities for "preventive" programs. Simply, the analysis of retardation from a behavioral perspective provides direction for further study, prescription for correction, and implications for prevention. As such the behavioral system must be considered legitimate and useful for purposes of etiological classification.

REFERENCES

Azrin, N. H., and Holz, W. C.: Punishment. In Honig, W. K. (Ed.): *Operation Behavior: Areas of Research and Application*. New York, Appleton, 1966, pp. 380-448.

Barrett, B. H., and Lindsley, O. R.: Deficits in acquisition of operant discrimination and differentiation shown by institutionalized retarded children. *American Journal of Mental Deficiency*, 67:424-436, 1962.

Baumeister, A. A.: Learning abilities of the mentally retarded. In Baumeister, A. A. (Ed.): *Mental Retardation: Appraisal, Education, and Rehabilitation*. Chicago, Aldine Publishers, 1967, pp. 181-211.

Bijou, S. W.: A functional analysis of retarded behavior. In Ellis, N. R. (Ed.): *International Review of Research in Mental Retardation*. New York, Academic, 1966, vol. I, pp. 1-18.

Bijou, S. W., and Baer, D. M.: *Child Development: A Systematic and Empirical Theory.* New York, Appleton, 1961.

Birnbrauer, J. S.: Exploration of operant conditioning in physical therapy. In American Association on Mental Deficiency and U. S. Public Health Service, Mental Retardation Branch: *Role of Physical Therapy in Mental Retardation,* proceedings of the workshop for physical therapists held at the 90th annual convention of the American Association on Mental Deficiency, Chicago, 1966, pp. 36-42.

Bostow, D. E., and Bailey, J. B.: Modification of severe disruptive and aggressive behavior using brief time-out and reinforcement procedures. *Journal of Applied Behavior Analysis,* 2:31-37, 1969.

Bowlby, J.: *Maternal Care and Mental Health.* Geneva, World Health Organization, 1952.

Ferguson, J. T.: The use of social group work to prepare residents for community placement. Paper presented at the 91st annual meeting of the American Association on Mental Deficiency, Denver, Colorado, May 15-20, 1967, 22 p. (Mimeographed).

Ferster, C. B., and Perrott, M. C.: *Behavior Principles.* New York, Appleton, 1968.

Ferster, C. B., and Skinner, B. F.: *Schedules of Reinforcement.* New York, Appleton-Century-Crofts, 1957.

Friedlander, B. Z.; McCarthy, J. J.; and Soforenko, A. Z.: Automated psychological evaluation with severely retarded institutionalized infants. *American Journal of Mental Deficiency,* 71(6):909-919, 1967.

Foxx, R. M., and Azrin, N. H.: The elimination of autistic self-stimulatory behavior by overcorrection. *Journal of Applied Behavior Analysis, 6:* 1-14, 1973.

Gerwirtz, J. L.: A learning analysis of the effects of normal stimulation privation and deprivation, on the acquisition of social motivation and attachments. In Foss, B. M. (Ed.): *Determinants of Infant Behavior.* New York, Wiley, 1961, pp. 213, 299.

Herbert, E. W.; Pinkston, E. M.; Hayden, M. L.; Sajuaj, T. E.; Pinkston, S.; Cordua, G.; and Jackson, C.: Adverse effects of differential parental attention. *Journal of Applied Behavior Analysis,* 6:15-30, 1973.

Harlow, H. F.: The development of affectional patterns in infant monkeys. In Foss, B. M. (Ed.): *Determinants of Infant Behavior II.* New York, Wiley, 1963, pp. 3-33.

Hernstein, R. J.: Superstition: A corollary of the principles of operant conditioning. In Honig, W. K. (Ed.): *Operant Behavior: Areas of Research and Application.* New York, Appleton, 1966, pp. 33-52.

Hess, E. H.: Imprinting. *Science, 130:*133-141, 1959.

Hopkins, B. L.: Effects of candy and social reinforcement, instructions, and reinforcement schedule learning on the modification and maintenance of smiling. *Journal of Applied Behavior Analysis, 1:*121-129, 1968.

Hubschman, E.: Experimental language development program at the nursery. Paper presented at the 91st annual meeting of the *American Association for Mental Deficiency*, Denver, Colorado, May 1967, 13 p. (Mimeographs).

Kirk, S. A.: *Educating Exceptional Children*. Boston, Houghton Mifflin Co., 1962.

Lindsley, O. R.: Direct measurement and prosthesis of retarded behavior. *Journal of Education, 147*:62-81, 1964.

Lorenz, K. Z.: The comparison in the bird's world. *Auk, 54*:245-273, 1937.

Lovaas, O. I., and Simmons, J. Q.: Manipulation of self-destruction in three retarded children. *Journal of Applied Behavior Analysis, 143*-157, 1969.

Lunzer, E. A., and Hulme, I.: Discrimination learning and learning sets in subnormal children. *British Journal of Educational Psychology, 37*(2): 75-187, 1967.

McConnell, J. V.: Psychoanalysis must go. *Esquire, 70*:176, 1968.

Millenson, J. R.: *Principles of Behavioral Analysis*. New York, Macmillan Co,, 1968.

Moltz, H.: Imprinting: Empirical basis and theoretical significance. *Psychological Bulletin, 57*:291-314, 1960.

O'Brian, F., and Azrin, N. H.: Developing proper mealtime behaviors of the institutionalized retarded. *Journal of Applied Behavior Analysis, 5*:389-399, 1972.

O'Brian, F.; Azrin, N. H.; and Bugle, C.: Training profoundly retarded children to stop crawling. *Journal of Applied Behavior Analysis, 5*:131-137, 1972.

Robinson, H. B., and Robinson, N. M.: *The Mentally Retarded Child: A Psychological Approach*. New York, McGraw-Hill, 1965, pp. 173-207.

Schumaker, J., and Sherman, J. A.: Training generation verb usage by imitation and reinforcement procedures. *Journal of Applied Behavior Analysis, 3*:273-287, 1970.

Scott, J. P.: A time to learn. *Psychology Today, 2*:46-50, 1969.

Sidman, M.: Avoidance behavior. In Honig, W. K. (Ed.): *Operant Behavior: Areas of Research and Application*. New York, Appleton, 1966, 448-499.

Skinner, B. F.: *The Behavior of Organisms*. New York, Appleton, 1938.

Skinner, B. F.: *Science and Human Behavior*. New York: Macmillan, 1953.

Skinner, B. F.: What is the experimental analysis of behavior? An address given at the 1964 meeting of the American Psychologist Association, Los Angeles, California.

Stolz, S. B., and Wolf, M. M.: Visually discriminated behavior in a "blind" adolescent retardate. *2*:65-77, 1969.

Stuart, R. B.: *Trick or Treatment*. Champaign, Ill., Research Press, 1970.

Terrace, H. S.: Stimulus control. In Honig, W. K. (Ed.): *Operant Behavior: Areas of Research and Application*. New York, Appleton, 271-345, 1966.

Turner, R. J., and Cumming, J.: Theoretical malaise and community mental health. In Cowen, E. L.; Gardner, E. A.; and Zax, M. (Eds.): *Emergent Approaches to Mental Health Problems*. New York, Appleton-Century-Crofts, 1967, pp. 40-62.

White, O. R.: *A Glossary of Behavioral Terminology*. Champaign, Ill., Research Press, 1971.

Zigler, E., and Philips, L.: Psychiatric diagnosis: A critique. *Journal of Abnormal and Social Psychology*, 3:607-618, 1961.

Chapter 3

MENTAL RETARDATION: A CRITICAL REVIEW OF PERSONALITY CHARACTERISTICS

WILLIAM I. GARDNER

ALMOST A DECADE AGO, Dr. Rue Cromwell stated in a conference similar to this one that ". . . research on basic personality variables in mental retardates has received relatively little attention" (p. 333). In 1964, Professor Heber in a review of research on personality characteristics of the retarded offered the following observations:

> Despite the generally acknowledged importance of personality factors in problem solving, there has been little experimental work relative to personality development and characteristics of the retarded. Not one of such commonly purported attributes of the retarded as passivity, anxiety, impulsivity, rigidity, suggestibility, a lack of persistence, immaturity, withdrawal, low frustration tolerance, unrealistic self-concept, or level of aspiration can be either substantiated or refuted on the basis of available research data (p. 319).

Although this is changing slowly, there is no question but that research in the personality area in mental retardation is still in an early stage of development. In glancing through the last three volumes of the *American Journal of Mental Deficiency*, I noted that less than 8 percent of the approximately 350 articles, including those of an abnormal, personality evaluation, psychotherapy, and social motivation orientation, could be viewed as concerned with personality characteristics of the retarded. The majority of

---

Note: Reprinted from H. J. Prehm, L. A. Hammerlynck and J. E. Crosson (Eds.) *Behavioral Research in Mental Retardation*. Rehabilitation Research and Training Center in Mental Retardation, University of Oregon, Monograph No. 1, February, 1968, 53-68. The original title of the paper was, Personality characteristics of the mentally retarded: Review and critique.

these few articles were isolated studies providing little in the way of substantive data.

As Dr. Heber suggested, there remain many misconceptions about the personality attributes or characteristics of the mentally retarded, and these misconceptions are prevalent even among those in the behavioral and social sciences. I presume one of the reasons for this lies in the assumption that the mentally retarded is subnormal, not only in intellectual or learning characteristics but in most other psychologic characteristics as well. The retardate is viewed as pathological, is described as being below the norm or as deviant along whatever dimensions of behavior a given personality theory or set of behavior constructs would provide. As he is subnormal in learning characteristics, his behavior is viewed as simple, fixed, rigid, and relatively unmodifiable. But, as Dr. Lindsley has shown, the behavior of the retarded can be modified, and sometimes to an astonishing extent.

In addition, statements such as the following contribute to the stereotyped conceptions which many hold for the retarded. Dr. Tredgold (1949), an Englishman and author of the textbook that every serious student of mental deficiency has read suggested:

> . . . the behavior of many imbeciles is abnormal even in infancy, some being markedly restless and excitable. These abnormal reactions are constitutional; they persist throughout life, and they enable us to differentiate two clinical types which we may term the *stable* or *apathetic* and the *unstable* or *excitable*. We have seen that a similar difference exists in the idiots, and we shall see that this is also the case of the feeble-minded. The stable imbeciles are harmless, inoffensive, stolid, and well-behaved persons who give no trouble, and who are tolerably industrious within the limits of their capacity. The unstable imbeciles on the other hand, are constantly chattering, running about, and generally interfering with everything and everybody (p. 304).

Earl (1961), another English specialist in mental retardation, has written, "The essential components of the inherently subnormal personality include weakness, poverty of the formative instinct of the urge to develop, and later poverty of libido, an inability to strive toward a goal, to persist in effort or withstand frustration" (p. 73).

These and literally hundreds of other descriptive labels and theoretical constructs could be used when discussing *some* retardates, just as they could when discussing *some* nonretarded persons. But it should be recognized that the sweeping generalizations which appear in the writings concerning the mentally retarded are mostly based on theoretic proclamation or on clinical observation of biased samples and not on data gathered in a scientifically suitable manner.

Permit me to elaborate upon representative generalizations that are easily acceptable on the basis of the apparent face validity of the statements, but which are not appropriate conclusions drawn from satisfactory observational procedures. A common statement is that behavioral disturbances—social and emotional adjustment difficulties—have a high rate of occurrence among the retarded, and furthermore that retardates attending special education classes demonstrate more satisfactory personality adjustment than those who attend regular classes. In reviewing the evidence, however, it becomes apparent that little is available which bears directly on the question of the occurrence of such disorders among noninstitutionalized mildly retarded children and adolescents. While some data are available on the institutionalized retarded, these can hardly be viewed as characteristic of those residing in the community, since behavioral disturbance is one of the major factors determining institutionalization.

In searching for data pertaining to this question I have been impressed with various statements concerning behavior disorders among the mentally retarded which do not appear to be justified on the basis of the supporting data provided. These are the types of statements which create and perpetuate inappropriate stereotypes.

Garrison and Force (1965), as an example, report, "There is considerable evidence that maladjustment looms large among mentally retarded children" (p. 446). These authors summarize the first of two studies presented in support of this conclusion as follows: "An early study by Lurie (1935) dealt with the types of problems encountered by 1,000 mentally retarded boys and girls referred to a child guidance clinic" (p. 447). Lurie's summary of the article, published in 1937, differs substantially from the previous statement: "In a series of 1,000 children studied at the Child Guidance Home, 15.7 percent rated as definitely feebleminded; 18 percent rated as borderline cases of probable mental defect; and 22.5 percent rated as subnormal" (p. 1033).

The object of the study was to determine the nature of problems of children who were intellectually subnormal as defined by intelligence quotients in the eighty to eighty-nine range. This study, while possibly suggestive of types of problems which may occur among the mentally retarded, offers nothing of a reliable nature to support the statement "that maladjustment looms large among mentally retarded children." The second study presented by Garrison and Force in support of the maladjustment statement was of even less pertinence than the first.

A statement by Johnson (1963) provides a second illustration of an error in appropriately representing reported data relative to the question of behavioral adjustment levels of the mentally retarded. In considering personal adjustment differences between mentally retarded children attending regular classes with those in special classes, Johnson states, "Blatt compared mentally retarded children in special classes with those in regular classes. He found the special class children are socially more mature and emotionally stable" (p. 471). Although Johnson's statement is taken almost verbatim from the Blatt reference, Johnson neglected to include Blatt's (1958) highly limiting qualification that "comparisons were based on scales that have no established validity or reliability . . ." (p. 818). The scales referred to were the New York Scales of Social Maturity and Emotional Stability. In addition, Blatt presented other evidence which does not support the Johnson statement. He indicated that neither California Test of Personality scores nor school records and teacher interviews revealed differences between regular and special class children.

Although one could readily question the adequacy of the California Test of Personality as a measure of personal and social adjustment of mentally retarded children, it would appear that greater reliance could be placed on this test and the teacher interviews than on "Scales that have no established validity or reliability." Apparently, Johnson was not of this opinion, although in a later study (Johnson, 1961) he did use the California Test of Personality in evaluating personal adjustment of the retarded.

As a final example, Hutt and Gibby (1965) state:

> the mentally retarded child may show unusually severe behavioral reactions during puberty, even more so than those shown by the child of more average intelligence. This is demonstrated by a study by Foale on the incidence of psychoneuroses in mentally retarded children. He pointed out that while only six percent of normal adolescents develop psychoneurotic reactions, twelve percent of mentally retarded adolescents show such personality involvements (p. 233).

An examination of the Foale (1956) reference reveals the statement "According to Burt six percent of normal adolescents are neurotic, but twelve percent of mental defective adolescents" (p. 868). As Foale did not include a reference list, the basis for the Burt statement could not be identified. That is, contrary to the Hutt and Gibby statement, Foale did not conduct a study. Furthermore, the source of the Foale statement is unavailable to a person interested in examining the data.

It is evident, contrary to the textbook and research review summary statements, that there is little of a conclusive nature that would suggest that mildly retarded children are characterized by an unusual incidence of emotional or behavioral adjustment problems.

In reviewing some twenty additional studies (Gardner, 1966) using a variety of techniques including projective-clinical evaluations, checklist and rating scales, sociometric procedures and personality inventories, I can only conclude that although I agree with the generally held opinion that personal and social adjustment problems are of sufficient prevalence and magnitude among the retarded to merit special consideration, if challenged to support this opinion concerning rate of occurrence, I would have no alternative other than to conclude that such evidence is not available. Furthermore, in view of *numerous* methodological deficiencies in available studies, it can only be concluded that the question of behavior adjustment differences between special and regular class students is presently unanswered.

Hutt and Gibby (1965) provide a final example of a personality description which is not supported by evidence. These writers, in discussing emotional disorders among the mentally retarded, conclude that the retardate is more prone to depressive reactions due to rejection and inconsistent mothering. In a search for epidemiologic data which would shed some light on this possibility, I was able to locate four studies of some relevance (Craft, 1959; Davis, 1964; Penrose, 1938; Pollock, 1945). While each study contained obvious, and perhaps serious, sampling defects which limit the meaningfulness or generality of findings, all were consistent in reporting a *low rate* of occurrence of depressive reactions among the mentally retarded—a rate considerably less than that characteristic of the general population.

These examples could be multiplied considerably. Such a state of affairs does emphasize, as stated earlier, the early developmental stage of most research efforts devoted to personality variables. It must be concluded, in light of present evidence, that there are no specific categories or behavioral characteristics which describe all retardates or even most retardates, except, of course, that all have certain "retarded behaviors," to use Bijou's (1966) term, in the general intellectual or learning area as well as certain deficits in the adaptive behavior area—and these are present by definition.

But even within these categories of similarity, there resides considerable variability. I would assume, until provided evidence to the contrary, that the retarded exhibit the same range of behavioral characteristics as that observed in the nonretarded population. The retardate is not a simple personality, but rather a complex one. The scientific study of the personality characteristics of the retarded is just as demanding as the study of the normal personality. In fact, in some respects it is more demanding as many of the usual techniques of personality study have definite limitations when used with the retarded.

PROBLEMS OF PERSONALITY MEASUREMENT

Many techniques and procedures designed to provide personality and personal-social adjustment status data are of questionable value when used with the retarded due to such subject characteristics as limited language skills (reading, verbal and conceptual-cognitive deficits), limitations in self-perception, and those of time-boundedness and stimulus-boundedness. Gallagher (1959) suggested that the feeling tones verbalized by the retarded are more likely a reflection of immediate experience rather than being representative of "a deeper core of personality." Similarly, Guthrie, Butler, Gorlow, and White (1964), in recognition of the limited ability of the retarded to verbally report feelings and thoughts, suggested, ". . . their reports do not give us sufficient material to identify the patterns of attitude which they have developed toward themselves and toward others" (p. 42). Burg and Barrett (1965) concluded, "assessing the interest patterns of mentally retarded is complicated by their inability to read, questionable comprehension, poor attention span, and lack of abstractive power" (p. 552).

As one example of the difficulties encountered when a self-report procedure is used with the retarded, I shall briefly review the use of the California Test of Personality. I have identified some twelve or so studies in which the CTP is used to obtain personality data on the mentally retarded (Gardner, 1967). The frequency of use of the CTP in personality research with the mentally retarded has increased considerably within the last few years apparently because the test is relatively easy to administer and does yield quantitative results.

A number of questions arise, however, when the CTP is used with the retarded. Initially, which level of the test should be used? Due to the lower mental age, reading and general language skills, problems arise when a CA-appropriate level is administered. When an MA-appropriate level is used, some obvious difficulties are created by the nature of the items and their meaningfulness or appropriateness to such a CA level group. Some researchers have used a level closely corresponding to the mental age characteristics of the sample studied while others have used a CA-appropriate level. Blatt (1958), for example, apparently in an effort to use the MA-appropriate level, administered the primary level to a mentally retarded group with a CA range from 8-6 years to sixteen years and with a mean IQ of sixty-eight. Many items at this level (e.g. "Do you feel like crying when you are hurt a little?" "Is it all right to cry if you cannot have your own way?" "Does someone usually help you dress?"), may well be appropriate for the typical child in the five- to nine-year-old age range for which this level is recommended, but is of questionable appropriateness when used with a sixteen-year-old adolescent with a mental age of twelve. In contrast, Cassidy and Stanton (1959) selected the intermediate level, recommended for use with adolescents in grades seven to ten, for use with a mildly retarded group in the twelve to 14-11 CA range. Again, items at this level (e.g. "Do your friends seem to think that your folks are as successful as theirs?" "Would you rather stay away from parties and social affairs?" "Do you like to go to school affairs with members of the opposite sex?"), appear to be rather inappropriate for the retarded whose intellectual and social age levels are quite below the level for which the test was designed.

Concerning the retest reliability of the CTP, I administered the elementary form of the test to 105 mildly retarded children ranging in age from ten to sixteen with Stanford-Binet or Wechsler IQ scores of fifty-one to eighty. On a two-week retest approximately 30 percent of the items were changed, with no differences in the direction of change. This amount of change over a relatively short period of time would surely suggest that only limited confidence could be placed in individual items or even subtest scores as up to one-third of the items may be changed if retested within a few days. I would emphasize the hazard of comparing groups on the basis of items or subtest scores as has been done in some studies or using the pre- and post-test treatment scores as has been done in others.

Finally, certain characteristics of the test items would suggest the hypothesis that the test is not an appropriate instrument for use with the retarded. First, the test items reflect a middle-class set of values (e.g. "Would you rather stay away from most parties?" "Is it necessary to thank those who have helped you?" "Should people be nice to people they don't like?" "Do others decide to which parties you may go?" "Do you usually act friendly to people you do not like?" "Do you visit many of the interesting places near where you live?" "Is it all right to do what you please if the police are not around?"). As the great majority of the retarded are from low income, culturally deprived families, questions concerning parties, social graces, and respect for middle-class authority are of questionable value in evaluating general personal-social adjustment. Should the retarded be viewed as maladjusted if he does not respond in terms of the values reflected by the item content? There obviously is no easy or categorical answer to this question, but at least those who use this test with the retarded should examine their concepts of normality and personal-social adjustment prior to interpreting CTP scores.

In addition, other items if answered realistically in terms of the typical experience of retardates, especially those who attend regular classes, would be scored as deviant responses (e.g. "Do your classmates think you cannot do well in school?" "Is your work often so hard that you stop trying?" "Is school work so hard that you are afraid you will fail?" "Do your classmates and friends usually feel that they know more than you do?" "Do people often think that you cannot do things very well?" "Do you feel that most of your classmates are glad that you are a member of the class?" "Do most of your friends and classmates think you are bright?"). Again, realistic answers to these questions would lower the CTP adjustment score of the retardate. Thus, the retarded is viewed as having adjustment problems if he does not deny reality. If, on the other hand, he denies what is present, his adjustment score is enhanced. This type of procedure would appear to be an inappropriate approach to defining and evaluating adjustment-maladjustment with the mentally retarded.

REVIEW OF RESEARCH PROGRAMS

In these introductory comments I have attempted to emphasize (1) that the position which assumes the behavior characteristics of the retarded to be simple and of little variability has little or no validity and (2) that personality study with the mentally retarded is a complex undertaking. With these established, I shall devote my remaining remarks to a review of research. As it would not be possible to provide a comprehensive review of the research in such a broad area as "personality," I shall review some of the most recent research in a *few* different areas and in so doing hopefully provide you with the flavor of the questions being asked and the types of research being conducted.

It may be of interest to note that the majority of the personality research has been concerned with identifying behavioral differences between the retarded and the normal—that the retarded is more or less anxious, more or less influenced by social reinforcement, produces similar or dissimilar free operant behavior, has more or less behavior problems, has a different locus of control, is more outer directed or has a poorer self-concept. A few studies, however, are less concerned with comparative data and more concerned with the type of question, "I wonder what the retarded is like along certain behavioral dimensions." Personally, I am more impressed by studies of this nature than by comparative studies. We cannot learn what the retarded are like by studying the normal. We learn about the retarded by studying the retarded. As Baumeister (1967) stated recently, "If we aim to understand, predict, and control the behavior of retarded individuals we need to know how they behave, not how they differ. Furthermore, a principle is no less important, meaningful or reliable because it is established with reference to a group of retardates" (p. 875).

The works of Dr. Edward Zigler and colleagues at Yale and Dr. Rue Cromwell of Peabody and Vanderbilt are notable. Both have been the impetus for a series of studies designed to provide answers to a set of related questions. Dr. Zigler (1966) states that it is his view "that many of the reported behavioral differences between familial retardates and normal children of the same MA are a product of a variety of differences in the motivational systems of these two types of children rather than a result of any immutable effects associated with mental retardation per se." Dr. Zigler continues:

> It has been increasingly popular for theoreticians to conceptualize the familial retardates as pursuing not only a slower and more limited course of cognitive development, but as suffering from a variety of specific physiological or quasi-orgasmic defects as well. . . .

Maturational differences between normal and retarded children, which are themselves the result of differences in environmental histories, must be ruled out before any differences in performance can be considered *prima facie* evidence in support of a defect position. Over the years, then, our goal has been to discover the part played by differences in the experimental histories in producing the differences in performance so frequently noted in comparisons of normals and retardates of the same MA (pp. 77-78).

Zigler and colleagues initially evaluated the "defect" position advanced by Lewin and supported by Kounin. These formulations concerning the cognitive-rigidity characteristics of the mentally retarded have created considerable interest among researchers in mental retardation chiefly because the position did represent a theoretic position from which hypotheses could be generated concerning behavioral differences between normals and retardates. The theory represented the retarded child as having fewer regions in the cognitive structure than a normal child of the same CA. Lewin further stated that ". . . the major dynamic difference between a feebleminded and a normal child of the same degree of differentiation consists in a greater stiffness, a smaller capacity for dynamic rearrangement in the psychical system of the former" (Lewin, 1936). Thus, due to this rigidity within the system, the mentally retarded person would be expected to exhibit more rigid behavior over a wide range of tasks in comparison with the normal individual possessing an equal degree of differentiation.

Zigler and colleagues, beginning in 1957 and extending through some fifteen studies over the decade to follow, rejected the rigidity hypothesis of Lewin and Kounin and advanced a social deprivation motivational hypothesis (see Zigler, 1962; 1966). Simply stated, differences in rigid behavior between normal and retarded individuals of the same MA may be related to differences in Ss's motivation to obtain adults' contact and approval rather than to differences in cognitive rigidity. The basic assumption made was that ". . . institutionalized retarded children tend to have been relatively deprived of adult contact and approval and have a higher motivation to procure such contact and approval than do normal children" (1966, p. 83). After obtaining support for this basic hypothesis, Zigler advanced the additional hypothesis that: "The greater the amount of pre-institutional social deprivation experienced by the feebleminded child, the greater will be his motivation to interact with an adult, making such interaction and any adult approval or support that accompany it more reinforcing for his responses than for the responses of a feebleminded child who has experienced a lesser amount of social deprivation" (1966, p. 84). Following studies which supported this hypothesis, Zigler concluded that "the studies . . . clearly indicate that certain behaviors of the institutionalized retarded that previously have been attributed to their inherent rigidity can more parsimoniously be viewed as a product of the greater social deprivation experienced by the institutionalized child" (1966, p. 85). Further, to deal with co-satiation effects, an additional motivation construct, the negative-reaction tendency was advanced. The institutionalized mentally retarded subject enters an experimental task with a positive-reaction tendency higher than that of normal Ss. In addition they begin a new situation with a higher negative-reaction tendency than that of normal Ss. This is due, it was speculated, to the wariness of adults which stems from the more frequent negative encounters which he experiences at the hands of adults.

In further studies Zigler obtained data in support of the following hypotheses:

(a) Due to the environmental differences experienced by institutionalized retarded children, the positions of reinforcers in their reinforcer hierarchy will differ from the positions of the same reinforcers in the reinforcer hierarchy of normal children.

(b) Institutionalized retarded children have learned to expect and settle for lower degrees of success than have normal children.

(c) Finally, retarded children are more outer-directed in their problem-solving. That is, they are more dependent upon the direction provided by others for gaining solutions to problems. This orientation is a result of the experience of the child.

As suggested earlier, Dr. Cromwell and colleagues have, for the last decade, conducted some twenty-five to thirty studies that began with a concern for the effects of success and failure experiences in influencing the behavior of the mentally retarded.

Rotter's Social Learning theory has been used to produce hypotheses and to organize data as gathered. This research program and the resulting integrative statements presented by Dr. Cromwell, represent in my view, the most sustained, sophisticated effort by a group of researchers to deal with possible meaningful personality characteristics of the retarded. As the specifics of these studies are available in Dr. Cromwell's writings, most notable in his chapter "A Social Learning Approach to Mental Retardation" in the *Handbook of Mental Deficiency* (Ellis, 1963), I shall restrict my comments to a lengthy quote which summarizes these endeavors:

> Early consideration was given to the effect of failure and perceived failure on the retardates' self-evaluation and performance. Gradually, more refined notions were developed about the role of failure and success in human behavior. This led to a major phase of research which proceeded from an assumption that retardates typically experience more failure than average children and therefore have developed greater generalized expectancies for failure. Along with this came the assumption that retardates have stronger tendencies to be failure avoiders than success strivers. That is, the success-striving person, with a high generalized expectancy for success, was viewed as one who responded primarily to cues associated with continued success. The failure-avoiding individual, one with a low generalized expectancy of success, responds primarily to environmental cues which were related to avoiding failure.
>
> These assumptions led to research which presented evidence that retardates (1) enter a novel situation with a performance level which is depressed below their level of constitutional ability, (2) have fewer tendencies to be "moved" by failure experience than normals, and (3) have fewer tendencies than normals to increase effort following a mild failure experience. Evidence was also obtained which gave partial support to the notion of separate approach and avoidance motivational systems. Stronger avoidance tendency was sometimes but not always shown by retardates. From this research there gradually developed a theoretical formulation which posited a success-approach and failure-avoidance motivational system which was separate from the hedonistic system typically described in terms of primary and secondary drives.
>
> This formulation gave rise to a study which investigated relationships between locus of control, delay of gratification, and tendency to return to interrupted versus completed tasks. The developmental aspects of these variables were demonstrated with mental, rather

than chronological, age being the important developmental variable. This research focused attention on the construct locus of control, which has come to be investigated in various ways. Further formulations were then developed which afforded predictions of marked differences in serial learning rates as a function of locus of control in the subject and success versus failure emphasis on the learning situation (pp. 86-87).

Finally, Dr. Cromwell has presented a summary postulate system comprised of nine basic postulates with supporting corollaries and theorems. This system serves to focus on some of the controversial interpretations of evidence in this line of research.

REVIEW OF RESEARCH AREAS

I shall now turn from data gathered in systematic research programs to a brief encounter with specific areas of research concerned with personality "organization and dynamics." Following a review of studies concerned with a structural concept, that of *self-concept,* attention will be directed to a more dynamic construct, *anxiety.* Finally, a few additional illustrations of studies and related problems in the personality evaluation or measurement area will be followed by a consideration of the question of why research on personality characteristics of the mentally retarded has not been more extensive and productive.

Self-Concept. Concern for self-attitudes, a construct which assumes a central role in some personality theories, has provided direction for a few studies in mental retardation. Guthrie, Butler, and Gorlow (1961) in developing a self-attitude questionnaire for use with the mentally retarded, found that institutionalized adolescents and young adults do not develop a single set of views of themselves. Several clusters were identified, some denoting positive views and others indicating themes of worthlessness and weakness. In comparing the differences between institutionalized and non-institutionalized retardates, these same authors (1963) found that females in the institutions have a much more negative set of self-attitudes than those who remain in their homes. They see themselves as of less value and as more dominated by their own needs, and as less able to acknowledge angry feelings.

Under the general hypothesis that self-attitudes of retardates represent a major *determinant* of behavior and perceptions, Gorlow, Butler, and Guthrie (1963) sought to identify *correlates* of self-attitude differences among samples of institutionalized women between the ages of sixteen and twenty-two. Small, but significant, positive relationships were found between self-acceptance and measures of intelligence, school achievement, success in the institutional training program and success on parole. In addition, retardates who were separated from their parents at an early age expressed more negative self-attitudes. Finally, there was a tendency for those expressing high degrees of self-acceptance to express less need for the support of others.

Recognizing the limitations of using a questionnaire procedure which relied on S's response to a relatively undisguised question, Guthrie, Butler, Gorlow, and White (1964) departed from the usual measurement procedures and presented retarded Ss with a series of pairs of pictures. Each pair was designed to show situations in which various needs were expressed. S selected the picture which was more like her and later the picture in which the person was doing the best thing. Responses were factor analyzed. Self-attitudes were organized around themes of popularity, acceptability to the opposite sex, compliance, friendliness with peers, being ignored, respected, or dominant, giving but not receiving, and being angry with peers. The ideals revealed themes of self-confidence, popularity, being helpful, loyal, assertive and aware of others.

At least three studies (Bacher, 1965; Mayer, 1966; Meyerowitz, 1962) have investigated the relationship between self-concept and placement in special education classes. None found, contrary to speculation, a more favorable self-concept to characterize those who attended special class. Nor did length of time in special class relate to self-concept. Meyerowitz (1962) found the educable mentally handicapped more derogatory of themselves than normal children and Ringness (1961) found mental retardates to have a less realistic self-concept than bright or average children. Mayer (1966), however, reported that the mean self-concept scores did not support the assumption that retarded children in general have negative self-concepts. Snyder (1966), in evaluating self-concept differences between high and low

achieving mildly retarded adolescents, found a positive relationship between adequate self-concept and high achievement.

The final self-concept study, one by McAfee and Cleland
(1965), evaluated the possible relationship between level of
psychological adjustment and the level of discrepancy between
self-concept and ideal-self. The Bills, Vance and McLean Index
of Adjustment and Values was used to evaluate self-concept and
ideal-self. The writers concluded that the use of the discrepancy
between self and ideal-self to estimate the psychological adjustment of institutionalized educable mentally retarded males was
not a feasible technique. Furthermore, no difference was found
in the self-concept between the two groups differing in level of
behavioral adjustment.

The major barrier to successful research with a phenomeno-
logical construct such as self-concept lies in obtaining suitable
measures from which meaningful (reliable) inferences can be
drawn. The present writer has not been impressed with the procedures used in the studies reviewed. As an example of the difficulties encountered when a procedure is used which requires the
verbal comprehension and responsiveness of the retarded, one
writer (Ringness, 1961) reported ". . . Mentally retarded subjects
did not always immediately understand the import of the rating
scales and were aided by the examiner, after suitable probing,
in making their ratings. Average and bright children were given
assistance only upon request" (p. 454). The influence of the
probing and assistance of the examiner on the ratings made by
the retarded subjects is, of course, unknown. It was hardly surprising to find that the reliability of the self-concept measures
of the retarded was lower than that of the normal Ss.

Anxiety. The role of anxiety in personality theory, both as a
drive or motivational construct relating to learning effectiveness
and as a variable involved in general personality functioning,
hardly needs elaboration. It is not surprising, therefore, that a
number of studies in mental retardation have been devoted to
questions of measurement, comparisons with normals as to relative level of anxiety and relation of anxiety to institutionalization, school achievement and learning efficiency.

It has been suggested that children residing in the structured environment of an institution would be less anxious than retarded children residing in the community and in daily competition with more adequate peers. Others argue that an institutional setting will increase anxiety as adjustment to family life is hard to extinguish. Using the Test Anxiety Scale for Children, Knight (1963) found no difference between institutional and non-institutional groups of retarded children. Malpass (1960), in contrast, found institutional retarded children to be more anxious, as measured by the Children's Manifest Anxiety Scale, than noninstitutional controls.

A frequent statement concerning the retarded is that he experiences considerable anxiety in attempting to compete with normal children as he has less ability to handle stress situations. Malpass (1960) and Cochran and Cleland (1963) using the Children's Manifest Anxiety Scale and Knight (1963), using the Test Anxiety Scale for Children, obtained test evidence of greater anxiety among retarded children than among matched groups of normal children. Feldhusen and Klausmeier (1962) also reported higher mean anxiety scores for retardates. Lipman (1960), however, obtained no significant difference in CMAS scores between retarded and normal males of approximately equal mental ages.

In examining the relationship between anxiety level and academic achievement, Wiener, Crawford, and Snyder (1960) found poor achievement in groups of adolescent retardates related to high test anxiety but not to high general anxiety level. These writers also noted a negative relationship between both measures of anxiety and performance on a visual-motor test. Huber (1965), using the Children's Anxiety Pictures with groups of mildly retarded adolescents from two different residential schools found no relationship of anxiety scores to academic achievement levels in one school. In the other school a relationship was found between high scores on the reading, spelling, and arithmetic tests and *high* anxiety scores. Feldhusen and Klausmeier (1962), using the Children's Manifest Anxiety Scale with a group of special class mildly retarded children, found no relation between anxiety scores and Wechsler Intelligence Scale for Children IQ, reading, or language scores. A positive relationship was found, however, between anxiety and arithmetic achievement.

Wiener, Crawford, and Snyder (1960) found that the Test Anxiety Scale for Children scores related to intellectual performance. Finally, Lipman and Griffith (1960) found Children's Manifest Anxiety Scale scores of institutionalized retardates to be negatively related to performance on a concept formation test. These results supported the hypothesis that heightened anxiety produces poorer performance in a complex learning situation. These results do not agree, however, with those obtained by Cantor (1960) in a study designed to evaluate the effect of competition with members of the same and opposite sex on a motor performance task. Assuming that heterosexual competition would be anxiety-evoking for the retarded, he speculated that such competition would increase the anxiety-drive level and thus interfere with task performance. No differences were found, however, as a function of heterosexual competition on the Minnesota Rate of Manipulation Test.

Silverstein and Mohan (1964), concerned about the use of the Test Anxiety Scale for Children with the retarded, sought to answer the question ". . . what does this scale measure?" Results of a factor analysis of scores obtained on a sample of institutionalized retarded children revealed a complex factor structure. The writers suggested the TASC be more appropriately viewed as a measure of generalized school anxiety than of test anxiety.

Matthews and Levy (1961) in an effort to assess the applicability of the Children's Form of the Manifest Anxiety Scale to a mentally retarded sample, administered the test on a test-retest basis along with a response set scale. On the basis of this study, the writers conclude ". . . that the scores of retardates on the CMAS are strongly influenced by response sets, as well as situational and capacity variables, and that the test, therefore, is not appropriate for a retarded, institutionalized population" (p. 583).

It can be concluded from this brief review of studies involving the anxiety construct, that definitional, measurement and sampling differences render meaningful generalizations difficult if not impossible.

Additional Measurement Problems. It is evident that problems of personality research with the retarded do not differ in kind from the problems characteristic of similar research with any group of human subjects. As suggested, however, the general language deficits characteristic of the mentally retarded render many techniques of personality measurement of questionable value. Sternlicht and Silverg (1965), for example, obtained an average of twenty-eight words per story on the Thematic Apperception Test for institutionalized retarded in the IQ range of fifty to sixty-nine. Stories were frequently simply enumerative of what was on the card. In an effort to evaluate differences in fantasy aggression between a group of acting out, hostile, and destructive adolescents in an institutional setting and a group of peers who were docile and of conforming behavioral reactions, these writers (Sternlicht and Silverg, 1965; Sternlicht, 1966) administered a battery of projective tests, including drawing and thematic tests. About the only difference reported was that the females tended to draw more cats and the males more dogs—a result hardly startling or revealing. These results were similar to those obtained by Lipman (1959). The Picture-Frustration Study and the Children's Manifest Anxiety Scale were administered to groups of institutional *Ss* identified as behavior problems or as behavior models. No differences between groups were found, as in the Sternlicht and Silverg studies, on any of the measures.

Most will agree in light of this state of affairs that considerable effort must be invested in the personality/behavior evaluation area prior to or at least concomitant with research in personality development, organization, and functioning.

CONCLUSION

In summary, it is evident that the approach to the study of the significant personality characteristics of the mentally retarded is not different from the approach followed in studying the problems of any other group of people presenting general social problems. For example, in work with the delinquent, the physically handicapped or the emotionally disturbed, an attempt is made to identify the characteristics which define the difficulty, to relate these to other characteristics of the individual, and to delineate the conditions under which, and the behavioral processes by which, these characteristics develop. There is no evidence to suggest that the same general approach should not be followed in researching the significant personality variables involved in mental retardation. Such questions as the following are representative of those which need investigation: "What are the behavioral characteristics which preclude vocational-social adjustment of the adult retardate?" And we must get beyond the explanation that this is due to personality difficulties. "What are the characteristics of the school-age retardate which interfere with his school success and account for his interpersonal and social difficulties?" Once the significant behavioral characteristics have been described, and reliable measures devised, research concerned with development of these behaviors should coincide with research concerned with improved remediation techniques.

In view of the recognized need and in light of the attention which personality research has received in the social sciences in general, why then has research on personality characteristics of the mentally retarded not been more extensive and productive?

1. Until the last decade only a limited number of researchers have been interested in the retarded. The retarded were viewed as a simple, sterile group, an exception to the rule, with little of value which could attract or excite the personality researcher. Even within the last decade, with few exceptions like Zigler and Cromwell, interest has been limited. Personality researchers have been more involved in developing general principles of behavior. But as Baumeister (1967) has suggested, ". . . a principle is no less important, meaningful, or reliable because it is established with reference to a group of retardates" (p. 875).

2. Relatively too much research has been with the residential population. Location of personnel interested in mental retarda-

tion and the availability of subjects are important factors in this state of affairs. However, as only a small percentage of retardates ever reside in institutions and as most institutionalized retardates are obviously a biased representative of retardates in general, a greater proportion of research effort must be directed toward the retardate who resides in the community if knowledge about this group is to accrue.

I am sure that most any unbiased observer from the field of general psychology who studied the articles appearing in the *American Journal on Mental Deficiency* over the last five years would conclude that many of the studies, and especially those conducted on institutional samples, were designed because the population was available to someone who found it necessary to "conduct research" and not because a systematic research program guided the question asking and data gathering process. I believe, however, that this is changing as larger and longer term projects are receiving support from public and private agencies and as a larger number of successful researchers are selecting mental retardation as a field of inquiry.

3. Research has tended to be *too comparative* in nature, and frequently with rather inappropriate matching procedures. As suggested earlier, it is of legitimate interest to know how the retarded differ from other groups along numerous behavioral dimensions other than the ones used as defining criteria of the condition, although the interest may be somewhat esoteric at times, *but* it would be quite valuable from a practical point of view to know what he is *like*. The rehabilitation counselor, educator, clinical psychologist, social worker, and psychiatrist faced with the task of providing a set of experiences for the retardate or group of retardates which will result in more optimal behavioral development or adaptation to environmental expectations, must know what the retardate is like, how to identify or measure these characteristics, how they interact with other factors, and how they interact with certain environmental conditions created to produce behavioral change. It may be unquestionably of scientific or even of more general societal value to know that institutionalized retardates ". . . begin a new situation with a higher

negative-reaction tendency than that of normals" or that retarded children are ". . . more outer-directed, more dependent upon the direction provided by others for gaining solutions to problems than are normal children," *but* what are the implications of such general comparative data for the vocational counselor, for example, when he plans for and interacts with a particular retardate or group of retardates.

Dr. Cromwell and colleagues did get beyond this general descriptive-comparative level and experimented not only with the development of a meaningful procedure for describing a retardate along an internal versus external locus of control dimension, but furthermore sought to identify covariants and interactions of this personality construct. This is the *type* of research which holds great promise for contribution to those in our society concerned with development and remediation of adaptive behaviors, that is, the social welfare, educational and vocational and personal rehabilitation agencies.

4. Finally, it would appear that too much research has been aimed at the identification of characteristics which are descriptive of all retardates, or of all institutionalized or trainable or brain-injured, e.g. all are highly anxious, all have low frustration tolerance, poor self-concepts or general feelings of inferiority. No one has been successful to my knowledge in identifying either characteristics which are unique to the retarded or those which describe all or even most retardates. An alternative, seemingly productive, strategy would consist of focusing on the identification of behavioral or personality deficits or excesses and on the systematic study of remediation or behavior change procedures. Another concern may be focused on the development of these behavioral characteristics.

Again, I wonder of what value it is to know that "the" retarded is different from the nonretarded in five or eight or twelve ways. Does this not serve merely to solidify, or render more rigid, the construct that is difficult to apply reliably due to problems of definition and measurement? Would it not be better to study dimensions of behavior and to seek relationships among variables which hold promise of being more reliable and less cluttered than such broad behavior categories as, for example, mental retardation or emotional disturbance? The focus of attention would not be on attempting to discover the essence of mental retardation but rather on discovering relationships among such behavioral constructs as locus of control, expectancy of success, frustration tolerance, self-concept, or negative reaction tendency *and* such other variables as mental age, an index of adaptive behavior, an index of interpersonal relations, as well as historical, other subject, or environmental variables. With this orientation perhaps we could avoid the temptation to discover what *the* retarded is "really" like.

REFERENCES

Bacher, J. H.: The effect of special class placement on the self-concepts, social adjustment, and reading growth of slow learners. *Dissertation Abstracts, 25:*70-71, 1965.

Baumeister, A. A.: Problems in comparative studies of mental retardates and normals. *American Journal of Mental Deficiency, 71:*869-875, 1967.

Bijou, S. W.: A functional analysis of retarded development. In Ellis, N. R. (Ed.), *International Review of Research in Mental Retardation.* New York, Academic Press, 1966, vol. I, pp. 1-19.

Blatt, B.: The physical, personality, and academic status of children who are mentally retarded attending special classes as compared with children who are mentally retarded attending regular classes. *American Journal of Mental Deficiency, 62:*810-818, 1958.

Burg, B. W., and Barrett, A. M.: Interest testing with the mentally retarded: A bi-sensory approach. *American Journal of Mental Deficiency, 69:* 548-552, 1965.

Cantor, G. N.: Motor performance of defectives as a function of competition with the same and opposite-sex opponents. *American Journal of Mental Deficiency, 65:*358-362, 1960.

Cassidy, V. M., and Stanton, J. E.: *An Investigation of Factors Involved in the Educational Placement of Mentally Retarded Children.* Columbus, Ohio State University, 1959.

Cochran, I. L., and Cleland, C. C.: Manifest anxiety of retardates and normals matched as to academic achievement. *American Journal of Mental Deficiency, 67:*539-542, 1963.

Craft, M.: Mental disorder in the defective: A psychiatric survey among inpatients. *American Journal of Mental Deficiency, 63:*829-834, 1959.

Cromwell, R. L.: A methodological approach to personality research in mental retardation. *American Journal of Mental Deficiency, 64:*333-340, 1959.

Davis, B. B.: The occurrence of depressive reactions in an institutionalized adult retarded population. Unpublished thesis, University of Mississippi, 1964.

Earl, C. J.: *Subnormal Personalities.* London, Bailliere, Tindall, and Cox, 1961.

Ellis, N. R. (Ed.): *Handbook of Mental Deficiency.* New York, Mc-Graw-Hill, 1963.

Feldhusen, J. F., and Klausmeier, H. J.: Anxiety, intelligence and achievement in children of low, average, and high intelligence. *Child Development, 33:*403-409, 1962.

Foale, M.: The special difficulties of the high grade mental defective adolescent. *American Journal of Mental Deficiency, 60:*867-877, 1956.

Gallagher, J. J.: Measurement of personality development in preadolescent mentally retarded children. *American Journal of Mental Deficiency, 64:* 296-301, 1959.

Gardner, W. I.: Social and emotional adjustment of mildly retarded children and adolescents: Critical review. *Exceptional Children, 33:*97-105, 1966.

Gardner, W. I.: Use of the California test of personality with the mentally retarded. *Mental Retardation,* 1967 (in press).

Garrison, K. C., and Force, D. G., Jr.: *The Psychology of Exceptional Children,* 4th ed. New York, Ronald Press, 1965.

Gorlow, L.; Butler, A.; and Guthrie, G. M.: Correlates of self-attitudes of retardates. *American Journal of Mental Deficiency, 67:*549-555, 1963.

Guthrie, G. M.; Butler, A.; and Gorlow, L.: Patterns of self-attitudes of retardates. *American Journal of Mental Deficiency, 66:*222-229, 1961.

Guthrie, G. M.; Butler, A.; and Gorlow, L.: Personality differences between institutionalized and non-institutionalized retardates. *American Journal of Mental Deficiency, 67:*543-548, 1963.

Guthrie, G. M.; Butler, A.; Gorlow, L., and White, G. N.: Nonverbal expression of self-attitude of retardates. *American Journal of Mental Deficiency, 69:*42-49, 1964.

Heber, R.: Research on personality disorders and characteristics of the mentally retarded. *Mental Retardation Abstracts, 1:*304-325, 1964.

Huber, W. G.: The relationship of anxiety to the academic performance of institutionalized retardates. *American Journal of Mental Deficiency, 69:* 462-466, 1965.

Hutt, M. L., and Gibby, R. G.: *The Mentally Retarded Child,* 2nd ed. Boston, Allyn and Bacon, 1965.

Johnson, G. O.: *A Comparative Study of the Personal and Social Adjustment of Mentally Handicapped Children Placed in Special Classes with Mentally Handicapped Children Who Remain in Regular Classes.* Syracuse, Syracuse University, 1961.

Johnson, G. O.: Psychological characteristics of the mentally retarded. In

Cruickshank, W. M. (Ed.): *Psychology of Exceptional Children and Youth*, 2nd ed. Englewood Cliffs, Prentice-Hall, 1963, pp. 448-483.

Knight, R. M.: Test anxiety and defensiveness in institutionalized and non-institutionalized normal and retarded children. *Child Development, 34:* 1019-1026, 1963.

Lewin, K.: *A Dynamic Theory of Personality*. New York, McGraw-Hill, 1936.

Lipman, R. S.: Some test correlates of behavioral aggression in institutionalized retardates with particular reference to the Rosenzweig Picture Frustration Study. *American Journal of Mental Deficiency, 63:*1038-1045, 1959.

Lipman, R. S.: Children's manifest anxiety in retardates and approximately equal mental age normals. *American Journal of Mental Deficiency, 64:* 1028-1029, 1960.

Lipman, R. S., and Griffith, B. C.: Effects of anxiety level on concept formation: A test of drive theory. *American Journal of Mental Deficiency, 65:*342-348, 1960.

Lurie, L. A.: Conduct disorders of intellectually subnormal children. *American Journal of Psychiatry, 93:*1025-1038, 1937.

Malpass, L. F.; Mark, S.; and Palermo, D. S.: Responses of retarded children to the Children's Manifest Anxiety Scale. *Journal of Educational Psychology, 32:*577-584, 1961.

Matthews, C. G., and Levy, L. H.: Response sets and manifest anxiety scores in a retarded population. *Child Development, 33:*77-81, 1966.

Mayer, C. L.: The relationship of early special class placement and the self-concepts of mentally handicapped children. *Exceptional Children, 33:* 77-81, 1966.

McAfee, R. O., and Cleland, C. C.: The discrepancy between self-concept and ideal-self as a measure of psychological adjustment in educable mentally retarded males. *American Journal of Mental Deficiency, 70:*63-68, 1965.

Meyerowitz, J. H.: Self-derogations in young retardates and special class placement. *Child Development, 33:*443-451, 1962.

Penrose, L. A.: A clinical and genetic study of 1280 cases of mental deficit. *Medical Research Council Special Report*, series, no. 229. London: H.M.S.O., 1938.

Pollock, H. M.: Mental disease among mental defectives. *American Journal of Mental Deficiency, 49:*477-480, 1945.

Ringness, T. A.: Self-concept of children of low, average and high intelligence. *American Journal of Mental Deficiency, 65:*453-461, 1961.

Silverstein, A. B., and Mohan, P. J.: Test anxiety or generalized school anxiety. *American Journal of Mental Deficiency, 69:*438-439, 1964.

Snyder, R. T.: Personality adjustment, self-attitudes, and anxiety differences in retarded adolescents. *American Journal of Mental Deficiency,* 71:33-41, 1966.

Sternlicht, M.: Fantasy aggression in delinquent and nondelinquent retarded. *American Journal of Mental Deficiency,* 70:819-821, 1966.

Sternlicht, M., and Silverg, E. F.: The relationship between fantasy aggression and overt hostility in mental retardates. *American Journal of Mental Deficiency,* 70:486-488, 1965.

Tredgold, A. F.: *A Textbook of Mental Deficiency,* 7th ed. reprinted. London, Bailliere, Tindall, and Cox, 1949.

Wiener, G.; Crawford, E. E.; and Synder, R. T.: Some correlates of overt anxiety in mildly retarded subjects. *American Journal of Mental Deficiency, 64:* 735-739, 1960.

Zigler, E.: Rigidity in the feebleminded. In Trapp, E. P., and Himelstein, P. (Eds.): *Readings on the Exceptional Child.* New York, Appleton-Century-Crofts, Inc., 1962, pp. 141-162.

Zigler, E.: Research on personality structure in the retardate. In Ellis, N. R. (Ed.): *International Review of Research in Mental Retardation.* New York, Academic Press, 1966, vol. I, pp. 77-108.

REHABILITATION AND
MENTAL RETARDATION

In recent years, efforts have increased to maximize the number of mildly retarded who "disappear" into the normal community, and to provide conditions under which the moderately and severely retarded can attain to an adult status of partial productivity, social assimilation and independence. Perhaps the most striking outcome of recent programs of rehabilitation of the retarded has been the frequency with which the success of clients has exceeded expectations.

Cobb, H. V.: *The Forecast of Fulfillment: A Review of Research on Predictive Assessment of the Adult Retarded for Social and Vocational Adjustment.* New York: Teachers College Press, 1972, p. 1.

OVERVIEW

THE FORWARD MOVEMENT of rehabilitation over the past two decades has brought about vital changes with respect to the lives of disabled Americans. Society's understanding and acceptance of the disabled has been enhanced; the government's responsibility for assisting handicapped citizens has increased significantly through major legislation; a new helping profession has evolved; and more comprehensive services are now being delivered to an increasing number of persons with handicapping conditions. The growth and development of this "helping" field has, indeed, been one of the most exciting social movements within the past twenty years.

Definitions of the term "rehabilitation" have evolved parallel to the changing concepts and practices which have occurred throughout the movement. These periodic changes have thus led to a historic accumulation of divergent viewpoints, the common thread continuing to be the generic position that rehabilitation is a change agent directed toward lessening the person's disabling and/or handicapping condition. The more specific definition chosen for this book considers rehabilitation as a process encompassing a coordination of services planned to develop and/or restore disabled persons' physical, mental, social, and vocational usefulness to the extent of their capability.

This definition expands the use of the term, which has traditionally been associated with restoration (re-learning), to include the concept of development or new learning. Consequently, rehabilitation is used in place of or interchangeably with habilitation throughout the book. The definition also views rehabilitation as a holistic approach by including the major life domains of the person. The recognition that man's physical, mental, social and vocational self are not exclusive entities is one of the more healthy attributes of the field. However, this philosophy and practice is seen in light of the fact that the primary

67

goal of rehabilitation continues to be the realistic and permanent vocational adjustment of the disabled. This long standing characteristic is germane to this section in that major attention is devoted to the vocational considerations of the retarded.

Until the early 1960's, the mentally retarded were only superficially recognized and affected by the field of rehabilitation. However, they now have come to represent one of a number of disability groups upon which the movement has had a direct and visible impact. The next eight chapters reflect upon the influence of rehabilitation and its fairly recent intervention into the field of mental retardation.

The major thrust for bringing the mentally retarded into the mainstream of this social service has been the federal government. Chapter 4 is a historically-documented account of the government's role and impact with respect to a variety of programs, i.e. Rehabilitation Research and Demonstration Projects, Rehabilitation Research and Training Centers in Mental Retardation, Developmental Disabilities Program, Federal Employment Program, Rehabilitation Facilities, Work-Study Programs, and the Federal-State Vocational Rehabilitation Program. This chronicle of rehabilitation programs and activities provides a developmental overview, reflecting the rapid and expansive growth which occurred within the last decade.

During this period, one of the most important programs to emerge was that of prevocational services in the educational setting. Popularly known as "work-study" programs, they represent a viable approach to augmenting the developmental process of rehabilitation with the retarded. First, they serve as a source for secondary prevention; through early prevocational orientation and training, the need for additional specialized rehabilitation services may be precluded for many youngsters following high school graduation. Second, they help to better prepare those students who need continued assistance once their educational program has been terminated. For these cases, the importance of such programs in facilitating the habilitation process is clear, especially because two-thirds of the retarded clients served by rehabilitation agencies are under twenty years of age. Chapters 5 and 6 are both addressed to this "early" emphasis on the working world and the retarded.

Once graduated, the majority of persons of less intelligence acquire sufficient independent skills for gainful employment. A sizeable portion of this group receives some assistance in achieving this goal through rehabilitation agencies. Chapter 7 provides an extensive and descriptive profile of former special education students served through the Division of Vocational Rehabilitation. Nevertheless, there are some who temporarily need a controlled work environment and still others for whom such a setting is of permanent necessity. These opportunities often are provided for in transitional and terminal sheltered workshops. Central to this type of rehabilitation facility is Chapter 8, which introduces a behavioral approach to vocational programming. The application of this technology continues to demonstrate that retarded persons can achieve levels of vocational success which often exceed expectations.

Another important tool for increasing the effectiveness of rehabilitation is a uniform system which incorporates the many ramifications of the world of work. Since work represents such a complex domain, failure to think and apply a comprehensive yet manageable framework may curtail the quality of practice and research. Recognizing this dilemma, Chapter 9 presents an integrated approach for conceptualizing, describing and understanding the vocational success or work adjustment of the retarded.

Probably the most frequent question pertaining to the rehabilitation of the retarded has been about factors, variables or conditions related to its successful outcome. This line of inquiry has comprised a major body of research, the combined results of which leave the question still largely unanswered. Discussed in Chapter 10 are plausible methodological explanations for this discouraging note, in addition to recommendations for future research endeavors in the area.

So far, the described chapters have been couched mainly in the past and present. Even though the future is a topic which is considerably more vague and confusing, rehabilitationists must recognize that they cannot afford to base all their thinking and actions on current and previous experience. Forecasting is essential to long-range planning, which is necessary if we are to provide for the future welfare of the handicapped. Chapter 11 confirms this position in a bold attempt to predict the future direction of rehabilitation with the retarded.

Except for the presentation of the practitioner's role, which is covered in the beginning of the next and final section, these eight chapters are a select overview of mental retardation considerations and activities within the field of rehabilitation. For the convenience of the reader who is interested in a more extensive coverage, additional bibliographic resources are provided, i.e. thirty-five basic readings on rehabilitation and mental retardation (Appendix A), 188 rehabilitation research and demonstration projects in mental retardation (Appendix B), and a description of fifteen films on rehabilitation and counseling with the retarded (Appendix C).

Chapter 4

REHABILITATING THE MENTALLY RETARDED: AN OVERVIEW OF FEDERAL-STATE IMPACT

PHILIP BROWNING

ESTHER BRUMMER

THE EARLY 1960's MARKED the beginning of what was to become an active and historic role assumed by the Federal government in confronting the long neglected nation-wide problem of mental retardation. The stage was officially set when a panel appointed by John F. Kennedy issued a plan containing over ninety recommendations for a comprehensive, coordinated national attack upon the problem (*Report to the President,* 1962). The impact of this event is evident today throughout the agencies and programs of the Department of Health, Education, and Welfare, which was given a major role in implementing the plan.

Comparison of monies allocated for mental retardation before and after its prioritization as a national problem provides dramatic evidence of one aspect of the government's increased involvement. Whereas $40,476,209 was obligated by the Department for mental retardation activities during fiscal year 1960, $878,951,000 has been estimated for mental retardation in 1973 (*Mental Retardation Activities,* 1972). From 1963 to 1973, approximately four and one-half billion dollars has been obligated for mental retardation activities alone. These monies have been channeled through a multitude of agencies within the Department and directed to a wide range of diversified activities. For a comprehensive view of the Department's multi-dimensional role, the reader is referred to *Mental Retardation Activities,* an annual publication made available through the U. S. Government Printing Office, and *Mental Retardation Financial Assist-*

71

ance Programs (1971), which reports fifty-four separate sources for funding within the Department.

The focus of this chapter is on only one of the Department's five main agencies, emphasizing its past and present involvement with and impact upon the rehabilitation of the mentally retarded. More specifically, attention is directed to: (1) selected mental retardation programs administered through Social and Rehabilitation Service, the major "helping" agency for the disabled; and (2) selected mental retardation programs administered through Rehabilitation Services Administration, one of the five major agencies under Social and Rehabilitation Service.

SOCIAL AND REHABILITATION SERVICE

The Social and Rehabilitation Service (SRS) was established in August, 1967, by the Secretary of the Department of Health, Education, and Welfare. The primary objective of this agency is to provide a unified approach to the problems of needy Americans, with a special emphasis on the family, the aged, the handicapped, and children. In essence, SRS aims to provide an integrated system of mutually supporting services to people in need.

As one of five main administrative offices of the Department of Health, Education, and Welfare, SRS is responsible for the largest portion of funds allocated for mental retardation grants, services, and public assistance. This is clearly reflected in Figure 4-1.

Although SRS monies for mental retardation are channeled to a wide range of programs, including public assistance, medical, social, and rehabilitation, this section is concerned with just two of the rehabilitation-related activities: Rehabilitation Research and Demonstration, and Rehabilitation Research and Training Centers.

Rehabilitation Research and Demonstration

The Rehabilitation Research and Demonstration (R-D) program was authorized in 1954 as part of the amendments to the Vocational Rehabilitation Act. The research projects were intended to contribute new knowledge, principles, techniques and devices to the field of rehabilitation. The demonstration proj-

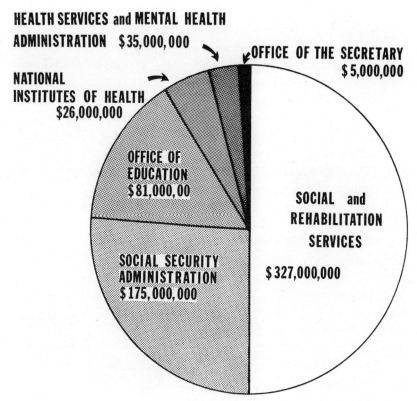

HEALTH SERVICES and MENTAL HEALTH ADMINISTRATION $35,000,000

OFFICE OF THE SECRETARY $5,000,000

NATIONAL INSTITUTES OF HEALTH $26,000,000

OFFICE OF EDUCATION $81,000,00

SOCIAL and REHABILITATION SERVICES

$327,000,000

SOCIAL SECURITY ADMINISTRATION $175,000,000

Figure 4-1. Financial obligations for mental retardation programs administered through the U. S. Department of Health, Education, and Welfare (fiscal year 1971). Source: *Mental Retardation Activities.* Office of the Secretary, Office of Mental Retardation Coordination, U. S. Department of Health, Education, and Welfare, Washington, D. C. 20201, March, 1972, pp. 48-49.

ects, on the other hand, were to apply the results derived from previous research or practice for the purpose of developing and evaluating the effectiveness of new rehabilitation procedures for the handicapped. The major objectives of these grants are (*Mental Retardation Activities,* 1967):

1. the development of new information devices and methods to reduce the physical, psychological and social components of disability, and to evaluate, train, and place in employment disabled persons;

2. the creation of new job opportunities demonstrating the ability and capacity of the disabled to work effectively in employment areas previously closed to them;
3. developing greater public understanding and increased community cooperation and financial support through demonstrations of what can be accomplished by new methods and knowledge; and
4. providing information to administrators and policy makers in State agencies, enabling them to broaden their perspective and apply new methods in the development of the State vocational rehabilitation program (p. 66).

The R-D program expanded Federal participation in the rehabilitation of the mentally retarded. Since its inception in 1954, approximately 2,300 separate R-D projects in vocational rehabilitation have been funded (Jackson, 1971), 188 of which have been directed to the area of mental retardation. For an annotated listing of these 188 projects, the reader is referred to Appendix B.

Only twenty-two or 11.7 percent of these 188 projects were funded prior to 1960. The significant increase in the number of R-D projects directed to the retarded during the decade of the 60's can be traced to President John F. Kennedy's interest in and commitment to this disability group.

Work-study programs, which were practically nonexistent prior to the early 1960's, now represent one of the more prominent clusters of R-D projects for the mentally retarded. To date, there have been forty-three R-D projects (forty-one funded by SRS) directed to this type of program. A detailed account of each of these Federally sponsored work-study projects has been provided by Berard and Halpern (1970). As will be discussed later, these R-D projects contributed to the momentum that resulted in the proliferation of this type of rehabilitation program for the retarded.

Rehabilitation Research and Training Centers

Authorized in 1962, the Regional Rehabilitation Research and Training Centers represent another of the special rehabilitation programs administered through SRS. There are nineteen Research and Training (R-T) Centers geographically distributed throughout the United States, each with an emphasis on a certain type of disability (e.g. spinal cord injury, deafness, mental retardation) as a major focus for training and research. Three R-T Centers are concerned specifically with mental retardation: the Oregon Center, which has been in operation since 1966; the Wisconsin Center, also in operation since 1966; and the Texas Center, which began operations in 1971.

The training accomplishments of the Oregon and Wisconsin Centers were reflected upon by Heber (1972) during a conference commemorating the Research and Training Center Division's tenth anniversary. He noted:

> The two Centers have cooperated in the sponsorship of 165 specialized short-term training institutes which have varied from a few days to four weeks in length. These institutes have helped fill a great void in the twenty states we serve in that they have been attended by 9,200 practitioner-type trainees representing every conceivable specialty with a contribution to make to rehabilitation of the mentally retarded. In addition, approximately forty doctoral fellows have completed training programs in the two centers and most of these persons have gone on to assume significant positions of leadership in rehabilitation (p. 157).

The research at both Centers has been geared primarily to the rehabilitation concerns of the "cultural-familial" or "socio-cultural" retarded. In addition, the research approach can be described as problem-centered and programmatic. Some of the ongoing problem-centered areas of investigation are: verbal learning, work-study programs, program evaluation, behavioral analysis, community live-in facilities, and high-risk populations. This latter area of study deserves brief mention since it represents the oldest and most significant research of the R-T Centers in mental retardation.

Upon inception, the Wisconsin Center established a High-Risk Population Laboratory to study the problems of "socio-cultural" retardation. Center staff began with several extensive surveys in Milwaukee's inner core area which comprised about 2½ percent of the population of Milwaukee, but yielded approximately one-third of all Milwaukee children identified as mentally retarded by the public schools. The survey data showed that the extraordinarily high prevalence of mental retardation attributed to poverty or otherwise disadvantaged groups is not randomly distributed, but rather, is largely accounted for by a relatively small proportion of parents who are, themselves, of low intelligence and who produce an above average number of children, many of whom become identified as mentally retarded. This survey data has performed a significant service to the poor and the minority groups by "destroying the myth that the soil of poverty is somehow, in and of itself, the breeding ground of mental retardation" (Heber, 1972, p. 160).

Following the survey, the Wisconsin staff undertook a longitudinal study regarding critical determinates of cultural-familial retardation. The essential purpose of the study, which is in its fifth year, is:

> to determine whether a program of "comprehensive family rehabilitation" is an effective means of (1) vocationally rehabilitating "slum dwelling" retarded adults who, generally, have not been sufficiently motivated to seek out, participate in, or profit from the usual rehabilitative resources in the community; and (2) to determine whether intervention in the family is effective in preventing consequent rehabilitation problems in children reared in "high-risk families" (p. 160).

The findings regarding the first objective of the study have been favorable in that the experimental families have shown positive results on measures of community adjustment, e.g. legal infractions, attention of social agencies, marital stability, home ownership, etc. However, the most dramatic impact of this comprehensive family program is with the experimental children, most of whom have been in a stimulated and enriched program for a little over five years. The experimental children are on every measure of intelligence, and on every standardized and experimental test of language and learning far superior to the control children. More specifically, from twenty-seven months of age and on, the IQ difference between experimental and control group children has varied between twenty-four and thirty IQ points, and at age five, the mean IQ for the experimental children is approximately 123. By contrast, about one-half of the control group, or children whose sole source of stimulation is their retarded mother, are testing in the seventies and eighties and the decline in measured intelligence is continuing with increasing age. So far the data strongly suggest that this type of cultural-familial mental retardation can be *prevented*. For further information on this significant Federally funded project the reader is referred to the following sources (Heber et al., 1970; *MR 71*, 1972; and *Time*, 1972).

Unfortunately, space does not allow for elaboration on other Center research projects. However, these activities are fully described in the *Research Directory of the Rehabilitation Research and Training Centers* (1973).

REHABILITATION SERVICES ADMINISTRATION

Rehabilitation Services Administration (RSA) is one of five major agencies under Social and Rehabilitation Service. Although all but one of these agencies have major responsibilities in the area of mental retardation, this section is concerned with the programs administered through RSA—Developmental Disabilities, and Federal-State Vocational Rehabilitation.

Developmental Disabilities

The Developmental Disabilities Services and Construction Act (*Programs for the Handicapped*, 1970; *Developmental Disabilities*, 1972) was signed into law by President Nixon in 1970. This legislation markedly expands the scope and purposes of the Mental Retardation Facilities Construction Act in 1963 and represents a new thrust on the part of the Federal government in providing for all mentally retarded and other developmentally disabled citizens.

As revealed in *Programs for the Handicapped* (1970), "developmental disability" is defined in the Disabilities Act as:

a disability attributable to mental retardation, cerebral palsy, epilepsy or another neurological condition of an individual found by the Secretary to be closely related to mental retardation or to require treatment similar to that required for mentally retarded individuals . . . (pp. 5-6).

In addition, the disability must constitute a substantial handicap to the individual, must have originated before age eighteen, and must be expected to continue indefinitely.

As further disclosed, "services" for persons with developmental disabilities mean:

> specialized services directed toward the alleviation of a developmental disability or toward the social, personal, physical, or economic habilitation or rehabilitation of the individual with such a disability . . . (p. 6).

These services are practically all-inclusive, ranging from diagnosis, evaluation and treatment, through socio-legal services, to the transportation necessary for the delivery of these services.

The greatest proportion of the 170 million dollars authorized for appropriations in 1973 is directed to two sources: Grants to States, and University Affiliated Facilities.

Grants to States

The Developmental Disabilities Act is designed to provide states with a broad responsibility for planning and implementing a comprehensive program of services and to afford local communities a voice in determining needs, establishing priorities, and developing a system for delivering services. The funds granted may be used for providing services, supporting state and local planning, providing administrative and technical assistance, training specialized personnel, demonstrating new service techniques, and constructing community facilities, according to the discretion of the local communities.

Some data pertaining to the construction of community facilities will serve to illustrate the significance of this Act for the future of the mentally retarded. By December 31, 1970, the Federal government had already approved 362 construction projects. It has been estimated that upon completion these projects will provide services to more than 114,000 retarded persons, 57,000 of whom have never received these services in the past (*Mental Retardation Construction Program*, 1971).

University Affiliated Facilities

The University Affiliated Facilities (UAF) contribute to the diagnosis, care, education, training and rehabilitation of the retarded through the provision of facilities essential to the clinical training of professional and technical personnel. In addition, a comprehensive interdisciplinary approach is being taken by the UAF's in directing a total effort to the field of mental retardation.

As of 1971, twenty UAF's had been approved for funding. The Developmental Disabilities Act also extended the authority to construct new UAF's through June 30, 1973, and authorized a new grant program to cover the costs of administrating and operating demonstration facilities and interdisciplinary training programs within the facilities (*Mental Retardation Construction Program*, 1971).

Federal-State Vocational Rehabilitation Program

The Federal-State program has had a profound effect upon the rehabilitation of the mentally retarded. This impact has been most keenly felt via direct rehabilitation services to mentally retarded clients at the local level, overseen by rehabilitation counselors implementing their specialized knowledge to enhance the vocational and community adjustment of their clients.

Growth

Although the mentally retarded became eligible for state rehabilitation services as early as 1943, a number of years passed before any serious effort was directed to serving this client population. In recognizing the problem, the President's Panel reported:

> Many states hesitate to use any substantial portion of the funds currently available under the Federal-State program for vocational rehabilitation to extend services for the mentally retarded, because they consider themselves committed to longstanding services in other areas of disability and because their communities may not have fully accepted the need to develop this area more fully. . . . A major in-

crease in vocational rehabilitation services for the mentally retarded can be brought about under the incentive of a more substantial and directed program of Federal financial assistance (*Report to the President*, 1962, p. 120).

The Panel's recommendation set the stage for a rapid increase in the number of mentally retarded clients served by vocational rehabilitation agencies, as demonstrated by a statistical item from fiscal year 1963. While the number of rehabilitations for the nonretarded increased 6 percent over the previous year, there was an increase of 33 percent in the number of rehabilitations for the mentally retarded.

Indeed, perhaps the most eloquent way of communicating the continued and rapidly increasing involvement of the Federal-State program with the retarded is through numbers. As shown in Figure 4-2, the number of vocationally rehabilitated clients with mental retardation as a primary disability rose from 175 in

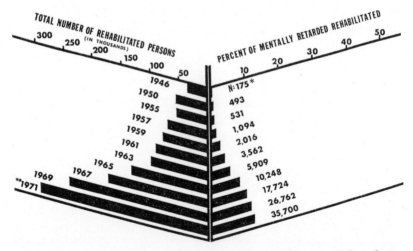

Figure 4-2. The increase in the number of mentally retarded and non-retarded clients rehabilitated since 1946. *In 1946, 175 mentally retarded clients were rehabilitated. This represented .05 percent of the approximate 35,000 rehabilitated persons during that year. **Estimated. Source: *Statistical History: Federal-State Program of Vocational Rehabilitation (1920-69)* Division of Statistics and Studies, Rehabilitation Services Administration, Social and Rehabilitation Service, U. S. Department of Health, Education, and Welfare, Washington, D. C. 20201, June, 1970.

1946 to an estimated 35,700 in 1971. These figures represent .05 percent of the total number of rehabilitated persons in 1946 and 12.5 percent of the estimated total number of rehabilitated persons in 1971. A total of 155,743 mentally retarded clients were rehabilitated by vocational rehabilitation agencies between the years 1945 and 1970. It is remarkable that 145,230 of them, or 93 percent, were rehabilitated during the decade of the 1960's.

Economic Benefits

Two pillars, the humanistic and economic, constitute powerful forces in supporting the vocational rehabilitation program. Every member of a democratic society has an inherent "right" to the opportunity to earn a living and make his contribution to society. An "obligation" is thus imposed on the American people to provide specialized services in order that disabled persons can prepare to participate in the privileges and responsibilities of American citizenship. Furthermore, "one of the purposes of a formally-established program of rehabilitation is to prevent long-term expenditures of tax money by making the individual capable of self-support" (McGowan and Porter, 1967, pp. 6-7).

One cannot help but be impressed with the economics of rehabilitation. For example, of the approximately 208,000 disabled men and women rehabilitated in 1968, nearly 79 percent had no earnings whatsoever at time of acceptance into a rehabilitation program, while all but 17.5 percent were working and earning wages at the time of closure. The mean earnings of all clients (including those with no earnings) amounted to $11.86 per week at time of acceptance and increased to a mean of $55.34 per week at closure. Also, it has been estimated that every $1,000 of public and private funds invested in a client's rehabilitation represents an increase of $35,000 in life earnings (*Rehabilitation: A Blue Chip Investment*, N. D.).

Cost benefits regarding the economic justification of vocational rehabilitation services for the retarded vary in relation to reported estimates. Nevertheless, they all lend themselves to the conclusion that the provision of rehabilitation services to this disability group is economically sound.

Fraenkel (1961) reported estimated annual earnings based on

2,942 retarded persons who participated in the Federal-State vocational rehabilitation program during the four-year period
from 1954 to 1957. These figures are presented in Table 4-I.

TABLE 4-I

ESTIMATED EARNINGS OF 2,942 RETARDED CLIENTS
BEFORE AND AFTER REHABILITATION

	Rehabilitation	
	Before	After
1954-1957	$124,800	$4,829,000
Per year	$ 31,200	$1,207,675

Another set of data, provided in a document by the Department of Health, Education, and Welfare's Division of Statistics
and Studies (*The Rehabilitated Mentally Retarded,* 1964), is
presented in Table 4-II. These figures (which are based on all
but seven of the total rehabilitants) show that 85 percent of the
rehabilitants with retardation as a secondary disability reported
no earnings before receiving rehabilitation services, whereas 89
percent were receiving wages after rehabilitation, nearly half of
them earning over $40 per week. These figures are comparable
to those reported for the mean weekly earnings of rehabilitated
mentally retarded clients served in 1969, when mean weekly
earnings rose from $3.70 at time of acceptance to $51.27 at closure (*Statistical Notes,* 1971).

TABLE 4-II

WEEKLY EARNINGS AT ACCEPTANCE AND AT CLOSURE OF
REHABILITANTS (N = 1,152) WITH MENTAL RETARDATION AS
A SECONDARY DISABILITY (FISCAL YEAR 1963)

Weekly Earnings	*At Acceptance*	*At Closure*
No earnings	978	127
Less than $10	54	63
$10-$19	42	134
$20-$39	47	326
$40-$59	17	262
$60-$79	5	108
$80 and over	2	31

In a study conducted by Social and Rehabilitation Service
(Garrett and Griffis, 1971), a cost rate of 3.58 to 1, based on annual earnings, was reported for the rehabilitated client popula-

tion in general. This means that for every thousand dollars spent on case services there was an increase of $3,580 in a rehabilitant's earnings. In the same study a ratio of 4.7 to 1 was reported for mentally retarded rehabilitants. In other words, retarded rehabilitants were found to return more in wages than the rehabilitated population in general, for each thousand dollars spent on services.

As a final comment on the cost benefits of rehabilitation, it has been pointed out that the average rehabilitated mentally retarded person will return seven to ten dollars in income taxes for each dollar spent on his rehabilitation (Wolfensberger, 1967).

Federal Employment Program

Under the leadership of President Kennedy in 1963, a program was initiated to employ the mentally retarded in the Federal government (*Handbook of Selective Placement,* 1970; *Employment of the Mentally Retarded,* N. D.). The U. S. Civil Service Commission directs the program working in cooperation with the Federal-State program. In order to place as many retarded clients as possible, typical civil service requirements for potentially employable retarded clients are waived and are replaced by a certification of job readiness made by the client's vocational rehabilitation counselor.

Several figures pertinent to its growth will afford a general picture of the extent of the program's success: over 2,800 placements were made under the program during its first three years and over 5,200 placements had been made by 1968. Rates of retention (62 percent) and advancement (40 percent) are further validation of the vocational potential of mental retardates when training and placement processes are carefully considered. Further information relative to the growth and success of the program is provided in a final R-D report of a national follow-up study (Cole, 1968).

Rehabilitation Facilities

A tremendous growth in rehabilitation facilities occurred during the decade of the 60's. This is dramatically evidenced by the increased utilization of rehabilitation facilities by state agencies as shown in Figure 4-3 (Hunt, 1969). In 1959, 9,102 clients or 3.2 percent of all state agency clients were served in rehabilitation facilities during their program of services; whereas 64,920 or 11.4 percent of all state agency clients were served in rehabilitation facilities in 1967 (p. 11).

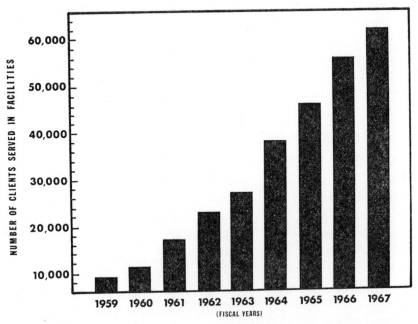

Figure 4-3. Number of state agency clients served in rehabilitation centers and workshops in fiscal years 1959 through 1967. Adapted from chart in Hunt, 1969, p. 11.

The increased utilization of these rehabilitation facilities has particular importance with regard to the mentally retarded as a disabled client population. For example, 39.5 percent of the mentally retarded clients served by state agencies during the 1969 fiscal year were provided services in rehabilitation centers and/or workshops as compared to only 16.5 percent of the state agency client population in general (*Statistical Notes*, 1971).

Members of the President's Panel on Mental Retardation recognized that the majority of rehabilitation services for the mentally retarded were undertaken in grossly inadequate quarters which were often located in deteriorated and sometimes unsafe buildings. Consequently, one of the Panel's recommendations to the President was (*Report to the President,* 1962):

> A Federal program should be established to provide financial support for construction, equipping, and initial staffing of sheltered workshops and other rehabilitation facilities (p. 121).

This recommendation was implemented by the Vocational Rehabilitation Act amendment in 1965. The Rehabilitation Services Administration was given the responsibility for administering an extensive program for construction and improvement of rehabilitation facilities. The increased number and continued improvement of these facilities serves as one explanation for the increased utilization of them by state agencies (Table 4-III).

TABLE 4-III

WORKSHOP IMPROVEMENT GRANTS

Fiscal Year	Number of Sheltered Workshops	Amount Awarded
1966	40	No figure
1967	15	400,215
1968	171	3,422,000
1969	182	4,068,000
1970	155	3,900,000

These figures were taken from *Mental Retardation Activities,* 1967, 1968, 1969, 1970, and 1971.

Another type of rehabilitation facility improvement activity resulting from the 1965 Act is Federal financial assistance in training grants. This program may assist in the cost of such services as training in occupational skills, work evaluation, work testing and provision of occupational tools and equipment necessary for training purposes and job tryout. Table 4-IV gives an account of Training Service Grants awarded between 1967 and 1970 to sheltered workshops and other rehabilitation facilities serving the mentally retarded as well as other disabled persons.

Staff of the Regional Rehabilitation Research Institute at Cornell University conducted an extensive investigation of sheltered workshops in the United States (Button, 1970). Based upon a

TABLE 4-IV
TRAINING SERVICES GRANTS

Fiscal Year	Number of Facilities	Amount Awarded
1967	13	2,000,000
1968	36	6,000,000
1969	36	5,730,000
1970	41	5,860,000

These figures were taken from *Mental Retardation Activities* 1968, 1969, 1970, and 1971.

systematic collection of data, they estimated that the number of organizations offering vocational services under the generic title "sheltered workshops" to be 1,200 for the year 1968. In addition, they noted that these workshops were serving approximately 100,000 people each day or 200,000 persons during an average year.

For an extensive study regarding the characteristics of sheltered workshops, they selected 196 workshops or 16.3 per cent of the national population of workshops. On the basis of the statistical characteristics of the sample of workshops, they extrapolated to an estimate of the characteristics of the 1,200 workshops throughout the United States.

In essence, they found that the distribution of disabling conditions of 14,767 clients for whom information was available from the 196 workshops and the disability conditions of 1967 rehabilitants, that a considerably greater proportion of mentally retarded persons were served by these workshops than the rehabilitated disability population in general. More specifically, 4,447 or 30.1 percent of the persons served were mentally retarded. Assuming that 16.3 percent of the total population provides an adequate sample from which population characteristics can be estimated, then approximately 30,000 mentally retarded persons are being served in sheltered workshops each day and approximately 60,000 mentally retarded persons during an average year.

In summary, the Federal government's participation in the construction and improvement of rehabilitation facilities has played a most significant role in the rehabilitation of the mentally retarded.

Work-Study Programs

The initial thrust of work-study programs can be traced to one of the recommendations made in the *Report to the President* (1962) regarding the need to coordinate education and vocational rehabilitation services. It was reported that:

> . . . it is clear that the first line of attack is through the educational system, and that vocational rehabilitation for the mentally retarded must be coordinated with our secondary educational system. We must seek "habilitation" rather than "rehabilitation." What is needed for vocational preparation is a program starting during the teens which coordinates special education, evaluation, and guidance with prevocational training and vocational training (p. 125).

As previously mentioned, the forty-three Research and Demonstration work-study projects, which resulted following the above recommendation, provided significant momentum in the rapid development of this type of rehabilitation program for the mentally retarded.

Apparently, there are no records pertinent to the total number of work-study programs or retarded students served by them during the past decade. However, in order to afford the reader some appreciation for what has occurred, a national survey on work-study programs deserves mention (*State Agency Exchange*, 1969). In 1969, state administrators of vocational rehabilitation programs were asked to report their cooperative agreements with work-study programs. There was among the thirty-seven states represented in the survey a total of 515 cooperative agreements with county or city school systems, 471 agreements with school districts, and 348 agreements with local schools. A total of 96,604 students were served through these cooperative work-study programs. These figures are indeed impressive, especially when one realizes that they represent only a conservative estimate of the current status of work-study programs since (1) only thirty-seven states were represented in the survey, (2) not all work-study programs have cooperative agreements with the state departments of vocational rehabilitation, and (3) the number of work-study programs has increased considerably since 1969.

Professional Training

The shortage of specialists in mental retardation was recognized by the President's Panel on Mental Retardation as a serious impediment to mounting a rapid and expansive national program to effectively confront the problem. Recognizing that there should be rehabilitation specialists to work with the retarded, the Panel offered the following recommendation (*Report to the President*, 1962, p. 126):

> The vocational rehabilitation training program has proven to be an effective mechanism for increasing the available pool of skilled manpower, and it should be expanded to include:
> 1. Increased emphasis on knowledge of the social and vocational adjustment of the mentally retarded in the curriculum for the training of rehabilitation counselors.
> 2. The training of personnel for workshops after studies to determine the competencies needed.
> 3. Preparation of personnel in rehabilitation and related professions for research careers.

In response to this recommendation, the Vocational Rehabilitation Administration (now the Rehabilitation Services Administration) initiated a program of long-term training grants in mental retardation. Training programs in such areas as rehabilitation counseling, social work, psychology, and speech pathology and audiology were encouraged to expand their programs to include professional training in the rehabilitation of persons with mental retardation. Included within the professional training grants program are:

1. Grants to educational institutions to employ faculty or otherwise expand or improve their instructional resources (teaching grants);
2. Grants to educational institutions for traineeships (stipends) to students;
3. Grants to State residential institutions for the mentally retarded and State vocational rehabilitation agencies for in-service staff training;

4. Contracts with educational institutions and other agencies to support short-term training programs;

5. Grants to public and private nonprofit agencies and organizations for a program of student work experience and training in mental retardation (*Mental Retardation Activities,* 1970).

The information provided in Table 4-V is offered to give the reader a selected "glimpse" at what has resulted.

TABLE 4-V

PROFESSIONAL LONG-TERM TRAINEESHIPS IN MENTAL
RETARDATION OFFERED THROUGH REHABILITATION
SERVICES ADMINISTRATION*

Year	Number of Traineeships	Number of Graduates
1963	3	
1964	93	44
1965	178	83
1966	235	110
1967	283	133
1968	466	219
1969	249	117
1970	289	136
1971	268	126
1972	231	109

* Special appreciation is extended to Mr. Terry Kopp, Manpower Training and Development, Rehabilitation Services Administration, Social and Rehabilitation Service, Department of Health, Education, and Welfare, for providing this information.

Prior to 1963 there were no RSA traineeships in mental retardation. Since that time however 2,295 traineeships have been awarded and an estimated 1,077 students have graduated. In considering the proportion of graduates to traineeships, one should take into account the fact that many students' professional training extended beyond a year. Consequently, they were awarded more than one stipend.

As a final indicator regarding the Federal government's involvement in manpower training, combined figures taken from *Mental Retardation Activities* (1967, 1968, 1969, and 1970) indicated that for the fiscal years 1966-1969, approximately 7,200,-000 dollars was awarded for professional training grants in mental retardation through the Rehabilitation Services Administration.

Through this Federally-sponsored manpower training program, significantly greater leadership has developed for rehabilitation services and research for the mentally retarded.

Rehabilitation Process and Outcome

The first comprehensive profile of selected characteristics of mentally retarded clients rehabilitated by vocational rehabilitation agencies was published in 1964 (*The Rehabilitated Mentally Retarded*, 1964). This final discussion draws upon subsequent profiles in order to provide the reader with concise, updated information on mentally retarded clients who are served by state rehabilitation agencies. This information will include: referral sources; types and costs of services; and outcomes, in terms of personal and economic benefits and job placements. In addition, Chapter 7 reports similar data based on an extensive follow-up of 1,338 former special education pupils.

The referral stage represents the initial phase of the rehabilitation process. The graph in Figure 4-4 represents referral sources for 237,812 clients rehabilitated during fiscal year 1969, 26,762 of whom were mentally retarded.

There is relatively little variation among referral sources for the nonretarded rehabilitated client population. On the other hand, educational institutions served as the referral source for over 50 percent of the retarded rehabilitated clients. This can be explained, in part, by the recent proliferation of work-study programs, many of which have cooperative agreements with the state vocational rehabilitation agencies.

Frequently, there is a reticence among counselors regarding the mentally retarded as rehabilitation clients because of such considerations as the types of services that are needed, their cost, and the amount of time required for positive results to occur. In studying Figure 4-5, however, one learns that mentally retarded clients do not differ significantly from other disabled client populations in terms of types and costs of services.

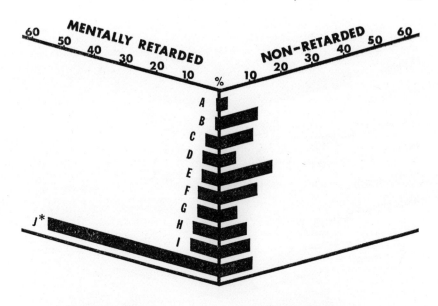

A. SOCIAL SECURITY F. OTHER SOURCES

B. PHYSICIANS G. OTHER HEALTH AGENCIES

C. SELF REFERRAL H. WELFARE AGENCIES

D. STATE EMPLOYMENT SERVICE I. INDIVIDUAL

E. HOSPITALS & SANITORIUMS J. EDUCATIONAL INSTITUTIONS

Figure 4-4. Referral sources for the rehabilitated retarded and non-retarded client population (fiscal year 1969). *In 1969, 54.8 percent of the rehabilitated retarded clients were referred to the agency from educational institutions. Source: A Profile of Mentally Retarded Clients Rehabilitated During Fiscal Year 1969. *Statistical Notes*, #29, Rehabilitation Services Administration, Social and Rehabilitation Services, U. S. Department of Health, Education, and Welfare, September, 1971.

Furthermore, a difference of only 1.7 months for rehabilitating both groups is reported in *Statistical Notes* (1971), with the mentally retarded group taking an average of 15.2 months from acceptance to closure and all other client groups taking an average of 13.5 months.

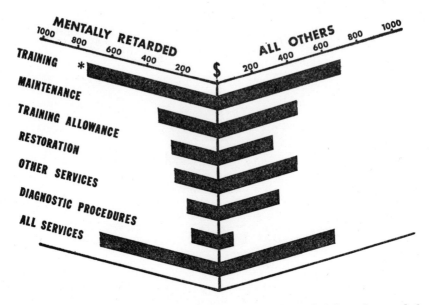

Figure 4-5. Types and costs of services for the rehabilitated retarded (N=26,762) and non-retarded client (N=237,812) populations (fiscal year 1969). *In 1969, the mean costs of training services for mentally retarded clients was 749 dollars. Source: A Profile of Mentally Retarded Clients Rehabilitated During Fiscal Year 1969. *Statistical Notes,* #29, Rehabilitation Services Administration, Social and Rehabilitation Service, U. S. Department of Health, Education, and Welfare, September, 1971.

The ultimate goal of vocational rehabilitation is to enhance the physical, mental, social, vocational, and economic adjustment of the handicapped individual. Figure 4-6 reports one set of data regarding the extent to which this goal is achieved for both mentally retarded and nonretarded clients.

Both groups of clients were reported to have experienced their most significant rehabilitation benefits in the areas of economic improvement and personal adjustment. It is interesting to note that the mentally retarded show greater benefits in all categories except for physical adaptation, the area in which they were less likely to require and to receive services.

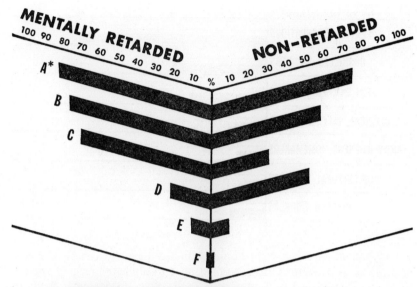

A. ECONOMIC IMPROVEMENT

B. PERSONAL ADJUSTMENT

C. EDUCATIONAL DEVELOPMENT

D. PHYSICAL ADAPTATION

E. COMMUNICATION IMPROVEMENT

F. NO BENEFITS

Figure 4-6. Vocational rehabilitation benefits reported for rehabilitated retarded (N=26,762) and non-retarded client (N=237,812) populations (fiscal year 1969). *In 1969, 82.3 percent of the rehabilitated retarded clients were reported to have experienced economic benefits as a result of their vocational rehabilitation. Source: A Profile of Mentally Retarded Clients Rehabilitated During Fiscal Year 1969. *Statistical Notes*, #29, Rehabilitation Services Administration, Social and Rehabilitation Service, U. S. Department of Health, Education and Welfare, September, 1971.

A final question pertains to the types of jobs in which mentally retarded clients are placed. For a partial answer to this question, the reader is referred to Figure 4-7.

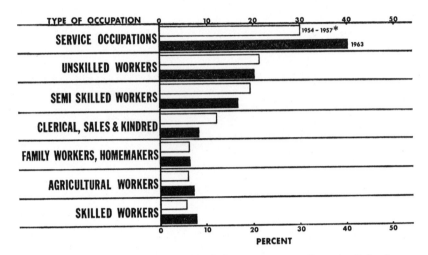

Figure 4-7. Occupations held by rehabilitated mentally retarded clients. *During fiscal years 1954-1957, 30 percent of rehabilitated mentally retarded clients were placed in service occupations. Sources: Mentally Retarded Persons Rehabilitated During Fiscal Years 1954 and 1957. *Facts in Brief,* Office of Vocational Rehabilitation, Rehabilitation Services Series (discontinued), 1958. *The Rehabilitated Mentally Retarded,* Vocational Rehabilitation Administration (now the Rehabilitation Services Administration), Division of Statistics and Studies, U. S. Department of Health, Education, and Welfare, Washington, D. C. 20201, April, 1964.

A more detailed and updated account of occupations held by 26,840 rehabilitated mentally retarded clients in 1969 is provided in Table 4-VI. This table also provides a comparison of occupational settings with the 210,972 nonretarded clients rehabilitated in the same year (*Statistical Notes,* 1969).

As reflected in Figure 4-7 and Table 4-VI, the mentally retarded client is more likely than not to be placed in a service occupation. Reed and Weiss (1969), who found similar results, do not see this as a positive sign and admonish against stereotypic job placement practices. In essence, they state that the wide range of fields in which the mentally retarded have been placed suggests the high concentration of placements in service and unskilled areas is not justified, and that further broadening of job opportunities for the retarded can and should be achieved.

TABLE 4-VI

OCCUPATIONS HELD BY REHABILITATED MENTALLY RETARDED
AND NON-RETARDED CLIENTS IN 1969

| | Percent Distribution | |
| | Retarded | Non-Retarded |
Occupations	*(N = 26,840)*	*(N = 210,972)*
Professional, technical and managerial		
Architecture & engineering	.1	1.4
Medicine and health	.1	1.2
Education	.1	1.9
Administration and management	.4	2.6
All other professional, technical and managerial		
occupations	.3	3.0
	1.0	10.1
Clerical		
Stenography, typing, filing, etc.	1.2	4.7
Computing and account recording	.5	3.8
All other clerical occupations	4.0	4.0
	5.7	12.7
Sales	1.6	4.3
Service		
Domestic	4.2	4.6
Food and beverage preparation	12.8	5.1
Building	6.9	3.0
Apparel and furnishings	4.1	1.6
Lodging	1.9	1.0
Barbering and cosmetology	1.2	1.7
All other service occupations	5.6	4.2
	36.7	21.3
Agriculture	3.8	3.8
Industrial		
Skilled	5.0	9.1
Semi-skilled	3.2	3.6
Unskilled	28.2	16.9
	36.4	29.6
Homemakers	5.0	15.3
Unpaid family workers	3.5	2.1
Sheltered workshop workers	6.1	.9

SUMMARY

The early 1960's marked the emergence of mental retardation
as a national priority. Under the leadership of President John
F. Kennedy and the Panel he appointed, concerted efforts were

undertaken to combat this problem. Specific recommendations concerning areas ranging from prevention through rehabilitation were made and implemented. Multi-agency and multi-disciplinary, the Federal approach committed vast resources, financial and technical, to the integrated provision of services. In addition, research, professional training, and construction of facilities were all necessary concomitants of this comprehensive program.

Significant strides have been made as a result of these efforts. More retarded persons are being served more effectively. Research is providing new insights regarding the complexity of problems related to this disability group. Tens of thousands of persons with retardation are contributing to their communities in ways and to degrees unthought of ten years ago.

As is true of the ecology of all human conditions, attention paid to some problems serves to raise others, previously unforeseen. A multitude of questions have been answered regarding the mentally retarded; still more are being asked. It is the task of those concerned with mental retardation to consolidate the gains made during the 1960's and to expand those gains toward the ultimate goal of serving more persons more comprehensively.

REFERENCES

Berard, W. R., and Halpern, A. S.: *Abstracts of Federally Sponsored Work/Study Programs for the Mentally Retarded.* Austin, Texas, The University of Texas, Rehabilitation Research and Training Center in Mental Retardation, Monograph No. 3, December, 1970.

Button, W. H.: Sheltered workshops in the United States: An institutional overview. In *Rehabilitation, Sheltered Workshops, and the Disadvantaged: An Exploration in Manpower Policy.* Ithaca, New York, Cornell University. New York State School of Industrial and Labor Relations, Regional Rehabilitation Research Institute, 1970, pp. 3-48.

Cole, L. B.: *A National Follow-up of Mental Retardates Employed by the Federal Government.* The Department of Vocational Rehabilitation Government of the District of Columbia, Washington, D. C. 20005, 1968, R-D project no. 2425-G, Social Rehabilitation Service, U. S. Department of Health, Education, and Welfare, Washington, D. C. 20201.

Developmental Disabilities. Rehabilitation Service Administration Social and Rehabilitation Service, U. S. Department of Health, Education, and Welfare, Washington, D. C. 20201, 1972.

Employment of the Mentally Retarded in Federal Service. Office of Public Policy Employment Programs, Manpower Sources Division, U. S. Civil Service Commission (BRE-7), Washington, D. C. 20415, N. D.

Facts in Brief: Mentally Retarded Persons Rehabilitated in Fiscal Years 1954 to 1957. Office of Vocational Rehabilitation, Rehabilitation Service Series (Discontinued), U. S. Department of Health, Education, and Welfare, Washington, D. C. 20201, 1958.

Fraenkel, W. A.: *The Mentally Retarded and Their Vocational Rehabilitation: A Resource Handbook.* New York, National Association for Retarded Children, Inc., 1961.

Garrett, J. F., and Griffis, B. W.: The economic benefits of rehabilitation of the mentally retarded. *Welfare in Review, 9*:1-7, 1971.

Garrett, J. F.: Economic benefits of programs for the retarded. *Programs for the Handicapped.* Secretary's Committee on Mental Retardation. U. S. Department of Health, Education, and Welfare, Washington, D. C. 20201, January 8, 1971.

Handbook of Selective Placement in Federal Civil Service Employment of the Physically Handicapped, the Mentally Restored, the Mentally Retarded, the Rehabilitated Offender. United States Civil Service Commission (BRW-12), Washington, D. C. 20415, August, 1970.

Heber, R.: Research and training center accomplishments in mental retardation. In Leshner, M. (Ed.): *Developing an RT Center Program Strategy to Improve the Effectiveness of Rehabilitation Services.* Conference of the Rehabilitation Research and Training Centers, Temple University, Philadelphia, Pennsylvania, February, 1972.

Heber, R.; Dever, R.; and Conry, J.: The influence of environmental and genetic variables on intellectual development. In Prehm, H. J., Hamerlynck, L. A., and Crosson, J. E. (Eds.): *Behavioral Research in Mental Retardation.* Eugene, Oregon, University of Oregon, Rehabilitation Research and Training Center in Mental Retardation, Monograph No. 1, 1970, pp. 1-22.

Hunt, J.: A decade of progress. *Journal of Rehabilitation,* January-February: 9-12, 1969.

Jackson, D. G. (Ed.): *Research 1971: An Annotated List of SRS Research and Demonstration Grants (1955-1971),* Research Utilization Branch, Office of Research and Demonstration, Social and Rehabilitation Service, U. S. Department of Health, Education, and Welfare, Washington, D. C. 20201, 1971.

McGowan, J. F., and Porter, T. L.: *An Introduction to the Vocational Rehabilitation Process.* Rehabilitation Services Administration, Social and Rehabilitation Service, U. S. Department of Health, Education, and Welfare, Washington, D. C. 20201, July, 1967.

Mental Retardation Activities. Office of the Secretary. Secretary's Committee on Mental Retardation. U. S. Department of Health, Education, and Welfare, Washington, D. C. 20201, January, 1967.

Mental Retardation Activities. Office of the Secretary. Secretary's Committee on Mental Retardation. U. S. Department of Health, Education, and Welfare, Washington, D. C. 20201, January, 1968.

Mental Retardation Activities. Office of the Secretary, Secretary's Committee on Mental Retardation, U. S. Department of Health, Education, and Welfare, Washington, D. C. 20201, January, 1969.

Mental Retardation Activities. Office of the Secretary, Secretary's Committee on Mental Retardation, U. S. Department of Health, Education, and Welfare, Washington, D. C. 20201, January, 1970.

Mental Retardation Activities. Office of the Secretary, Secretary's Committee on Mental Retardation. U. S. Department of Health, Education, and Welfare, Washington, D. C. 20201, January, 1971.

Mental Retardation Activities. Office of the Secretary, Secretary's Committee on Mental Retardation. U. S. Department of Health, Education, and Welfare, Washington, D. C. 20201, January, 1972.

Mental Retardation Construction Program. Office of the Secretary, Secretary's Committee on Mental Retardation, U. S. Department of Health, Education, and Welfare, Washington, D. C. 20201, February, 1971.

Mental Retardation Financial Assistance Programs. Office of the Secretary, Secretary's Committee on Mental Retardation, U. S. Department of Health, Education, and Welfare, Washington, D. C. 20201, July, 1971.

MR 71: Entering the Era of Human Ecology. The President's Committee on Mental Retardation, Washington, D. C. 20201, 1972, pp. 10-12.

Programs for the Handicapped. Developmental Disabilities Services and Facilities Construction Act (Public Law 91-517). Secretary's Committee on Mental Retardation. U. S. Department of Health, Education, and Welfare, Washington, D. C. 20201, December 7, 1970.

Programs for the Handicapped. Social and Rehabilitation Service, Mental Retardation Research, Secretary's Committee on Mental Retardation, U. S. Department of Health, Education, and Welfare, Washington, D. C. 20201, February 29, 1972.

Reed, M. H., and Weiss, D. J.: Counseling Outcomes for Mentally Retarded Clients, Psychology Department, University of Minnesota (Mimeographs), 1969.

Rehabilitation: A Blue Chip Investment. Social and Rehabilitation Service, U. S. Department of Health, Education, and Welfare, Washington, D. C. 20201 (Pamphlet), N. D.

Report to the President: A Proposed Program for National Action to Combat Mental Retardation. The President's Panel on Mental Retardation, Washington, D. C. 20201, October, 1962.

Research Directory of the Rehabilitation Research and Training Centers. Social and Rehabilitation Service. U. S. Department of Health, Education and Welfare, Washington, D. C. 20201, February, 1971. (Prepared by Don Bowers and Irwin Mohler, Biological Sciences Communication Project, The George Washington University Medical Center in cooperation with the George Washington University Research and Training Center.)

State Agency Exchange. Published by Rehabilitation Interagency Focus, 1522 K. Street, N. W., Room 1120, Washington, D. C. 20005, December, 1969.

Statistical History: Federal-State Program of Vocational Rehabilitation (1920-1969). Division of Statistics and Studies, Rehabilitation Services Administration, Social and Rehabilitation Service, U. S. Department of Health, Education, and Welfare, Washington, D. C. 20201, June, 1970.

Statistical Notes: A Profile of Mentally Retarded Clients Rehabilitated During Fiscal Year 1967. U. S. Department of Health, Education, and Welfare, Social and Rehabilitation Service, Rehabilitation Services Administration, No. 10, February, 1969.

Statistical Notes: A Profile of Mentally Retarded Clients Rehabilitated During the Fiscal Year 1969. U. S. Department of Health, Education, and Welfare. Social and Rehabilitation Service, Rehabilitation Services Administration, No. 29, September, 1971.

The Rehabilitated Mentally Retarded. Vocational Rehabilitation Administration (now the Rehabilitation Services Administration) Division of Statistics and Studies, U. S. Department of Health, Education, and Welfare, Washington, D. C. 20201, April, 1964.

Time, 1972, 99, January 3, p. 56.

Wolfensberger, W.: Vocational preparation and occupation. In Baumeister, A. A. (Ed.): *Mental Retardation: Appraisal, Education, Rehabilitation.* Chicago, Aldine Publishing Company, 1971, pp. 232-273.

Chapter 5

PRE-VOCATIONAL CONSIDERATIONS IN REHABILITATING THE MENTALLY RETARDED

R. WILLIAM ENGLISH
PHILIP L. BROWNING

QUITE COMMONLY, in a variety of interpersonal encounters, adult Americans are asked two questions: (1) What is your name? and (2) What do you do? The latter question highlights the importance of work in our highly industrialized society. Status in our culture is based on achievement versus ascription, and nearly all achievement is to some degree reflective of work. For most men, and for an increasing majority of women, vocational success, especially in "meaningful" work, is life's most consistent uplifting psychological reward. Rehabilitation-habilitation is based largely upon this philosophical premise of the importance of work to all persons, including individuals with handicapping conditions.

In addition to the critical role that work plays in contributing to self-esteem and basic human dignity, work has other values for adolescent and adult retardates. These have been enumerated by Wolfensberger (1967, p. 233):

> A working retardate is generally a happier person. Work contributes to self-esteem and feelings of accomplishment and worth.
>
> Work lends adult status to a retardate, and thus adds to his dignity in the sight of others.
>
> In our work-oriented society, positive attitudes will generally be expressed toward the worker, and negative ones toward the drone. Thus, the retardate's adjustment will be enhanced by the community attitudes he encounters.
>
> The family of the working retardate is, generally, a better adjusted family. Since work tends to make the retardate more acceptable, it engenders positive attitudes in the family benefiting the retardate indirectly.

A retardate capable of working will be less likely to become an economic burden to his family or society.

A working retardate contributes to the economic welfare of society.

A working retardate has disposable earnings which enable him to share in the material benefits enjoyed by the majority of our citizens.

Work frees individuals from idleness which can lead to nonadaptive or maladaptive behavior.

The process of preparing young people to be responsible, productive adults in a complex society should begin in their early formative years. This is true especially of the mentally retarded, the majority of whom need special prevocational education and training before they finish school and begin to receive vocational rehabilitation services. Heath (1970) clearly makes this point by stating

> Vocational guidance for the mentally retarded student cannot wait until he reaches the age of fifteen or sixteen and becomes a candidate for services by the Vocational Rehabilitation Counselor. It must be begun very early in life in the home and followed throughout all of his school years if he is to develop the proper attitude toward work, good work habits, and skills (p. xi).

The primary purpose of this chapter is to discuss the habilitation process as it relates to the mentally retarded, with particular attention directed to prevocational considerations. Special emphasis will be given to: (1) a need for improved coordination between special education and rehabilitation; (2) the habilitation process with respect to a model or system which incorporates prevocational components; and (3) avocational habilitation, a too often neglected but essential part of the total process.

COORDINATION

The coordination between special education teachers and the rehabilitation counselors is of utmost importance since the vocational habilitation process is developmental and originates prior to the students' high school graduation. Of course, the assumption is that coordination will aid the developmental process and facilitate the youth's transition between the school and work. Too many vocational rehabilitation counselors have unfortunate stories to relate about some retarded person who has been referred abruptly in the last months of his high school tenure for rehabilitation services, yet who is not ready to assume an independent adult role. In many such instances, the youth is not ready because he has been improperly prepared by his teachers and guardians.

Unfortunately, many university teacher preparation programs fail to appropriately equip their students in training with the type of curriculum needed for adequately preparing high school students for eventual vocational and social adjustment. Thus, special education students in their secondary schooling too often receive only a watered-down version of a conventional academic curriculum. This is a main reason that university-based secondary level teacher preparation curricula needs to focus on areas such as vocational education and vocational rehabilitation, in addition to the regular teacher preparation courses. One of the more recent and promising signs in this direction is a project funded by the Office of Education's Bureau of Education for the Handicapped (Brolin, 1972). The purpose of this project was to study the need for a new training model for teachers of the secondary EMR. In the final report, the proposed teacher training model utilizes strengths from vocational education and vocational rehabilitation, in addition to a number of other non-traditional teacher education areas.

Through improved coordination and cooperation, rehabilitation counselors can assist in improving the quality of school services for the retarded, if teachers use them as resource consultants to plan curriculum, do sporadic counseling, and disperse their knowledge of jobs and resources in the local community. In addition, they can provide more effective and efficient guidance, counseling, and placement service to older adolescents if they have access to specific behavioral observations made by teachers who have known the youngsters professionally for some time. Because of the large number of potential applicants to the public vocational rehabilitation program, counselors can justify making a substantial time and energy commitment to working directly with special educators in inservice education on a non-fee consultant basis. Such arrangements have been tried in some cities and found to be successful.

Perhaps, the problem of cooperation and coordination is less serious in the early 1970's than it was in the early 1960's, when Peters and Rhode (1964) reported that only about 33 percent of special educators and rehabilitation counselors had an on-going working relationship. This statement is based, in part, upon recent publications which are germane to the problem. For example, the proceedings of an institute sponsored by the Western Interstate Commission for Higher Education were printed and titled *Exploring Rehabilitation—Special Education Relationships* (1968). In addition, Younie and Rusalem (1971) published a book entitled *The World Atlas of Rehabilitation: An Atlas for Special Educators*. This lively illustrated book provides a speedy and informative introduction to the stages of the rehabilitation process and the mission of the state-federal vocational rehabilitation program.

In actual practice, the single most important event to improve the coordination between special education and rehabilitation of the retarded was the origination of work-study programs. These programs were practically nonexistent prior to 1960. However, by 1969, a survey "conservatively" indicated over 96,000 handicapped students were being served by them (*State Agency Exchange*, 1969). These 1,334 work-study programs were based on a cooperative agreement between state vocational rehabilitation agencies and school districts. The following chapter provides an overview of this type of program which has served as a major habilitation vehicle in improving the retarded students' transition from school to work.

In spite of these improvements in the coordination between special education and rehabilitation, much remains to be done to insure the successful outcome of the habilitative process for the mentally retarded. The following models are intended to enhance the educational-vocational continuum and insure that the retarded student will

> progress sequentially through a series of activities designed to meet his special learning needs, including content that will assist him to move successfully across the gap that frequently exists between the world of school and the world of work (Younie and Rusalem, 1971, p. 19).

THE PROCESS OF HABILITATION

Skillful planning and programming are essential to eventual successful vocational habilitation and thus should be grounded in the following basic assumptions:

Habilitation-rehabilitation can and should be *ahistorical* in its approach to individuals.

Effective habilitation-rehabilitation planning and programming is based on an *individualized* approach throughout the process.

Learning is sequential in nature and retarded persons are prepared for rehabilitation by a longitudinal developmental process; thus, planning and programming should be built on an orderly approach from the general to the specific.

The major component parts (e.g., evaluation, training) of an effective habilitation-rehabilitation plan and program are interdependent and in practice often occur simultaneously.

In keeping with these propositions, it must be understood that what follows is not a rigid blueprint. A perfect master plan cannot be developed and implemented which will effectively meet the needs of every retardate in every setting. With this in mind, the following approaches should be integrated into the realities of specific work situations, in accord with the particular needs of the individual retardates involved.

An outline of the pre-habilitation-rehabilitation system or model appears in Table 5-I, followed by a select and brief description of its components.

TABLE 5-I

AN APPLIED MODEL FOR IMPLEMENTING THE PRE-VOCATIONAL
HABILITATION-REHABILITATION PROCESS WITH
RETARDED ADOLESCENTS

Stage	Component Parts
I.	The Pre-Vocational Education Process
	A. Mastering of academic skills
	B. Introduction to occupations
	C. Orientation to work
II.	The Pre-Vocational Training Process
	A. A generic strategy
	B. A behavioral strategy

Stage 1: The Pre-Vocational Education Process

A sound pre-vocational educational program has three basic ingredients: first, a grounding in basic academic skills; second, a cursory but comprehensive introduction to occupations; and third, an orientation to work. A more thorough and comprehensive orientation to curriculum considerations for pre-vocational education at the secondary level than appears here may be found in Brolin's (1972) *Preparing Teachers of Secondary Level Educable Mentally Retarded: A New Model.*

Mastery of Academic Skills

Functional skills in reading and math at about the fourth grade level appear to be valuable, if not necessary, in many jobs held by the retarded. It is the functional nature of these abilities that is important, however, and most existing special education curricula should *deemphasize* rather than increase academic studies. Follow-up research, conducted by Dinger (1961) in the Detroit area, shows that a large number of former special education students work in jobs which utilize little, if any, of their formal academic training. Thirty-three percent of the students that Dinger followed up worked in jobs that required *no* reading skills, and almost all the rest worked in jobs that required little more than word recognition. For example, the most frequent requirements were reading printed tags, signs, inventory sheets, and labels on boxes. And only 31 percent of the retardates had to perform any writing other than signing a check or completing a job application.

Arithmetic appears to be the most critical of basic academic skills important to the working retardate, but here again only a minimal and functional performance level is usually necessary. While 90 percent of the working retardates in Dinger's study were required to perform some type of math, frequently (47%), the skill level was no higher than that of counting. Furthermore, 10 percent of the working retardates had no arithmetic to perform and only 5 percent used any math process higher than that of third or fourth grade. Complementary research by Bobroff

(1956) suggests that these rudimentary skills are generally within the scope of retardates and are provided by special education programs. In the follow-up study of former special education students in Detroit, Dinger found that 81 percent of retarded pupils had, at the time of graduation, arithmetic skills between the second and fifth grade level with a mean of grade 4.2. Generally, the mastery of these basic academic skills should be accomplished by the completion of the seventh or eighth school grade.

Introduction to Occupations

Educational-vocational curricula should offer a broad exposure to most of the major occupational areas. This is crucial because of evidence (Hurley, 1969) that most retardates are hindered in their preparation for work by substantial experiential deficits. In addition, Jeffs (1968) has demonstrated that occupational counseling has positive value to retarded adolescents. In this research, he experimentally studied the effects of occupational information counseling upon the occupational aspirations and goal selection of mentally retarded and slow learning senior high school boys. The reported results suggest that the use of occupational information (1) promotes a greater congruence between interest patterns and occupational choice, (2) influences students to look for occupational goals which are more appropriate to their interest patterns and abilities, and (3) promotes more appropriate occupational aspirations.

Among the broad occupational groupings that might be included in such an introduction are: trades, sales, manufacturing, clerical, agriculture, fishing, construction, transportation, and service, e.g. domestic, food, recreation. A variety of stimulus materials presented by different kinds of communications media might contribute to making such an orientation more interesting and effective. Such teaching methods as lectures, audio and video tapes, films, industrial tours and vocational readings could be used.

Orientation to Work

Orienting the retarded to work is closely related to providing them with an introduction to work. The first provides them with general information upon which to express vocational interest and the latter provides them with general and specific knowledge that will be critical to their performing adequately as employees. A number of general curricula areas for job orientation are described by Dinger (1961) and consist of imparting the following information: (1) use of banking services; (2) job opportunities and employment procedures, e.g., methods of job seeking, interviewing and the filling out of applications; (3) dating, engagement, and preparation for marriage (although Dinger does not mention directly the issue of sex education, this might be the appropriate content area in which to introduce it); (4) rights and duties of a citizen; (5) family health; (6) fundamentals of insurance; (7) transportation techniques; (8) communication techniques, e.g., how to write letters and appropriately use the telephone, telegraph, radio, tape recorder, etc.; (9) budgetary techniques; (10) military service; (11) shopping techniques; (12) community resources, e.g. agencies involved in providing services in health, education, and welfare, employment, rehabilitation, and recreation; (13) credit buying; (14) renting and purchasing housing; (15) home economics; and (16) home repair.

Before beginning a new job, the retarded worker should be provided with a highly-focused "nuts and bolts" orientation to his work surroundings. Some of the particular areas for such specific job orientation are described by Graggert (1962) as: (1) time clocks; (2) work hours; (3) lunch hours and eating areas; (4) work breaks and areas; (5) restroom and locker room location; (6) specific rules of work conduct; (7) fire regulations; (8) location of first aid equipment; and (9) procedures for entering work grievances. Although skills in these areas need to be learned as required by each specific job, they can be introduced in a general sense into the educational program as part of the student's vocational preparation.

Stage II: The Pre-Vocational Training Process

The most promising current approaches to vocational education and habilitation are developmental, behavioristic approaches which include comprehensive programs of evaluation, training, placement, and follow-up. The unique aspects of each approach can be integrated and applied by practitioners, e.g. special education teachers, vocational educators, rehabilitation counselors, in a variety of settings, e.g., schools, workshops, state rehabilitation agencies. Each approach has a solid base in theory and research, has been used successfully, and is adaptable to both retarded and nonretarded persons.

A Generic Strategy: The Guide to Jobs Approach

At the American Institute for Research in Pittsburgh, Pennsylvania, Peterson and Jones (1960 and 1964) developed a system which delineates four stages to the vocational habilitation process with the mentally retarded. Their manual *Guide to Jobs for the Mentally Retarded*, describes the stages as selection and evaluation, training, job identification, and placement.

In the *first stage*, rehabilitants receive an applied vocational *evaluation* at the initial point of selection, at an interim point of diagnostic evaluation, and at a subsequent point of placement evaluation. The initial preliminary screening is intended to provide a rough approximation of student-client skills, whereas the interim evaluation is intended to provide information about specific areas for further job training. The final placement evaluation assesses the person's skills as they relate to one or two specific jobs.

The selection and evaluation process is an applied assessment, making extensive use of general and specific work samples so as to give rehabilitants the opportunity to improve their performance with practice and recognize a realistic threshold of ability. Peterson and Jones feel that superficial assessment results in false negative thresholds of ability and frequent errors in training and placing of an individual in a job for which he is inately overqualified.

The *Personal Characteristics Requirement Scale* is used frequently during this first stage of selection and evaluation. This scale provides the opportunity to rate workers on nineteen job related characteristics, on a three-point trait dimension measure: minimal, moderate, and major. The nineteen personal characteristics reflect: (1) social skills (self-expression, sociability, work independence, physical appearance, and team work); (2) time skills (pace, attendance, simultaneity, and timing); (3) performance skills (accuracy, dexterity, choices, direction, memory, and caution); and (4) tolerance requirements (repetitiveness, perseverance, and stamina).

In the *second stage,* rehabilitants receive vocational *training:* first work adjustment training which is intended to develop basic work habits and skills, then general skill training which provides the potential worker with competencies in fairly common work activities, and finally, specific job training which prepares the worker for one or two jobs and utilizes on-the-job training techniques.

Peterson and Jones recommend that during job analysis, procedures be utilized to break down specific jobs into a sequential chain of tasks related to successful job performance. Often this is best accomplished by the professional person first doing the job himself, simultaneously making careful notes on the steps involved.

The *Job Activity Requirements Scale* can be a useful measure in general and specific job training and is tangentially related to job analysis. This instrument identifies the jobs most commonly held by retarded persons. Each activity is rated according to the extent that it is required (minimal, moderate, or major) to meet its unique features (hazard to person, hazard to material, cannot be supervised, and other), and to the ideal location for training (on the job, orientation, workshop, or school). Job activity requirement scales are provided for the 131 jobs most commonly held by retardates.

The *third stage* of the approach involves *locating appropriate jobs* and *employers* within a local community and laying the groundwork for eventual job placement of a specific retardate. These authors offer a number of hints to facilitate this particular part of the habilitation process. First, they suggest that practitioners collect information about jobs in the local community, emphasizing semi-skilled and unskilled work. The Chamber of Commerce is one potential source for such information. Further, it is suggested that their job requirement profiles be reviewed and new profiles be developed where the existing ones are incomplete. A second suggestion is to review job opportunities with specific employers where the focus is on selling the retarded. A third hint involves summarizing the general job opportunity picture as reflected within the local community. This summarization should include delineation of jobs by type and sex, a summary of the job activity requirements for all jobs, and the personal characteristics requirements as well as the frequency and nature of the special considerations involved in successful employment. Finally, it is suggested that employers be kept informed and that employment data be continuously reviewed and updated.

A useful list of those jobs most commonly held by retarded persons is provided by Bobroff (1956), Dinger (1961), Peters and Rhode (1964), Peterson and Jones (1960 and 1964), and *Statistical Notes* (1969). In addition, a pictorial graph based on two surveys is presented on page 94 of this book. In spite of the usefulness that these job lists may serve, the practitioner must be aware of the fact that, to some degree, they are a sign of stereotypic job placement practices with the retarded. As Reed and Weiss (1969) and Elo and Hendel (1972) have stated, one is not justified in placing persons into service and unskilled areas simply on the basis of a "mental retardation" label. Even though service and unskilled occupations represent the major job placements for the retarded, a further broadening of job opportunities for the retarded can and should be achieved.

The best timing for job identification is subject to debate. A rule of thumb, however, might be to finish most basic job identifications before beginning training and attempting a specific job placement.

The *fourth* and last *stage* of the habilitation process described by Peterson and Jones is *vocational placement,* which involves extensive work in preparing individual retardates and substantial contact with specific employers where appropriate and necessary. The general availability of community jobs appropriate to a specific retardate should be reviewed, specific employers identified, and information relevant to the application solicited.

Specific emphasis should be placed on the initial contact of the retardate with the employer, and counselors may wish to invoke role playing techniques to approximate real life situations and improve client's interviewing skills. Contact with employers may be necessary before some preliminary interviews, and occasionally it may be desirable for the rehabilitationist to accompany the client to the job interview. In addition, it is suggested that the counselor preview the interview with the client and the employer and to follow-up interviews with the employer if the client is hired for the job. However, direct employer contact should be minimized because, in general, it tends to perpetuate client dependency and to project a weaker image of the client in the employer's eyes. In essence, unnecessary counselor intervention is viewed as counter-productive to successful vocational placement.

The Peterson and Jones (1964) approach to vocational education and rehabilitation provides a logical system for the vocational evaluation, training and placement of retarded and non-retarded persons. The specific profile developed on the jobs most commonly held by the retarded is helpful in its own right, but perhaps the greatest value of their entire approach is flexibility. That is, the basic approach can be applied to new jobs not delineated in the *Guide,* and it can be used to redesign existing jobs presently not held by retarded persons. Thus, it appears to be a very adaptable approach, one which fits nearly all communities and nearly all capable practitioners.

A Behavioral Strategy: Transenvironmental Programming

In recent years a number of attempts have been initiated to operationalize the principles of learning theory to the habilitation-rehabilitation of retarded persons. These treatments which carry a variety of terms, e.g. behavior modification, behavior analysis and operant conditioning, focus on teaching individuals adaptive coping behaviors as well as helping them to extinguish or control undesirable behaviors. One of the more cogent examples of this type of habilitation programming has been practiced by a group from the University of Oregon Rehabilitation Research and Training Center in Mental Retardation. A complete description of their approach, which is called "Trans-environmental Programming," is found in Chapter 8.

The developers of this program suggest that successful habili-tation must begin with specification of terminal performances desired of clients, followed by delineation of the specific skills and behaviors necessary to successfully complete these outcomes. Such skills and behaviors must be arranged in their proper se-quential order within a training hierarchy, and only then can a selection of appropriate training procedures relevant to the training hierarchies be made. In other words, this approach be-gins by defining the product desired, e.g. competitive workers, and then designs the machinery necessary to manufacture the product itself, e.g. improving poise, dexterity, etc.

This general description of transenvironmental programming is operationalized in six specific program stages: *evaluation* and *pretraining; pre-vocational programming; contract workshop; pre-placement training;* and *in-placement programming.* Again, each of these phases receives detailed elaboration in the referred to chapter.

This behavioristic model represents one of the more scientifi-cally based approaches to programming the vocational process with mentally retarded clients. It is precisely defined, rigorously based on learning theory, and empirically has been found to be a viable approach. The following represent only a few of the many studies which demonstrate the efficacy of the behavioral approach with the retarded.

White (1968) reports the results of a study designed to train a severely retarded male to perform the duties of "job helper" in a local bakery. In this case, the subject was trained on the job to check bread dough as it dropped into trays, fill empty contain-ers, straighten the dough if needed, and then place the trays (each containing four pans) onto racks of fifty trays each. The rate of machine production was approximately fifty trays every 4.5 minutes or about 11.1 trays per minute. Previously, the man-ager of the bakery had employed retarded clients for two posi-tions which, in the opinion of the supervisor, required less skill, coordination, or discriminative ability than the "job helper" position. It is interesting to note that the two previously employed retardates required approximately three and six months of training, respectively, whereas, the subject in this study was trained in a period of two and one-half weeks. Within this short period of time he was performing at the machine rate without instructions, imposed aids or props, or direct supervision.

Crosson (1969) reports the success of vocationally training a severely retarded person in a workshop. The client learned to operate a drill press in less than two hours with this approach. He progressed from performing an average of 60 percent out of one hundred successful operants to 90 percent accuracy after only six trials, and he obtained completely errorless vocational task behavior after eighteen trials.

Peterson (1969) reports the results of behavioral training procedures applied to a trainable retarded youth with a mental age of six. The subject who was enrolled in a sheltered workshop, was trained to polish rental roller skates for a local skating rink. The analysis and programming of this vocational task was a twenty-nine step procedure. In thirteen sessions which occurred over a month's duration, he learned this task, as well as the use of city bus service to transport himself to and from the job. The trainee was employed at the rink for six months and, based on follow-up data, his production rate remained above the criterion level.

Probably one of the more enlightening results of the behavioral approach is that with the proper techniques and procedures retardates are capable of learning much more than was originally expected. For more information about this strategy to the rehabilitation process and its results, three sources are especially suggested: (1) Gardner, W. I., *Behavior Modification and Mental Retardation: A Behavior Modification Approach to the Education and Rehabilitation of the Mentally Retarded* (1971); (2) Gardner, J. M. and Watson, L. S., *Behavior Modification of the Mentally Retarded: An Annotated Bibliography* (1969); and (3) Gold, M. W., *Research on the Vocational Habilitation of the Retarded: The Present, the Future* (1973). Additional related materials may be found in Pigott (1969), Durfee (1969),

Cushing (1969), Ayllon and Azrin (1968), Zimmerman, Overpeck, Eisenberg, and Garlick (1969), and Zimmerman, Stuckey,
Garlick, and Miller (1969).

Some personnel working in the field of rehabilitation may
question themselves and be questioned by others regarding the
humaneness of applying behavioristic techniques to the retarded. Behaviorism has been actively criticized since its first experiments with animals in laboratories, but critics of behaviorism
generally have been unable to utilize more effective or efficient
procedures for assisting disabled persons to higher levels of self-
sufficiency and social progress. Furthermore, such criticism over-
looks the fact that all forms of education and habilitation involve some type of covert or overt manipulation on the part of
the so-called helper.

Both the generic and behavioral models discussed here include
the vocational placement process which represents the culmination of all previous educational and training efforts. Because of
the importance of this final phase of the vocational habilitation
process, the reader is encouraged to look at Chapter 9, which presents a systematic and applied model of vocational placement.

AVOCATIONAL HABILITATION

This last area represents a slight departure from the previous
sections devoted primarily to pre-vocational education and training for the mentally retarded. However, failure to discuss the
avocational area would overlook its importance in the total habilitation process.

The importance of avocational habilitation, which focuses on
helping retardates (as well as nonretardates) become increasingly adept in making functional use of leisure time, was recognized by the panel appointed by President John F. Kennedy
(*Report to the President,* 1962):

> The adolescent's vital need for successful social interaction and
> recreational experiences is frequently intensified by isolation result-
> ing from parental overprotection, the numerous failure experiences
> in school and occupational pursuits, and by his exclusion by normal
> groups from their everyday play, group, and social activities. For the

retarded adult, opportunity in constructive use of leisure time may prove a factor in maintaining community adjustment (pp. 95-96).

Related to this area are three major sources which have evolved since the Panel's report: (1) Avedon, E. M. and Arje, F. G., *Socio-Recreative Programming for the Retarded* (1964), (2) Neal, L. (Ed.), *Recreation's Role in the Rehabilitation of the Mentally Retarded* (1970), and (3) Freeman, B. L., *Habilitative Recreation for the Mentally Retarded* (1971). In spite of these few efforts, we have yet to give serious consideration to this area of habilitation.

For some retardates, avocational habilitation *must* be a primary consideration and vocational habilitation secondary. This fact is due, in some instances, to the complexity of a particular individual's problems, while in others it relates to general and specific economic conditions. In still other cases, a combination of multiple client problems and economic conditions are involved. The employment problem in America results from the imbalance of the demand for jobs and the supply of workers to fill jobs. Childs (1966) noted that each year we are *less* successful in balancing the number of jobs with the number of job seekers. He reports that the labor force of the 1960's was half again greater than that of the 1950's. During the same period, unemployment advanced from 3 percent to 5.6 percent, and today it is consistently over 6 percent. Among the general population there may be a 10 percent to 15 percent unemployment rate by 1980, and by the year 2000, it may have soared to between 25 percent and 40 percent. How the retarded will be affected is subject to speculation. Although some people argue that employment levels will not decrease among the retarded, no one seems to be arguing that employment levels will be higher than they are today. This strongly suggests that avocational habilitation must become more than a catchy phrase, both for retarded as well as nonretarded persons.

Work, contrary to the wishes of some idealists, is not an inalienable right for retarded persons. What perhaps is an inalienable right is the *opportunity to achieve something intrinsically meaningful with one's life and to be publicly rewarded for it.* Status in most societies, and notably democratic societies, is conferred upon individuals who have achieved success in activities that the society values. Traditionally, work has been the only critical role for status achievement; however, this need not be the case, and because of increasing unemployment, cannot continue to be the case. Avocational status hierachies must be developed, in which individuals will be rewarded for achieving according to their individual goals and abilities. In other words, status would continue to be conferred according to success in competition; however, the competitive base for valued production would be broadened so that, ideally, people could compete against themselves, in vocational and avocational areas rather than against each other.

Perhaps it is not realistic to visualize such profound changes in societal values. However, critics may wish to consider some historical, cultural precedents in which work was devalued and avocational activities valued. When their empires were at fullest bloom, the Greeks viewed work as a curse, the Romans thought of it as vulgar, and the Hebrews considered work to be a drudgery (Childs, 1966). Finally, in a recent monograph entitled, *Mental Retardation and the Future*, McGovern (1972) stated

> The importance of avocational and leisure time activities cannot be ignored, for futurists have predicted that 20th and 21st Century man is entering an era of greater leisure time (p. 76).

Hopefully, our future will be a time in which persons can be recognized and appreciated for avocational as well as vocational accomplishments.

SUMMARY

Because vocational and avocational skills are so essential to societal recognition and self-satisfaction, the habilitation process of the mentally retarded should begin in early school years and be stressed throughout the educational and vocational program. Consequently, closer coordination between rehabilitation counselors and special education teachers is essential, as is greater emphasis on students' vocational development within teacher training curricula. Educational programs should give the student not only basic academic skills but also a broad introduction to possible future occupations and an orientation to specific job situations and skills.

Some pre-vocational training processes have been developed. In one by Peterson and Jones, the student's occupational abilities are evaluated through testing, possible jobs are broken down into specific skills, available jobs are located by a well-informed vocational counselor, and the student is prepared for interviews and specific placement. In addition, behavioral prevocational programs have demonstrated considerable success in training retarded individuals to work and to learn more than had been previously expected.

Although the vocational training and eventual placement are of vital importance, avocational preparation should be stressed, also, to promote adjustment and satisfaction in the retardate's life as a whole.

REFERENCES

Avedon, E. M., and Arje, F. U.: *Socio-Recreative Programming for the Retarded*. New York, Bureau of Publications, Teachers College, Columbia University, 1964.

Ayllon, T., and Azrin, V.: *The Token Economy: A Motivational System for Therapy and Rehabilitation*. New York, Appleton-Century-Crofts, 1968.

Bobroff, A.: Economic adjustment of 121 adults, formerly students in classes for the mental retardates. *American Journal of Mental Deficiency, 60:* 525-535, 1956.

Brolin, D.: *Preparing Teachers of Secondary Level Educable Mentally Retarded: A New Model*. Menomonie, Wisconsin, University of Wisconsin-Stout, Department of Rehabilitation and Manpower Services, School of Education, 1972 (Final Report Grant No. OEG-0-70-4818(603), Office of Education, U. S. Department of Health, Education and Welfare).

Childs, G. B.: Is the work ethic realistic in an age of automation. In Peters, H. J., and Hansen, J. C. (Eds.): *Vocational Guidance and Career Development*. New York, The Macmillan Company, 1966, pp. 3-12.

Crosson, J. E.: A technique for programming sheltered workshop environments for training severely retarded workers. *American Journal of Mental Deficiency, 73:*814-818.

Cushing, M.: When counseling fails then what? *Journal of Rehabilitation,* July-August:18-20, 1969.

Dinger, J. C.: Post adjustment of former educable retarded pupils. *Exceptional Child, 27*:353-356, 1961.

Durfee, R. P.: Another look at conditioning therapy. *Journal of Rehabilitation,* July-August:16-18, 1969.

Elo, M., and Hendel, D.: Classification as "Mentally Retarded": A determinant of vocational rehabilitation outcomes. *American Journal of Mental Deficiency, 77*(2):190-198, 1972.

Freeman, B. L.: *Habilitative Recreation for the Mentally Retarded.* University of Alabama in Birmingham, Center for Developmental and Learning Disorders, 1971.

Gardner, W. I.: *Behavior Modification and Mental Retardation. A Behavior Modification Approach to the Education and Rehabilitation of the Mentally Retarded.* Chicago, Aldine, 1971.

Gold, M. W.: Research on the vocational habilitation of the retarded: The present, the future. In Ellis, N. R. (Ed.): *International Review of Research in Mental Retardation.* New York, Academic Press, 1973.

Graggert, H. T.: Differential diagnosis, training, and job placement for the mentally retarded. *Journal of Rehabilitation, 30*:35-37, 1962.

Heath, E. J.: *The Mentally Retarded Student and Guidance* (Series V: Guidance and the Exceptional Student). Boston, Houghton Mifflin Company, 1970.

Hensley, G., and Buck, D. P. (Eds.): *Exploring Rehabilitation-Special Education Relationships.* Boulder, Colorado, Western Interstate Commission for Higher Education, May, 1968.

Hurley, R.: *Poverty and Mental Retardation: A Causal Relationship.* New York, Vintage Press, 1969.

Jeffs, G. A.: The effect of occupational information on the vocational aspirations of the retarded. In Wright, G. N., and Trotter, A. B. (Eds.): *Rehabilitation Research.* Madison, Wisconsin, The University of Wisconsin, 1968, pp. 167-174.

McGovern, K. B.: Rehabilitation, education, mental retardation and the future: A group analysis. In McGovern, K. B., and Browning, P. L. (Eds.): *Mental Retardation and the Future.* Eugene, Oregon, Rehabilitation Research and Training Center in Mental Retardation, University of Oregon, Monograph No. 5, April, 1972.

Neal, L. (Ed.): *Recreation's Role in the Rehabilitation of the Mentally Retarded.* Eugene, Oregon, Rehabilitation Research and Training Center in Mental Retardation, University of Oregon, Monograph No. 4, 1970.

Peters, J. S., and Rhode, H. J.: Successful work-study program for mentally retarded. *Rehabilitation Record, 8*:11-15, 1964.

Peterson, C. M.: Positive reinforcement in the vocational training of a trainable mental retardate: A case report. University of Oregon, Rehabilitation Research and Training Center in Mental Retardation, Working Paper No. 33, August, 1969.

Peterson, R. O., and Jones, M.: *Guide to Jobs for the Mentally Retarded.* Pittsburgh: American Institute for Research, 1960 and 1964.

Pigott, R. A.: Behavior modification and control in rehabilitation. *Journal of Rehabilitation,* July-August:12-15, 1969.

Reed, M. H., and Weiss, D. J.: Counseling outcomes for mentally retarded clients, Psychology Department, University of Minnesota (Mimeographed), 1969.

Report to the President: A Proposal Program for National Action to Combat Mental Retardation. The President's Panel on Mental Retardation, Washington, D. C., October, 1972.

State Agency Exchange. Published by Rehabilitation Interagency Focus, 1522 K Street, N. W., Room 1120, Washington, D. C. 20005, December, 1969.

Statistical Notes: A Profile of Mentally Retarded Clients Rehabilitated During Fiscal Year 1967. U. S. Department of Health, Education and Welfare, Social and Rehabilitation Service, Rehabilitation Services Administration, No. 10, February, 1969.

White, O. R.: The analysis and programming of vocational behavior. University of Oregon, Rehabilitation Research and Training Center in Mental Retardation, Working Paper No. 17, August, 1968.

Wolfensberger, W.: Vocational preparation and occupation. In Baumeister, A. A. (Ed.): *Mental Retardation: Appraisal, Education and Rehabilitation.* Chicago, Aldine, 1967, pp. 232-273.

Younie, W. J., and Rusalem, H.: *The World of Rehabilitation: An Atlas for Special Educators.* New York, The John Day Company, 1971.

Zimmerman, J.; Overpeck, C.; Eisenberg, H.; and Garlick, B.: Operant conditioning in a sheltered workshop: Further data in support of an objective and systematic approach to rehabilitation, *Rehabilitation Literature,* 30(11):326-334, November, 1969.

Zimmerman, J.; Stuckey, T. E.; Garlick, V. J.; and Miller, M.: Effects of token reinforcement on productivity in multiple handicapped clients in a sheltered workshop. *Rehabilitation Literature,* 30(2):34-41, February, 1969.

Chapter 6

WORK-STUDY PROGRAMS FOR THE MENTALLY RETARDED: AN OVERVIEW

Andrew S. Halpern

OVER THE PAST FIFTEEN YEARS, there has been a steadily increasing interest in high school work experience programs for the educable mentally retarded. The rationale for these programs is to provide retarded high school pupils with the kinds of experiences they need to move successfully from the school environment to adult community life.

In an overview of this type of rehabilitation program for the mentally retarded, specific attention needs to be directed to work-study programs in terms of their (1) goals, (2) administrative structure, (3) curriculum content and emphasis, (4) efficacy, and (5) current issues and their implications for the future.

GOALS

One important aim of special education, as of all education, is to prepare young people for the role of participating citizen. However, achieving this goal is frequently a problem for educable mentally retarded youth because of the lack of secondary school curricula that can mediate between school and the work world. One approach to solving this problem is the so-called work-study programs, conducted cooperatively by the public schools and local offices of state rehabilitation agencies. The general goal of these programs is to create a unified academic, social, and prevocational curriculum focused on preparing pupils for successful community adjustment.

A variety of specific goals have been suggested by those who staff existing programs. The best summary of these objectives is probably that found in a recent handbook for teachers in Cali-

120

fornia work-study programs (Campbell et al., 1971). The handbook stipulates that work-study programs should encourage the development of attitudes and skills that will:

Lead to the formation of habits enabling pupils to understand themselves and to get along with others.

Lead to the formation of habits promoting emotional security and moving pupils toward independence.

Lead to the formation of sound habits in physical development, health, safety, and sanitation.

Enable pupils to become adequate members of a family and to become future homemakers.

Enable all pupils to develop their maximum capabilities in the basic tool subjects through individualized instruction that helps them to apply the communication and computational skills in the solution of problems encountered in everyday living situations.

Enable pupils to express themselves through music, art, and drama and to appreciate and enjoy these and other arts.

Assist pupils in selecting and participating in wholesome leisure time activities.

Lead to the acceptance of civic responsibility as participating, productive members of their communities.

Enable pupils to participate in occupational and vocational experience within the school environment and within the community in developing economic self-sufficiency (p. 9).

ADMINISTRATIVE STRUCTURES

Understanding the service delivery patterns of work-study programs requires an examination of their administrative structures. Four major types of agreements have evolved among the agencies that participate in these programs. One of these is informal, whereas, the remaining three involve formal interagency contracts.

Two-Party Contract

The first type of formal agreement is a two party contract between the state division of vocational rehabilitation and a local school district. At the core of this agreement is the assignment by the school district of a secondary level teacher to function as a work coordinator. This teacher is then released from ordinary instructional activities for part of each day in order to perform a variety of other duties, which may include finding community work placements for pupils, supervising pupils on their work placements, participating in parent conferences or helping develop overall habilitation plans for their pupils. The rehabilitation agency then certifies the time spent by the teacher as a work coordinator as work done under its aegis. In addition, the rehabilitation agency certifies the teacher's salary for that time as state "in-kind" matching funds, which it can then use to generate additional federal funds. These federal monies are deposited in the state rehabilitation agency's general fund to be used in part to provide services to the pupils in the school district with whom the contract was negotiated.

In addition to providing a mechanism for generating federal funds, the two-party formal agreement has a number of administrative characteristics that help strengthen work-study programs. Certifying a portion of the teacher's time as a work coordinator helps to guarantee that these important activities in the habilitation process will be carried out. The contract also guarantees that *all* eligible pupils in the cooperating school district will receive rehabilitation services. Moreover, the counselors assigned by the rehabilitation agency to work with these programs usually have smaller caseloads than general agency counselors. All of these administrative characteristics increase the likelihood that a high quality of service will be delivered.

Three-Party Contract

The two other types of formal agreement are basically modifications of the two-party contract with an additional third or a fourth cooperating agency. Three-party formal agreements generally involve the state department of special education as well as the state division of vocational rehabilitation and a local school district. When the state department of special education is involved in these agreements, it serves primarily as a consultant to the individual school districts and thus helps insure more uniform contracts throughout the state. In addition, many state departments of special education become involved in developing curriculum and program guides for work-study programs in their state.

Four-Party Contract

Only a few four-party formal contracts have been negotiated to date. These involve the state department of vocational education in addition to the agencies of the three-party agreement. The state department of vocational education has participated in the general development of program guidelines and has also contributed financially to the support of individual programs. Although this type of agreement is not yet prevalent, it may come to be the preferred one because of today's strong movement to integrate the educable retarded into regular school programs, of which vocational education is surely the most appropriate type provided at the secondary level.

Informal Agreement

In contrast to the three types of formal contractual agreements, there is also an informal two-party model, which involves collaboration between a special education teacher and a rehabilitation counselor with a general caseload. In this type of arrangement, the special education teacher refers pupils to the rehabilitation counselor who may or may not accept these referrals, depending on whether he has vacancies in his caseload. Service to pupils in this type of program may be as good as that provided through contractual programs; however, the informal agreement cannot guarantee the availability of service.

There are three situations in which an informal agreement is likely to occur. The first is in a secondary school where there are too few EMR pupils to justify assigning part of a teacher's time to work coordination. The second, which is similar, is in the local rehabilitation office which does not have sufficient staff to assign a counselor to a work-study program that requires smaller caseloads. The third situation cuts to the heart of the problems of interagency collaboration in that it involves the issue of agency autonomy.

As mentioned above, the financial support of formally contracted work-study programs depends, in part, on certification of a portion of the teacher's time as a work coordinator who provides rehabilitation services. The salary for this time is further certified by the rehabilitation agency as a third-party match for generating federal funds. Federal regulations, however, stipulate that the work coordinator's certified time must be *supervised* by the rehabilitation agency. This requirement has caused many school districts to balk at entering into contractual agreements with the vocational rehabilitation agency. In Oregon, both the state department of special education and the vocational rehabilitation agree that the policy on supervision is one of the most serious hindrances to the development of strong work-study programs.

CURRICULUM

Although much has been written suggesting the allocation of pupil time within work-study programs (e.g. Kolstoe and Frey, 1965), there are very few descriptions of kinds of activities actually experienced by pupils in these programs. One exception is a study of the work-study programs in Oregon conducted by the Oregon Research and Training Center. Twenty-six of the fifty-nine work coordinators in Oregon participated in this study and provided information on the program activities of a total of 354 pupils (Halpern et al., 1972).

Between February and May 1972, the participating work coordinators provided information on the course of study of their pupils, the work placements of these pupils, and their pupils' achievement in various social and prevocational skills. The highlights of this study which follow are intended to provide an empirical picture of the content and emphasis of work-study programs.

Curriculum Content

During nine of the fifteen weeks of the study, twenty-five of the participating teachers kept detailed individual inventories of the curriculum that was provided to each of their pupils. Nearly three-and-one-half million minutes of classroom time were ultimately accounted for, as well as the time pupils spent on work placement and on interim activities such as lunch and passing between classes.

Some pupils received work placements during the study; others did not. The total day of those who spent part of their day on work placement can be described in four categories: (1) direct instructional time under the work coordinator; (2) direct instructional time under other classroom teachers; (3) time spent on work placements; and (4) time spent eating or moving between classes.

Each bar in Figure 6-1 shows the percent of time spent by pupils in that activity within each of the twenty-five participating schools. For example, the bar on the far left shows that in one school pupils receiving work placement during part of the day spent around 5 percent of their time receiving instruction from their work coordinator, around 55 percent in another school, and slightly over 30 percent in the median or thirteenth school. Looking at the time spent on work placement, there is again great variation among schools, ranging from 10 to 65 percent, with a median of around 35 percent. The message seems to be clear: teachers in Oregon vary tremendously in the kinds of experi-

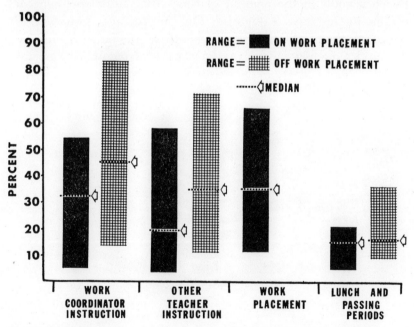

Figure 6-1. Distribution of time spent in school as a function of being on or off work placement.

ences they provide their pupils under the title of work-study programs.

The time pupils spent receiving instruction, from either the work coordinator or other teachers, was classified and recorded into seventy-four categories. To facilitate interpretation of this information, these categories have been grouped into nine major clusters: (1) communication skills, including reading, writing, spelling, and language arts; (2) employability, including work habits and job search skills; (3) economic self-sufficiency, including budgeting and purchasing skills; (4) family living, including home management and nutrition; (5) leisure time, including art, drama, and music; (6) citizenship, including social studies and current events; (7) personal habits, including grooming and hygiene; (8) self concept; and (9) other, a catch-all category including such things as physical education, driver's education, field trips, and counseling.

Figure 6-2 shows that there were again great differences between schools in the amount of time that pupils spent in each of the instructional categories. On the average, however, disregarding the catch-all category of "other," the largest percentage of pupil time was spent in the area of communication skills,

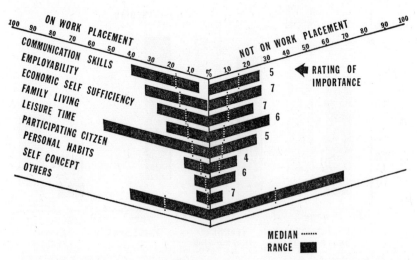

Figure 6-2. Curriculum emphasis for pupils on and off work placement.

followed by employability, economic self-sufficiency, family living, leisure time, citizenship, personal habits, and self-concept. This ordering of instructional emphasis was identical for all pupils, whether or not they were on work placement.

The numbers on the right side of Figure 6-2 indicate ratings of importance for each of the eight major curriculum clusters. These ratings were generated by the work coordinators, using a scale of increasing importance from one to seven.

A number of interesting discrepancies appear between the rated importance of certain areas and the amount of instructional time actually provided in these areas. For example, the highly-rated categories of self-concept and personal habits received relatively little instructional emphasis, whereas the lower rated category of communication skills, which encompasses much of traditional academics, received a disproportionately large instructional emphasis.

Work Experience

As shown in Figure 6-1, pupils who participated in work experience spent, on the average, one-third of their time in this activity. Of the 354 pupils in the sample, 259 (or 73 percent) received one or more placements during the period of data collection. Once again, the differences between schools were remarkable, some work coordinators finding at least one placement for all of their pupils while others placed only 25 percent of their pupils.

What distinguished the pupils who received work placements from those who did not? As might have been expected, older pupils were more likely to receive placements than younger ones (see Figure 6-3). However, the placement of many younger pupils on jobs may indicate a growing belief that early vocational experience is important to overall vocational development.

On the other hand, the sex, IQ levels, or cognitive and motor skills of pupils (as judged by teachers) did not appear to determine who received work placements. Since nearly all prediction studies on the mentally retarded have failed to find a significant relationship between IQ and level of vocational adjustment

(Goldstein, 1964; Wolfensberger, 1967; Cobb, 1972), it was especially encouraging to discover that the teachers did not base their selections on pupil IQ.

One interesting factor, however, did seem to influence the teacher's decision concerning who would and would not receive work placements. During the first week of data collection, work coordinators were asked to rate each of their pupils on a set of adjectives which described pupil attitudes and personality characteristics. The placement rates for pupils who received check marks on the various adjectives were then compared with the placement rate of 73 percent for the total sample. As can be

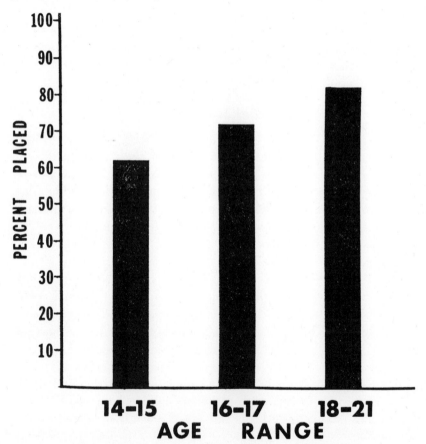

Figure 6-3. Work placement as a function of pupil age.

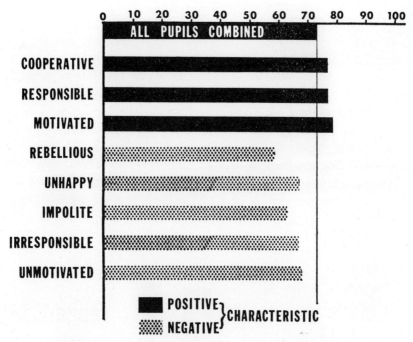

Figure 6-4. Percent of pupils receiving work placement.

seen in Figure 6-4, pupils *less* likely to receive work placements were those who were rated by their teachers as rebellious, unhappy, impolite, irresponsible. Pupils *more* likely to receive work placements were those who were rated by their teachers as cooperative, responsible, or motivated. The likelihood that pupil success was a selection criterion for teachers in deciding who should receive work placements is strongly suggested.

Efficacy

Having examined the curriculum and the work experience components of work study programs, at least as far as Oregon is concerned, the question remains concerning the efficacy of these programs. Two kinds of evidence will be presented: short-term results within the classroom and long-term follow-up results within the community.

Short-Term Evidence

One of the primary objectives of the Oregon study was the development of a battery of tests measuring pupil achievement in social and pre-vocational skills. Data from these tests provide some short-term classroom results within the Oregon study.

From the eight curriculum clusters, ten specific abilities have thus far been developed into tests of pupil achievement. The first five tests assess skills in banking, purchasing, health care and nutrition, functional signs, and job seeking. The second five tests include budgeting, home management, work habits, personal hygiene, and the perception of social cues. The tests are easily administered in small groups, requiring approximately fifteen minutes per test.

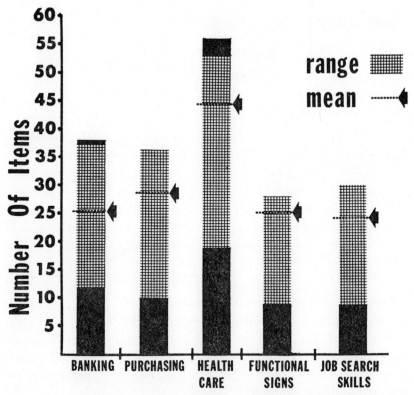

Figure 6-5. Level of mastery on first five tests.

The results of the first five tests show that most pupils in the Oregon work-study programs have a mastery of banking, purchasing, health care, functional signs, and job search skills. The mean scores in all cases exceed 75 percent correct answers, and, in the case of functional signs, the mean is only three points below the maximum possible score. Results from the second five tests are still being analyzed so were not available at the time of this writing.

An expected positive correlation was found between IQ level and each of the five tests. The correlations ranged from .4 to .5, which is typical of the relationships usually found between IQ and tests of academic achievement. A positive relationship was also expected between age and achievement test proficiency, under the assumption that older pupils would attain higher test scores. However, with the exception of the test of recognition of functional signs, there was no apparent relationship between age and test proficiency, which suggests that the skills measured by these tests may have been learned by many of the pupils before they reached high school. This possibility is currently being investigated by administering the tests to three hundred junior high EMR pupils in twenty-two Oregon classrooms.

In order to fully trust the results of these paper and pencil tests, it is necessary to establish their validity. Therefore, all graduating seniors from work-study programs in Oregon are being tested on the full battery of ten tests, with a follow-up study to be conducted in one year to determine the level of community adjustment of each former work-study pupil. Then test scores will be correlated with measures of community adjustment in order to estimate the predictive validity of the tests.

Follow-up Evidence

The ultimate test of work-study programs is how they prepare their pupils for adult community adjustment. A number of follow-up studies, three of which are considered below, have investigated the efficacy of such programs.

As mentioned in Chapter 4, forty-three Research and Demonstration projects have been funded by the Federal government in the area of work-study programs. In a recent study (Halpern, 1972), the final reports from projects were analyzed in order to evaluate their collective impact. Within the various projects, the pupils who received a full complement of services were distinguished from those that were only partially served. Therefore, comparison of the former with the latter could be used as one test of the efficacy of the program. When the projects were rank ordered according to their employment outcomes, it was found that 75 percent of the fully served pupil-clients in the median positioned project were employed, whereas only 52 percent of those who were partially served in the same project were employed. Since comparable employment rates for nonretarded but economically disadvantaged adolescents were around 80 percent, these R and D projects provided favorable evidence of the efficacy of the fully implemented work-study model.

During the summers of 1969 and 1970, a follow-up study was conducted on two groups who had terminated from work-study programs in Oregon one year previously (Halpern, 1972). For each subject, an employment index was constructed which reflected his degree of employment during the twelve-month period following high school termination. The employment records of the graduates were found to be superior to those of the dropouts.

A third follow-up study conducted in Kansas (Chaffin et al., 1971) examined the employment status of former work-study pupils two years after their high school termination. Two groups were compared: one which participated in a work-study program and the other which experienced a high school program without a work-study component. At the time of the follow-up, 83 percent of the work-study group was employed whereas 75 percent of the comparison group was employed, suggesting little difference between the two groups with respect to *degree* of employment. The *level* of employment for the two groups, however, was substantially different, the work-study group showing a mean gross weekly wage of $90.54 and the comparison group only $62.84.

Although research is still needed to pinpoint the specific processes that are maximally effective within work-study programs, the above cited studies provide support for the continuing use of this model as a means of delivering effective rehabilitation services to the mentally retarded.

CURRENT ISSUES AND PROBLEMS

There are a number of important issues that should be discussed in the areas of administrative structures, curriculum, work experience, and efficacy. Some of them are discussed in an excellent paper by Deno (1970).

With respect to administrative structures, there seems little doubt that, in most instances, formal contracts are more likely than informal agreements to result in interagency collaboration and high quality services. However, the requirement that the high school work coordinator be supervised by the rehabilitation agency has frequently caused bad feelings between the parties of existing contracts and, at times, has even prevented the consolidation of a contract. Not only is the autonomy of a school district threatened by this regulation, but the teacher assigned as work coordinator often has more experience in the vocational training of the retarded than the rehabilitation counselor who is assigned as his "supervisor." One possible solution to this problem is waiving the requirement for supervision of third-party matching funds (i.e. the work coordinator's salary) in the case of work-study programs. Another solution is encouraging alternate methods of financing rather than relying, as at present, on federal funding that requires certifying the work coordinator's salary for the purpose of matching.

One of the most interesting findings of the Oregon study was the great variation in curriculum provided to pupils, all within the context of work-study programs. Both the type and the amount of instruction varied greatly from classroom to classroom; it appears that although there may be agreement on the broad philosophical goals of work-study programs, the actual methods of implementing such programs are by no means uniform.

In spite of this variation in curriculum, some general trends were discernible. The most interesting was the strong emphasis on traditional academic subjects, such as reading, writing, spelling, and arithmetic, despite the participating teachers considering traditional academics less important than social and pre-vocational training. However, since teachers are typically unprepared to provide social and pre-vocational instruction, they may emphasize academic subjects more of necessity than by choice.

Whatever the reason for the curriculum emphasis of Oregon teachers, the ideal balance of academic, social, and pre-vocational instruction remains an unknown. In fact, the professional literature reveals two current, different directions. One is toward increased integration of EMR's into regular school programs (Dunn, 1968; Lilly, 1970), which, if successful, should include a continued emphasis on academic subjects as well as on vocational education. The other is toward the development of curricula specifically for EMR's, with a strong, almost exclusive, emphasis on social and pre-vocational skills (Goldstein, 1972; Heiss and Mischio, 1972). Perhaps it is good that these divergent approaches are being developed simultaneously, since it is possible that no single curriculum can ever apply to *all* mildly retarded pupils.

The work experience component of work-study programs also raises a number of problems. One of these identified by the Oregon study, relates to criteria for selection. That is, given the fact that not every pupil in a work-study program experiences a work placement, what distinguishes the pupils who do from those who do not?

Twenty-seven percent of the pupils in the Oregon study did not receive any work placements over a fifteen-week period. As might have been expected, younger pupils were more likely to be in this group than older pupils. An unanticipated finding, however, was that pupils perceived by their teachers to have a variety of negative attitudes tended not to receive work placements. If, in fact, teachers consciously deny work placements to pupils who may be troublesome to employers, they would be withholding an important experience from those who may need it the most. On the other hand, teachers cannot afford to alienate employers whose cooperation is essential to work-study programs.

Once a decision has been made to locate a pupil on work placement, the objectives of that placement must be questioned. An old issue related to this question is whether vocational training for the mentally retarded should emphasize skill training or the development of work habits. Strong voices have argued in favor of work habits (Goldstein, 1964; Wolfensberger, 1967), citing evidence that poor vocational adjustment can frequently be attributed to poor work habits. But do poor habits result from an *inability* to perceive accurately and respond appropriately to the social demands of a work environment, or could there also be motivational factors, including a retarded worker's boredom with his job? Evidence shows that most job opportunities for the mentally retarded are clustered within a narrow range of vocational categories, with the greatest concentration in the area of services (Elo and Hendel, 1972). In the Oregon study, approximately one-third of all the pupil job placements were in the category of food services. Does this mean that retarded workers are only capable of this kind of job or, that by our neglect of skill training, we have forced them into vocational patterns that do not fully develop their potential? There is some evidence supporting the latter explanation (Oswald, 1968) which raises an interesting question about the relationship between skill training and the development of good work habits; would the poor work habits that have been attributed to mentally retarded workers disappear if a retarded worker had a job that tapped his true abilities?

Another issue relating to work placements is whether or not they should be in the community. In many work-study programs, initial placements are made in the school building (e.g. as cafeteria worker or janitor's helper) with subsequent placements in the community. The assumption is that the pupils who progress to community placements are more likely to achieve ultimate vocational success. One study, however (Howe, 1967), suggests that some pupils do not need community placements. Because community placements are usually much more cumbersome to administrate than in-school placements, a further investigation of this question would be especially useful.

The problem implicit in all these issues is whether teachers and rehabilitation counselors have the ability to implement effective programs. This may, in fact, be the most critical problem since there is clearly a lack of counselor and teacher training programs that focus on work-study programs. During the late 1960's, there were a number of special grants for training rehabilitation counselors to work with the mentally retarded, but these have been phased out. Moreover, most special education departments in the country have not developed strong training programs for secondary level teachers. One promising exception is the teacher-training model recently developed by Brolin (1972) and implemented at Stout State University in Wisconsin. Additional efforts in this area are clearly required if work-study programs are to improve their service.

In response to these problems and issues, there will undoubtedly be changes in the financing and administration of work-study programs, in the kinds of curriculum and work experiences that are provided to pupils in these programs, and in the training that is provided to teachers and counselors who run the programs. But a good foundation has been laid, so that we reasonably can anticipate that work-study programs, with renewed effort and commitment, will continue to help prepare our retarded adolescents for as successful a level of community adjustment as is possible.

REFERENCES

Brolin, D.: Preparing Teachers of Secondary Level Educable Mentally Retarded: A New Model. Menomonie, Wisconsin, University of Wisconsin-Stout, Department of Rehabilitation and Manpower Services, School of Education, 1972 (Final Report Grant No. OEG-0-70-4818(603), Office of Education, U. S. Department of Health, Education and Welfare).

Campbell, W. L.: *Work-Study Handbook for Educable Mentally Retarded Minors Enrolled in High School Programs in California Public Schools.* California State Department of Special Education, Division of Special Education, 1971.

Chaffin, J.; Davison, R.; Regan, C.; and Spellman, C.: Two follow-up studies of former mentally retarded students from the Kansas work-study project. *Exceptional Children, 37:733-738, 1971.*

Cobb, H.: *The Forecast of Fulfillment.* New York, Teachers College Press, 1972.

Deno, E.: The school-work experience approach to rehabilitation. In Prehm, H. J. (Ed.): *Rehabilitation Research in Mental Retardation.* Rehabilitation Research and Training Center in Mental Retardation, University of Oregon, Eugene, Oregon, 1970.

Dunn, L.: Special education for the mildly retarded—Is much of it justifiable? *Exceptional Children, 35:*5-22, 1968.

Elo, M., and Hendel, D.: Classification as "mentally retarded": A determinant of vocational rehabilitation outcomes? *American Journal of Mental Deficiency,* 77:190-198, 1972.

Goldstein, H.: Social and occupational adjustment. In Stevens, H. A., and Heber, R. F. (Eds.): *Mental Retardation: A Review of Research.* Chicago, University of Chicago Press, 1964.

Goldstein, H.: Construction of a social learning curriculum. In Meyer, E.; Vergason, G.; and Whelen, R. (Eds.): *Strategies for Teaching Exceptional Children.* Denver, Love Publishing Co., 1972.

Halpern, A.: *The Impact of Work-study Programs on Employment of the Mentally Retarded: Some Findings from Two Sources.* Rehabilitation Research and Training Center in Mental Retardation, University of Oregon, Working Paper No. 61, 1972.

Halpern, A.; Raffeld, P.; and Littman, I.: *Longitudinal Evaluation of Work-study Programs for the Educable Mentally Retarded in Oregon: Progress Report.* Rehabilitation Research and Training Center in Mental Retardation, University of Oregon, Working Paper No. 62, 1972.

Heiss, W., and Mischio, G.: Designing curriculum for the educable mentally retarded. In Meyer, E.; Vergason, G.; and Whelen, R. (Eds.): *Strategies for Teaching Exceptional Children.* Denver, Love Publishing Co., 1972.

Howe, C.: *A Comparison of Mentally Retarded High School Students in Work-study Versus Traditional Programs.* Project 6-8148, Grant OEG-46-068148-1556. Long Beach, California, 1967.

Kolstoe, O., and Frey, R.: *A High School Work-study Program for Mentally Subnormal Students.* Carbondale, Illinois, Southern Illinois University Press, 1965.

Lilly, S.: Special Education: A teapot in a tempest. *Exceptional Children,* 37:43-49, 1970.

Oswald, H.: *A Follow-up Study of Mental Retardates Employed by the Federal Government.* Project RD-2425. Social and Rehabilitation Services, DHEW, 1968.

Wolfensberger, W.: Vocational preparation and occupation. In Baumeister, A. (Ed.): *Mental Retardation: Appraisal, Education and Rehabilitation.* Chicago, Aldine Publishing Co., 1967.

Chapter 7

THE REHABILITATION OF FORMER SPECIAL EDUCATION STUDENTS: A DESCRIPTIVE REPORT

Patrick J. Flanigan

Edward J. Pfeifer

James E. Allen

THERE HAVE BEEN NUMEROUS studies of the post-school adjustment of mildly mentally retarded (classified as educable mentally retarded in most educational settings) individuals indicating that a significant percentage are capable of independent functioning as adults and that vocational opportunities for them are not limited to either unskilled or semiskilled jobs. However, both descriptive and evaluative investigations have been consistent in stating the need for a systematic effort to evaluate, train, place, and follow up mentally retarded clients as an integral factor in the educational-habilitative process (Bhatia, 1966; Kolstoe and Frey, 1965; Peck, 1966). A study by Cowen and Goldman (1959) reports results which indicate that a group of retarded clients who received vocational training and selective placement from the Division of Vocational Rehabilitation (DVR) had a significantly larger number of vocationally successful clients than did a control group of untrained retarded clients who received no services from DVR.

In the state of Wisconsin, as in many states, formal and informal agreements exist between the public schools, the DVR, and the state education agency to provide a program of pre-vocational and vocational adjustment services to the mentally retarded adolescent. The available literature not only supports

Note: Research supported in part by Grant 16-P-56811/5-08, from the Rehabilitation Services Administration of the Social and Rehabilitation Service of the Department of Health, Education and Welfare.

such work-study programs but also emphasizes the importance of interagency cooperation in their operation and continued implementation (Chaffin, Smith and Haring, 1967; Crawford and Cross, 1967).

The primary purpose of the present study was to examine the outcomes of referrals recommended to DVR through local school systems which had certified special education classes during the 1965-66 school year in the state of Wisconsin. The study was designed to provide descriptive information regarding referrals received by DVR during the three years following completion of the 1965-66 school year, as well as data concerning the outcomes of DVR services which were provided those EMR clients who had "completed" their education. In addition, yearly breakdowns by districts within the state were undertaken to furnish data on the characteristics of referrals, referral services, rehabilitated closures and case service costs. It was anticipated that the descriptive data thus provided would be of value to any state agencies involved in cooperative educational-rehabilitative programs for the EMR. Similar data reflecting national profiles is reported in Chapter 4.

METHOD

Subjects

The names of all mildly mentally retarded (EMR) students between the ages of fifteen (on or before 9/1/65) and twenty inclusive who were certified through the Division for Handicapped Children (DHC) in special classes throughout Wisconsin during the 1965-66 school year were obtained from individual school enrollment forms on file at DHC. This age group was selected because it comprised those students potentially eligible for DVR services during the three-year period studied.

The names of all mildly retarded clients who were active cases during the 1965-66 fiscal year and each of the three succeeding fiscal years were procured from DVR. The subjects for this study were identified by comparing the DVR computer printout of all referrals within the specified age limits to the DHC list of names to determine which DHC students were referred to the process of referral for DVR services. Those individuals who appeared on both lists comprised the population utilized in this study.

Procedure

The individual DVR client numbers were used to retrieve pertinent computer data. Printouts from the 1966-67, 1967-68, and 1968-69 computer tapes were utilized. The 1965-66 computer tape was not used because this was the year during which the computer system was first implemented and the stored information was fragmented and largely unintelligible. For each of the client numbers submitted, the following information was requested: district, referral source, major disability, weekly earnings at closure, date of referral and date of closure, total case service costs. The retrieval of computer data on each client did not include types of services or their individual costs, since this information was stored on a separate computer tape and would have demanded a prohibitive amount of time and money to program.

RESULTS

Referral Information

Date and Number of Referrals

Data obtained from enrollment forms on file at DHC indicated that there were 2,638 students between the ages of fifteen and twenty inclusive enrolled in EMR classes in Wisconsin public schools during the 1965-66 school year. Of this number approximately 1,338 were referred for DVR services prior to June 30, 1969, the end of the 1968-69 fiscal year. This figure includes forty-five clients who had been closed once but returned for services at a later date.

Table 7-I shows the basis for the derivation of figures on referrals and closures. The total figure of 1,338 cases referred for services was arrived at by adding the number of active cases at the beginning of the 1966-67 fiscal year (413) to the number of referrals in 1966-67 (485), 1967-68 (238) and 1968-69 (101); the total thus reached 1237, 101 fewer than the 1338 stated above. These 101 cases represent the difference between the number of active cases at the beginning of the 1966-67 fiscal year and the

TABLE 7-I

DERIVATION OF FIGURES ON REFERRALS AND CLOSURES

Number of DHC students, aged 15-20, in EMR classes during 1965-66 . . .	2638
Number of those EMR cases referred for DVR services before the end of 1968-69	1338
Number of EMR students who received services more than once	43

Actual number of EMR students referred for DVR services before the end
of 1968-69 1295

Active cases at the beginning of 1966-67	413	
Referrals in 1966-67	485	
Referrals in 1967-68	238	824
Referrals in 1968-69	101	

1237

Unclassified cases at the beginning of 1967-68 101

1338

Referral information is based on total classified referrals over
1966-67 to 1968-69 824
Closure information is based on the total cases referred for services 1338

number of active cases at the beginning of the 1967-68 fiscal
year. These cases were not classified because no referral information was available, due to a programming problem in initial
storage of the desired information. However, the 1338 figure
will be used throughout the study because it represents the total
number of cases referred for service.

The following referral information is based on the 824 individuals who were referred during 1966-67, 1967-68, and 1968-69
fiscal years. Not included are the 413 clients referred prior to
1966-67 and the 101 clients not classified or unknown with respect to exact level of retardation prior to 1967-68. Information
on these cases was available at the time of closure and therefore
is included in the section on closures.

Referral Source

Table 7-II indicates the percentage of DVR referrals from
major sources. Most of the referrals were made by the public
schools: 71 percent (584) over the three-year period. Information on the 413 referrals made prior to the 1966-67 fiscal year
was not available, though a high percentage of these cases were

TABLE 7-II

PERCENTAGE OF DVR REFERRALS FROM MAJOR SOURCES

Source	% Referrals
Public schools	71
Special schools for the handicapped	4
Wisconsin State Employment Service	1-8
Public welfare agencies	2-13
Correctional agencies or institutions	1
Private mental retardation organizations	1

probably school referrals. This would tend to raise the overall percentage of referrals in the fifteen to eighteen age range.

Further inspection of the data on referral source revealed that special schools for the physically and mentally handicapped made 4 percent (33) of the total referrals. Referrals from the Wisconsin State Employment Service ranged from 1 percent (7) of the total in 1966-67 to 8 percent (8) in 1968-69. The same trend holds for referrals from public welfare agencies, which ranged from 2 percent (10) in 1966-67 to 13 percent (13) in 1968-69. Only 1 percent (10) of the total number of referrals for the three-year period studied were from correctional agencies or institutions, and 1 percent (7) came from private mental retardation organizations.

Referrals by District

The distribution by district of DVR referrals over the three-year period is illustrated in Table 7-III. During the period prior

TABLE 7-III

DISTRIBUTION BY DISTRICT OF DVR REFERRALS
OVER THE THREE-YEAR PERIOD

	Total	Percent
Milwaukee	370	30
Madison	302	24
Green Bay	189	15
Racine	149	12
Eau Claire	109	9
Fond du Lac	108	9
Wood County	10	1

Note: This table does not include 101 cases not classified by the computer.

to July 1, 1969, the Milwaukee district received approximately 30 percent (370) of the total referrals to DVR, the Madison district received 24 percent (302), the Green Bay district received 9 percent (109), Fond du Lac district received 9 percent (108), and Wood County received 1 percent (10). These percentage figures are based on the total number of cases (1237) for which referral information was available.

Data on the district comparison of DVR referrals is contained in Table 7-IV. There were four districts which served over 50 percent of the EMRs reported within their respective areas: Madison, 53 percent (302); Milwaukee, 52 percent (370); Green Bay, 51 percent (189); and Eau Claire, 61 percent (109); yet Eau Claire had within the counties it served only 7 percent of the total number of EMR's reported. In two districts, the percentage of EMR's served was considerably less: Racine, 38 percent (149); and Fond du Lac, 27 percent (108); this suggests a more serious referral problem in the two districts. Yet in the four districts which served over 50 percent of the EMR's in their areas, what happened to the 40 percent or 50 percent who were not referred to DVR for services? Were services not needed by this group, or were the public schools unaware of the services available to the mentally retarded through DVR?

The Milwaukee and Racine districts, in particular, tended to work with the mentally retarded early in their high school program since 82 percent and 75 percent of the referrals, respectively, were received prior to July 1, 1967, the beginning of the second fiscal year studied. On a statewide basis, of the 824 referrals made during the three years studied, 59 percent (485) of the referrals occurred during the first year. This predominance of early referrals is further supported by the fact that 413 referrals were made prior to July 1, 1966.

Rehabilitated Closures

Degree of Major Disability

Of the 1338 people referred for DVR services, 974 were closed prior to July 1, 1969. Of the total number closed, 85 percent (818) were closed as rehabilitated; that is, each client had

TABLE 7-IV

DISTRICT COMPARISON OF DVR REFERRALS AND CLOSURES—
REHABILITATED AND NOT REHABILITATED

District	Referrals to DVR		Rehabilitated Closures		Non-Rehabilitated Closures	
	Number	% of EMR's Reported	Number	% of Referrals	Number	% of Referrals
Madison	302	53	177	59	33	11
Milwaukee	370	52	276	75	39	11
Green Bay	189	51	116	61	27	14
Eau Claire	109	61	78	72	16	15
Racine	149	38	105	70	12	8
Fond du Lac	108	27	63	58	24	22
Wood County	10	59	3	30	5	50
State Total	1,237*	47	818	66	156	13

* This figure does not include 101 cases not classified by the computer.
Note: There were 974 cases closed; the remainder of the total (1,338) were not closed.

TABLE 7-V

TOTAL CASE OUTCOMES FOR THE DVR SAMPLE

Outcome		Total	Percent
Closed—rehabilitated		818	84
Closed—not rehabilitated		156	16
Prior to acceptance		144	92
After acceptance		12	8
Total cases referred for DVR services	1,338		
Total cases closed prior to July 1, 1969	974		
Total cases—not closed	364		

achieved a satisfactory vocational placement commensurate with his individual abilities. Table 7-V shows these total case outcomes for the DVR sample.

The relationship between employment outcome and degree of major disability is charted in Table 7-VI. The table reveals that of the clients rehabilitated during the three years studied, 73 percent (595) were identified as mildly retarded; 24 percent (198) were moderately retarded; 3 percent (25) were severely retarded, as defined in DVR Case Process Guide (1969). These figures evidenced little variation from one year to the next.

A comparison of competitive and noncompetitive employment closures indicates that 84 percent of the mildly retarded clients who were closed as rehabilitated were placed in competitive employment. The percentages of the moderately and severely retarded placed in competitive employment were 73 percent and 48 percent respectively. Of the 659 clients closed as competitively employed over the three-year period, 76 percent (503) were identified as mildly retarded, 22 percent (144) as moderately retarded and 2 percent (12) as severely retarded. Of the noncompetitively employed, 58 percent (92) were identified as mildly retarded, 34 percent (54) as moderately retarded, and 8 percent (13) as severely retarded.

Total Case Service Costs by District

The total case service costs for the 818 clients closed as rehabilitated amounted to $1,083,747; the average cost per rehabili-

TABLE 7-VI

EMPLOYMENT OUTCOME AND DEGREE OF MAJOR DISABILITY

Degree of Major Disability	Rehabilitated		Percent of Disability Group Competitively Employed	Group Composition					
				Competitive Employment		Noncompetitive Employment		Not Accepted by DVR (Known)	
Mildly retarded	595	73%	84	503	76%	92	58%	103	72%
Moderately retarded	198	24%	73	144	22%	54	34%	8	6%
Severely retarded	25	3%	48	12	2%	13	8%	1	1%

tated closure was $1,325. A district comparison shows considerable variation in average costs per closure, ranging from a low of $423 in the Green Bay district for 1966-67 to a high of $3,021 in the Milwaukee district for 1968-69. Wood County shows a high of $3,591 per closure in 1968-69 and a low of $67 in 1966-67. However, during the three years studied, Wood County had a total of three rehabilitated closures; therefore, these figures are not used in making cost comparisons among districts.

For the three fiscal years combined, the average cost per rehabilitated closure varied from a low of $834 (Eau Claire district) to $1,920 (Milwaukee district). These figures raise questions regarding the types and costs of services provided within various districts. The duration of services or time interval from referral to closure does not explain the high average costs in some districts, since duration of services in the high-cost districts only slightly exceeds or is considerably less than the statewide average for a given year.

Work Status

A yearly comparison of statewide rehabilitated closures according to work status and gross weekly earnings in dollars for the three-year period under consideration is provided in Table 7-VII. Of the 818 clients closed rehabilitated, 81 percent (659) were closed in competitive job situations as indicated by numbers 1, 3, and 4; 19 percent (159) were closed in noncompetitive job situations as indicated by numbers 2, 5, and 6. Numbers 7 and 8 designate those cases not employed and are not applicable to rehabilitated closures.

Weekly Earnings

Of the 659 clients closed in competitive employment during the three-year period, the gross weekly earnings at the time of closure for 30 percent (199) of these individuals was $50 or less; this figure varied from 46 percent (73) of the clients in 1966-67 to 20 percent (51) in 1968-69. This data is very disturbing since the poverty indicator for a single person as determined by the U. S. Department of Labor (1969) is a net amount of

TABLE 7-VII

YEARLY COMPARISON OF STATEWIDE REHABILITATED CLOSURES ACCORDING TO WORK STATUS AND GROSS WEEKLY EARNINGS IN DOLLARS FOR THE 1966-67, 1967-68 AND 1968-69 FISCAL YEARS

Year		Total Closures	Work Status								Gross Weekly Earnings				
			1	2	3	4	5	6	7	8	0-25	26-50	51-75	76-100	101+
1966-67	Number	189	156	10	2		10	11			41	63	66	17	2
	%-State Total	100	81	5	1		5	6			22	33	35	9	1
1967-68	Number	308	249	17	1		17	24			77	56	137	33	5
	%-State Total	100	81	5	1		5	8			25	18	44	11	2
1968-69	Number	321	250	28	1		16	26			76	43	155	36	11
	%-State Total	100	78	9			5	8			24	13	48	11	4
Cumula.	Number	818	655	55	4		43	61			194	162	358	86	18
Total	%-State Total	100	80	7	1		5	7			24	20	44	10	2

Work Status Codes

1—Wage or salaried worker (competitive labor market)
2—Wage or salaried worker (sheltered workshop)
3—Self-employed
4—State agency, managed business enterprise
5—Homemaker
6—Unpaid family worker
7—Not working–student
8—Not working–other

$1,600 per year or $30.77 per week. The majority of individuals closed as competitively employed received gross earnings between $51 and $75 per week at the time of closure; this figure varied from 42 percent (66) of the total number closed in 1966-67 to 61 percent (153) in 1968-69. There was little difference between the mildly and moderately retarded in the percentage of people grouped in the various gross weekly earnings categories. The earnings of the severely retarded tended to be low.

DISCUSSION

The purpose of this study was to examine the Division of Vocational Rehabilitation involvement with a population of educable mentally retarded adolescents who were in special education classes in Wisconsin during the 1965-66 school year. Information on referrals to DVR and outcome of services provided was gathered on those EMR's between the ages of fifteen and twenty who were in special education classes during the 1965-66 school year and referred to DVR sometime prior to the end of the 1968-69 fiscal year. During this period DVR received approximately 49 percent of the 2,638 EMR students listed on the 1965-66 enrollment forms on file at the Division for Handicapped Children.

An area of concern and one for further investigation is the 51 percent of the 2,638 EMR's listed who were never referred to DVR during the period studied. Further research is needed to determine whether this number reflects a need for more cooperative programming between the schools and DVR or simply reflects those EMR students who do not require DVR services. If, indeed, a need exists for more interagency communication, it must be determined if schools are unaware of the services available through DVR or if they choose not to participate for one reason or another.

A district comparison of referrals received showed that referrals are more of a problem in some districts than in others. Four districts each served between 50 percent and 60 percent of the EMR's reported by schools located in their respective areas. In two districts, the percentage served was considerably less; 38 percent and 27 percent respectively. The determination of the factors which account for the comparatively low percentage of EMR's served in these two districts merits further investigation.

The average case service costs varied considerably among districts. These differences raise questions regarding the types of services provided as well as their costs within the respective districts. For example, it may be the case that some districts use rehabilitation facilities (e.g. sheltered workshops) more extensively than others, that is, for larger numbers of clients and/or for longer periods of time. District policies regarding reimbursement for on-the-job training may also be an important factor.

This study reported that 81 percent of the rehabilitated closures were closed as competitively employed; however, only information on work status and earnings was reported. It would be interesting to study these closures more comprehensively to determine what intellectual, social, and vocational skills are required to function successfully on the job and to what extent previous training contributed to job placement. Such a study, particularly if implemented on an ongoing basis, could supply data on the effectiveness of VR services and could identify factors associated with success and failure. The results would contribute to improved services and an increased proportion of successful outcomes.

One of the most important findings of this study was that approximately 30 percent of the clients closed in competitive employment had gross earnings of $50 per week or less at time of closure. Many of these people, therefore, fell at or below the poverty level indicator. The question arises as to whether or not these clients should be closed as rehabilitated and DVR services terminated if their earnings are that low. It would seem that for many of these people very serious problems remain. It is interesting to note that there was little difference between the mildly and moderately retarded in the percentages of people grouped in the various earnings categories.

A relatively small number of Wisconsin's public school districts reporting EMR's in special education programs had formal occupational adjustment programs during the period studied. In

1965-66, seventeen schools throughout the state had such programs; this number rose to thirty-one in 1966-67, forty-one in 1967-68, and sixty-five in 1968-69. In spite of this continued expansion, there arises a serious question as to why more schools are not making use of DVR services through the occupational adjustment program.

The problems encountered in gathering data for the present study attest to the need for an efficient information retrieval system organized to permit all agencies concerned with retardation programming to collect and exchange basic information. A major problem in gathering data for this study was that names on file at the Division for Handicapped Children could not be used to obtain computerized information from the Division of Vocational Rehabilitation on referrals received and individual services provided. Without the DVR client number no information could be retrieved. This necessitated a clumsy, time-consuming process of comparing by hand the DHC list of student names with a DVR printout of all MR's served to determine which students were referred to DVR and to record the corresponding DVR client numbers so that information pertinent to the study could be obtained. It is essential that a central data bank for storage and retrieval of information be established to enable all state agencies concerned with retardation programming to coordinate their efforts in program evaluation, planning, and implementation.

REFERENCES

Bhatia, B. D.: Preparation and placement of the mentally retarded in normal employment. *Journal of Rehabilitation in Asia,* 7(3):46-49, 1966.

Bobroff, A.: Economic adjustment of 121 adults formerly students in classes for mental retardates. *American Journal of Mental Deficiency,* 60:525-535, 1956.

Carriker, W. R.: *A Comparison of Post-School Adjustment of Regular and Special Class Retarded Individuals Served in Lincoln and Omaha, Nebraska Public Schools.* Contract No. SAE-6445, U. S. Department of Health, Education and Welfare, Washington, D. C. 1957.

Cassidy, V. M., and Phelps, H. R.: *Postschool Adjustment of Slow Learning Children: A Study of Persons Previously Enrolled in Special Classes in Ohio.* Columbus, Ohio, Bureau of Special and Adult Education, Ohio State University, 1955.

Collman, R. D., and Newlyn, D.: Employment success of educationally subnormal ex-pupils in England. *American Journal of Mental Deficiency,* 60:733-743, 1956.

Cowan, L., and Goldman, M.: The selection of the mentally deficient for vocational training and the effect of this training on vocational success. *Journal of Consulting Psychology,* 23:78-84, 1959.

Crawford, W. L., and Cross, J. L.: *Guidelines: Work-Study Programs for Slow Learning Children in Ohio Schools.* Ohio Department of Education, Columbus, Ohio, Blank Book Company, 1967.

Goldman, M. S.: Identification of barriers and facilitators in the vocational habilitation of educable mentally retarded youth. Unpublished doctoral dissertation, University of Wisconsin, 1969.

Keeler, K. F.: Postschool adjustment of educable mentally retarded youth educated in San Francisco. *Dissertation Abstracts,* 25(2):936-937, 1964.

Kennedy, R. J. R.: The social adjustment of morons in a Connecticut city. Millport, Conn., Commission to Survey Resources in Connecticut, 1948.

Kennedy, R. J. R.: *A Connecticut Community Revisited: A Study of the Social Adjustment of a Group of Mentally Deficient Adults in 1948 and 1960.* Research Project No. 665, Vocational Rehabilitation Administration, Washington, D. C., 1962.

Kolstoe, O. P., and Frey, R. M.: *A High School Work-study Program for Mentally Subnormal Students.* Carbondale and Edwardsville, Southern Illinois University Press, 1965.

Oswald, H. W.: *A National Follow-up Study of Mental Retardates Employed by the Federal Government.* Grant RD-2425-G, Department of Vocational Rehabilitation, Washington, D. C., 1968.

Peck, J. R.: The work-study program—A critical phase of preparation. *Education and Training of the Mentally Retarded,* 1(2):68-74, 1966.

Peterson, L., and Smith, L. L.: A comparison of the post-school adjustment of educable mentally retarded adults with that of adults of normal intelligence. *Exceptional Children,* 26:404-408, 1960.

Phelps, H. R.: Post-school adjustment of mentally retarded children in selected Ohio cities. *Exceptional Children,* 23:58-62, 1956.

Statewide Planning for Vocational Rehabilitation. Final report of the ad hoc committee on mental retardation. Madison, Wisconsin, 1967.

U. S. Department of Labor, Manpower Administration. Subject: Definition of the term disadvantaged individual. Manpower Administration Order No. 1-69, Washington, D. C., 1969.

Wisconsin Department of Health and Social Services. Vocational rehabilitation case process guide. Wisconsin Division of Vocational Rehabilitation, 1969.

Chapter 8

REHABILITATING THE MENTALLY RETARDED: A BEHAVIORAL APPROACH

JAMES E. CROSSON

C. DUANE YOUNGBERG

OWEN R. WHITE

SOME EIGHT YEARS AGO the American Psychological Association, in cooperation with what was then the Office of Vocational Rehabilitation, jointly sponsored a conference on research in the psychological aspects of rehabilitation (Lofquist, 1960). One of the several working committees of this conference was composed of research psychologists representing the fields of learning and behavior. Within the context of this committee's report are several statements underscoring concepts which were, at that time, unique in the field of rehabilitation. For example, it was noted that both the rehabilitation client and the rehabilitation process might be defined in behavioral terms. That is, "the problems of the disabled person require the acquisition of new behaviors, the maintenance of adequate behaviors, and the extinction of inadequate or deficient behavior." Additionally, it was suggested that researchers "forget the idealized conceptions of research, the cookbooks and stereotypes . . ." and "encourage research that is frankly exploratory or descriptive" (Meyerson, 1960, p. 70-71).

This chapter describes one example of this philosophy in operation. The application will be described in the context of an approach to rehabilitation programming which incorporates and

---

Note: Reprinted from H. J. Prehm (Ed.): *Rehabilitation Research in Mental Retardation*. Rehabilitation Research and Training Center in Mental Retardation, University of Oregon, Monograph No. 2, July, 1970, 19-34. The original title of the paper was, Transenvironmental programming: An experimental approach to the rehabilitation of the retarded.

blends behavioral principles and research strategies. The term "Transenvironmental Programming" has been coined to identify the operational model resulting from this approach for reasons that will be made clear in the following pages.

A BEHAVIORAL MODEL FOR REHABILITATION SERVICES

The logic of behaviorism seeks to explain the determinants of behavior—those influences which produce, direct, maintain, and otherwise control behavior—in terms of functional relationships between behavioral and environmental events (Skinner, 1953). In keeping with this, the basic premises underlying transenvironmental programming define the rehabilitation client as essentially a behaving organism whose behavior occurs as a function of environmental events and conditions. Within this framework, abnormal behavior (e.g. retardation) is assumed to be no different than normal behavior with respect to its acquisition, maintenance, or potential for change (Bijou, 1968; Ullmann and Krasner, 1969). Or, as Lindsley (1964) has suggested, the individual is not retarded—only his behavior is *sometimes* retarded in *average* environments (author's emphasis).

The program to be used as an example is being carried out in cooperation with the Pearl Buck Center, a private, nonprofit day care center for trainable mentally retarded children and adults.* The clients typical of this particular program are drawn from the population of individuals for whom existing rehabilitation and educational services were shown to be ineffective with respect to the attainment of rehabilitation objectives. However, this fact is not considered to have importance with respect to program objectives. The clients are viewed simply as presenting an admixture of deficient and deviant behaviors comprising a repertoire which is largely incompatible with the economic and social demands of the community. At the point of entry into the program no assumptions are made regarding limitations in their aptitude or rehabilitation potential. Rather, they are viewed

---

* Appreciation is accorded to Mrs. Elisabeth Waechter, founder and Director of the Pearl Buck Center, without whose confidence and cooperation this paper could not have proceeded beyond a purely theoretical discussion.

within the framework of the conceptual problem which is to discover and implement clinical procedures which will bring about the alteration of the deficient and deviant behaviors. The terminal objective is the same for all clients; that of affecting a more appropriate matching of the client's repertoire to the adaptive requirements of his anticipated community.

It should be noted that the guidelines for the procedures are drawn from a long history of productive behavioral research (e.g. Skinner, 1953) which has more recently developed into an innovative applied science (Baer, Wolf, and Risley, 1968). More specifically, an extensive background of work by such individuals as Bachrach (1962), Birnbrauer and Lawler (1964), Krumboltz (1966), Lindsley (1964), Michael and Meyerson (1962), and Premack (1965) has provided the background upon which are based the technologies to be described in the outline immediately following.

The Specification of Training Objectives

Within the framework of a behavioral model, the term rehabilitation connotes the alteration of behaviors to conform to a specific set of behavioral criteria. It follows, then, that the prerequisite to a rehabilitation program is to specify the desired or predicted terminal performance. Following this, the precise skills or behaviors requisite to the successful completion of the rehabilitation effort must be determined. Thirdly, these skills and behaviors must be identified in terms of their relative positions within a training hierarchy, and finally a selection of training procedures relevant to the training hierarchies must be made.

Transenvironmental programming is the term given to the above processes, and the resultant program of training. The program, it should be recalled, has the objective of preparing retarded individuals for a successful adaptation to the social and economic demands of the community. Since the ability to maintain oneself in productive work is seen as a basic requirement for survival in the community, the first step in specifying the program objectives was to identify the kinds of work placements which would be available to retarded clients within the immediate geographic area encompassed by the program services. Consultation with rehabilitation counselors and others who had been involved in the vocational training and placement of retarded individuals led to the specification of fifty-four placements representing fourteen job areas as defined by the *Guide to Jobs for the Mentally Retarded* (Peterson and Jones, 1964).

It is recognized, of course, that each job area includes a variety of different specific tasks requisite to maintenance in such job placements. Adequate performance of the various tasks involved in a specific job placement would therefore constitute the terminal objectives for job training. The *Guide to Jobs for the Mentally Retarded* was again employed to obtain a listing relevant to the previously identified fifty-four potential job placements. Approximately three hundred task activities were identified. However, grouping those activities which had similar descrip-

TABLE 8-I

BASIC TASK

Task Name	Job Classes (Letter) and Job Placements (Numeral) Represented by Task
Burn trash	C2 C5 D5 D9 F2 H1 H4 H5 N1 V3 V5
Dust	C2 H1 H2 H4 H5 V2 V3 V5 V6
Hose floors	C2 C5 F4 H1 H5 V5
Lift	V3 D1 D3 D4 D6 D8 D10 C5 F4 W3 C5
Load	A1 A2 A3 A8 A9 A10 A11 A12 A13 A14 17 19 I10 I11 I12 K5 V3 R2 V3 V2 V3
Mop floors	D D2 D3 D4 D5 D6 D8 D9 F4 H1 H2 H4 H5
Transport by hand	C5 H1 H2 H4 H5 V3 V5
Perform simple carpentry	I9 I10 I11 I12 R2 R3 V3
Scrub floors (hand)	C4 D5 D9 H1 H2 H5
Scrub floors (machine)	C2 D5 D9 H1 H2 H5
Sweep	C2 H1 H2 H4 H5 N1 V2 V3 V5 V6
Tie	A2 A8 A9 A10 A11 A12 A13 A14 K5 P1
Transport by cart	I7 K9 I10 I11 I12 L4 L6 A2 A3 A8 A9 A10 A11 A12 A13 A14 R2 R3
Unload	A1 A2 A3 A8 A9 A10 A11 A12 A13 A14 K7 I9 I10 I11 I12
Use telephone	A9 A10 A11 C1 C2 C3 C4 F4 V2 V3 V5
Vacuum	C2 F4 V2 V3 V5 V6
Wet, wipe surfaces	F4 H1 H2 H4 H5 C2 V3 C4 D5 D8 D9 D1 D2 D3 D8 D9
Wash windows	C2 C5 D5 D9 F4 H1 H2 H5
Wax floors (hand)	C4 D5 D9 H1 H2 H5
Wax floors (machine)	C2 D5 D9 H1 H2 H5

tions reduced the list by approximately one-third. The resulting list of task activities was then analyzed with respect to the degree of overlap across placement profiles and job classes. From this analysis, a set of twenty high overlap task activities was selected to comprise the behavioral targets for the initial training operations of the program. All clients who enter the program receive training on each of the twenty tasks, except those who are inappropriate by virtue of sex or physical disabilities. Completion of the training provides the client with a basic skills repertoire appropriate to a variety of potential job placements. Expansion of his skill repertoire to more adequately match a specific job placement as it occurs is accomplished through subsequent training within later stages of the program and through specific on-the-job programming at the appropriate time.

Task Analysis

Task activities, as defined in the *Guide* (e.g. sweeping) obviously incorporate a number of specific behaviors, each of which must occur in a relatively prescribed sequence in order for the task to be properly completed. Since the population of clients involved in transenvironmental programming usually manifests severe behavioral deficits, it is necessary to approach client training in a much more discrete manner than is typical of more traditional vocational training programs (Crosson, 1969). To achieve this, it is necessary to analyze each of the task activities into its requisite sequential behaviors.

In order that the resulting analysis may have more utility for the application of conditioning principles, a specialized form of task analysis is employed in which both the discrete task behaviors, or operants, and their correlated response-produced stimuli are specified. The resulting specifications of behavioral chains are then evaluated in terms of known or assumed limitations in the behavior repertoires characteristic of the client population, and initial adjustments are made in the analysis through adding or substituting response topographies or specifying means by which the correlated stimuli can be augmented artificially. Where the analyses are to be used to prepare training programs for large numbers of clients, as in the case of the basic tasks, a representative sample of clients is systematically exposed to the resulting stimulus components of the task and prompted or shaped to emit the associated behaviors. Further adjustments are then made in the analysis, and a set of training procedures designed to have utility for the majority of clients is prepared. In the case of subsequent training, the analyses are generally less discrete and are prepared for the particular client.

It should be noted that, while the preparation of such analyses and the related training procedures may appear laborious and time consuming, the actual preparation time is relatively brief—usually requiring only a few hours. More importantly, research has suggested that training programs based upon the analysis of operant chains greatly facilitate the acquisition of task behaviors in severely deficient clients (Crosson, 1969). Continued application of these procedures suggests this facilitation effect occurs as a function of the precise identification of task related operants which are deficient in the client's repertoire. In many cases, it has been shown that very few of the total requisite operants in a task are actually deficient in a repertoire. The immediate focus of training procedures upon only those operants which are in fact deficient appears to greatly reduce the error and time required in the training process.

Programming the Acquisition of Task Behavior

The task analyses described above are used to formulate training procedures. Typically, such training procedures are based upon adaptations of the technology associated with linear instructional programming (Holland, 1960).

Generally speaking, the procedures involve: (a) the specification of discrete conditioning operations relative to either discrete behaviors or brief sequences of behaviors which are determined to be deficient in the client's repertoire, (b) prompting of task operants or brief sequences under related task conditions until relevant task behaviors are reliably emitted in the presence of appropriate stimulus components, (c) fading augmented or artificial stimuli, (d) chaining response sequences, and (e) repeating the process until the entire chain of operants is reliably emitted under the "natural" task conditions.

Certain portions of the task may be trained out of sequence depending upon the information obtained during the initial sampling of the client's repertoire. Wherever possible reverse chaining is employed in the early training stages in order to maintain an optimal relationship between the emitted behaviors and terminal reinforcement. Quite often, it is possible to program early training sequences under simulated conditions outside of the actual task environment, thus permitting more precise control of the training operations. This has been found to be particularly helpful in the process of shaping difficult response topographies.

In initiating a program with a particular client, several trial runs are usually performed and response failures are noted in relation to particular stimulus features of the operant chain. Where discrimination consistently fails to occur, an attempt is made to increase the strength of the relative stimulus, and the resulting augmented stimuli are incorporated into the training procedures. Consistent discrimination failures and/or inadequate approximations to the terminal operants are attended to individually through additional stimulus building or shaping procedures.

Two general training paradigms are currently in use: (a) the programming of individual clients on a one-to-one basis, generally limited to the early stages of basic training and on-the-job placement; and (b) exposing groups of client-observers to the programming of an individual client, a technique typically utilized in the intermediary program stages. At this level of training, a previously-trained client may function as the trainer.

Social Correlates of Task Activities

It has been repeatedly stated that social interactions constitute a critical aspect of vocational adjustment (Windle, 1962). Experience with the behaviorally oriented transenvironmental program has tended to lend support to this contention. Beyond this, nonexperimental observations have suggested that social behavior characteristics, while perhaps partially client-specific, appear to be mediated to a certain extent by task conditions. This has led to the hypothesis that task environments may include social contingencies which operate concurrently with task requirements. Recent research, while limited and certainly incomplete, has tended to support this hypothesis (DeVoss, 1969). On this basis, efforts are currently under way to conduct an extensive analysis of social contingencies associated with potential job placements utilizing an experimental technique for the analysis of social contingencies currently under development at the Oregon Rehabilitation Research and Training Center. While the data are, at this time, far from classifiable in useful ways, the technique itself has been found helpful in the analysis of community work placements. The data yield includes information regarding the probabilities of specific consequences associated with worker emitted social and task behaviors. Similar data obtained in preplacement environments permit a direct comparison of existing and predicted social interaction patterns, and may permit the pinpointing of potential deficiencies in response to social contingencies which may lead to failure in work adjustment. It may then be the case that simulated conditions of social interaction may be arranged in the preplacement training environment to permit both the evaluation of client responses to social contingencies identified in the project work placement and the remediation of deficient responses.

Other classes of behavior which can best be described as social are more commonly recognized and identified under such rubrics as habits, attitudes, aptitudes, etc. These behavior classes may be thought of as being comprised of relatively specific responses under the control of stimuli which are not necessarily task or job specific. Punctuality, for example, which may be thought of in terms of both habit and attitude may be conceptualized as a pervasive responsiveness to temporal stimuli. Mobility, as an aptitude which permits the client to get to his job, may be conceptualized in terms of long sequences of responses under the control of specific topographic stimuli such as landmarks, street signs, directionality, etc. The list could go on to include such things as an appreciation for the value of money (which for many clients certainly requires a rather careful programming of experience with conditioned reinforcers); health and grooming; effective use of leisure time; and so on. Certain of these behaviors are pervasive requirements in any vocational situation. In recognition of this fact continual training in what might be termed work habits and attitudes are incorporated into all training phases of the transenvironmental program. Where other behaviors are requisite to a particular placement, such requirements usually tend to become apparent without formal analysis. Where deficiencies in the client behavior exist, they also are usually apparent. In the rather limited experience so far acquired, such behavioral factors have played a significant role in adapting a client to a particular job placement. Necessary corrective treatments have ranged from extinguishing a cigarette "bumming" habit to establishing with a parent a token economy whereby money earned was systematically associated with social reinforcement. Such deficiencies, in other words, have tended to be highly client specific as is likely the case with any rehabilitation program. Programs for the modification of such behavioral deficits are therefore, in actuality, supplemental to the transenvironmental program.

Programming Adaptation in Community Placements

Survival in a community work placement, and all that this encompasses, constitutes the terminal program objective for all clients. To facilitate this outcome, active contact is maintained with potential employers, and placement contacts emphasize discussion of known skills and abilities of available clients rather than disabilities. Prior to affecting a placement the specialized procedures to be employed in on-the-job training are explained to the potential employers and their use justified on the basis of assisting clients having inadequate work histories to achieve a rapid adaptation to the work setting.

Once a placement is identified, a task analysis of the type described previously is performed in the work setting, except that: (a) there is no attempt to "standardize" the analysis with several clients as is done in the case of the basic training tasks; and (b) additional descriptive information regarding the "natural" skill and social contingenices (as discussed previously), and the classes and schedules of reinforcement operating in the work setting is obtained. This information is used in comparison with the available training history of prospective clients to assist in matching the trainee to the job and in determining the necessary pretraining and on-the-job training programs. Training procedures employed in on-the-job training are essentially the same as those described previously, except that the training is identified and speeded up considerably. This is possible because of the prior training histories of the clients selected for placement.

Typically, a trainer initiates the program in a simulated work situation in the pretraining environment, then moves with the client to actual daily on-the-job training which may range from two to four hours initially. The principal program emphasis in on-the-job training involves the fading of "artificial" contingencies employed in training, permitting effective maintenance of performance under the "natural" contingencies of the work setting. With the more dependent client, the fading process may also involve working with the employers and/or parents to establish performance maintaining contingencies incorporating schedules of conditioned reinforcement designed to supplement the "naturally" reinforcing economy. Following the termination of the training program, periodic follow up of the client is performed to insure transfer of training and stability of the maintaining contingencies. Generally speaking, in the limited experience accrued to date, maintenance has definitely not been a problem. Where post placement intervention has been requested by an employer, the objective has been to train the client to perform additional tasks.

Programming Motivation for Work

The behavioral model underlying the transenvironmental program incorporates reinforcement as its pervasive casual principle. That is, while perhaps not a sufficient condition (as when stimulus control is a factor) reinforcement is the necessary condition requisite to an explanation of the continued emission of

behavior. Reinforcement is said to occur when a particular behavior produces, or is followed by, a stimulus change which has
the demonstrated power to affect the future probability of the
behavior. The stimulus change (or stimulus) so defined is known
as a reinforcer. A variety of reinforcers exist in the context of
the transenvironmental program (e.g. food or candy, money and
other tokens, and free time). In order to make maximal use of
the principle of reinforcement in the operation of the training
program, a multi-stage token economy is employed. Specific reinforcers employed in the training program vary as a function
of the client's position in the training sequence.

Generally speaking, when a client is first introduced to the program, his motivational levels (as reflected by rate of responding)
are tested with respect to a variety of potentially reinforcing
stimuli. A list of the most effective and easily dispensed reinforcers is then compiled for utilization in subsequent training.
After the effectiveness of the reinforcers has been rechecked in
actual training situations, the reinforcers are replaced by coins.
At the end of each session, the client exchanges the coins for any
of the previously identified back-up reinforcers. When performances have stabilized at the coin level of the token economy, the
client is then introduced to paper substitutes in which the coins
are symbolized by check marks on a slip of paper. Initially, the
client exchanges the check for a coin, followed by exchanging
the coin for the back-up reinforcers.

Once the client's performance has been stabilized under the
paper economy, progressively longer delays are programmed between the delivery of the token and the purchase of the back-
up. This assures that subsequent performances will maintain in
the absence of immediate reinforcement—a condition similar
to that in most natural work environments. Concurrently, the
client is encouraged to save a certain amount of paper tokens,
or checks which he receives. Clients are reinforced for that behavior with an interest of 10 percent compounded weekly. This
rather excessive interest rate is gradually reduced as the client ac-
crues sufficient savings to purchase progressively more costly (and
desirable) back-ups.

As the client's performance repertoire becomes progressively expanded and stabilized, the schedule of token reinforcement is extended from continuous reinforcement of task components to completed tasks, to quarter-day, half-day, daily, weekly, and eventually in some cases, to monthly payment. This progression corresponds to the client's advancement through initial training on the basic tasks, through performance generalization, skill expansion, habit and attitude training, and preplacement programming.

Since recent research (DeVoss, 1969) has suggested that the probability of social reinforcement is extremely low in selected potential job placements, and because the typical client is relatively "dependent" upon praise, attention, etc., the proportion of social reinforcement is gradually reduced as he progresses through the program. At the point the client is ready for a community job placement, it should be the case that very minor adjustments in schedules of extrinsic and social reinforcers must be made to match those operating in the projected replacement.

It should be noted that it is likely that the client's terminal performance in a community job placement is not maintained solely by the monetary reinforcement he receives. Intuitively, one must assume that certain classes of reinforcers sometimes referred to as "intrinsic" are also operating, perhaps on a somewhat richer schedule than either money or praise. Recent experience has, in fact, suggested that this is the case, and that perhaps not all "intrinsic" reinforcers are as elusive as might be supposed. For example, nonexperimental observations suggest that stimulus changes associated with task components and perhaps completed tasks within a sequence of tasks may operate as conditioned reinforcers. So far as the authors are aware, however, this remains to be demonstrated.

PROGRAM OPERATIONS

In designing the transenvironmental program, the technological procedures described above were incorporated into a six-phase sequence of program operations distributed across a linear continuum ranging from client intake to terminal community placement. The program outline follows.

Phase I: Evaluation and Pre-Training

The initial operation for all clients consists of a mapping of his functional repertoire. Functional dimensions evaluated include: (a) specific behavior skills and deficits; (b) critical processes, including the client's responsiveness to reinforcement operations, stimulus control operations, etc.; and (c) social adaptiveness. Each client is seen in evaluation, following which a determination is made as to the appropriate level of placement within the transenvironmental program. Where remediation of specific functional operations is indicated, basic therapeutic or prosthetic programs are applied prior to placement in a higher phase of programming.

Phase II: Pre-Vocational Programming

This program is directed toward a systematic strengthening of the client's functional repertoire with respect to both work skills and social adaptiveness. Clients are trained on a sampling of approximately twenty specific tasks each representing a minimum of three job classes and five specific potential job placements. Their performance relative to these job samples is evaluated with respect to criteria established on the basis of "normal" performance. Subsequent to training on basic tasks, the client is exposed to "advanced" tasks which incorporate the basic tasks in the context of broader and more diversified applications.

Phase III: Contract Workshop

This program phase emphasizes performance under varying situational demands and incentive conditions. Within these dimensions, such performance variables as rate, stability, and accuracy are critically evaluated and, where necessary, remedial programming is implemented. Particular attention is given to the transfer of performance control from the relatively artificial social and realistic intrinsic and monetary reinforcement schedules.

Phase IV: Pre-Placement Training

Each community placement that becomes available is analyzed with respect to skill requirements, social contingencies, and available reinforcement classes and schedules. A client is then selected on the basis of his prior performance history (e.g. skill repertoire, adaptiveness, apparent vocational preference, etc.) and his current performance assessed with respect to the proposed job demands. Critical elements of the proposed placement are, where possible, simulated in the rehabilitation center to permit pre-training and adaptation with respect to specific behavior deficits demonstrated by the client.

Phase V: In-Placement Programming

Following a brief period of pre-placement programming, the client is assigned to a trainer who goes with him to the work situation. The trainer begins a process of shaping remaining deficit skills and arranging contingencies to facilitate the client's adaptation to the work situation. Where possible, and when necessary, this on-the-job training begins on a part-time basis while the client continues his pre-training activities at the rehabilitation center. As the client's performance begins to match the requirements of the community placement, the supporting contingencies are faded to the "natural" incentives and monetary reinforcement operable in the work setting, through family support, etc. Following this, the client's work schedule is increased to full time.

Phase VI: Follow-up

Periodic follow-up is made on each client placed throughout the duration of the project. Client performance is systematically evaluated, and where necessary, remedial programs implemented. Similarly, if necessary, additional programs are initiated to broaden the client's functional repertoire to include additional work roles within the job setting.

All clients admitted to the program are initially assigned to Phase I for purposes of evaluation. Following evaluations, a client may be assigned to Phase II, III, or IV. For the typical client, however, it is necessary to program him through each subsequent phase. Programming is individually paced for each client, permitting as rapid advancement as his progress dictates.

While progression through the six phases is defined in terms of a developmental continuum of aptitude and adaptiveness, intermediate phases each have a set of general entry criteria. For entry into Phase I, the only requirements are that the client be ambulatory and of an appropriate age. As a prerequisite to entry into Phase II, the client must respond appropriately to the paper substitutes as conditioned reinforcers, perform at least one complex task at criterion level, and respond appropriately to certain classes of social stimuli (e.g. verbal directives).

Advancement to Phase III is contingent upon the client's demonstrated ability to: (a) perform three contract tasks at or above a minimal criterion rate (in addition to criterion performance on all designated Phase II tasks) and (b) maintain rate over a three week period under a delayed schedule of reinforcement. Criteria for assignment to Phase IV include (a) the ability to maintain performance rates (under Phase III reinforcement economy) at less than .10 level of social reinforcement density, (b) "save" at least 40 percent of his pay for a minimum of one week, (c) operate efficiently under minimum reinforcement delay of one work day, (d) perform at a criterion level on at least 75 percent of available contract jobs, (e) maintain an error ratio at less than the .10 level, (f) maintain peer interaction level at less than the .50 level of working day (excluding breaks), and (g) maintain sustained performance rates at criterion level for a minimum of two consecutive hours.

For entry into Phase V, the client must meet the following criteria: (a) maintain performance rates at criterion level for a minimum for four consecutive hours, (b) maintain peer interaction at less than the .10 level during working day (excluding breaks), (c) maintain criterion performance under delayed token reinforcement interval of one work week, with social reinforcement frequency not exceeding two per day, and (d) maintain error ratio at or below criterion level for minimum periods of four consecutive hours.

It is obvious that the entry criteria for a given phase constitutes, in effect, the terminal behavioral objectives for the preceding phase. The program operations of Phase I through IV are, therefore, essentially designed to produce the designated criterion behaviors. As can be seen from the discussion, the over-all training program can be conceptualized as a process of advancing the client through a sequence of essentially different environmental conditions, each designed to systematically shape and extend appropriate behavior repertoires while fading forms of reinforcement and stimulus control to levels and classes closely approximating the "natural" work environment. Hence the term, Transenvironmental Programming.

DATA COLLECTION AND UTILIZATION

The systematic collection of behavioral data is a critical function in all phases of the program. At the intake stage, continuous operant rate data are taken relative to various simple and complex operants under differing conditions of reinforcement and stimulus control. The data collection instruments employed at this level of operation usually consist of simple counting and timing devices. The resulting data are used to map the client's aptitudes relative to the critical processes previously referred to and to assist in the specification of maximally effective back-up reinforcers.

As the client moves from evaluation to the skill building program (Phase II), the data collection model is expanded to permit the specification of performance error, the occurrence of prompts and other antecedent events, and the class and frequency of reinforcers presented in addition to the usual behavior rate measures. A specially designed checklist is employed at each training session which also permits the analysis of the above variables relative to the specific sub-components of a given task. This checklist is also employed in conjunction with program operations of Phases IV and V. A somewhat simplified data collection process, wherein measures are limited to performance rate, error ratio, and reinforcement density is employed in the "advanced" stages of Phase II, and in Phases III and VI. Since the focus of interest at these levels is on maintenance, rather than acquisition of behavior, the data are collected on a random time sampling basis. All rate, error ratio, and reinforcement density data are regularly plotted for each client and displayed in the staff workroom, a process which permits precise monitoring of

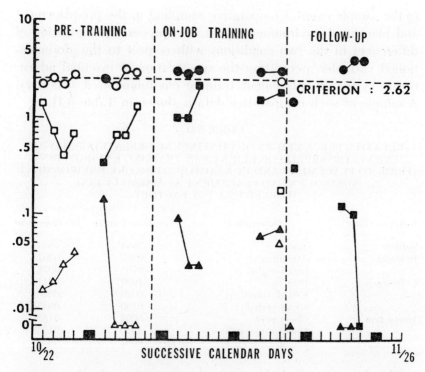

Figure 8-1. Relative distribution of performance, error, and reinforcement measures obtained for client P across stages of preparation and follow up for community job placement as assembly line worker in a toy factory. The legend is: ○ performance rates (total responses/total time); □ reinforcement density (total reinforcements/total time); and △ error ratio (total responses/total errors). Open figures (○ □ △) identify data obtained in the pre-training (simulated) environment. Closed figures (● ■ ▲) identify data collected in the community work environment.

client progress. An example of such data obtained across Phases IV and V for a specific client is shown in Figure 8-1.

During the operation of Phases IV and V, data regarding job-related social and work contingencies are obtained by use of the experimental instrument mentioned previously. This technique incorporates a field-unit model wherein the relative frequency of coded behavior transactions are recorded in a series of brief time samples. The derived measures provide indices of subject behavior, subject-person interaction, and consequation relative to the sample event. Comparative sampling in the pre-placement and placement environments permits a precise determination of differences in the two conditions with respect to the aforementioned variables, permitting the specification of essential adjustments in the pre-placement training environment, if necessary. A sample of such comparative data is shown in Table 8-II.

TABLE 8-II

RELATIVE PERCENTAGES OF CONTINGENCY-RELATED BEHAVIOR
EVENTS OBSERVED FOR CLIENT P IN TRAINING ENVIRONMENT
PRIOR TO PLACEMENT AND IN A COMMUNITY WORK ENVIRONMENT
SUBSEQUENT TO PLACEMENT AS ASSEMBLY LINE
WORKER IN A TOY FACTORY

Behavior Class	Description	Training Center	Job Placement
Subject	Task	.7854	.9634
Behavior	Attending	.0687	.0201
	Social-verbal	.0791	.0076
Consequence	Directive	.1000	.0211
	Verbal rnfmt.	.0029	.0000
	Social-verbal	.0750	.0048
Interaction	Client-peer	.0062	.0182
	Client-supervisor	.1520	.0125
	Unconsequated task behavior	.6687	.9576

The data described above are quite useful in closely monitoring a client's progress. They may often lead to reduced error in programming and, consequently, improved training efficiency. However, a second major value is realized in the provision of precise measures permitting a truly experimental approach to the rehabilitation of each client, and ultimately the generation of valuable research operations which are derived directly from the rehabilitation process and can feed directly back into it.

INTERDEPENDENCE OF PROGRAM OPERATIONS AND RESEARCH

It is certainly the case that clients thus far involved in the rehabilitation process described herein have learned. It is equally certain those responsible for their programming have learned a great deal. This is likely the case in any situation wherein relatively inquisitive people function as agents of change. Indeed, much of what is seen as innovation may well be derived from such essentially serendipitous person-environment interaction. A vignette of an actual case may serve to illustrate this point: A young man was in the process of on-the-job programming, and nearing the completion of the Phase V operations. At about this point, unforeseen things began to happen. For example—money, for the young man, was not an effective reinforcer. The staff was forced to quickly arrange a set of operations whereby money would acquire the properties of a generalized reinforcer. It was learned that to do this effectively, it would be necessary to train his mother to establish and maintain certain contingencies in the home. Secondly, it became acutely apparent that a prior history of reinforcement, perhaps having nothing to do with work, can very directly influence work adaptation, as when the client's rather catastrophic response to a dog who merely wished to share his hamburger at a drive-in restaurant resulted in his being escorted to work by a policeman. These events necessitated somewhat of an expansion of training procedures, and in fact the client acquired in his thirteen half days of training something of an improved social adaptation. These rather unfortunate events also taught the staff something in regard to both what to look for in an evaluation program, and what to aim for in a training program.

Within this context of serendipity, the rather stringent data-orientation of the present program is quite advantageous in that it permits one to make the most of serendipity, and perhaps add a few carefully-planned investigative strategies in the bargain. In the case of Transenvironmental Programming, this has become such a powerful reality that maximum program efficiency has, in a very real sense, become dependent upon research strategy and methodology. For example, it is not uncommon to overhear staff discussing the implementation of baseline, treatment, and even reversal phases in regard to a relatively minor program adjustment for an individual client. It is true, of course, that the perpetually incoming data renders this almost a matter of routine.

Further, since the research alluded to is generally applied in nature, it is in turn very dependent upon program operations.

Without the program, there could be no research, and, it seems, without the research there would be a less efficient and less effective program. This reciprocity is what is meant by the term "experimental" in the title of this paper, the operational model of which is presented in Figure 8-2.

From this model, it becomes clear that investigative strategies and research methodologies of a more general nature than that utilized for specific treatments of individual clients can be directly related to each of the program phases. The phase operation and related research are schematized in Figure 8-3. Beyond this, it becomes feasible to conceptualize what has been referred to here as experimental rehabilitation as an integral, if perhaps limited by client population, aspect of what has been described as a general strategy for programmatic research in rehabilitation (Crosson, 1968). This strategy has, as its molar problem, the ecology of adjustment, which is defined as the systematic identification of environmental and behavioral parameters relevant to the rehabilitation process, and the analysis of the functional interaction of these parameters as variables mediating the maintenance of rehabilitation clients in target environments. Within the framework of this model, and particularly its various components presented herein, it should become possible to make use of program-produced information, through research, to improve both the efficiency and effectiveness of rehabilitation services.

CONCLUSIONS

This paper has described an experimental model for vocational training and placement. The model is based upon behavioral principles and emphasizes the specification of terminal behavioral objectives as a beginning point of the rehabilitation process. Program operations dictated by the model consist of a set of developmentally-oriented sequential experiences which are closely related to actual requirements of community adaptation. The program is highly flexible, and emphasizes individual programming. It has been shown to be efficient in that training typically progresses rapidly, and effective in the sense that severely disabled clients typically acquire skills which would normally be as-

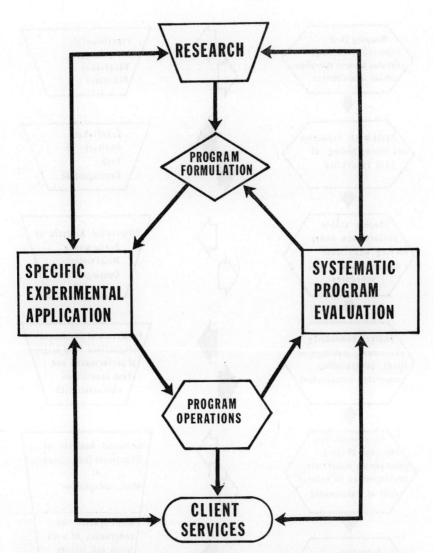

Figure 8-2. Operational model showing functional interdependence of program operations and research in the provision of rehabilitation client services. The rectangular and trapezoidal figures identify functions utilizing research strategies and methods. The remaining figures identify functions specifically oriented to clinical processes and client services. Arrows represent directionality of informational output and the consumer source of the various functions.

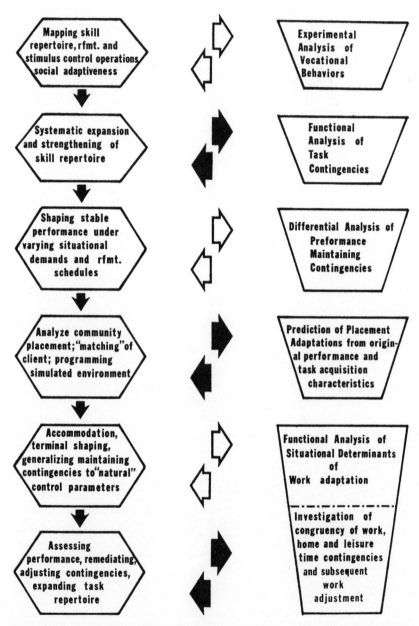

Figure 8-3. Interrelationships of program operations and research strategies in an experimental rehabilitation program.

sumed to be beyond their abilities. Most importantly, the program emphasizes the individual client's abilities rather than his disabilities and negates the reliance on present performance as an index of behavioral potential.

A major value of the program is a continuous, in-process interdependence between program and research operations. This is facilitated through systematic data collection procedures, which permits an efficient experimental approach to rehabilitation without disruption of the rehabilitation process. The model as a whole is seen as potentially leading to improved efficiency and effectiveness of rehabilitation services.

REFERENCES

Bachrach, A. J.: Some applications of operant conditioning to behavior therapy. In Wolpe, J. et al. (Eds.): *The Conditioning Therapies.* New York, Holt, Rinehart, and Winston, 1962, pp. 62-78.

Baer, D. M.; Wolf, M. M.; and Risley, T. R.: Some current dimensions of applied behavior analysis. *Journal of Applied Behavior Analysis, 1:*91-97, 1968.

Bijou, S. W.: The mentally retarded child. *Psychology Today, 2:*46-51, 1968.

Birnbrauer, J. S., and Lawler, J.: Token reinforcement for learning. *Mental Retardation, 2:*275-279, 1964.

Crosson, J. E.: A strategy for multi-disciplinary research on behavioral ecology of the mentally retarded. In Ayers, G. E. (Ed.): *Program Developments in Mental Retardation and Vocational Rehabilitation.* Proceedings of the Vocational Rehabilitation Subdivision Meetings, American Association on Mental Deficiency, Boston, 1968, pp. 6-9.

Crosson, J. E.: A technique for programming sheltered workshop environments for training severely retarded workers. *American Journal of Mental Deficiency, 73:*814-818, 1969.

DeVoss, H.: A study of social contingencies observed in work-study environments of mentally retarded high school students. Unpublished doctoral dissertation, University of Oregon, 1969.

Holland, J. G.: Teaching machines: An application of principles from the laboratory. *Journal of the Experimental Analysis of Behavior, 3:*275-287, 1960.

Krumboltz, J. E. (Ed.): *Revolution in Counseling: Implications of Behavioral Science.* New York, Houghton Mifflin, 1966.

Lindsley, O. R.: Experimental analysis of social reinforcement: Terms and methods. *American Journal of Orthopsychiatry, 33:*624-633, 1963.

Lindsley, O. R.: Direct measurement and prosthesis of retarded behavior. *Journal of Education, 147*:62-81, 1964.

Lofquist, L. H.: *Psychological Research in Rehabilitation.* Washington, D. C., American Psychological Association, 1960.

Meyerson, L.: Learning, behavior and rehabilitation. In Lofquist, L. H. (Ed.): *Psychological Research in Rehabilitation.* Washington, D. C., American Psychological Association, 1960, pp. 68-111.

Michael, J., and Meyerson, L.: A behavioral approach to counseling and guidance. *Harvard Education Review, 32*:383-402, 1962.

Peterson, R. O., and Jones, E. M.: *Guide to Jobs for the Mentally Retarded.* Pittsburgh, American Institute for Research, 1964.

Premack, D.: Reinforcement theory. In Levine, D. (Ed.): *Nebraska Symposium on Motivation.* Lincoln, Neb., University of Nebraska Press, *13*:123-180, 1965.

Skinner, B. F.: *Science and Human Behavior.* New York, The Free Press, 1953.

Ullman, L. P., and Krasner, L.: *A Psychological Approach to Abnormal Behavior.* Englewood Cliffs, N. J., Prentice-Hall, 1969.

Windle, C.: Prognosis of mental subnormals. *American Journal of Mental Deficiency.* Monograph Supplement 66: 180 pp., 1962.

Chapter 9

THE WORK ADJUSTMENT OF THE MENTALLY RETARDED: A FRAME OF REFERENCE FOR PRACTICE AND RESEARCH

PHILIP L. BROWNING

IN THE PAST DECADE the mentally retarded and the world of work has become an increasingly popular topic among professionals in the rehabilitation community. This growing interest is reflected, in part, by the publications which emerged during the 1960's (e.g., Fraenkel, 1961; Mackie Williams, and Dabelstein, 1961; Heber, 1963; Goldstein, 1964; Peterson and Jones, 1964; Gunzberg, 1965; Galazan, 1966; DiMichael, 1966; Wolfensberger, 1967; Stahlecker, 1967; Cobb, 1969). Prior to that time, professional literature with such titles as *The Mentally Retarded and Their Vocational Rehabilitation: A Resource Handbook, Special Problems in Vocational Rehabilitation of the Mentally Retarded, New Vocational Pathways for the Mentally Retarded, Vocational Preparation and Occupation* (for the retarded), and *The Predictive Assessment of the Adult Retarded for Social and Vocational Adjustment* were rare indeed. However, it is surprising to note that in the literally hundreds of recently written pages devoted to the topic, practically no attention has been directed to the development or utilization of vocational-occupational-work-related *theory*.

When delving into the area of vocational rehabilitation research with the retarded it becomes apparent that a voluminous accumulation of research results has been gathered from hundreds of studies. It is difficult not to be dismayed, therefore, when one learns that practically all of these investigations have been atheoretical in nature (Browning, 1971).

The lack of positive recognition toward theory is also evident

177

in the field of practice. Over the past six years, short-term training has been provided through the University of Oregon's Rehabilitation Research and Training Center for over two thousand
practitioners working with the mentally retarded in some form
of helping capacity. As a result of working directly with these
trainees, the author has come to the definite conclusion that practitioners are by and large highly resistant to the term "theory."
I have, in fact, observed that when referring to its potentialities
as a tool for practical use, the mere mention of the word "theory" seems to produce an adverse reaction among practitioners,
often to the point of creating a "mental block."

One can only guess at the reasons for the lack of recognition,
acceptance, and utilization of theory in the field of vocational
rehabilitation with the mentally retarded. Are the literature providers simply not cognizant of its relevance, or have they concluded that because of the relative newness of the topic there
are more important concerns to write about? Have the practitioners experienced a sour dosage of theory? Have they been introduced to a theory which is nonfunctional for them, or have they
simply not been provided an adequate translation of theory into
practice? Are the researchers unaware of the literature related
to longitudinal vocational research and theory-building which
has been in progress for the past several decades and has come
to represent a respectable body of knowledge in vocational psychology?

It is the author's contention that theory is an essential ingredient to be incorporated into practice and research activities related to the vocational rehabilitation of the mentally retarded. The
purpose of this chapter, therefore, is to focus on theory as it relates to the mentally retarded and their world of work. More
specifically, attention is directed to: (1) the nature of theory
with respect to its definition and function; (2) presenting an actual theory of work adjustment; and (3) discussing the implications of this theory as a frame of reference for both the practitioner and researcher working toward the vocational adjustment of the retarded.

THEORY

As a result of considerable experience in serving practitioners in an instructional capacity, I have come to recognize the important role that semantics play in communication. The mere choice of words often has a direct bearing upon the listener's reaction to the information imparted. For example, the use of the term "theory" inevitably raises many specters: an academician in his ivory tower fashioning theories to "hand us folks down here"; intellectualizers engaging in abstract thought which has little relevance to the real world; etc. It is especially unfortunate that semantics can elicit such a negative reaction when one considers that, as in this case, when the term "theory" is replaced with such words as "blueprint," "flowchart," "map" or "model," the practitioner is often quite receptive. The semantic problem coupled with the fact that few practitioners deny the need for a cogent framework, plan or guide for organizing, systematizing, and integrating their work into a more coherent whole, highlights what is often an irrational basis for aversion to theory in the field of practice.

With these thoughts in mind, let us take a closer look at theory and the question of its usefulness in everyday practice and research.

A Definition of Theory

Kerlinger (1964) defined theory as ". . . a set of interrelated constructs (concepts), definitions, and propositions that present a systematic view of phenomena by specifying relations among variables, with the purpose of explaining and predicting the phenomena" (p. 11). According to this definition, a theory is a system or model characterized by a collection of assumptions, statements, or propositions consisting of defined parameters, constructs, or variables which are systematically interrelated to operate within a *coherent framework*.

The Function of Theory

Theory serves to reduce the complexity of a phenomenon into a specified and limited number of events. Essentially, it is a means of preventing the observer (practitioner or researcher) from being "dazzled" by the full blown complexity of events (Hall and Lindzey, 1957). This is especially critical when one considers that phenomena, such as the vocational success of the retarded, for example, often represent multiple events which occur both simultaneously and concomitantly. Thus, there is a need for a sorting-out mechanism, a model if you will, which allows one to deal with phenomena in a more manageable way.

A theory will also influence one's choice of events to be observed and interpreted. In other words, it will suggest the explicit criteria for determining what is relevant and what is irrelevant. If a person does not have a theory which supplies him with a systematic frame of reference, then on what grounds can he make such decisions? In addition, a theory can facilitate one's ability to observe in an orderly fashion. The counter to this is that nonsystematic observations lead to nonsystematic procedures and practices.

There are two functions of theory which seem to have particular relevance to the researcher: A theory can lead to the collection of relevant empirical relations not yet observed and permit the incorporation of known empirical findings within a logically consistent and reasonably simple framework (Hall and Lindzey, 1957).

In summary, then, theory: (1) provides the user with a systematic frame of reference, thus facilitating nonrandom practices (observations, interpretations, interventions, predictions); (2) breaks down the complexity of the task and provides a manageable set of guidelines for practice; (3) serves as a yardstick for decision making and problem solving; and (4) is like a map in that it suggests how the user might best go about reaching his objective (destination).

A THEORY OF WORK ADJUSTMENT

This section will provide a general overview or skeletal framework of an actual theory of work adjustment that the author feels could be appropriately and meaningfully applied to vocational rehabilitation practice and research with the mentally retarded. Since 1957, the University of Minnesota has received federal funding for a continuing series of research investigations which have come to be known as the *Minnesota Studies in Vocational Rehabilitation.* One of the highlights of this longitudinal research project has been the development of the Theory of Work Adjustment. The first formulation of the theory was published in 1964 (Dawis, 1964), followed by a revision in 1968 (Lofquist et al., 1968). Since the development of this theory, a major objective of the project has been to devise instruments to measure the major constructs of the theory and to investigate the propositions it has generated.

The Theory of Work Adjustment represents what many refer to as a matching model, i.e. correspondence between the worker and the work setting. Degree of correspondence can be described in terms of (1) how well the person fulfills the requirements of

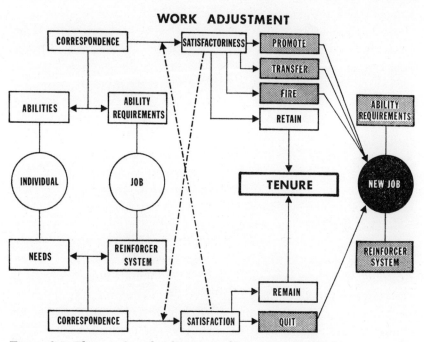

Figure 9-1. Theory of work adjustment. [Courtesy of publishers, copyright 1968]

the work (abilities to meet the job requirements) and (2) how well the work environment fulfills the requirements of the person (reinforcement system to meet his needs or preferences for stimulus conditions in the environment). Thus, the greater the correspondence between the person's work behavior and the work environment, the greater the probability that requirements at both levels will be met.

The degree of correspondence between the individual and the job is represented by employer satisfactoriness (external indicator of success) and employee satisfaction (internal indicator of success). It follows that the greater the degree of correspondence between abilities and job requirements and needs or preferences and reinforcement system, the greater the probability of satisfaction at each respective level.

The stability of correspondence between the individual and the job is reflected as tenure on the job. The probability of tenure increases as correspondence increases.

In short, the Theory of Work Adjustment is like a map. It reveals that two roads must be traveled when the ultimate destination is job tenure for the client. The first is the route of the employer, in which at least minimal connections must be made between the abilities of the client and of the job; otherwise, the employer will either promote or fire the client, imposing the detour or a dead-end on the course toward the desired destination. The second is the route of the client, in which at least minimal connections must be made between his preferences and the job's reinforcement system; otherwise, he will probably stray off course before his vocational objective is adequately met.

In line with the purposes of this paper, the above description has been limited to a well-defined, although brief sketch, of the Theory of Work Adjustment. Those who are interested in acquiring further information about the theory are referred to the series of monographs which have been generated by the Minnesota project. Also recommended is a recently published book providing a synopsis of this work (Lofquist and Dawis, 1969). The remainder of the chapter sets forth both the practical and research implications of the Theory of Work Adjustment.

IMPLICATIONS
Practice

The discussion of the implications of the theory in terms of its practical utility will show how the model serves as a frame of reference for definitions of disability and work adjustment as well as for workers in the areas of evaluation and training, counseling and placement.

Disability and Work Adjustment

The staff of the Rehabilitation Research and Training Center frequently engage their trainees in the task of defining both the disability conditions (e.g. mental retardation) of those whom they serve and goals (e.g. work adjustment) of their practice. The many discussions which this task has generated among trainees have played an important part in leading to the author's appreciation of the extent to which a practitioner's viewpoints concerning these two concepts govern his professional approach. Even though some persons hold definitions to be of little practical importance to their work, the truth is the practitioner's attitudes, assumptions, expectations and decisions often reflect the definitions which he consciously or unconsciously included in his frame of reference. The discussions have also revealed that frequently there are as many interpretations of the two terms (i.e. mental retardation and work adjustment) as there are persons providing them.

The practitioner who incorporates the Theory of Work Adjustment into his approach will equip himself with a frame of reference for viewing disability and vocational success. He will begin to see disability as the interaction of client and work environment as opposed to medical diagnostic categories (Lofquist et al., 1964). In other words, disability will be viewed in terms of its effects or consequences upon the client's adjustment to his work. Further, disability will be defined in terms of vocationally relevant dimensions. This runs counter to a recent experience of mine wherein I requested a group of rehabilitation counselors to define mental retardation within the context of work. Not unexpectedly, many of the definitions placed primary emphasis on medical criteria such as central nervous system pathology, while lesser importance was attached to adaptive behavioral dimensions related to work. Kauppi and Weiss (1967) have commented on the narrow possibilities that the disability construct or term "mental retardation" has for the vocational counselor aside from informing him that the client is below average on verbal skills:

> The label says little about other abilities, interests, needs or potential. Thus, effort should be spent on finding ways to measure vocationally relevant dimensions in the mental retard and to relate these dimensions to the world of work. The job potential of mental retards can be broadened sometimes simply by not cutting off opportunities, sometimes by providing compensatory training, and sometimes by eliminating unnecessary verbal demands from non-verbal jobs. Most important is the recognition that a single measure (e.g., IQ) or a single level is not enough for careful vocational counseling or the study of vocational adjustment (p. 8).

As defined within the Theory of Work Adjustment, the term "mental retardation" serves as a point of reference for overcoming the problems and limitations encountered with the narrower usage of the term. Specifically, congenital or developmental disabling conditions such as mental retardation are seen as (Lofquist, 1964):

> . . . resulting in sets of abilities and needs that are similar to those of the average individual, but are perhaps more limited in range and pattern and perhaps at a lower level. These abilities and needs result from structured social-educational experiences in the same fashion as for "normal" individuals. The individual is not really disabled in the sense of a decrease in ability strengths as a result of trauma, although he has experienced a disabling condition. He has, however, probably experienced a more limited range of reinforcers than the "normal" individual (p. 6).

That vocational success is a concept lacking consistent definition among practitioners is indeed remarkable, particularly since the ultimate goal of the vocational counselor is the vocational success of his client. Practitioners all seem to have their own idiosyncratic views of vocational success, which vary according to their philosophical positions. The following questions illustrate the wide range of issues:

1. Should a single criterion of success apply to all retarded clients in all settings?
2. Against what baseline should vocational success be measured, e.g. middle-class norms, norms for the retarded client population, or goals specific to the individual client?
3. Is the employer's satisfaction an adequate indicator of work adjustment of the client?

The Minnesota theory provides the practitioner with one way of viewing work adjustment. It defines work adjustment as the ongoing process by which an individual seeks to achieve and maintain correspondence with his work environment (Lofquist and Dawis, 1969). Thus, the achieving of minimal correspondence or matching enables him to remain in a work environment. The greater the correspondence the greater the probability that he will remain on the job (tenure). Consequently, the ultimate goal of the vocational counselor who employs the model will be job placement in which the client can meet the requirements of the job and the job can meet the requirements of the client. This objective includes both an internal (client) and an external (employer) indicator of success. Tenure on the job will reflect the degree to which they are both satisfied.

Evaluation and Training

The evaluator plays an important role in the engineering of the rehabilitation plan, and many view him as the prescriber and predictor of the events which hopefully lead to a successful outcome. Therefore, it is essential that the evaluator be cognizant of the critical ingredients which influence successful placement. He must ask: "What are the critical ingredients or factors that facilitate successful rehabilitation outcomes; or what are the predictive variables for successful job placement?" In dealing with this question, he must assess the important dimensions and on the basis of his evaluation, make specific recommendations regarding the nature and course of the rehabilitation plan for a given client.

Considering the importance of evaluation as a service component, the significance of evaluation to the overall rehabilitation
process, and the critical role of the evaluator, means of increasing the effectiveness of evaluation should be explored. The author believes that the incorporation of a vocational model to
serve as a frame of reference for practice would be meaningful
to this effort. The Theory of Work Adjustment represents an important available model from which to choose.

First of all, the model recognizes work personality or behavior
as being two dimensional, i.e. abilities and needs. This suggests
that the evaluator should not only look at the retarded client's
specific work abilities or job skills but should also assess his repertoire of needs or preferences for stimulus conditions which
are reinforcing to him. Secondly, the model suggests that the
evaluator should not limit his evaluation to client variables. This
is an important consideration, particularly since it is now recognized that non-subject variables may play a crucial role in determining whether the person is successful on the job (Butler and
Browning, 1970). This model also recognizes the importance of
assessing the work environment, i.e. job requirements and the
job's reinforcement system.

In addition to the guidelines which the theory sets forth regarding what to evaluate, there is available a set of vocational
instruments which have been designed to measure the major elements or constructs of the theory (see Instrumentation, p. 192).
Even though the theory is only experimentally operational at
this stage, it is the author's opinion that these measuring tools
could add significantly to the evaluator's "shelf" of instruments
for assessing the vocational behavior of the retarded.

Two major implications for training are derived from the
theory. First, since the theory recognizes persons with mental retardation as being limited in their patterns of abilities and needs
(work behavior) the model suggests broadening their patterns
of work abilities and preferences through training experiences.
Second, the model, being a matching one, suggests that the emphasis is not on changing the client to fit the world of work;
rather, the major task is to find a job to which the person best

corresponds in order that the requirements of the work and the client will be met.

Counseling

Professional literature and practitioners in the field frequently touch upon two issues in the area of counseling the retarded. The first questions whether or not retarded individuals can benefit from counseling. For the purpose of this paper, it is enough to assume that the answer is affirmative. Counselors who have worked with the retarded and provided them with a supportive psychological climate know that this often results in a rewarding learning experience for many of them. For the reader who wishes to further explore the many ramifications of this issue, however, reference is made to Gardner (1967), Halpern (1968), Browning and Butler (1970), and Browning (1971).

The second issue questions whether or not counseling techniques for the retarded are different from counseling techniques in general. The author supports the position of Halpern and Berard (1972) who suggest that the answer is "no." In other words, the wide variety of counseling techniques that have been used with the retarded are the same techniques with which clinicians are familiar, for example, individual verbal counseling, group counseling, and play techniques. Likewise, the Theory of Work Adjustment in terms of its implications for vocational counselors provides a frame of reference which is no different for retarded clients than for clients in general.

The theory views counseling as a major technique or vehicle for achieving the goal of the client's work adjustment, i.e. placement on a job in which he will be both satisfied and satisfactory and tend to remain for a reasonable length of time. In essence, counseling serves as a means of facilitating correspondence between the person's work behavior and job environment. As a facilitator, the counselor is not devoted to "changing" the client but rather to appropriately matching or fitting a client and job.

Thus, one implication of the theory is that the counselor should have sufficient knowledge in the area of work personality and work environment. He must have a grasp and understanding

of the psychological parameters of work (e.g. career development, occupational interests, job skills), as well as understand
and be familiar with the labor market (e.g. job analysis, work
availability, employer attitudes). The counselor's expertise in vocational information should also include competencies in vocationally related psychometrics (e.g. Multi-Factor Tests such as
the General Aptitude Test Battery) as well as technical material
related to the working environment (e.g. *Worker Trait Requirements for 4,000 Jobs, Dictionary of Occupational Titles*). This
type of information-based competency will enhance his ability
to more appropriately facilitate correspondence between clients
and jobs.

The theory also implies that the counselor should have expertise in interview skills. It is through good interview skills that
he will be able to more effectively gather and impart (especially
to the client) the vocational information important to decision-
making. Special attention to specific procedures and techniques
of the interviewing process within the context of the Theory of
Work Adjustment has been given by Lofquist (1969).

To summarize, the theory provides the vocational counselor
with a model for working with mentally retarded clients (and
clients in general). This frame of reference suggests not only
what the counselor and counselee communicate about (work personality and work environment) but also toward what end they
establish a relationship (work adjustment) (Dawis, 1967).

Placement

The vocational placement counselor working with retarded clients is responsible for persons who have had an undue excess of
failure. Consequently, it is critical that he consider every alternative for reducing the retarded individual's chances for another
defeating experience.

Being essentially a placement model, the Theory of Work Adjustment lends particular emphasis to this latter stage of the rehabilitation process (Dawis, 1967). More specifically, the theory
views vocational success or work adjustment as being facilitated
by and resulting from the placement of clients in appropriate
jobs. The appropriateness of placement is best indicated by the

degree of correspondence between the person's work behavior and his work environment (see Figure 9-2). The closer the matching the more assured one can be that the requirements of the job and the client will be mutually met, resulting in tenure and success.

In looking at Figure 9-2 it also becomes apparent that a major characteristic of the theory is the recognition of individual differences, both in terms of persons and jobs. The author feels

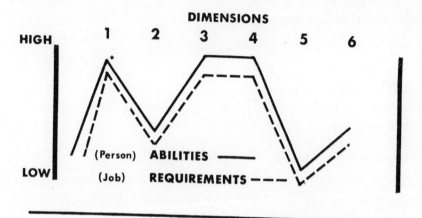

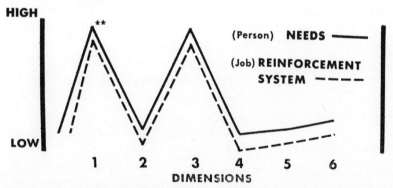

Figure 9-2. Differential profile of work adjustment. *Close correspondence between the person's strong ability (dimension No. 1) and the skill required to do the job, e.g. fine motor dexterity. **Close correspondence between the person's high need (dimension No. 1) and the stimulus condition in the work environment which has reinforcement value to that need or preference, e.g. money.

that the significance of this point cannot be overemphasized when considering the mentally retarded and their working world. Even though retarded individuals may have limited abilities and needs, they represent a most heterogeneous segment of the population. Moreover, there is considerable variation among the types of work environments in which they have proven successful, despite the fact that these jobs generally represent the occupational classifications of unskilled and semi-skilled work. The point is that job placement should be no less selective and differential for retarded than for nonretarded clients.

Research

The discussion of the research implications of the Theory of Work Adjustment will be in terms of a framework for empirical findings, a systematic basis for variable selection, instrumentation, and hypotheses generation.

Framework for Empirical Findings

As previously indicated, one of the functions of theory is to provide a logically consistent and reasonably simple framework for the incorporation of known empirical findings. An abundant amount of empirical data from rehabilitative prognostic studies with the retarded has been collected, and a framework for the incorporation of the more sound empirical findings—if any exist—is currently needed. Hundreds of predictive and criteria variables have been investigated, creating a vast fund of data in need of some sort of systematic organization. It appears that the Theory of Work Adjustment may have some utility in serving this need.

Systematic Basis for Selection

Another function of theory alluded to earlier was that it not only provides a limited number of events to be observed but determines in a non-random fashion the explicit criteria for determining relevant vs. irrelevant events. Cobb (1969) discusses the importance of this aspect of theory as it relates to the problem of variables selected in vocational outcome studies with the retarded:

> . . . predictors are in the nature of independent variables and therefore may logically be any measures whatsoever which can show a statistical relationship to a criterion variable. The investigator can choose to explore anything that suits his fancy, and many a test has no better rationale than that it "works" in the sense that a relationship with a criterion or dependent variable can be shown at some acceptable level of probability. However, it is hardly economical research to explore any and every possible variable at random, without some theoretical basis for a reasonable hypothesis. What we are really searching for in the end is a systematic account of determiners of the behavioral outcomes that we are interested in. Consequently, out of the wide universe of all possible measures we (should) select those which are consistent with already known (empirical) relationships or those which are selected by or derivative from a theoretical orientation to the problem at hand (p. 11).

For those engaging in rehabilitation research in mental retardation, the Theory of Work Adjustment may serve as a viable alternative for dealing with the problem.

Instrumentation

Researchers engaged in vocational investigations with the retarded have been plagued by the lack of vocationally-related instruments which are appropriate for this population. A few efforts, however, have been made to remedy the problem. A project was initiated in 1959 at the MacDonald Training Center in Tampa, Florida, the purpose of which was to ". . . develop, validate, and standardize a vocational capacity scale which would assess the training assets, limitations and potential of young adults handicapped by mental retardation (Pinkard, 1963, p. 3)." The resultant Vocational Capacity Scale, which consists of eight subtests, represents one of the few vocationally related batteries of instruments involving extended evaluation (Pinkard, 1961; Dayan, 1968). Peck, Stephens and Fooshee (1964) developed what is known as the Texas Screening Battery, which they used to evaluate the personal, socio-economic, and vocational success of mentally retarded youth. It was used specifically in an attempt to answer the following research questions (Stephens and Peck, 1968, p. 1):

  —Upon what did the success of male educable mental re-
    tardates depend?
  —What cluster of personality and cognitive attributes existed
    in successful male retardates?
  —Did subjects who had habilitation training achieve greater
    success that those who had no training?
  —Were graduates of certain habilitation training programs
    more successful than graduates of other programs?

An attempt has also been made to develop a vocational interest test for the retarded (Becker, 1971). The general purpose of this study was to develop a non-reading technique for assessing the vocational preference of educable mentally retarded youth.

The staff at the Work Adjustment Project have also directed their attention to the adaptation of vocational instruments for the retarded (Lofquist and Dawis, 1970). They conducted a series of studies to modify the instruments used to measure the work personality (abilities—General Aptitude Test Battery; needs—Minnesota Importance Questionnaire) of the retarded. This investigative effort of programmatic research seems to have direct implications for researchers concerned with the vocational prognosis of the retarded. A set of vocational instruments has been designed to measure the major constructs of a theory. Thus, a set of measuring tools is available which will allow the investigator to begin testing some of the propositions or hypotheses generated by a theory.

Generation of Hypotheses

A good theory will generate research questions or a set of hypotheses that may be tested to determine the usefulness of the theory. The Theory of Work Adjustment meets this criterion, and the following propositions (Lofquist and Dawis, 1969, p. 50-53) represent only a few which are generated by this model:

  —An individual's work adjustment at any point in time is in-
    dicated by his concurrent levels of satisfactoriness and sat-
    isfaction.

—Satisfactoriness is a function of the correspondence between an individual's abilities and the ability requirements of the work environment, provided that the individual's needs correspond with the reinforcer system of the work environment.

    a. Knowledge of an individual's abilities and of his satisfactoriness permits the determination of the effective ability requirements of the work environment.

    b. Knowledge of the ability requirements of the work environment and of an individual's satisfactoriness permits the inference of an individual's abilities.

—The probability that an individual will be forced out of the work environment is inversely related to his satisfactoriness.

—The probability that an individual will voluntarily leave the work environment is inversely related to his satisfaction.

More specific hypotheses which stem from the theory might be investigated with the retarded population. For example:

—Average tenure for a retarded population should be higher for a correspondent group (matching of work ability-job requirements and needs-work reinforcement system) than for a non-correspondent group.

—The proportion of retarded individuals fired for lack of satisfactoriness should be higher for a non-correspondent group (work ability-job requirements) than for a correspondent group.

—The proportion of retarded individuals who quit voluntarily should be higher for a non-correspondent group (needs-work reinforcement system) than for a correspondent group.

These represent only a few of the hypotheses which appear to have direct implications for researchers interested in the vocational prognosis of the mentally retarded.

To summarize, there is a definite need for rehabilitation researchers concerning themselves with the vocational world of the retarded to begin considering theory-based research. In fact, this has been considered as a major recommendation resulting from a critical analysis of methodological issues in the prediction of rehabilitation outcome with the retarded (Butler and Browning, 1970).

SUMMARY

This chapter was based on the author's (1) recognition that, within the field of vocational rehabilitation of the mentally retarded, theory has received minimal attention from researchers and support from practitioners, and (2) opinion that theory is an essential ingredient to be incorporated into vocational practice and research activities related to the retarded. In an attempt to meet this dilemma, the reader was first provided an orientation to the nature of theory, i.e. definition and function. In essence, theory was viewed as a "map" which serves to provide the user with a more systematic frame of reference for his professional practice. Secondly, an actual theory of work adjustment was presented. This occupational, vocational, or work-related theory was selected not only because of its desirable attributes (e.g. comphensiveness, explicitness, parsimony) but also because of its utility for practitioners and researchers working with the retarded in a vocational capacity. The remainder of the paper was devoted to discussing the practical and research implications of the theory. The practical implications related to the definition of terms or concepts (i.e. mental retardation and work adjustment), evaluation and training, counseling and placement. The research implications focused on a framework for empirical findings, systematic basis for variable selection, instrumentation, and hypotheses generation. In light of the numerous implications brought out, it is hoped that the concept of theory will receive closer scrutiny as a useful and viable tool for providing a frame of reference for practitioners and researchers in the vocational rehabilitation of the mentally retarded.

REFERENCES

Becker, A. L.: *Reading—Free Vocational Interest Inventory.* Columbus, Ohio, Ohio Department of Mental Hygiene and Correction (Final Report, Project No. 452227, Grant No. OEG-0-8-080188-4421), Office of Education, Bureau of Research, 1971.

Browning, P. L.: Rehabilitation research with the mentally retarded: A consideration for theory. In Jaffe, J. (Ed.): *Challenges in Vocational Rehabilitation and Mental Retardation.* Proceedings of the Vocational Rehabilitation Subdivision Meetings held at the American Association on Mental Deficiency Annual Meeting, Washington, D. C., May 25-30, 1970, February, 1971, pp. 19-30.

Browning, P. L., and Butler, A. J.: Process research in counseling the retarded. In Prehm, H. J. (Ed.): *Rehabilitation Research in Mental Retardation.* Eugene, Oregon, Rehabilitation Research and Training Center in Mental Retardation, Monograph No. 2, July, 1970, pp. 35-47.

Browning, P., and Keesey, M.: Experimental Studies in Counseling the Retarded: A Critical Analysis. Rehabilitation Research and Training Center in Mental Retardation, University of Oregon, Working Paper No. 52, September, 1971.

Butler, A. J., and Browning, P.: Methodological issues in the prediction of rehabilitation outcome with the mentally retarded. In Prehm, H. J. (Ed.): *Rehabilitation Research in Mental Retardation.* Eugene, Oregon, Rehabilitation Research and Training Center in Mental Retardation, Monograph No. 2, July, 1970, pp. 49-69.

Cobb, H. V.: *The Predictive Assessment of the Adult Retarded for Social and Vocational Adjustment: A Review of Research, Part II—Analysis of the Literature.* Research Project RD-1624-P, Final Report, Rehabilitation Services Administration, Social and Rehabilitation Service, U. S. Department of Health, Education and Welfare, 1969.

Dawis, R. V.: A theory of work adjustment. *Minnesota Studies in Vocational Rehabilitation,* Monograph No. XV, 1964.

Dawis, R. V.: The Minnesota studies in vocational rehabilitation. *Rehabilitation Counseling Bulletin XI,* 1-10, September, 1967.

Dayan, M.: *Validation of the Vocational Capacity Scale Utilizing Institutionalized Retardates.* Pineville, Louisiana, Pinecrest State School (Report on Project VRA-RD-1619-P), 1968.

DiMichael, S. G. (Ed.): *New Vocational Pathways for the Mentally Retarded.* American Rehabilitation Counseling Association, Division of American Personnel and Guidance Association, 1966.

Fraenkel, W. H.: *The Mentally Retarded and Their Vocational Rehabilitation: A Resource Handbook.* New York, National Association for Retarded Children, Inc., 1961.

Galazan, M. M.: Vocational rehabilitation and mental retardation. In Philips (Ed.): *Prevention and Treatment of Mental Retardation.* New York, Basic Books, Inc., 1966.

Gardner, W. I.: What should be the psychologist's role? *Mental Retardation,* 5:29-31, 1967.

Goldstein, H.: Social and occupational adjustment. In Stevens and Heber (Eds.): *Mental Retardation: A Review of Research.* Chicago, The University of Chicago Press, 1964, pp. 214-258.

Gunzberg, H. C.: Vocational and social rehabilitation of the sub-normal. In Clarke and Clarke (Eds.): *Mental Deficiency: The Changing Outlook.* New York, The Free Press, 1965.

Hall, C. S., and Lindzey, G.: *Theories of Personality.* New York, John Wiley and Sons, Inc., 1957.

Halpern, A. S.: Why not psychotherapy? *Mental Retardation,* 6:48-50, 1968.

Halpern, A. S., and Berard, W. R.: Counseling the Mentally Retarded: A Review for Practice. Rehabilitation Research and Training Center in Mental Retardation, University of Oregon, Working Paper No. 55, February, 1972.

Heber, R. (Ed.): *Special Problems in Vocational Rehabilitation of the Mentally Retarded.* Rehabilitation Service Series No. 65-16, Vocational Rehabilitation Administration (now the Rehabilitation Services Administration), U. S. Department of Health, Education and Welfare, 1963.

Kauppi, D. R., and Weiss, D. T.: The Utility of the Classification "Mentally Retarded" in Vocational Psychology. Paper presented at the 75th Annual Meeting of American Psychological Association, Division 17, September, 1967.

Kerlinger, F.: *Foundations of Behavioral Research.* New York, Holt, Rinehart and Winston, Inc., 1964.

Lofquist, L. H. et al.: Disability and work, *Minnesota Studies in Vocational Rehabilitation,* Monograph No. XVII, October, 1964.

Lofquist, L. H.: Techniques of counseling. In Malikin and Rusalem (Eds.): *Vocational Rehabilitation of the Disabled: An Overview.* New York, New York University Press, 1969, pp. 217-238.

Lofquist, L. H. et al.: A theory of work adjustment (a revision), *Minnesota Studies in Vocational Rehabilitation,* Monograph No. XXIII, 1968.

Lofquist, L. H., and Dawis, R. V.: *Adjustment to Work: A Psychological View of Man's Problems in a Work-oriented Society.* New York, Appleton-Century-Crofts, Educational Division, Meredith Corporation, 1969.

Lofquist, L. H., and Dawis, R. V.: *Assessing the Work Personalities of Mentally Retarded Adults.* Department of Psychology, University of Minnesota, Minneapolis, September, 1970, Final Report RD-2568-P.

Mackie, R. P.; Williams, H. M.; and Dabelstein et al. (Eds.): *Preparation of the Mentally Retarded Youth for Gainful Employment.* Washington, D. C., U. S. Department of Printing Office, Superintendent of Documents, Rehabilitation Service Series No. 507, 1961.

Peck, J. R.; Stephens, W. B.; and Fooshee, D. K.: *The Texas Screening Battery for Subnormals.* Austin, 1804 Raleigh, 1964.

Peterson, R. O., and Jones, E. M.: *Guide to Jobs for the Mentally Retarded* (Revised Edition). Pittsburgh, American Institute for Research, 1964.

Pinkard, C. M.: *Predicting Vocational Capacity of Retarded Young Adults.*

Tampa, MacDonald Training Center Foundation, Research Division, 1963.

Pinkard, C. M.: *Second Progress Report and Continuation Application Development of Vocational Capacity Rule for Use in Sheltered Workshops Serving Young Adults Handicapped by Mental Retardation*. Tampa, MacDonald Training Center Foundation, 1961.

Stahlecker, L. V.: *Occupational Information for the Mentally Retarded*. Springfield, Ill., Charles C Thomas, 1967.

Stephens, W. B., and Peck, J. R.: *Success of Young Adult Male Retardates*. The Council for Exceptional Children, CEC Research Monograph, 1968.

Wolfensberger, W.: Vocational preparation and occupation. In Baumeister (Ed.): *Mental Retardation: Appraisal, Education, Rehabilitation*. Chicago, Aldine Publishing Company, 1967, pp. 232-273.

Chapter 10

PREDICTIVE STUDIES ON REHABILITATION OUTCOME WITH THE RETARDED: A METHODOLOGICAL CRITIQUE

ALFRED J. BUTLER

PHILIP L. BROWNING

THE REHABILITATION PROCESS may be viewed as a planned sequence of services provided to assist an individual in movement from a handicapped to a less handicapped condition. The outcome of this process has been one focal point of research in the area of rehabilitation and mental retardation. Windle (1962, p. 3) underlines the importance of such research undertakings when he states that "In most cases, the more accurately probability of outcome can be estimated, the more effectively practical decisions can be made" and that "Practitioners also need to know what variables are related to favorable outcome so they may concentrate upon developing or augmenting these variables."

Each practitioner and researcher has his own idiosyncratic view or definition of rehabilitation outcome. Consequently, research on predictions of outcome warrants a number of philosophical and methodological considerations. The following questions illustrate the range of issues:

To what extent does rehabilitation outcome subsume the concept of personal and socio-civic success as well as vocational success?

Note: Reprinted from H. J. Prehm (Ed.), *Rehabilitation Research in Mental Retardation*. Rehabilitation Research and Training Center in Mental Retardation, University of Oregon, Monograph No. 2, July, 1970, 49-69. The original title of the paper was, Methodological issues in the prediction of rehabilitation outcome with the mentally retarded.

To what extent does rehabilitation success reflect the objectives of the individual or the objectives of society?

Against what baseline should rehabilitation success be measured, e.g. middle-class norms, norms for the retarded population, or goals specific to the individual client?

Should a single success criterion apply to all clients in all settings?

This chapter is directed to these and related issues in research on rehabilitation outcome with the mentally retarded. Our purpose is to review the current status of research in the prediction of rehabilitation outcome and to identify areas in which expenditures of future efforts might be fruitful. More specifically, an attempt is made to treat, in part, the following questions:

What research has been reported on the prediction of rehabilitation outcome with the mentally retarded, and what generalizations may be formulated from these studies?

What methodological dimensions should be considered in assessing the investigations which have been undertaken?

How are these methodological dimensions illustrated in selected outcome studies?

What recommendations can be made for future research strategy?

RESEARCH OVERVIEW

A comprehensive answer to the first question requires presentation of material now available in several reviews, particularly those by Windle (1962), Goldstein (1964), Charles (1966), Cobb and Epir (1966), Cobb, Epir, Dye, and Streifel (1966), Wolfensberger (1967), Stahlecker (1967), and Cobb (1969). For the purpose of this paper, nineteen studies were selected as representative of research focusing on rehabilitation outcome of the mentally retarded. Table 10-I describes the major methodological characteristics of these studies.

The outstanding feature of this area of research endeavor is the diversity of findings and the lack of consensus among investigators concerning dimensions of and underlying reasons for the rehabilitation success of the retarded. Thus, the conclusions

TABLE 10-I

SELECTED ORIGINAL STUDIES OF REHABILITATION OUTCOME
AND THEIR MAJOR METHODOLOGICAL CHARACTERISTICS

Reference	Major Methodological Characteristics
Baller (1936)	Longitudinal study over a three-year period of three non-institutional groups representing three levels of intelligence. Only intelligence was related specifically to outcome informally described in terms of vocational, personal and social functioning.
Baller, Charles and Miller (1967)	A thirty-year follow-up of the three non-institutional groups reported by Baller (1936). Some vocational, personal and social outcome criteria.
Bobroff (1956)	Follow-up study after twelve years of special class students, male and female, IQ range 40-94; outcome criteria primarily vocational and economic; outcome criteria related only to program level, i.e., "Special B."
Charles (1953)	A fifteen-year follow-up of three groups reported by Baller (1936). Same vocational, personal and social outcome criteria.
Cohen (1960)	Follow-up of an institutional group after placement in a short-term residential training school, age and intelligence levels not reported. Informal description of outcome and of factors influencing outcome.
Cowan and Goldman (1959)	Follow-up comparing outcome of twenty Ss receiving vocational training through a state rehabilitation program and twenty Ss receiving no vocational training and served by private agencies. Outcome defined as being employed at minimum wage level. Outcome related to training, intelligence and level of education by chi-square analyses.
Dinger (1961)	Follow-up of one-hundred male and female secondary special education class students, from one to eighteen years after completion of school. Outcome criteria included occupational, economic and social adjustment. Characteristics of sample described in terms of IQ, age, sex, types and requirements of positions, but not systematically related to outcome.
Hartzler (1953)	A ten-year follow-up of 191 females following institutionalization. Successful outcome defined as ability to be self-supporting and avoiding conflict with law. Predictors informally related to outcome included age at admission, age at discharge, IQ, change in IQ, years on parole, and degree of delinquency pre-admission.
Jackson and Butler (1963)	A two-year follow-up of 191 females following institutionalization. Successful placement defined as six months of uninterrupted employment. Predictors which included seventeen maturational and environmental variables were related to outcome by t-test and multiple regression analyses.

Kolstoe (1961) — Follow-up of eighty-two male rehabilitation clients of a short-term training and evaluation program. Outcome defined in terms of obtaining employment following training. Thirty-five predictors including experimental, familial, maturational, medical, and achievement variables were related to outcome by t-tests.

Madison (1964) — Follow-up of twenty-nine males and females following temporary discharge from an institution. Outcome success defined as receiving permanent discharge or being returned to the institution. Thirty-four predictors including demographic, family, medical, psychometric, behavioral, and educational and training variables were related to outcome by chi-square analyses.

O'Connor and Tizard (1956) — Two investigations reported with two male institutional groups, N = 104 and 100 respectively. Concurrent studies of predictor and criterion variables. Two criteria used: (1) neurotic tendency rated on basis of psychiatric diagnosis and behavior record; (2) employment success ratings based primarily on day work assignments from institution. Twenty-seven predictor variables including age, physical, motor, intelligence, and personality measures were related to criteria by correlational and multiple regression analyses.

Peterson and Smith (1960) — Follow-up study of special education class graduates. Forty-five mentally retarded were compared with forty-five normals from a low socio-economic status. Groups were compared informally on work, home and family, social and civic outcome characteristics.

Phelps (1956) — Follow-up of 163 male and female special education class students. Outcome based on personal interviews and interviews with employers informally described in terms of wages earned, quality of work, work behavior, appearance, etc. A number of predictor variables related to receiving wages above the median by chi-square analyses.

Porter and Milazzo (1958) — Follow-up of seventeen male and female students who attended special classes and thirty-two retarded who attended regular classes. Outcome informally described in terms of vocational, social and civic variables. Differences in two educational groups informally assessed.

Shafter (1957) — Follow-up of 205 male and female institutionalized patients. Outcome defined as complete discharge from the institution. Fifty-six predictors including demographic, experiential, medical, behavioral, intellectual, achievement and training variables were related to outcome by chi-square analyses and analysis of variance.

Stephens (1964) — Concurrent study of five non-institutional groups (N = 125), four groups receiving special educational and/or vocational training, one group from regular school classes. Outcome defined in terms of eighty variables including a wide range of vocational, personal and socio-civic measures. Predictors included seventy-eight intellectual, perceptual-motor, family status and personality measures.

Reference	Major Methodological Characteristics
	Factor analysis was used to reduce criterion and predictor measures to a smaller number of identifiable factors. Predictors related to criteria by analysis of variance, chisquare and multiple regression analyses.
Windle, Stewart and Brown (1961)	Follow-up over a four-year period of three institutional groups, total N = 296, one group on vocational leave, one on home leave and one on family care. Outcome criterion defined in terms of maintaining leave versus re-institutionalization. Reasons for failure analyzed in terms of patient's actions, health reasons and environmental lack of support. Three groups informally compared on each specific reason for failure.
Wolfson (1956)	Follow-up over an eight-year period of 223 male and female institutional patients. Outcome informally described in terms of vocational and social adjustment. Four levels of adjustment compared informally on age on admission, years in residence, and IQ.

that there remains severe limitations in the knowledge of the relevant factors critically related to vocational adjustment (Goldstein and Heber, 1961) and that there is no single measure which can predict vocational success with anything approaching reasonable certainty (Heber, 1963; Wolfensberger, 1967) are not surprising. It is distressing that these conclusions are still valid today.

When taking into account studies using broader definitions of rehabilitation outcome, e.g. release of retardates from institutional settings, the only variables that appear to have any reasonably consistent value in outcome prediction are age, time of admission into the institution, age at time of discharge from the institution, sex, IQ, and difference in verbal and performance IQ (Windle, 1962). However, even these indices have a very low statistical relationship with successful outcome, no matter how success is defined.

Cobb's most recent work (1969) reflects a most thorough and comprehensive analysis of the literature regarding rehabilitation outcome research with the mentally retarded. The reader is referred to his report in which he summarizes the research in a series of twenty statements which appeared to him to represent the most significant developments in the area. As for a broader generalization, he stated:

From the review of research studies in the preceding chapters (which are representative of rehabilitation outcome studies with the mentally retarded), it should be readily apparent that no neat and certain formulas for predicting adult success in the retarded have been achieved. To the contrary, if there is one clear conclusion to be drawn from this array of studies, it is that no simple formula for prediction is possible, that the relationship between predictors and criteria are enormously complex, and that outcomes in terms of personal, social, and vocational success are the product of manifold interactive determinants (p. 138).

Finally, Goldstein (1964, p. 229) stated:

> Only one broad generalization may be derived with any degree of confidence—the probability is that the majority of higher grade mentally retarded inmates of public institutions will make a relatively successful adjustment in their communities when training, selection, placement, and supervision are all at an optimum.

The fact that there have been only a few tentative generalizations, most of which are global in nature and non-helpful in practice (other than seriously questioning assumptions often held by the practitioner, e.g. the importance of the IQ as a predictor of success) is not surprising in view of the diversity among studies on a number of methodological characteristics. These dimensions are considered in the following section.

METHODOLOGICAL ISSUES

The major methodological dimensions which appear to account for most of the difference in findings of the outcome studies reviewed are populations sampled, predictors, outcome criteria, statistical design, and research strategy. The major methodological characteristics differentiating outcome studies are presented in Table 10-II.

Population

In assessing research investigations in rehabilitation outcome and determining their applicability or generalizability, the population that was represented in a particular study must be considered. For example, in deriving information from a sample that represents one population, one cannot necessarily infer its applicability to another population. Samples used in a number of re-

TABLE 10-II

MAJOR CHARACTERISTICS DIFFERENTIATING STUDIES OF
REHABILITATION OUTCOME OF THE MENTALLY RETARDED

Dimension	Variable Studied
Population	Institutional and non-institutional placement
	Intelligence: severely, moderately, and mildly retarded
	Type of employment placement
Predictors	Intellectual, e.g. test scores and academic achievement
	Personal, e.g. appearance, habits, attitudes, strength, and motor coordination
	Biographical (background), e.g. race, sex, age, and socio-economic level
	Social, e.g. relationship with peers, and relationship with supervisors
	Vocational skills, e.g. specific and related
	Non-subject variables, e.g. type of training program, amount and type of specific treatments, community characteristics
Outcome criteria	Vocational
	Personal
	Socio-civic
Statistical Design	Univariate approach
	Multivariate approach
Research strategy	Longitudinal or follow-up studies
	Retrospective studies
	Concurrent studies
	True predictive studies

habilitation outcome studies are very diverse and may be differentiated by a number of characteristics. Particular consideration may be given to the appropriateness of generalizing from institutional to non-institutional populations, and from one level of intellectual functioning to another. Of the many other factors which limit generalization, one is the type of job placement(s) considered in the sample. In other words, the critical factors related to success on one job may not be relevant to another job.

Predictor Variables

An even greater source of diversity of findings in outcome studies may be attributed to the variables selected to differentiate the successfully from the unsuccessfully rehabilitated. Predictive variables may be considered under the following three headings: subject variables, non-subject or situation variables, and interaction or subject X non-subject variables.

Subject Variables

Most of the attention has been focused on subject variables as predictors of vocational success with the mentally retarded. Appell, Williams, and Fishell (1962) stated that variable categories which had been surveyed for differentiating employed from unemployed retardates were level of intelligence, personality characteristics, and specific vocational skills. Kolstoe and Shafter (1961) have presented a more specific categorization of subject variables: (1) intellectual (e.g. test scores and academic achievement); (2) personal (e.g. appearance, habits, attitudes, strength); (3) biographical (e.g. race, sex, age, socio-economic level); (4) social (e.g. relationship with peers and relationship with supervisors); and (5) vocational skills (e.g. both specific and related skills). As stated by Wolfensberger (1967), outcome predictors have been most frequently based on the naive assumption that outcome is largely a function of subject variables. In discussing the relation of subject predictors to rehabilitation outcome, he suggested that the strength of the variables be considered as a potential dimension. This dimension refers to the "softness-hardness" of the variable which may be arranged along a continuum. The soft predictors are those which are inherently unstable and subject to modification, such as the retardate's initial motor performance. Hard predictors are those with a promise of stability. Very often the unstable characteristics are ones chosen as potential predictors, and yet those less stable variables are likely to change in the process of rehabilitation. Thus, the extent to which the soft subject variable is related to rehabilitation outcome will vary according to the state of that variable at a given point in time.

Non-subject Variables

In general, little attention has been given to non-subject or situational variables in the prediction of rehabilitation outcome. Job success or failure may well depend on situations or factors over which the retarded individual has no control. Cohen (1960) presented evidence to this effect and concluded that one of the most important factors in determining good adjustment in the community was the image the community had of the individual. Goldstein (1964) stated that community attitudes were an essential area to consider when predicting successful outcome for the retarded.

In addition to community attitudes, Cowan and Goldman (1959) suggested the following situational variables which may influence vocational success of the retarded: (1) the personality of the trainee in combination with the personality of the instructor; (2) the relationship between the trainee and the instructor; (3) the type of training given; and (4) the effort and ability of the placement counselor who works with the trainee. In his review, Wolfensberger (1967) concluded by stating that in order for outcome studies to be fruitful, the variables of training, placement process, and placement situation should be considered.

Interaction of Subject and Situational Variables

The word "interaction" refers to certain subject variables which may be differentially related to certain non-subject or situational variables. In elaborating on the differential interaction, special attention is given to jobs as the non-subject factor.

Investigators have been interested in predictive variables which were related to jobs in *general*. Consequently, they have frequently used samples in which the subjects represented a wide array of jobs. Findings resulting from this approach have allowed generalizations across many occupations. When this type of representative sample is employed, the following assumptions are made:

1. that success means the same for all jobs represented in the sample since only one criterion or set of criteria for success is used in the study.
2. that jobs held by the retarded are homogeneous in terms of work requirements;
3. that both the success and failure groups across a number of jobs are homogeneous in terms of certain subject variables which differentiate the two groups.

The first assumption is highly questionable since success may

very well mean different things for different jobs, e.g. units produced versus interpersonal relationships. As for the second assumption, it is doubtful that semi-skilled and unskilled jobs are
homogeneous in terms of job requirements even though they
fall within the same occupational classification level. Assuming
diversity among jobs suggests that factors which may be required
for success on one job may have little bearing on the success of
another job. Consequently, the validity of the third assumption
is doubtful since subjects comprising the failure or success
groups may well have failed or succeeded on the job for reasons
which were specifically job connected. The emphasis given differential prediction (Kolstoe and Shafter, 1961; Windle, 1962)
results in one questioning the assumption that groups who are
either successful or unsuccessful on jobs are homogeneous.

There may be subject variables which are essential for success
across most jobs held by the retarded. However, the significance
of these variables to specific jobs may vary. Thus, as a *predictive
schema,* there may be a hierarchy of general subject predictive
variables which are differentially related to the success and failure groups across many jobs. However, the position or value of
each of the predictors in the hierarchy may vary for different
jobs.

Outcome Criteria

As stated in the introduction, outcome criteria represent a
wide range of concepts. The selection of which variable to study
is a complex process. The stress given vocational, personal, or
socio-civic success as rehabilitation outcome indices may reflect
both one's goals for the mentally retarded as well as one's ability
or willingness to develop measures of the criteria.

A detailed examination of individual studies revealed a wide
range of criteria and considerable variability in the ability to
measure these criteria both reliably and validly. Another more
subtle difference among the many outcome studies has been the
ability of the investigator to make his predictors conceptually
congruent with his criterion measure. An obvious illustration of
incongruence is the attempt to relate motor skills to an outcome
criterion of personal adjustment. A more congruent approach

would be to relate a subject variable reflecting personality structure to eventual personal adjustment.

Outcome criteria represent one of the important methodological dimensions that need to be considered in rehabilitation outcome studies with the retarded. Little advancement in this area of research can be anticipated until there is some unanimity in selection of criteria and greater attention given to their measurement.

Statistical Design

Predictive studies have varied considerably in their use of statistical design and may be classified according to whether they use a univariate or a multivariate approach, i.e. a single predictor to one outcome criterion versus multiple predictors to outcome criteria. Depending upon the scaling (i.e. nominal; ordinal; interval; or ratio) of independent (predictor) and dependent (outcome) variables, selection of statistical methods such as chi square, t-tests, correlations, factor analysis, analysis of variance, and multiple regression is determined. Results across studies have varied, in part, as a function of the statistical designs selected. While in general the multivariate approach may be considered more efficient, it requires certain assumptions concerning the scaling of both the predictor and criterion measure which may be unwarranted; consequently, leading to potentially false positive results. The univariate approach, while less efficient, has the advantage of making the statistical design appropriate to the scaling of the predictor and criterion measure.

Research Strategy

There have been essentially four different research strategies incorporated in various research investigations on vocational predictive studies for the mentally retarded. These are: (1) longitudinal or follow-up studies, (2) retrospective studies, (3) concurrent studies, and (4) true predictive studies. They differ primarily in terms of the time at which the predictor and the criterion measures were taken during the life span of the subjects. For example, longitudinal or follow-up studies involved those in which the predictor variables were applied early in the life span of the individual without, usually, the specific criterion measure in mind. Criterion measures, which were selected at a later point in time, were taken and related to these predictors. Retrospective studies refer to those in which observations were made at the time the criterion measures were taken. For these studies, life histories of the individuals were inspected to obtain predictive measures which might or might not have been available in the case file. Concurrent studies are those in which predictor and criterion measures were made simultaneously. True predictive studies resemble longitudinal studies in terms of the time dimension. Predictor measures were taken earlier in the life span and criterion measures made later. They differ from longitudinal studies, however, insofar as the selection of both criterion and predictors were planned.

Research strategies represent one of the more important methodological considerations because of (1) the potential limitations upon availability of data on which predictor and/or criterion measures are based; (2) the limitations placed by some of the methods by attrition of subjects; (3) the differences in ability of methods to relate, conceptually, predictors and criteria; and (4) the differences in generalizability as a function of the difference in time between observations of the predictor measures and observations of the criterion measures.

ILLUSTRATIVE STUDIES

In discussing the following studies, attention is drawn to differences in methodological approaches which account, in part, for the differences in results and interpretations. The four studies critiqued are: Shafter (1957), Jackson and Butler (1963), Dinger (1961), and Stephens (1964).

Shafter (1957) initiated his study by a survey of criteria used by institutions for the mentally retarded for release of patients to community placement. These criteria were classified and supplemented by variables identified in the literature as correlates of rehabilitation outcome. These characteristics included such items as age at admission, type of admission, previous residence, father's occupation, type of home, nationality, religion, sibling rank and number of sibs, family history of institutionalization, reason for admission, intelligence quotient, impressions of psychometrician, educational attainment and where educated, work record, behavior in hospital, sterilization, family interest, area of placement, etc. In all, sixty-six characteristics of this type were objectified and made available for statistical test purposes.

Data were obtained on 75 males and 130 females who were patients of the Woodward State Hospital and School in Woodward, Iowa. All subjects were diagnosed as mentally retarded but not epileptic. All had been placed by the hospital's social service department in accordance with standard practices for placement.

A single criterion was used to determine successful placement; namely, complete discharge from the hospital. A comparison between 111 successful and 94 unsuccessful placements was made using all predictor variables. Chi-square analysis was used for each comparison.

Table 10-III lists the twelve release characteristics which were found to differentiate successful from unsuccessful placements. These included good behavior, escaping from the institution, quarrelsomeness in the institution, truthfulness, obedience, carelessness, stealing, etc. No relationship was found between success on placement and intelligence and age. Fifteen other characteris-

TABLE 10-III

RELEASE CHARACTERISTICS DIFFERENTIATING SUCCESSFUL
AND UNSUCCESSFUL PLACEMENTS (SHAFTER, 1957)

Behavior Characteristics in the Hospital	Weight for Characteristics		
	Plus Two	Plus One	Zero
Behavior problem	No	Unknown	Yes
Escaped	No	Unknown	Yes
Quarrelsome with employees	No	Unknown	Yes
Quarrelsome with patients	No	Unknown	Yes
Fight with patients	No	Unknown	Yes
Truthful	Yes	Unknown	No
Ambitious	Yes	Unknown	No
Obedient	Yes	Unknown	No
Careless	No	Unknown	Yes
Punishment record	No	Unknown	Yes
Steals	No	Unknown	Yes
Evaluation of work	Good	Fair or unknown	Poor

tics which had been reported elsewhere as differentiating between successful and unsuccessful placement were not found to be significant in this study.

Shafter's study is of interest for several reasons. It represents a traditional approach to the prediction of rehabilitation outcome in that the variables were selected on an empirical rather than a theoretical basis and were derived from data already available and not collected specifically for the purpose of the prediction study. Most of the ratings on behavior were based on case notes and not on systematically compiled data. It is surprising, in view of the informal manner in which the data were collected that they were related to any measure let alone the criterion itself.

The use of case history notes and other daily records which presumably reflect important events in the client's institutional life should, however, not be ignored in predictive studies. Their "real life" quality, as opposed to the artificiality of objective tests of personality and ratings of behavior, may well be a secret of their success. The major quarrel, if any, with Shafter's study is not with the selection of the predictor variables which have greater content validity than is represented by many studies, but with the contamination of the criterion measure with the release policies of the institution. It was probable that many of the professional staff who contributed to the decision to discharge a client were the same persons who contributed substantially to the case history notes; moreover, it was quite possible that they were making the same sort of value judgments in discharging a client as they were in assessing the everyday behavior of the client. The relationships and criteria must be scrutinized carefully in all studies of institutionalized retardates in which the outcome is controlled by institutional staff.

From another methodological standpoint, Shafter's study also suffers in that a univariate approach was taken in which the relationship of each predictor with the criterion was assessed independently. This approach, which has been the rule rather than the exception in outcome studies, does not permit any investigation of interactive or suppressor variables. Examination of the

twelve behavioral traits which were found to be predictive suggests that there might have been a fewer number of underlying
personality factors.

Jackson and Butler's (1963) study represents a different approach and, concomitantly, many different types of problems.
This investigation was also based on an institutional population.
The sample consisted of 191 women who ranged in age from
sixteen to twenty-two and in IQ from forty to eighty. Approximately 90 percent were committed by the courts for an indefinite
period, mainly for "self-protection" or for minor instances of
delinquent behavior. In selecting the predictive variables, an attempt was made to represent individual differences in skill and
personality, as well as differences in environmental conditions
and treatment. More specifically, the variables studied included:
age, intelligence, academic achievement, length of institutionalization, early environmental conditions, and certain dimensions
of personality. In Table 10-IV, twenty-two variables are listed.
Data for the experimental variables (separation from parents
during the first five years of life and separation from parents
during the second five years of life, rural-urban preadmission
residence, age, length of institutionalization, and institutional
work certificates earned) were taken from case histories and institutional records. Early home conditions (personal cleanliness
and health, moral and social standards, economic standards, edu-
cational-occupational level, general environment) were assessed
on a three-point scale yielding ratings of unsatisfactory, low average, and average. Intelligence and personality measures were
obtained from the psychological files. All measures were taken
prior to and independent of assessment of the criterion measure.
The criterion—successful community placement—was defined
as the completion of at least six months' total time on community placements without return to the institution because of inadequate adjustment. Of the original sample of 191, eighty-two
were successful according to this criterion. Of the remaining 109
subjects, ninety-three were considered by the staff as unready for
community placement, and sixteen of those selected for trial
placement remained in the community for periods of six weeks

TABLE 10-IV

COMPARISONS OF SUCCESSFUL AND UNSUCCESSFUL PLACEMENTS
ON 22 VARIABLES (JACKSON AND BUTLER, 1963)

Variables	Successful Placements Mean	SD	Unsuccessful Placements Mean	SD	t
Early home conditions	N = 82		N = 109		
1. Personal cleanliness and health .	1.09	0.84	0.97	0.99	0.92
2. Moral and social standards	0.56	0.66	0.43	0.72	1.30
3. Economic standards	0.84	0.85	0.71	0.81	1.08
4. Educational and occupational level	0.61	0.78	0.49	0.76	1.09
5. General environment	3.10	2.49	2.58	2.70	1.35
6. Sep. from parents: 1-5 years of age[1]	0.92	0.28	0.73	0.45	3.58†
7. Sep. from parents: 5-10 years of age[1]	0.76	0.41	0.57	0.50	3.09†
8. Urban-rural residence[2]	0.40	0.49	0.58	0.60	2.28
9. Length of institutionalization ...	2.70	1.91	1.80	1.60	3.48†
Intelligence, achievement, age					
10. Wechsler Verbal IQ	70.1	7.41	67.1	8.45	2.63†
11. Wechsler Performance IQ	72.6	9.22	68.8	9.96	2.68†
12. Wechsler Full Scale IQ	68.9	7.21	65.3	8.25	3.16†
13. Reading Achievement	4.46	1.25	4.02	1.23	2.41*
14. Arithmetic Achievement	4.52	1.04	4.13	1.11	2.53†
15. Age	19.0	1.89	17.9	2.02	3.72*
16. Certificates earned	1.29	1.27	0.85	0.91	2.66
Personality (social value-need scale factors)	N = 42		N = 60		
17. I passive, compliant, responsible	47.5	20.6	43.6	25.9	0.78
18. II loyal, protective	14.2	8.48	10.9	9.02	1.86
19. III submissive-author, aggressive-peer	49.9	14.7	43.1	17.3	2.11*
20. IV honesty, moral courage	22.9	7.14	22.4	7.50	0.34
21. V dominant with peers	2.89	5.30	3.32	6.15	0.39
22. VI negative-rebellious	−90.2	28.1	−82.7	30.6	1.24

* p = .05
† p = .01
[1] Separation from parents = 0, remaining with parents = 1.
[2] Rural residence = 0, Urban residence = 1.

or less. In terms of successful community experience, then, there was a fairly clearcut dichotomy. Tests of significance using the standard t-test for difference between successful and unsuccessful placement revealed significant differences on twelve of the twenty-two variables.

To determine if a small number of independent variables could predict successful community placement, a multiple regression analysis was completed. A multiple correlation of .43 was obtained. Significant beta weights were found for only four variables; namely, age, verbal IQ, urban-rural pre-admission residence, and remaining with parents to age five. It was noted (p. 216) that:

> Prediction of successful community placement may be made, in part, on selected maturational, experiential and personality variables. However, as in other studies reviewed . . . the level of prediction is not high. Prediction may be improved by combining the variables of age, intelligence, and early family experiences with measures of later behavioral adjustment, and with greater attention being paid to the relation of individual attributes and the demands of the placement situation.

Like Shafter's study, this investigation may be questioned on several points. The first problem is the generality of the findings. This institutional sample was not fully defined and it is doubtful that the parameters of the population could be adequately identified. In view of the changing nature of institutional populations, it is doubtful that future studies such as the two just reviewed will continue to be justified; however, they have been useful in identifying variables which should be considered in better and more broadly defined populations.

The sampling of predictor variables in Jackson and Butler was not as inclusive as that in Shafter, but did attempt to take into consideration early environmental circumstances which may have influenced the rehabilitation outcome. A close review of this study reveals that the instruments used were very crude and ratings of early home conditions were made on case history notes which were often sketchy and unsystematic. Reliability of these ratings was low and significant results were not obtained. Parenthetically, it should be noted that on all six ratings the trend was in favor of the successful placements. Family stability, as represented by the family's ability to keep the child in the home in early life, appeared to be a promising construct.

This study was also limited by the criterion measure itself. The artifactual relation between the predictors and criterion is not as obvious as in Shafter's study, however. Characteristics such as age, intelligence, and certain types of behavior which might be related to early environment may well have influenced professional staff decisions in attempting to place the client in a certain setting. While such restraints exist in a limited way "on the outside," it may be assumed that the non-institutionalized retardates have a greater freedom of movement which permits them to match their attributes to the opportunities available.

The multivariate approach, as demonstrated by use of the multiple regression analysis, suggests that prediction might well be made on a smaller and more manageable number of variables. At the same time, the investigators are subject to criticism for using parametric statistics on data that do not meet the assumptions underlying the statistic. The use of multiple regression is also open to challenge insofar as these authors did not demonstrate linearity of the relationship among the predictive variables.

Dinger (1961) reported on the follow-up of one hundred former pupils of the Altoona, Pennsylvania special education program. His study is included here, in part, because it was based on a population of non-institutionalized retarded. In his introduction (1961, p. 353) he quoted Doll (1934) who stated:

> Our approach to the problem of mental deficiency today is limited to a body of knowledge gained from the social *failures* within this class. Less than 10 percent of all the feeble-minded and probably not more than 5 percent ever reach our public institutions. We cannot much longer overlook the fact that the remaining 90 to 95 percent do not reach our institutions and are not *all* social failures even though their success may be only at a low cultural level.

He justifiably made this point in support of his follow-up study. However, he might have done some disservice to this group by certain methodological approaches which were more obvious in this study than in other follow-up studies of non-institutionalized retardates. The disservice, if any, resulted from his sampling procedures (Dinger, 1961, p. 355):

> A random sample of 614 names was selected from the 1,500 total names recorded in the special education files of former pupils of that

department. A mailing address was located for 421 of these subjects or their parents and a brief personal data questionnaire was sent to these people. Three hundred and thirty-three, or 79.3 percent of the 421 persons provided the desired information and an analysis of it revealed the following:

> 274 or 83.2% were employed (employed plus school full-time housewives).
>
> 43 or 12.9% were unemployed
>
> 16 or 4.8% were deceased or whereabouts were unknown to parents.
>
> ——— ———
>
> 333 100.0%

Since the scope of the problem limited the study to former pupils who were *employed* and *residing* in the city of Altoona, only 144 of these 333 persons met these criteria for inclusion in the sample population. The first one hundred of the total potential 144 subjects to be found at home at the time of the writer's unannounced visitation determined the final study population.

After examining the distribution of age and intelligence of this final group of one hundred, he considered that they paralleled a normal distribution of IQ from fifty to eighty-five and were typical of the average secondary class for the educable retarded in Pennsylvania. He asserted that the sample represented a "somewhat selected group in terms of employment and resident status and hence the data resulting from the study may not be representative of all mentally retarded adults [p. 356]."

In view of the process used to obtain one hundred subjects from the original file of 1,500, it becomes a matter of opinion as to how selective the group was. He subsequently reported on educational experiences and attitudes, military experiences and attitudes, occupational histories, marital histories, financial histories, community participation, and leisure-time activities. Generally, a descriptive approach was taken with no relationship between client and other characteristics to the criterion measures assessed. His conclusions were usually optimistic and included such statements as the following:

> Adult retardates are capable of successful occupational adjustments to unskilled and semi-skilled jobs which have few academic

requirements. . . . These retarded adults are capable of independent economic adjustments at a comfortable level. . . . These subjects as a group were not identifiable by the writer as being mentally retarded when judged by such factors as their appearance, homes, jobs, conversation, dress, wives and children (p. 357).

While Dinger acknowledged some of the dangers inherent in this type of follow-up study, further qualifications must be made because of several methodological problems. The primary problem is one of sampling. In studies of this type attrition rate will probably be high (for reasons which are identifiable by close examination of Dinger's approach). Attrition must be considered a potential problem in similar types of investigations.

First, a random sample was made of an original population of 1,500. In many school systems it would be impossible to obtain a random sample with sufficient information to warrant proceedings to the next step. Lack of information in the case file itself might be a biasing factor. The next step in obtaining the cooperation of subjects was the identification of addresses. Mobility and/or lack of an identifiable address is very probably a biasing factor. The next step involved the questionnaire. Ability and/or willingness to respond can be considered a biasing factor. The next selection factor was being employed and residing in the city. The final selecting factor was being at home at the time of the writer's unannounced visit. It should be pointed out that *all* these selective factors were reported by Dinger and may be justified on the basis of expedience due to limited budget. This does not reduce their impact on the outcome of the study, however.

A further criticism of follow-up studies such as these is that critical data concerning the client's original status are not usually available in a systematic form, thereby seriously limiting prediction of rehabilitation outcome. It is possible that studies such as Dinger's are more likely to be conducted in a progressive school system in which training and placement are optimal; thus even without the selective factors noted, a more optimistic picture may be obtained than is warranted by examination of the general population.

One of the more thorough and comprehensive studies of rehabilitation outcome is that reported by Stephens (1964). Her study had several advantages in that the predictor variables were comprehensively sampled and based maximally on theoretical considerations. Also, multiple criteria were used. This study was based on after-training success of 125 young male retardates. The research was designed to test four hypotheses which have grown out of the literature about mental retardation, as well as relevant knowledge and theories of human development with reference to the relative success of habilitation among mentally retarded male youth. The design involved gathering several kinds of predictive and criterion data from five sample populations, four of whom were experimental in nature (habilitation program graduates from Harbridge Foundation, State Schools, South Texas Habilitation Center, and special education public school classes). These four experimental groups of twenty-five subjects each were contrasted with a comparable control sample population of twenty-five subjects drawn from mentally retarded males who attended public schools that offered no special education vocational training.

With the foregoing sample in mind, the purpose of the research was set forth by asking a number of succinct questions: (1) Upon what did the success of educable mental retardates depend? Were personal, socio-civic, and vocational success separate aspects of individual functioning, or were they highly interrelated? (2) What clustering of personality and cognitive attributes existed in successful retardates? Were measures of these attributes useful predictors of success? (3) Did subjects who had habilitation training achieve greater success that those who had no training? (4) Were graduates of certain habilitation training programs more successful than graduates of other programs?

The total sample of 125 was composed of twenty-five individuals drawn from each of the five groups specified above, aged eighteen through twenty-six, with IQ's from fifty to seventy-five. In all, a total of seventy-eight predictor variables and eighty criterion variables which could be reduced to interval scaling were used. In order to reduce both predictor and criterion variables to a workable number, factor analytic procedures were followed. The results of this analysis was the identification of the twenty-one predictor factors and seventeen criterion factors listed in Table 10-V. A number of predictor and criterion variables were not appropriate for interval scaling, i.e. they were based on mutually exclusive dichotomies or categories. As a result, a rather complex analysis was necessary to relate all predictors to all criterion variables.

In her statement of conclusions, Stephens pointed out that the factor analytic study offered evidence that both success and contributors to success were multi-dimensional, with seventeen predictor and twenty-one criteria variables. In all, seventy of the eighty-point scale and continuous criterion variables had major loadings on criterion factors which were predicted significantly. Significant prediction was achieved for thirty-five of the sixty-one dichotomous criterion variables.

She offered a number of interesting conclusions and observations which may be relevant to future rehabilitation outcome research, but which are too detailed and complex to present here

TABLE 10-V

PREDICTOR AND CRITERION FACTORS (STEPHENS, 1964)

Predictor Factors	Criterion Factors
Controlled awareness	Effectiveness of employee
Convergent thinking	Responsible work orientation
Interpersonal competence	Functional autonomy
Unstable temperament	Parental ambivalence
Divergent thinking	Job satisfaction
Body image	Dependence upon authority
Responsiveness	Task orientation (withdraw syndrome)
Social maturity	Dependence upon religious inst.
Age-graded independence	Family irresponsibility
Self-realizing achievement	Escape from responsibility
Habilitation training	Work versus gregarious satisfaction
Alienation syndrome	Borderline functioning
Openness to stimuli	Acquiescent as to placement
Absence of superego	Successful job performance
Orderliness of concept formation	Self-directed responsibility
Motivated flexibility	Failure syndrome
Physical stamina	Laborer syndrome
Absence of learned social maturity	
Optimum performance	
Reaction to physical stimuli	
Conformity of character	

except in summary form. Stephens made a valuable contribution by pointing out the complexity (multi-dimensionality) of both predictors and criteria. However, whether these are really as complex as she indicated is open to question. In approaching both sets of variables from the perspective of content validity, the sampling should be noted for comprehensiveness and for recognition of theoretical constructs which further assure comprehensiveness, but which might be questioned on balance. Before utilizing her work as a basis for future research, it would be necessary to first reduce the criteria to a workable number. The number of predictor variables that would be necessary could then be substantially reduced both from empirical and logical bases.

The second point to be noted is the fact that this study considered "treatment" effect, that is, the type of training. She did so by examining the success of her five basic groups, but did not proceed to the second step of examining interaction of treatment with the client status variables.

A third point is sampling. Generalizations can be made only to the treatment populations sampled, and not to the mentally retarded in the general population.

A fourth point concerns the adequacy of certain measures designed to assess certain personality dimensions selected on the basis of theory. It would be unfair to criticize this study unduly because only a few adequate and appropriate personality measures for the mentally retarded are available. The fact that significant relationships were established between her personality measures and success, points to the potential usefulness of further research on personality measurement.

A final and major concern with the Stephens study is that it is not, by the usual definition, a "predictive" investigation. A large proportion of the predictor variables were measured, and reflect the status of the subject at the time criterion measures were taken. A close examination of predictor and criterion variables indicates that there is a considerable artifactual relationship across these two sets. Despite the negative aspects cited, this may be considered one of the most substantial and well-controlled studies in the field.

Critical Overview

At this point it is appropriate to summarize some of the methodological problems which may account for the wide range of results and conclusions reported in the literature. The four studies discussed above—two based on institutional samples (one of these based on both sexes, one on one sex alone), one based on a post-special education class population, and one based on a mixed population—illustrate that sampling differences between studies alone could account for most of the differences in results.

The studies by Shafter and by Jackson and Butler were selected because of their focus on an institutional population. In view of the fact that institutional populations are now shifting considerably in terms of the population served, it is difficult to generalize results to any well-identified segment of the population at large. Unless one unique contribution can be made, it is doubtful whether such outcome studies should be continued at a substantial level. However, they have made certain major contributions to our knowledge of the correlates of rehabilitation outcome. This has been due in part to the fact that, being captive samples, the clients are able to provide more extensive data, particularly that related to around-the-clock behavior. Also, by and large, greater attention has been paid to this group by professional personnel. Case history information covering substantial periods of time is available for researchers. Future studies of institutional populations, however, should be limited to those which exploit unique aspects of the data available.

Another dimension of sampling relates to attrition of subjects over time. The amount and type of attrition is largely a function of the research strategy employed. Dinger's retrospective study is an excellent example of the problems associated with attrition. Future studies must take into consideration causes of attrition, whether due to mobility (both geographic and economic), unwillingness to cooperate, inability to follow instruction, and so forth. Greater effort in tracing clients is absolutely essential.

A second issue to be resolved is the concept of content validity and construct validity in the selection and development of predictor variables. Of the studies examined above, three based their selection of predictors primarily on empirical bases, with Stephens giving greater consideration to theoretical concepts. Too often the selection of predictors seems to be based on expediency. This expediency is probably due in large part to financial considerations and time. However, it may often be due to lack of ingenuity on the part of the investigators or to sheer impatience with detail and unwillingness to exert that extra effort needed to trace critical history data, obtain cooperation of recalcitrant clients, or develop skills necessary for more sophisticated psychological evaluation. In order for future research to be fruitful, it must be based on the selection and measurement of predictor variables in a more systematic and comprehensive manner. One basic consideration is the theoretical relationship with the criterion measures. The second is a reconceptualization of predictors so that there will be a balance between client (both fixed and modifiable) and situational (training, treatment, family support) characteristics.

The third issue, that of the selection of criterion variables, is as much a philosophical issue as a methodological one. Whether one stresses vocational, personal, or socio-civic success reflects as much one's goals for the mentally retarded as it does the ability or willingness to develop measures of these criteria. In the four studies examined above, four quite different approaches to criteria were taken. Shafter's "complete discharge" cut across all three major dimensions without specifying relative weights of each. Jackson and Butler stressed vocational success. Dinger took into consideration all three dimensions but utilized a quite informal assessment. Stephens' seventeen factors specified several independent dimensions for each of the three. Obviously the adequacy of future research depends on the number of criteria selected and the ability to measure these reliably.

One solution to this problem would be to select a single criterion measure of a rather global nature, namely one of the following: amount of income, percentage of time employed under standard conditions of compensation, or an estimate of the per-

centage of financial contribution to the subject's own maintenance and/or to the maintenance of those dependent upon him.
Any one of these three criteria can be measured with a reasonable degree of reliability, has a high probability of being related
to personal satisfaction and adjustment (insofar as most retarded
in the educable range probably have much the same value system as the general population), and would be reflective of society's major responsibility in preparing the mentally retarded
for independent living.

A fourth issue is the selection of statistical tests used to analyze the relationships between predictors and criteria. To date,
a patchwork of conventional techniques has been used, sometimes with appropriate recognition of scaling of the variables
and basic assumptions. There is a critical need, however, for a
technique that will treat all predictors simultaneously and consider interactions among them. Multiple regression and factor
analysis are inappropriate with nominal data and, furthermore,
do not reflect interaction effects. Multiple analysis of variance
has the advantage of assessing interaction effects; but with a
fixed effect model, there is a limit on the number of variables
which may be considered simultaneously. Two techniques not
previously used in this specific field are the Bayesian theorem and
the interaction detection analysis. These permit "pattern" analysis by using categorical data in which classification is based upon
membership in subgroups defined by two or more variables. Regardless of the technique used, cross-validation is essential. Lack
of cross-validation has contributed substantially to the present
confusion of results and conclusions.

A final issue concerns the relative merits of various research
approaches, longitudinal or follow-up, and retrospective. These
approaches vary in basic purpose, time at which the sample population is identified, and times at which predictors and criteria
are observed. Each of these approaches has made and can make
a contribution to our knowledge of rehabilitation outcome. But
none alone can give a complete or accurate picture. While one
approach can better assess treatment effects, another can better
reflect the role of fixed client traits, another the role of modifi-

able traits. One approach or combination may be more appropriate for program planning (based on statistical prediction); another for individual planning (based on clinical prediction).

SUMMARY AND RECOMMENDATIONS

The focus of this presentation has been research on prediction of rehabilitation outcome of the mentally retarded. Four questions were posed:

What research has been reported on the prediction of rehabilitation outcome with the mentally retarded and what generalizations can be made from these studies?

What methodological dimensions should be considered in assessing the investigations which have been undertaken?

How are these methodological dimensions illustrated in selected outcome studies?

What recommendations can be made for future research strategy?

Review of representative research in the field revealed a general lack of definitive findings and an absence of consensus among researchers concerning correlates of rehabilitation success. An analysis of methods indicated that this lack of consensus was a function of the diversity in studies with respect to populations sampled, predictor and criteria variables selected, statistical techniques employed, and the research strategy followed. Based on this review the following recommendations for future research strategies can be made.

Sampling

Greater attention must be given to sampling truly representative segments of the total mentally retarded population. Less emphasis on institutional samples is recommended except in instances where unique contributions can be made. Sample sizes should be increased to permit adequate blocking of both subject and non-subject variables and for cross-validation. Greater consideration to causes and effects of subject attrition is stressed.

Predictor Variables

Emphasis should be given to systematic and comprehensive selection based on theory as well as prior empirical evidence

(Browning, 1970). Greater attention must be given to non-subject or situational variables, e.g. training, treatment, work conditions and community environment.

Outcome Criteria

Great effort needs to be made to develop more comprehensive yet statistically operational outcome measures. A reasonably reliable outcome measure reflecting economic independence should be considered.

Statistical Design

The relative economy and appropriateness of univariate and multi-variate approaches in assessing relationship between predictors and criteria must be considered. Attention should be directed to techniques not previously used in this field; for example, use of the Bayesian theorem and the interaction detection analysis.

Research Strategy

A multi-faceted approach in which longitudinal, retrospective, concurrent, as well as true predictive studies, should be used in a complementary manner giving maximum consideration to their unique disadvantages and advantages. The obvious need is for better planned, long-term predictive studies, based on some unifying theory such as the Minnesota theory of work adjustment (Lofquist and Dawis, 1969). Such studies must be designed to meet our ultimate objective, whether this be to provide guidelines for program planning or for individual case planning.

REFERENCES

Appell, M. J.; Williams, C. M.; and Fishell, K. N.: Significant factors in placing mental retardates from a workshop situation. *Personnel and Guidance Journal, 41:*260-265, 1962.

Baller, W. R.: A study of the present social status of a group of adults, who, when they were in elementary school, were classified as mentally deficient. *Genetic Psychology Monographs, 3:*165-244, 1936.

Baller, W. R.; Charles, D. C.; and Miller, E. L.: Mid-life attainment of the the mentally retarded: A longitudinal study. *Genetic Psychology Monographs, 75:*235-329, 1967.

Bobroff, A.: Economic adjustment of 121 adults, formerly students in classes for the mental retardates. *American Journal of Mental Deficiency, 60:*525-535, 1956.

Browning, P.: Rehabilitation research with the mentally retarded: a consideration for theory. Paper presented at 94th Annual Convention of the American Association on Mental Deficiency, May 27, 1970.

Charles, D. C.: Ability and accomplishment of persons earlier judged mentally deficient. *Genetic Psychology Monographs, 47*:3-71, 1953.

Charles, D. C.: Longitudinal follow-up studies of community adjustment. In DiMichael, S. G. (Ed.): *New Vocational Pathways for the Mentally Retarded.* Washington, D. C., American Personnel and Guidance Association, 1966.

Cobb, H. V., and Epir, S.: Predictive studies of vocational adjustment. In DiMichael, S. G. (Ed.): *New Vocational Pathways for the Mentally Retarded.* Washington, D. C., American Personnel and Guidance Association, 1966.

Cobb, H. V.; Epir, S. S.; Dye, G.; and Streifel, S.: *The Predictive Assessment of the Adult Retarded for Social and Vocational Adjustment: Part I Annotated Bibliography.* Vermillion, South Dakota, Department of Psychology, University of South Dakota, A Research Demonstration Project RD-1624-P of the Vocational Rehabilitation Administration, Department of Health, Education, and Welfare, Washington, D. C., 1966.

Cobb, H. V.: *The Predictive Assessment of the Adult Retarded for Social and Vocational Adjustment: Part II Analysis of the Literature.* Vermillion, South Dakota, Department of Psychology, University of South Dakota, A Research Demonstration Project RD-1624-P of the Vocational Rehabilitation Administration, Department of Health, Education, and Welfare, Washington, D. C., 1969.

Cohen, J. S.: An analysis of vocational failures of mental retardates placed in the community after a period of institutionalization. *American Journal of Mental Deficiency, 65*:371-375, 1960.

Cowan, L., and Goldman, M.: The selection of the mentally deficient for vocational training and the effect of this training on vocational success. *Journal of Consulting Psychology, 23*:78-84, 1959.

Dinger, J. C.: Post-school adjustment of former educable retarded pupils. *Exceptional Children, 27*:353-360, 1961.

Doll, E. A.: Social adjustment of the mentally subnormal. *Journal of Educational Research, 28*:26-43, 1934.

Goldstein, H.: Social and occupational adjustment. In Stevens, H., and Heber, R. F. (Eds.): *Mental Retardation: A Review of Research.* Chicago, The University of Chicago Press, 1964.

Goldstein, H., and Heber, R. F.: Preparation of mentally retarded youth for gainful employment. Washington, D. C.: United States Printing Office, 1961.

Hartzler, E.: A ten-year survey of girls discharged from the Laurelton State Village. *American Journal of Mental Deficiency, 57*:512-517, 1953.

Heber, R. F. (Ed.): *Special Problems in Vocational Rehabilitation of the Mentally Retarded.* Washington, D. C., U. S. Department of Health,

Education, and Welfare, Vocational Rehabilitation Administration, 1963.

Jackson, S. K., and Butler, A. J.: Prediction of successful community placement of institutionalized retardates. *American Journal of Mental Deficiency*, 68:211-217, 1963.

Kolstoe, O. P.: An examination of some characteristics which discriminate between employed and not-employed mentally retarded males. *American Journal of Mental Deficiency*, 66:472-482, 1961.

Kolstoe, O. P., and Shafter, A. J.: Employability prediction for mentally retarded adults: A methodological note. *American Journal of Mental Deficiency*, 16:287-289, 1961.

Lofquist, L. H., and Dawis, R. V.: *Adjustment to Work: A Psychological View of Man's Problems in a Work-oriented Society.* New York, Appleton-Century-Crofts, Education Division, Meredith Corporation, 1969.

Madison, H. L.: Work placement success for the mentally retarded. *American Journal of Mental Deficiency*, 69:50-53, 1964.

O'Connor, N., and Tizard, J.: *The Social Problem of Mental Deficiency.* London, Pergammon Press, 1956.

Peterson, L., and Smith, L. L.: A comparison of the post-school adjustment of educable mentally retarded adults with that of adults of normal intelligence. *Exceptional Children*, 26:404-408, 1960.

Phelps, H. R.: Post-school adjustment of mentally retarded children in selected Ohio cities. *Exceptional Children*, 23:58-62, 1956.

Porter, R. B., and Milazzo, T. C.: A comparison of mentally retarded adults who attended a special class with those who attended regular school classes. *Exceptional Children*, 24:410-412, 1958.

Shafter, A. J.: Criteria for selecting institutionalized mental defectives for vocational placement. *American Journal of Mental Deficiency*, 61:599-616, 1957.

Stahlecker, L. V. (Ed.): *Occupational Information for the Mentally Retarded.* Springfield, Ill., Charles C Thomas, 1967.

Stephens, W. B.: *Success of Young Adult Male Retardates.* Austin, Tex., University of Texas, 1964.

Windle, C. D.: Prognosis of mental subnormals: A critical review of research. *American Journal of Mental Deficiency (Monograph Supplement)*, 66:1-80, 1962.

Windle, C. D.; Stewart, E.; and Brown, S. J.: Reasons for community failure of released patients. *American Journal of Mental Deficiency*, 66:213-217, 1961.

Wolfensberger, W.: Vocational preparation and occupation. In Baumeister, A. A. (Ed.): *Mental Retardation: Appraisal, Education, and Rehabilitation.* Chicago, Aldine, 1967, pp. 232-273.

Wolfson, I.: Follow up studies of 92 male and 131 female patients who were discharged from the Neward State School in 1946. *American Journal of Mental Deficiency*, 61:224-238, 1956.

Chapter 11

REHABILITATING THE MENTALLY RETARDED: PREDICTING THE FUTURE

GEORGE E. AYERS

THE FUTURE, PARTICULARLY the latter part of the present decade, has been portrayed as a time of rapidly accelerating technological and sociological change. A large number of people representing many fields of thought are currently in the process of prognosticating the direction and impact of change in the years ahead. The quest is for meaningful ways to respond to change. It seems imperative that each of us concerned with the dynamic process of rehabilitating the mentally retarded also involve ourselves in planning for change.

At the 136th meeting of the American Association for the Advancement of Science recently held in Boston, the speakers reflected on the impending sense of emergency and uncertainty overwhelming mid-twentieth-century man. They spoke of the misdirections of man's efforts in a variety of areas, such as balancing food and population and controlling the proliferation of pollution and waste. Perhaps most intriguing to those in our field of concern was a presentation by Dr. H. B. Glass, Academic Vice-President of the State University of New York at Stony Brook. Dr. Glass spoke of a process he termed "reversed Darwinism," which might tend man toward the survival of the least fit and weakest; of a reversal in evolution which has been brought about through the scientific advances which save the lives of persons who formerly would have died because of genetic defects; of diabetic children who, prior to insulin would not have lived long enough to be married, have survived and passed defective

Note: Reprinted from K. B. McGovern and P. L. Browning (Eds.): *Mental Retardation and the Future*. Rehabilitation Research and Training Center in Mental Retardation, University of Oregon, Monograph No. 5, April, 1972, 37-44.

genes to their offspring. He projected an increase of genetic defects causing a large percentage of the population in the year 2000 to be supported on drugs and other special aids to maintain life. And he suggested that this inverted evolution might be reversed by limiting couples to two children until it could be shown that their children were mentally and physically sound (Webster, 1970).

One might question whether Dr. Glass's concept of "reversed Darwinism" is related to the antiquated and obsolete "anatomical whole" approach to life. Is he reiterating the old Greek attitude that only the nonhandicapped should be provided an opportunity to fully participate in the mainstream of human life? Is he overlooking the contributions of rehabilitation in helping the physically and mentally handicapped in our society to be productive and to lead meaningful lives? Since the early 1900's rehabilitation has experienced many significant changes. They represent only the threshold of what the future may have in store. Traditional concepts and practices are eroding so rapidly that it is inevitable that rehabilitation for the mentally retarded in the future will be vastly different from what it is today.

Although the years ahead hold many unknowns and uncertainties, there appears to be no reason why man cannot effectively control his environment and provide for all of the needs of people. It is important that all of us concerned with rehabilitating the mentally retarded involve ourselves in some brainstorming and project the course on which we would like to travel during the 1970's and beyond. If we are alert to the dynamics of change, we may be able to direct the future of rehabilitation into a creative process that will aid in maximizing human potential.

It is the purpose of this chapter to submit some trends regarding the future in rehabilitating the mentally retarded. Some of the trends are already beginning to emerge and it will only be a question of when, not if, they will come into full fruition. Other trends are predictions that may be seen as probable developments. Although tremendous technological and social changes make it difficult to predict the future with any accuracy, there are trends which can be noted, expected, or hoped for. I realize that the view of these trends is largely influenced by our individual experiences and affected by our individual biases. But, as Wolfensberger (1969) suggests, we should not let our personal feelings, one way or another, stand in the way of attempts to assess reality. Anticipation of and preparation for likely future events is much more adaptive than an attitude of denial or impotent passivity.

PREDICTIONS AND TRENDS
Societal Attitudes

The myths, superstitions, and societal prejudices plaguing the retarded for centuries and resulting in their exploitation, extermination, and rejection are gradually dissipating and being replaced with positive and optimistic attitudes. I believe that in the future the principle of valuing the retarded person as a human being will become a reality. As he is provided with the opportunity to unfold his personality and develop his potentialities for his own sake and for the benefit of society, he will become respected and valued. At the same time, society will more fully realize and fulfill its obligation in establishing the kinds of community resources that will more completely meet his needs.

In thinking about the principle of valuing the retarded person as a human being, I am reminded of an article by Mal Johnson (1969) in which she discussed the Danish philosophy relative to the handicapped. She reported that the Danes not only feel for, but take action to help their fellow citizens, including the handicapped, to attain and lead lives as normal and full as possible. She praised Denmark's programs and techniques in rehabilitating the mentally retarded and noted that human rights as well as human dignity are highly respected. Further, she indicated that she is ashamed of America—an affluent society that moves so slowly in its research and spends so little time and money in caring for the retarded.

Can we replicate Denmark's philosophy? Can we advance similar progressive concepts of humanism in America? According to

Otto (1969), the most important task facing us today is the regeneration of our environmental and institutional structures such as school, government, and church. With increasing sophistication has come the recognition that institutions are not sacrosanct and that they have but one purpose and function—to serve as a framework for the actualization of human potential. It is possible to evaluate both the institution and the contribution of the institution by asking: "To what extent does the function of the institution foster the realization of human potential?" I think we will attain the level of humanism of which Johnson speaks, thus eliminating the roots of prejudice and developing more accepting attitudes toward the mentally retarded.

Integration of Services

There will be increasing coordination and synthesis of traditional and new programs and techniques in rehabilitating the mentally retarded. We will see many rehabilitation service organizations and agencies merge in an effort to eradicate the duplication and fragmentation of rehabilitation services. As a result, the comprehensiveness and effectiveness of services for the retarded will improve considerably.

An illustration of this merger trend at the federal level is the recent incorporation of the Vocational Rehabilitation Administration with four other agencies—the Administration on Aging, Assistance Payments Administration, Children's Bureau, and the Medical Services Administration—to become the Social and Rehabilitation Service. This new organization, in which all of the component agencies except the Assistance Payments Administration have major responsibilities in the area of mental retardation, was designed to join the income support programs and the social and rehabilitation programs for needy Americans under the single leadership of the Department of Health, Education, and Welfare. It represents a constellation of programs whose objectives are solely and absolutely directed toward individuals— toward extending their capacity for a full life (*Mental Retardation Activities*, 1969).

At the national level, we will see increased cooperation among the many large associations dealing with the problems of retardation, such as the National Association for Retarded Children, American Association on Mental Deficiency, United Cerebral Palsy Association, and the National Rehabilitation Association. I predict that in the near future some of these professional organizations will merge. Since many of them are involved in similar goals, consolidation may be desirable. An unrelated but important factor here is that the survival of a few of the professional organizations is being threatened today because of lack of adequate financial support.

We will also experience increased coordination and synthesis of traditional and new programs in the area of cooperative school programs. Up until now, with few exceptions, cooperative school programs have been limited to special education and vocational rehabilitation. The Vocational Education Legislation of 1968 seems to ensure that vocational education will play an important role in all the future vocational programming for the handicapped.

Since coordination cannot be achieved simply at the federal level, the community will become more committed and involved in the coordination of community services and rehabilitation programs for the retarded. The efforts that "pay the dividends" begin where the service is, where the need for it exists, and where a willingness to organize to improve services is essential— in the community. This concept has already been experimented with in five different cities where projects have demonstrated ways of effectively bringing together the services of agencies involved in programs for the retarded. Such coordination will incontestably result in the development and provision of comprehensive rehabilitation services in the future.

The synthesis of traditional and innovative techniques in the future will significantly influence the vocational adjustment of the mentally retarded. As already demonstrated by The Devereux Foundation, automated teaching methods combined with regular classroom work is more effective than machine methods or classroom instruction alone in enabling retarded students to utilize learned material in a practical work situation (*Mental*

Retardation Activities, 1969). I agree with Dickerson and Lewin (1969) that this approach is needed and has unlimited possibilities in cooperative school programs in teaching specific behaviors needed by the retarded while freeing the teacher to develop simulated socializing experiences and other programs.

In short, the increased coordination and synthesis of traditional and new programs and techniques in rehabilitating the mentally retarded will contribute to the actualization of the principle of a continuum of support for the retarded. In particular, the integration of available community resources and working relations among the various kinds of rehabilitation agencies will facilitate their personal, social, and vocational adjustment.

Interprofessional Cooperation

The jurisdictional disputes among professionals in the field of rehabilitation will gradually disappear and be replaced with positive elements of interprofessional cooperation. Professionals in the future will adopt the concept that the basic concern of rehabilitation is neither professions nor disciplines, facilities nor techniques, agencies nor programs, but people. I envision in the near future, for example, that special educators, rehabilitation counselors, and vocational educators concerned with cooperative school programs will enter into a partnership of mutual agreement to integrate and coordinate their expertise in rehabilitating the mentally retarded. The quality of this partnership will depend on improved channels of communication among the three professional groups. Joint exposure to a number of similar educational experiences during their professional training will help eradicate the barriers to communication and interprofessional cooperation. The seminar, "Education-Vocation Continuum," held by Younie (1966) at Teachers College, Columbia University, for special educators and rehabilitation counselors, and the seminar here this week represent the initial forward thrust for multidisciplinary educational experiences. We will see more of such seminars plus the modification of education curriculums in colleges and universities to become more interdisciplinary in the future.

Utilization of Support Personnel

There will be increased utilization of support personnel in re-habilitation programs for the mentally retarded. There is a criti-cal manpower shortage among rehabilitation professionals cou-pled with increasing demands of the retarded for new programs and more quality in existing ones. This makes it imperative that we examine the functions of professionals and clearly identify those that could be performed by persons with less professional qualifications. A number of rehabilitation programs have experi-mented with the use of support personnel and discovered that they represent a wealth of potential for increasing the effective-ness and expansion of rehabilitation services to the retarded. Many of these individuals have demonstrated good judgment and have functioned effectively in such areas as interviewing, casefinding, referrals, collection of essential data on potential clients, maintaining liaison with community agencies, assisting in job development and placement, and maintaining agency rec-ords.

The Division of Vocational Rehabilitation in the State of Minnesota has established a number of comprehensive vocation-al rehabilitation programs (CVRP) in residential institutions for the retarded where support personnel are widely used. They perform many of the activities described above and have been extremely effective in helping the rehabilitation professionals provide more qualitative and quantitative services to the retard-ed. I feel that such cooperative programs will increase signifi-cantly, not only in Minnesota, but in many other states as well.

Social Concepts of Disability

We have seen dramatic changes in the classification of the mentally retarded, and the concepts of disability as they relate to the retarded will go through yet another metamorphosis. In the future, increasing attention will be directed toward the so-cial aspects of mental retardation. Social isolation, for example, is an underrated aspect of the disability even today. As Switzer (1967) noted, it seems extremely unfair that superimposed over their real burden, the retarded should have this burden. Their isolation often begins with non-acceptance at school, continues with exclusion from athletic and social clubs, and ends with social handicaps on the job.

Peckham (1968) has suggested two new disability constructs of retardation—sociogenic retardation and sociogenic neurosis. "Sociogenic retardation" indicates a functional retardation in which the genesis is social. It is particularly endemic to the ghetto. The individual with such socially acquired retardation functions in all essential attributes as does the more conventionally categorized low IQ individual from the non-ghetto areas. He is naive about the world just beyond his limited orbit; in fact, the paucity of his resources for ever reaching or communicating with the outside world is often incredible. Typically, marked educational retardation, if not outright illiteracy, is common. Family relationships, if any, may vary across a broad spectrum of indifference, brutishness, or perversity, but in any event, there is ordinarily a singular lack of enhancing mental health principles in practice.

Peckham also speaks of "sociogenic neurosis," wherein the genesis of a neurotic condition is attributed to exceptionally weighted social stimulus. It implies that the dynamics of psychic erosion are massively arranged for impingement upon a cluster of individuals, such as a ghetto population. He feels that sociogenic neurosis may be distinguished, semantically at least, from the conventional psychoneurosis entity in that the types of stimuli or stress situations that the latter cannot handle seem not to be inherently threatening to the overall group with which that individual is otherwise identified. If this is correct, it may be presumed that the classical psychoneurotic is predisposed to an emotional illness because of a basic weakness in his own ego structure and that his tolerance for abrasion is individually weak. In sociogenic neurosis, however, even though "true" psychoneurotics would also abound, it might be presumed that only the very strong would be able to be relatively free of neurotic "taint" arising from a lifetime spent in the ghetto environment.

As concluded by Peckham, if psychiatrists and psychologists who are responsible for certifying disabilities accept the rationale that the diseases of sociogenic retardation and sociogenic neurosis are indeed identifiable disabilities, 75 percent of the unemployed manpower in all of the ghettos in America could be served by state vocational rehabilitation agencies.

In the future we will see the development of many constructs such as Peckham's to describe the mentally retarded who come from socially and culturally deprived environments. In fact, the Vocational Rehabilitation Amendments of 1968 have focused attention on the necessity for research on retardation as a function of cultural deprivation. Current programs of research and demonstration will continue to be increasingly concerned with new approaches to retardation in ghetto areas and model city neighborhoods.

There is indication that the key Mental Retardation Centers at the Universities of Wisconsin, Texas, and Oregon will continue to focus on the Department of Health, Education, and Welfare's priorities of model cities, neighborhood service centers, rural poverty, and other priority areas as they relate to mental retardation. As an example, a "high-risk" population laboratory has been established by the University of Wisconsin Research and Training Center in Milwaukee's economically and culturally deprived inner city, which is characterized by an extremely high incidence of mental retardation.

Service Delivery System

The service delivery system will be modified to increase the effectiveness of rehabilitation services provided to the mentally retarded. In particular, public rehabilitation agencies, such as the Divisions of Vocational Rehabilitation, will make innovations in the delivery system in an effort to meet the ever growing demands for vocational rehabilitation services for the mentally retarded. It is common knowledge that there are identifiable gaps in the current rehabilitation system which necessitate rectification. The Statewide Planning projects undertaken by states to plan a comprehensive rehabilitation system that will serve all handicapped persons by 1975 are a step forward in an effort to close the gap.

In modifying the rehabilitation service system for the retarded, two major factors will be considered. First, opportunities for a variety of learning experiences will be built into the system. Since many of the mentally retarded lack adequate experience in a variety of work related areas and have not had the opportunity to engage in meaningful activities, they often fail at the beginning of their work experience. Second, behavioral adjustment criteria will be developed. In the current rehabilitation system, evaluation criterion for client success is primarily focused on employment, and inadequate attention is directed to the behavioral changes that may take place while the client proceeds through the rehabilitation process.

In developing an effective rehabilitation service system, rehabilitation workers and agencies would benefit from critical review of various work preparation and employment programs under the auspices of other public and private agencies. Programs such as the National Alliance of Businessmen, MDTA, OEO, and the Department of Labor have been successful in serving mentally retarded people. We can draw upon the experiences of these programs and abstract the components which will contribute to an effective service delivery system.

Employment Opportunities

In the future, employment opportunities for the mentally retarded will increase. DiMichael (1967) stated:

> In my experience with rehabilitation programs, I am told by leaders in vigorous programs that there are more jobs which the retarded can do than there are retarded persons prepared and trained to fill them. My reflections on these facts lead me to believe that competent counselors, educators, and placement specialists are able to offer substantial help such as the retarded have not had before. Their assistance, not available as broadly or as well in the past, has had a marked influence. This "professional intervention" was not taken into account in the usual, all-too-apparent treatments on job trends for the retarded.

The greatest impetus in increasing employment opportunities will probably be the use of job specifications which emphasize abilities. Jobs can be broken down into parts and new job descriptions written to fit the particular abilities of the retarded. Also, increased awareness of the under-utilization of abilities among the retarded will overcome the tendency to place them in positions which do not fully realize their potential. Dr. Abraham L. Gitlow (1968) has suggested four steps which might expand job opportunities for the mentally retarded in the future: (1) realistic job hiring requirements, reducing the artificially high levels of education being demanded for lesser-skilled jobs; (2) better on-the-job training programs for unskilled workers; (3) job redesign, removing routine and repetition from high-skilled jobs and placing it in newly created positions that could be filled by the unskilled; and (4) active recruitment of unskilled workers to fill existing jobs.

During the next decade we will see the community assuming more of the responsibility for employment practices. Industry will provide imaginative leadership in redefining jobs which the retarded can perform, and will identify, if not actually provide, training appropriate to these jobs. Through coordination, facilitation, and education, the community will lower numerous barriers to the employment of retarded persons.

Speaking of community responsibility quickly reveals one of our most glaring weaknesses: the lack of adequate dissemination of information on the employability of the mentally retarded. We have already accumulated a vast amount of knowledge concerning the vocational preparation and placement of the retarded and we are adding to this sum daily. This accumulation of knowledge gives positive views of the rehabilitation of the mentally retarded and discloses insights leading to their participation in the world of work. This knowledge, however, is of limited value if it remains in the hands of professional rehabilitation workers only. It must be disseminated to the community, particularly to the employers and potential employers of the retarded. As pointed out in studies by Cohen (1963), Phelps (1965), and others, employer attitudes and the concept of mentally retarded employees present a challenge in public information for public schools, residential institutions, and rehabilitation agencies. If we hope to increase employment opportunities, therefore, we will have to strengthen our public information programs on the preparation and placement of the mentally retarded.

CONCLUSION

The specific predictions and trends that I have suggested in the rehabilitation of the mentally retarded are not to be considered comprehensive or inclusive. My time here today does not permit a more thorough discussion of them nor the inclusion of other areas, such as supervised residential living, eligibility requirements for rehabilitation service by state vocational rehabilitation agencies, work evaluation techniques, and counseling strategies. The predictions may or may not come true, but the trends appear to be in the air and are consistent with the direction in which we seem to be going. The trend of thought around us in almost every human endeavor is to develop new models for responding meaningfully to change. In so doing, we will participate in a creative rehabilitation process which will assist the mentally retarded in maximizing their human potential.

REFERENCES

Cohen, J. S.: Employer attitudes toward hiring mentally retarded individuals. *American Journal of Mental Deficiency, 67:*705-713, 1963.

Dickerson, W. L., and Lewin, S.: The future of work-study programs for the mentally retarded. In Heber, R. F.; Flanigan, P. J., and Rybak, W. S. (Eds.): *Changing Concepts in Mental Retardation: Pre-Vocational Evaluation of the Mentally Retarded.* Madison, Wisconsin, Rehabilitation Research and Training Center in Mental Retardation, The University of Wisconsin and Dixon, Illinois, Department of Mental Health, Division of Mental Retardation, Dixon State School, 1969, pp. 60-69.

DiMichael, S. G.: Are jobs for the retarded really decreasing? A viewpoint and an invitation. *Vocational Rehabilitation Newsletter, 1*(4):1-3, 1967.

Gitlow, A. L.: New approaches to employment of the mentally retarded. In *Minutes of Annual Meeting of President's Committee on Employment of the Handicapped.* Washington, D. C., May 2-3, 1968, p. 31.

Johnson, M.: Denmark stresses human rights: Love. *Children Limited, 18* (1):2, 1969.

Otto, H.: New light on the human potential. *Saturday Review, 14-17,* December 20, 1969.

Peckham, R.: Two "new" disabilities. *Journal of Rehabilitation, 34*(5):14-15, 1968.

Phelps, W. R.: Attitudes related to employment of the mentally retarded. *American Journal of Mental Deficiency, 69:*575-585, 1965.

Switzer, M. A.: Coordinations: A problem and a promise. *Journal of Rehabilitation,* 35(2):27-28, 1969.

U. S. Department of Health, Education, and Welfare. *Mental Retardation Activities of the U. S. Department of Health, Education, and Welfare.* Washington, D. C., Author, 1969.

Webster, J. D.: Editorial Comment, *Vocational Rehabilitation Newsletter,* Winter, 1970, pp. 1-3.

Wolfensberger, W.: Twenty predictions about the future of residential services in mental retardation. *Mental Retardation,* 7(6):51-54, 1969.

Younie, W. J.: Increasing cooperation between school programs for the retarded and vocational rehabilitation services: An experimental teaching approach. *Mental Retardation,* 4(3):9-14, 1966.

COUNSELING AND MENTAL RETARDATION

The counseling process for mentally retarded clients is essentially the same as for all disabled persons. They are amenable to and can profit from counseling. As with all developmental disabilities, life-long experiences of failure and rejection often create particularly difficult rehabilitation problems which can only be resolved through personal counseling.

> Heber, R. F. (Ed.): *Special Problems in Vocational Rehabilitation of the Mentally Retarded.* Rehabilitation Services Administration, Social and Rehabilitation Service, U. S. Department of Health, Education, and Welfare, January, 1968, p. 55.

OVERVIEW

THE ENTIRE PREVIOUS SECTION was directed to mental retardation considerations in the field of rehabilitation; e.g. history-development, philosophy-goals, programs-facilities, methods-techniques, and research. However, absent from this extensive coverage and saved for this final section, were two topics of paramount importance: The rehabilitation practitioner and counseling as a tool for practice.

The rehabilitation counselor is the retarded client's first-line advocate and supportive agent. He is the facilitator of the rehabilitation process and the implementor of services, having as his ultimate goal the client's fullest development and achievement of physical, mental, social and vocational usefulness. Chapter 12 provides an overview of his professional role and function. Coupled with this are some personal opinions held by a former rehabilitation counselor regarding his work with this disability group. It is not surprising that one area he discusses is counseling since survey studies report that rehabilitationists spend more time engaging in this activity than any other. The remaining three chapters center on this "helping" service for the retarded.

Traditional verbal counseling with the mentally retarded has been a much less popular psychological approach to treatment than with other client populations of average and above intelligence. This fact may be attributed, in part, to a variety of situational reasons: (1) graduate training programs in clinical and counseling psychology have exposed students only minimally, if at all, to this potential client population; (2) retarded persons are seldom self-referrals for psychological help; (3) a large portion of persons with retardation are of a low socioeconomic level, a characteristic historically unappealing to counselors; and (4) persons of less intelligence are ordinarily financially unable to pay for such services. Aside from these reasons, however, many counselors simply envision the retarded as unattractive clientele.

This prejudice is most often a result of their own contrived theory or clinical hunch, which prejudges the retarded as "unsuitable" clients for counseling. First is the assumption that the retarded are somewhat "incurable." Thus, its goal being change, counseling would be ineffective for them, or progress would be too slow to be worthwhile. Second, a lessening of "psychic distress" is often assumed to be concomitant with subnormal intelligence. Their lack of emotional pain makes relief through counseling unnecessary. Third, "talk" therapy requires certain verbal skills which this population supposedly lacks, e.g. vocabulary with which to express their "inner dynamics" and carry on a meaningful clinical conversation. Finally, the retarded are seen as unable to engage in abstract thinking and conceptually gain insight into their problem(s), which, for some counselors, is a "necessary" and "essential" condition for good client prognosis.

In spite of their invalidity, these assumptions represent the basic core of what many counseling professionals consider to be universal truths. Rather than refutation on theoretical and empirical grounds, select case material can be provided from which the reader may draw his own conclusions. The following are excerpts from four actual counseling sessions with a "borderline" retarded adolescent girl in a residential setting. Unfortunately, typescripts do not communicate the affective nonverbal and paralinguistic (tone, pitch) behavior, which I so vividly remember with this client.

EARLY SESSION

C I don't want to be different than any other person, I just want to be me.

T You know it seems to me . . .

C (interrupting) I can't be myself, they just won't let me.

T Here they won't let you just be yourself!

C Anywhere I go. The only place I get to be myself is with my parents, that's all. In the car when we're driving on the road, that's the only time I get to be myself, with nobody else bothering me, just with my mother and dad and I. I can get along just fine until we get around other people and then I can't.

T uh huh.

C I just can't associate with them. Now at home I don't dare go anywhere myself, except up to the park (pause), and I get stared at constantly. It seems like I got an ailment inside me nobody likes me. (pause) I'm always by myself.

MIDDLE SESSION

C I'm getting bored and want to go home because everybody is saying it's a mental retardation school. Every time S. ———— mentions it she just about scares me out of my pants. I don't want-to go-to be like that. I want to learn something. I don't want to be a mentally retarded child. (long pause) We are all mentally retarded at sometime or another, aren't we? We all could be—a little bit—couldn't we? (long pause) I don't know . . .

T (Interrupting) Do you think you are retarded?

C Uh-uh. Not—well—a little bit I could because I can't study as well. Everybody has to be don't they?

T Would you think that in some ways you might be a slow learner?

C That's the truth. I'm a slow learner.

MIDDLE SESSION

C (Sobbing) Well, at the beginning of school everything was so nice and all of a sudden everybody has been getting me into trouble and I've been getting angry and I haven't been behaving myself or nothing. All last year I was a real good girl and this year I'm fighting like anything. I don't know what's made me that way. I wish my parents could see what was going on but they can't. I try to tell my parents and then I start crying and can't tell them. They get real angry with me when I start crying. I try not to cry or nothing—show them my anger or nothing. I haven't got nerve enough to tell them. It seems like I'm not wanted anymore.

T Just nobody cares!

C That's right. But I care about myself, but seems like nobody else cares about me.

T I care about you.

C I know you do. (long pause)

T I care about you and I want us to work at this thing together. (long pause) I think you have grown up some since I first met you.

C Yeah, I have.

LATE SESSION

T Well, time flies by fast. It's up for today.

C Yeah. But we talked a lot and got a lot in.

T We did, didn't we. We sure did!
C And I had it all stuck in my mind what I wanted to talk about.
T Before you came down?
C Yeah, I'm beginning to keep ideas in my head now. You know
   what? My lessons are going much better now . . .

The message is clear: persons with retardation have the same psychological needs as any other human being. Unlike most of us, however, they experience undue and prolonged frustrations in meeting these needs. Being members of a society which places so much emphasis on "intelligence," "education," and "culture" results in a lifelong history of failure and rejection for many of them. Of course, this leaves scars such as poor self-image, lack of motivation, and frequent withdrawal. What additional evidence is necessary for us to recognize that counseling is a much needed and long overdue service for this group?

Chapter 13 offers sixteen recommendations for working with the retarded in a counseling capacity. The first five are relevant to the social and psychological behavior patterns of the retarded, with respect to their role in four different life settings, i.e. student, family member, peer-group member, and worker. In addition to understanding these social-psychological roles, the counselor also must have a wide variety of counseling techniques at his command. The remaining guidelines for practice are related to a number of such counseling approaches, e.g. individual verbal counseling, play techniques, group counseling, and role playing. Another technique discussed and fully covered in Chapter 14 is behavior counseling. Unlike traditional counseling models, this approach represents an empirical technology based on learning principles. Goals of counseling are operationally defined in behavioral terms, and procedures for effecting behavior change are systematic and completely delineated. This technique, which only recently has become a popular topic among counselors and clinicians working with the retarded, warrants serious consideration as a viable approach to counseling these people.

Research on counseling the mentally retarded has not kept pace with the research trends in the general field of counseling and psychotherapy. For example, over the past twenty years investigators have increasingly questioned the assumption that counseling is a unitary dimension, and thus studied the nature of the therapeutic process and its relation to outcome. However, such has not been the case in the field of mental retardation; major focus of counseling studies with this client group continues to be outcome research. In addition, the quality of this research, compared to that conducted in the general field, is seriously lacking. One explanation is that trained researchers in the professional field of counseling have simply been uninterested in the retarded client population. Likewise, researchers in the field of mental retardation have been unfamiliar with research trends and strategies in the general field of counseling.

A methodological shortcoming of counseling outcome studies with the retarded has been "research design." Chapter 15 identifies some of the design problems which have been evident in these investigations. In addition, seven outcome studies are critically analyzed with regard to how well they answered the "efficacy" question of counseling with this client group.

In summary, these four chapters comprise many of the considerations in counseling with the retarded. However, for the convenience of the reader who is interested in further pursuing this area, additional bibliographic resources are included in this volume, i.e. seventeen basic readings on counseling and mental retardation (Appendix A), 166 annotated references on counseling and mental retardation (Appendix B), and a description of fifteen films on counseling and rehabilitation with the retarded (Appendix C).

Chapter 12

REHABILITATION COUNSELING
WITH THE MENTALLY RETARDED:
PROFESSION AND PRACTICE

GILBERT FOSS

VOCATIONAL REHABILITATION-HABILITATION is generally defined as a process whereby the handicapped individual relearns or newly learns adaptive ways of enhancing his physical, mental, social, vocational, and economic condition to the fullest and most useful extent. Traditionally speaking, the process, which is a planned and orderly sequence of services, is directed toward the goal of realistic and permanent vocational adjustment.

The Federal-State rehabilitation program is the single most important agency for overseeing the rehabilitation process. This agency is comprised of a network of over one thousand state, district, and local offices throughout the United States. Through this network, rehabilitation services are obtained, generally by purchase, from the full span of community resources (see Chapter 4 for an overview of the Federal-State program and its impact in rehabilitating the mentally retarded).

The key practitioner in the Federal-State program is the rehabilitation counselor. He is the professional who purchases and coordinates the services, and counsels and guides the handicapped individual throughout the entire rehabilitation process.

The purpose of this chapter is to discuss the rehabilitation counselor as a practitioner. More specifically, attention is directed to (1) his role and function in the rehabilitation process, particularly with respect to serving mentally retarded clients; and (2) personal attitudes and opinions derived from his habilitative work with the retarded. The second section is based upon the author's personal experience as a rehabilitation counselor who served mentally retarded clients.

THE REHABILITATION COUNSELOR

Rehabilitation counseling as a profession began in 1954, with the passage of Public Law 565 of the Vocational Rehabilitation Act. One of the major provisions of this Act was long-term training grants to educational institutions for support of basic and advanced training of professional personnel for rehabilitation services. Since that time, approximately 8,600 rehabilitation counselors (Kopp, 1972) at the masters and/or doctoral level have graduated from rehabilitation counselor training programs in over ninety colleges and universities throughout the United States. In spite of this upgrading in the profession, masters level counselors still comprise only about 40 percent of the counselor practitioners employed by state vocational rehabilitation agencies (Jacques, 1970).

Rehabilitation counseling of the mentally retarded is a recent specialization within the profession; it was not until the early 1960's that the problems of the mentally retarded were given serious attention by the Federal-State program, the Division of Vocational Rehabilitation. In fact, 93 percent of the 155,743 mentally retarded clients rehabilitated through the Division of Vocational Rehabilitation (DVR) between the years 1945 and 1970, were served during the 60's (see Chapter 4). Because of the recency of this specialization, some of the unique problems of the counselor's role and function in serving the retarded are just beginning to emerge.

Role and Function

The rehabilitation counselor in a state vocational rehabilitation agency is responsible for integrating all the services into a total rehabilitation program. He works with the client throughout the entire rehabilitation process, from the initial interview through job placement and follow-up. Although the literature is replete with articles concerning the controversy of whether the rehabilitation counselor is primarily a counselor or a coordinator, there is little question that he is both. He helps his client adjust to his disability, studies medical, psychological, vocational, and other data, and then together with the client formulates a vocational plan geared toward successful job placement. Once agreement is reached between counselor and client on a vocational rehabilitation plan, the counselor coordinates the provision of services specified in the plan.

Recently, the American Personnel and Guidance Association undertook a study to determine the amount of time the rehabilitation counselor spends in various rehabilitation activities (Muthard and Solomone, 1969). In this study, 215 rehabilitation counselors employed by the Division of Vocational Rehabilitation (DVR) were surveyed in terms of the percentage of time spent in various job functions. Table 12-I is a tabulation of the responses given by these counselors employed in state vocational rehabilitation agencies.

The table clearly shows the multitude of tasks in which a rehabilitation counselor engages in the performance of his duties. The data demonstrate that the counseling function is the activity that takes up the greatest share (33.57%) of his time. For a more complete review of the rehabilitation counselor *generalist* and his role and function, the following sources are recommended: Patterson, 1960; McGowan and Porter, 1967; Wright, 1968; Patterson, 1969; Muthard and Solomone, 1969; Muthard, Dumas and Solomone, 1969; Jacques, 1970; and Cull and Hardy, 1972.

TABLE 12-I

REHABILITATION COUNSELOR ESTIMATES OF PERCENTAGE OF TIME
SPENT IN MAJOR COUNSELOR ACTIVITIES

Activity	Mean % of Time (N = 215)
Clerical work	10.61
Counseling and guidance	33.57
Overall planning of work	5.42
Professional growth	5.09
Public relations and program promotion	5.67
Recording	10.63
Reporting	4.33
Resource development	6.30
Travel	8.15
Placement	7.32
Supervisory and administrative duties	3.03
Total	100.12

Efforts to study the role and function of the counselor specialist working with the retarded have been limited. Twenty years ago, DiMichael and Terwilliger (1953) published the results of a study of the unique activities of vocational counselors working with this client population. A more recent attempt was undertaken by Carter (1972); however, the purpose of her study was to investigate the *perceived* role of the rehabilitation counselor with the retarded as seen by counselor educators, state directors of rehabilitation, and the counselors themselves. Of particular interest was the updated finding that the role of the counselor specialist was seen as similar to that of the generalist in that his primary activity was counseling and guidance.

The Rehabilitation Process

The outcome of the rehabilitation process rests, in large part, upon the counselor's clinical skills in planning and programming. One of the more important tools to assist him is the incorporation of a model which delineates the major elements in the vocational rehabilitation process. A number of such systems have been proposed. For example, Fraenkel (1961), in addition to identifying eight critical steps to be considered when working with the retarded in a vocational habilitation capacity, proposed three plans from which the counselor can draw. Another set of procedural guidelines is offered in Chapter 5. Even though some of its components are directed primarily to pre-vocational training, much of the applied model lends itself to the post-school phase of the vocational rehabilitation process.

A complicating factor in formulating a procedural "blueprint" is the diversity of settings in which the counselor serving the retarded functions. He may be found in institutions for the retarded, sheltered workshops, rehabilitation and training centers, half-way houses, and in cooperative programs involving the local school district and the Division of Vocational Rehabilitation.

However, in spite of these difficulties, certain generic yet crucial stages of the rehabilitation process can be delineated. These are case-finding, gathering and studying client data, the rehabilitation diagnosis, the rehabilitation plan, placement, and follow-up.

Casefinding

Casefinding is a process of locating handicapped individuals who may be in need of and eligible for vocational rehabilitation services. There is evidence that knowledge of vocational rehabilitation services is lacking among the general population, among professionals such as medical doctors, educators, and others who are in a position to identify and refer handicapped individuals to the rehabilitation counselor, and among handicapped individuals themselves. For example, a recent study indicated that fully 50 percent of the physicians questioned were unaware of the existence of the state vocational rehabilitation program (Stotsky, Goldin, Margolin, 1968). Hence, the rehabilitation counselor must spend a share of his time interpreting the objectives and services of the vocational rehabilitation agency to others in order to increase both the appropriateness and timeliness of referrals of handicapped persons for rehabilitation services.

One unique characteristic of retarded clients served by rehabilitation agencies is that over half of the retarded rehabilitants are initially referred from educational settings. However, this trend did not begin on a large scale until the early 1960's, at which time work-study programs, many of which are in cooperative agreement with state rehabilitation agencies, began to emerge.

In spite of this major referral agency, many retarded individuals who need services are still unknown. As indicated by Di-Michael (1966), one reason there are not more mentally retarded persons referred is their lack of "visibility." In contrast to the retarded, physically handicapped persons have an observable disability, which often increases the chances of their being referred to an agency designed to serve handicapped people. In addition, the disability of mental retardation, unlike many other handicapping conditions, often hinders the retarded person from referring himself for services.

Gathering and Studying Client Data

The initial need for information is the determination of eligibility for vocational rehabilitation services. A person is considered eligible when he meets the following criteria (McGowan and Porter, 1967):

1. The presence of a physical or mental disability;
2. The existence of a substantial handicap to employment; and
3. A reasonable expectation that vocational rehabilitation services may render the individual fit to engage in a gainful occupation (p. 54).

The primary decision regarding eligibility is the responsibility of the counselor, who utilizes information and consultation from a number of sources (i.e. doctors, psychologists, work evaluators, etc.) in making that decision. One of the more salient factors in his decision is: The prospective client must have a disability that poses a substantial handicap to employment, yet the disability must not be so severe that it cannot be remediated to the extent necessary for his gainful employment.

Because of the difficult and time-consuming nature of the eligibility assessment process with the mentally retarded, the 1965 amendments to the Vocational Rehabilitation Act included a provision that allowed the counselor up to eighteen months to determine the eligibility of the retarded for vocational rehabilitation services. Specifically, it was recognized that whether a retarded person is capable of gainful employment if rehabilitation services are provided often can be decided only after a period of prolonged observation. It is a recognized fact that the learning deficits of the retarded are most apparent in the early stages of task performance so that a judgment of vocational potential at this stage would be neither accurate nor fair to the prospective client. Hence, the counselor may need to place the retarded individual in a simulated work environment such as a sheltered workshop or rehabilitation center, for a period of time in order to observe the practical assets and limitations of the prospective client. Moreover, such an extended evaluation provides an assessment of the rate of learning of the retarded person. There is no shortcut to full diagnostic understanding through easily obtainable test scores. The extended evaluation for purposes of the determination of eligibility for services is a recognition of this fact.

When the person is found eligible for services, additional assessment procedures may be necessary in order to formulate a rehabilitation plan. A thorough *medical* evaluation, including specialist examinations, where indicated, is particularly important for the mentally retarded; research has shown that many secondary handicapping conditions often accompany mental retardation (Patterson, 1969). It is particularly important for the counselor to be aware of the residuals of any physical disabilities that may be present.

Psychological evaluations are generally mandatory for all mentally retarded clients as part of the determination of eligibility. However, the astute counselor can obtain much psychological information beyond that needed for eligibility purposes, for instance, an assessment of affective functioning, self-regard, frustration behavior, emotional disturbance, and motivation level (Heber, 1968).

Educational information is derived from examining all facets of the client's school history, not just from looking at courses and grades on a school transcript. An inquiry into such things as extracurricular activities, membership in organizations and clubs, social relationships with teachers and peers, as well as favored subjects can provide clues to possible vocational directions. Sometimes a conversation with an interested teacher or school counselor can provide relevant information obtainable in no other way.

The importance of the counselor's concern with the *sociocultural* milieu of the client is underscored by the fact that the majority of retarded persons living in the community carry a diagnosis of cultural-familial mental retardation (Robinson and Robinson, 1965). For this reason, the client's present family environment needs to be closely scrutinized in order to determine the value system that has influenced the client, particularly the attitudes of the family toward the world of work.

Vocational assessment is the culmination of all the information obtained in the medical, psychological, educational, and social areas, plus specific evaluation of vocational interests, manual dexterity, clerical aptitude, motor coordination, and others. Unfortunately, most of the vocational tests have been standardized on nonretarded populations. Because of this and other difficulties involved in using these tests, the work sample method of assessment, which permits direct observation of performance on selected tasks, has become increasingly popular as a vocational assessment technique.

Finally, a recent exhaustive analysis of the literature related to the predictive assessment of the social and vocational adjustment of retarded individuals concluded that no battery of tests, biographical data, or rating scales can provide actuarial probabilities of success or failure sufficient to relieve the rehabilitation counselor from the exercise of his best "clinical" judgment (Cobb, 1972).

Rehabilitation Diagnosis

A rehabilitation diagnosis consists of an identification of the problems which may interfere with the individual's ability to obtain and maintain satisfactory employment. The rehabilitation diagnosis is central to the entire process: The success of the rehabilitation plan is contingent upon accurate appraisal. The diagnosis is made by synthesizing all the essential case data that has been compiled with the diagnostic impressions gained through the counseling process.

The counseling function plays an integral part in the establishment of a rehabilitation diagnosis through the vital process of helping the client achieve an understanding of his aptitudes, interests, and personal characteristics as they relate to the world of work. The person most in need of understanding the problems that must be faced is the client, and the counselor must do everything in his power to facilitate client understanding through the counseling function.

The Rehabilitation Plan

In this phase of the process, a direct outgrowth of the rehabilitation diagnosis, the counselor must fit necessary and available services into a rehabilitation plan to meet the needs of the individual client. The rehabilitation plan details the provision of goods and services deemed necessary by the counselor and client to enable the client to become gainfully employed. The plan can be thought of as a contract (some counselors do, in fact, write up contracts with their clients) in which the client agrees to engage in certain activities (medical or physical restoration, vocational training, therapy, etc.) and the counselor, as representative of the agency, agrees to provide the services agreed upon.

Once the rehabilitation plan is implemented, the counselor maintains contact with the client and the providers of services throughout the duration of the plan. In many cases problems may arise, and the counselor must be alert to changes in conditions that might require modifications in the rehabilitation plan. Implementation of the plan involves new and often threatening situations for the client, so it is essential that the counselor "be there" when the client needs him.

Training is most often an integral part of the rehabilitation plan with the mentally retarded. Unfortunately, training resources are limited in most communities. The most obviously delimiting factor is the poor academic ability of the mentally retarded client which hinders his participation in academically oriented training institutions, not only the university but most of the technical-vocational and trade schools. Recognizing this problem, the Vocational-Educational Act of 1968 mandated 10 percent of its money in programs for the handicapped, resulting in the provision of vocational-technical training programs for the retarded now being offered by many community colleges and vocational-educational schools. Of course, some of the mentally retarded clients served by DVR have sufficient academic skills to succeed in regular programs of vocational schools serving the general **public.**

In practice, then, the counselor specialist with the retarded must exercise some ingenuity in securing the community resources necessary for the vocational training of his clients. In many cases, he actually must create training sites on an individualized basis. On-the-job training (OJT), in which the counselor pays an employer to train one or more of his clients, has proven a very effective training vehicle for this population. The OJT method has a built-in advantage of often leading to the employer hiring the person trained. However, OJT's are sometimes very costly, and their setting up and continued supervision can consume a great deal of the counselor's time. Other methods of vocational training are work-study programs through the school system, rehabilitation centers (such as Goodwill Industries) and sheltered workshops, and special programs that may exist through the auspices of voluntary groups such as the National Association for Retarded Children.

Placement

The philosophy of selective placement implies that the person engaging in this activity has a thorough knowledge of both the client and the job market in the area. Careful selection of job and employer is of particular importance with the retarded client because of his limited adaptability to new situations. Hence, the more successful the counselor and client are in locating a job that draws on the personal and vocational strengths of the client (a job that can accommodate him "just as he is"), the more likelihood there is of success.

Some rehabilitation counselors delegate this responsibility to a placement specialist within their agency, if one exists. However, it is usually only the counselor, through the relationship established during the entire rehabilitation process, that knows the retarded client to the degree necessary for successful placement. Of course, it is not always necessary to intercede for the retarded client; with proper training and sufficient self-esteem, many of these clients are able to place themselves. Self-placement of the retarded client may minimize the problems created by employer prejudice as the client's handicap generally is not "visible."

Further detail about the placement process is found in Chapter 9, which offers a selective placement model, with particular emphasis on its practical and research implications with mentally retarded clients.

Follow-up

After the placement, the counselor must maintain close contact with the employer who will in most cases need consultation about handling problems that arise with his new employee. Equally important is the role of providing support, consultation, and a receptive ear to the newly employed client. Follow-up is concerned not only with work behaviors. Interpersonal relations with co-workers and supervisors, physical health, family life, and leisure time activities are sometimes factors that decide the client's success or failure in his job. Of course, the counselor cannot solve all the problems of his client, but he often can help by educating the client about the agencies and resources which might help him to meet his needs.

The appropriate amount of time required for following the client before closing the case depends on the needs of the particular client. Keeping the client dependent on the agency by an extended follow-up period can be as damaging as closing a case before the client has fully adjusted to his new job. Agency regulations vary on this point, also. In some states, the counselor may close the case after only thirty days of successful employment; other states require ninety days. However, it is generally left to the counselor's discretion to decide when the client is sufficiently adjusted to his work and capable of making it on his own.

In short, the center and prime mover of the dynamic and complex process of vocational rehabilitation is the counselor. A deeper understanding of the problems and challenges involved in the vocational rehabilitation of the mentally retarded may be gained from the following works: Fraenkel's (1961) *The Mentally Retarded and Their Vocational Rehabilitation: A Resource Handbook;* Heber's (1968) *Special Problems in Vocational Rehabilitation of the Mentally Retarded;* Heath's (1970) *The Mentally Retarded Student and Guidance;* Murry and Michael-Smith's (1972) *Psychology in the Vocational Rehabilitation of*

the Mentally Retarded; and Daniel's (1972) *Vocational Reha-*
bilitation of the Mentally Retarded: A Book of Readings.

A PRACTITIONER'S PERSONAL EXPERIENCE

A description of the role and function of a rehabilitation
counselor may be clarified and embellished by an account of
some of this profession's most critical areas as seen by an experienced counselor. As a rehabilitation counselor of the retarded,
I was most concerned with three major areas. The first was the
problem of the mental retardation label and its implications for
the client, his parents and teachers, and the counselor. Another
major concern was providing opportunities for my clients to
learn through reality testing. Finally, there were the counseling
methods I found to be most effective.

Setting

As a rehabilitation counselor, I worked with mentally retarded
clients through a cooperative work-study program involving two
school districts and the Division of Vocational Rehabilitation.
In essence, this type of program used a two-phase approach to
the education and habilitation of the student-client: an in-school
education and pre-vocational component and an out-of-school
part-time work experience program. The high school teacher
took the major responsibility for the in-school aspects of the
program, while I as a rehabilitation counselor provided service
for the out-of-school work-placement activities. I was most active
with juniors and seniors, because these were the students most involved in out-of-school work placements and closest to graduation.* In addition, I had sole responsibility for those people who
still needed assistance after high school graduation.

The primary purpose of the program, or at least the criteria
by which the success of it was measured, was eventual gainful
employment. In order to achieve this objective, the first two years

---

* The philosophy of the agency (DVR) discourages counselor involvement
with the students below the eleventh grade level. Being vocational in its focus,
the agency reasons that students below the eleventh grade are too far removed
from the labor market to be the proper concern of DVR.

of the four year program generally focused on academic subjects (English, math, reading) combined with in-school work placements, such jobs as cafeteria worker, janitorial helper, and messenger. The last two years were much more vocationally oriented, including the core component of out-of-school work placement. The student spent at least half of each day working at a job in the community and in some cases the whole day, particularly during his senior year. Sometimes the student was paid by the employer, but there was no wage requirement as the theory behind the work-study program was that the student was working in the community for academic credit and a high school diploma. The program consisted of approximately fifty students between the ages of fourteen and nineteen with a general IQ of 50-80. For an extended account of this type of program and work setting, Chapter 6, "Work-Study Programs for the Mentally Retarded: An Overview" is suggested.

Label: Nebulous Term

When I began my work as a DVR counselor with a specialized caseload of educable mentally retarded (EMR) student-clients, I was especially aware of the "retarded" part of the EMR label. The label conjured up a set of expectations of how these students would be likely to act. Consequently, my initial approaches were based on the "diagnosis," the stereotype of mental retardation contained in my head.

However, it soon became apparent to me that knowing that the young person sitting in my office was labeled EMR told me very little about him, at least in terms of how I might assist him toward gainful employment. I began to view the EMR label as of benefit only to educators working with this kind of student in the school, and before long I began questioning that assumption as well. Because of the wide diversity of abilities, problems and ancillary handicapping conditions found within the group, it seemed that the EMR label helped all concerned very little in developing specific approaches to rehabilitation. The one useful function of the label was that it allowed the funds necessary to provide the special educational and vocational services needed by these students.

The EMR label is a nebulous one, which often generates misconceptions. The result is that persons who come into contact with individuals so labeled often perceive them according to their personal, stereotypic definition.

The high school EMR student in the special education class has to deal with his "differentness." He cannot help but be aware of the implications involved in how others perceive him. More importantly, how does he perceive himself? In my opinion, there is no reason to accept the viewpoint that lack of intelligence keeps the person unaware of his differentness. It was my experience that he knows he is different (or at least is considered so by others) and knows the nature of this difference. In short, he knows that others consider him "stupid" and the problem for him is whether to accept the far reaching ramifications of that definition. In trying to define himself, such a person may express himself in many different ways, all of which affect the work of the rehabilitation counselor.

Some EMR students I knew strongly resisted the implications of the EMR label by assuming unrealistic independence. All this student wants is for his "helpers" to leave him alone. He realizes that the safest way to avoid being "found out" (identified as being mentally retarded) is to limit his involvement with anyone connected with the special class, including the special education teachers and the DVR counselor, and, in some cases, fellow students. Consequently, he tends to confine his field of action to only those activities in which he can cope without help. This student can be distinguished from the truly independent one by his general defensiveness and the vehemence with which he insists that all is well. The DVR counselor is a threat to such a "pseudo-independent" student; yet the student is generally very much in need of vocational rehabilitation services.

Another reaction of the student resistant to the nebulous EMR label is the one generally labeled "passive-aggressive." Although this student neither openly rebels nor resists the efforts of his "helpers," neither does he cooperate. Such a reaction is often explained away as a function of the "lack of motivation" typically attributed to special education students. In my opinion, this student *is* motivated—to succeed and maintain his self-esteem in the only way he knows; defeating the efforts of those in authority over him. The DVR practitioner who forgets he is a counselor and engages this student in a power struggle injures his capacity to provide the student with the services he needs in order to succeed after leaving high school.

A third type of reaction displayed by the EMR student-client is the classic "passive-dependent" role. This student has given up the struggle and placed his fate in the hands of his "helpers." He has accepted completely the implications of disability in the EMR label, i.e. he becomes almost totally disabled. Through his passive cooperation, he may do well in school ("he is such a nice boy") but, he generally presents problems to the DVR counselor because of his inability to function independently.

A healthier and more useful adjustment to the EMR label is demonstrated by the student who refuses despite others' definitions of him to define himself. Realizing that he has some strengths he is not so defensive about his limitations. He is able to accept the help he needs from other people, but, at the same time, he knows he is responsible for his actions. This individual may need and profit from vocational rehabilitation services, particularly post-high-school vocational training, but his excellent adaptive skills often make it possible for him to succeed without the special help provided by DVR.

The maladaptive adjustments I observed seemed to be methods students used to maintain some self-esteem in what was for them an oppressive environment. The proverb "it is better to give than to receive" points out the inferior position of the receiver. The problem for the counselor and teacher, then, is offering the student-client the assistance needed without assigning him a position of inferiority.

Clearly, the reactions of the EMR youngster are contingent upon the definitions of the EMR created by his "significant others." Even if the student-client wanted to conform to a stereotype, it would be impossible for him because there are as many definitions of the EMR label as there are definers.

Another unfortunate effect of this label is its use, both by the labeled individual and by his associates, as an excuse for any of his undesirable behavior. In school, if the EMR student does not cooperate with the program or misbehaves, his retardation may be used as the sole explanation. However, if the "normal" student resists the school program, the teacher may at least consider examining the program to see how it can be improved. And when the "normal" student misbehaves, he is held responsible for his actions.

Similar dynamics often occur in the home. If the EMR family member does not perform his assigned tasks, his non-cooperation is often explained away as a function of his "disease." His "normal" sibling would be allowed to experience the consequences of his behavior. The fact that the EMR student may learn to use his disability to obtain special privilege is often not recognized, to the detriment of the student.

When the EMR student is not allowed to be a responsible member of his group, he does not learn the kinds of attitudes and behaviors necessary for success in the world of work. The parent, teacher, DVR counselor, and the student-client all can become victims of the nebulous EMR label. Then this label which should provide services that assist the person in achieving normal adjustment becomes the main obstacle to that achievement.

The rehabilitation counselor's efforts are affected directly by the attempts of others to define the EMR student-client. Because the client lives with his parents and spends most of his day with a very few teachers in the special education program, this small group of people influence him intensely. If they encourage attitudes and behaviors that lead toward healthy adjustment of the kind described above, the DVR counselor's job is much easier. If not, his job is nearly impossible. In this light, it appears that the DVR counselor must devote his time and efforts to the people surrounding his client as well as to the client himself.

Reality Testing

The client's experience of the work world is one of the major rehabilitation tools that the traditional DVR counselor (one who works with adults who have previously been successful workers) has had at his disposal. The adult client has "been there" and has some idea of what he needs to get back. Unlike the client who is relearning familiar material, the high school-aged EMR student-client with no work experience is acquiring new skills and understandings.

Without an understanding of the realities of the work world a person cannot even begin to decide whether he wants to become an active participant in it. The work study aspect of the special education program is primarily designed to expose the student to these realities. However, another of its functions is to provide an opportunity for the student to explore various occupations. When the student explores his interests and aptitudes for a variety of jobs, he does not stay at any one job long enough to experience fully its demands. To survive on a job, one needs more than work skills. He also needs to know how to relate to his co-workers and when to take a coffee break. While it is possible for the work-study program to provide the student with the work skills necessary for survival, it is usually not possible to provide him with an understanding of these explicit and implicit rules and regulations that make up the total reality of the working world. Consequently, the DVR counselor must be aware that the work-study world is only a partial facsimile of the real working world.

The vocational rehabilitation process is built on a model that cannot work without the client's deliberate reaching out for help. But the EMR student-client in the habilitation process does not have the experience necessary to identify his needs so he does not know what to reach for. As a result, the reality tool of work experience often is replaced by the counselor's authoritarian advice, e.g. "Take it from me, if you don't do as I say, you'll never hold a job." A study done in Carbondale, Illinois, in which factors leading to job success of the mentally retarded were studied, showed that an important factor for job success in the group studied was age (Kolstoe, 1965). Older clients (over age 19) tended to be more successful in holding down a job than younger clients, and this factor was more important than IQ, years and type of schooling, and academic achievement scores. Many hypotheses could be postulated to explain this finding, but it is possible that the actual experience of a year or two in the work world, gave the older client an understanding of that world's reality unavailable to even the most well-trained younger client. If this is true, then a main problem for the DVR counselor working with high school-aged EMR students is finding a way to bring reality into the habilitation process sooner and more effectively. Counseling is one of the tools he has at his disposal to achieve this objective.

Counseling Approaches

Many writers have claimed that insight therapy is not possible with the mentally retarded. While this *may* be true for the severely retarded, it certainly did not seem to be true for the high school aged EMR student. In fact, many of these students seemingly refused to go on to more concrete, behavioral objectives until they gained "insights" into things that were troubling them. Often the EMR student is ignored or pushed under the rug by the high school counselor who believes counseling the retarded is futile; consequently, the DVR counselor who is open to hearing the more personal concerns of his student-client finds plenty of opportunity to do so. In terms of individual counseling, it was my experience that the DVR counselor's approach must include techniques that vary from the setting up of a specific behavioral program ("I want to get to work on time, but I don't know how to do it") to assisting his client in the acquisition of insights into deeply troubling problems ("Why do other students call me retarded?").

Group counseling seems to be an especially effective technique with the EMR population. I believe the reasons for this are similar to the reasons given for the utility of group counseling for any teenaged person: Peer norms and peer pressure carry considerable weight with people in this developmental stage. Of course, the counselor must be aware that the dynamics of the group may not always move in the direction he might like. Suppose the group norm temporarily moves toward the notion, "It's not cool to work." If the counselor does not trust the growth potential of the group, fears loss of control of his student-clients, or sees his own success as inseparable from the success of his client, then counseling in a group may not be a wise choice.

However, if the counselor is free to allow the group to move where it will because he believes in the basic forward moving nature of each of his clients, group counseling can be a successful counseling method as well as an enjoyable experience. A good example of the value of a peer group is in the area of vocational choice. A frequently discussed question among vocational counselors and work evaluators of the retarded is, "How do I talk my client out of his unrealistic vocational choices and make him accept a realistic job?" I found that in a discussion of vocational choice in a group of equals, unrealistic choices simply did not appear very often, and when they did, their inappropriateness was quickly recognized. Students find it much easier to make unrealistic declarations to the teacher and DVR counselor ("I'm going to be an airline pilot") than to a group of peers ("You're going to be a *what?*"). In short, the counselor using the group process can move away from the role of the authoritarian educator and toward the role of the facilitator who leaves the responsibility for change with his student-clients.

The problem-centered group approach is an example of the important rehabilitation tool mentioned earlier; exposure to reality which enables the client to identify his needs. For the EMR student is no different from anyone else in that he cannot satisfy his needs until he honestly recognizes them. And only when he sees himself as a responsible person living in a realistic environment will he be able to identify those needs and reach out for assistance.

REFERENCES

Carter, J. R.: *The Perceived Role of the Rehabilitation Counselor of the Mentally Retarded.* Doctoral dissertation, Eugene, University of Oregon, 1972.

Cobb, H. V.: *The Forecast of Fulfillment: A Review of Research on Predictive Assessment of the Adult Retarded for Social and Vocational Adjustment.* New York, Teachers College, Columbia University, 1972.

Cull, J. G., and Hardy, R. E.: *Vocational Rehabilitation: Profession and Process.* Springfield, Ill., Charles C Thomas, 1972.

Daniels, L. K. (Ed.): *Vocational Rehabilitation of the Mentally Retarded: A Book of Readings.* Springfield, Ill., Charles C Thomas, 1972.

DiMichael, S. G. (Ed.): *New Vocational Pathways for the Mentally Retarded.* Washington, D. C., American Personnel and Guidance Association, 1966.

DiMichael, S. G., and Terwilliger, W. B.: Counselors' activities in the vocational rehabilitation of the mentally retarded. *Journal of Clinical Psychology, IX:*99-106, 1953.

Fraenkel, E. A.: *The Mentally Retarded and Their Vocational Rehabilitation: A Resource Handbook.* National Association for Retarded Children, 1961.

Heath, E. J.: *The Mentally Retarded Student and Guidance.* Boston, Houghton Mifflin Company, 1970.

Heber, R. (Ed.): *Proceedings of a Conference on Special Problems in Vocational Rehabilitation of the Mentally Retarded.* Rehabilitation Services Administration, Social and Rehabilitation Service, U. S. Department of Health, Education, and Welfare, Washington, D. C., January, 1968.

Jacques, M. E.: *Rehabilitation Counseling: Scope and Services.* Boston, Houghton Mifflin Company, 1970.

Kolstoe, O. P., and Frey, R. M.: *A High School Work-Study Program for Mentally Sub-Normal Students.* Carbondale, Illinois, Southern Illinois University, 1965.

Kopp, T.: Information provided through personal correspondence with Mr. Kopp, Manpower Training and Development, Rehabilitation Services Administration, Social and Rehabilitation Service, U. S. Department of Health, Education, and Welfare, 1972.

McGowan, J. F., and Porter, T. L.: *An Introduction to the Vocational Rehabilitation Process.* Rehabilitation Services Administration, Social and Rehabilitation Service, U. S. Department of Health, Education, and Welfare, Washington, D. C., July, 1967.

Murry, M., and Michael-Smith, H.: *Psychology in the Vocational Rehabilitation of the Mentally Retarded.* Springfield, Ill., Charles C Thomas, 1972.

Muthard, J. E.; Dumas, N. S.; and Solomone, P. R. (Eds.): *The Profession, Functions, Roles and Practices of the Rehabilitation Counselor.* Jacksonville, Florida, Convention Press, 1969.

Muthard, J. E., and Solomone, P. R.: *The Roles and Functions of Rehabilitation Counselors.* American Rehabilitation Counseling Association, Washington, D. C., December, 1969.

Patterson, C. H.: Methods of assessing the vocational adjustment potential of the mentally handicapped. *Rehabilitation Counseling: Collected Papers.* Champaign, Ill., Stipes Publishing Company, 1969.

Patterson, C. H. (Ed.): *Readings in Rehabilitation Counseling.* Champaign, Ill., Stipes Publishing Company, 1960.

Robinson, H. B., and Robinson, N. M.: *The Mentally Retarded Child: A Psychological Approach.* New York, McGraw-Hill, 1965.

Stotsky, B. A.; Goldin, G. J.; and Margolin, R. J.: The physician and rehabilitation: A survey of attitudes. *Rehabilitation Literature,* 29:295-299, 1968.

Wright, G. N. (Ed.): *Wisconsin Studies in Vocational Rehabilitation.* Madison, Wis., University of Wisconsin, Regional Rehabilitation Research Institute, Series 1, Monograph II-X, 1968.

Chapter 13

COUNSELING THE MENTALLY RETARDED: A REVIEW FOR PRACTICE

ANDREW S. HALPERN
WALTER R. BERARD

T HE HISTORY OF COUNSELING and psychotherapy for the mentally retarded has not been impressive. Theoreticians have tended to ignore the mentally retarded or to argue against the feasibility of their benefiting from psychotherapy. Although a few practitioners and researchers have ventured into this area, the level and extent of service have generally been low. The purpose of this chapter is to review and synthesize the available literature that relates both directly and indirectly to counseling the mentally retarded. Recommendations will be offered concerning those future directions which seem most profitable to pursue.

The term "mental retardation" designates a very broad range of behaviors, from persons with practically no adaptive skills up to those who only marginally fall short of some, but not necessarily all, of society's demands. The focus within this chapter is on those people in the upper portion of this range, designated most frequently as "mildly" retarded or "educable." These individuals account for 75 to 80 percent of those labeled retarded.

Definitions and classification systems vary widely; but the educable retardate to whom we refer usually has an IQ of between 50 and 75, and if he comes from the lower socio-economic class, also usually is referred to as "cultural-familial." The reader is referred to Heber (1961), Robinson and Robinson (1965), and Brison (1967) for thorough reviews of definition and classification.

The mildly retarded person is most often found in the public school classroom for the educable mentally retarded, if these facilities exist. Otherwise, he will be found in the regular class quietly (sometimes not so quietly) waiting for convenient and legal time to leave school. His identity can be difficult to establish, as he seldom manifests detectable neurological or physical anomalies. He typically lives at home with at least part of his family. Although his family may belong to the middle or upper socioeconomic class, more typically they will belong to the lower socioeconomic class (Meyerowitz and Farber, 1966).

Looking at the retardate as a functioning human provides one with an indirect glimpse of his counseling needs. Like all humans, the retardate fulfills many social roles. To look at each role exhaustively would be beyond the scope of this paper, but inasmuch as role effectiveness is the crux of human adjustment, it seems important to discuss some of the relevant social and psychological parameters of retardate behavior as a prelude to discussing appropriate counseling techniques. These behavior patterns will be examined from the perspective of four different settings in the life of the retardate: (1) as a student; (2) as a family member; (3) as a peer-group member; and (4) as a worker.

AS A STUDENT

The retarded pupil will usually have been initially diagnosed sometime between the second and eighth grades. He will frequently have a speech or language problem, including limited vocabulary, nonstandard dialect, or difficulties in speech production. Academically, he will usually be performing below *mental-age* expectations.

The retarded pupil may also display one or many of a full range of emotional problems. The incidence of emotional disturbance has been thought to be greater among retardates than among normals, but research results are mixed (Beier, 1964). It is our opinion, however, that the retardate encounters more crisis situations during development than the nonretarded child.

As with the normal pupil, the retardate can possess a variety of counseling needs. Perhaps most important is the need to understand his difficulties in a regular classroom or his placement in a special class, and to receive help in adjusting to the school environment. For the retardate, school experience is one of repeated failure in the classroom. He encounters more and more frustration, humiliation, and defeat—all experiences which tend to precipitate lowered self-esteem and strong aversions to learning and the classroom. The counselor should be especially aware that the retarded child has been so labeled by the school primarily because he has failed. The psychological impact of failure must somehow be alleviated if he is going to succeed in the special or regular classroom.

> Recommendation 1: The counselor who works with retarded pupils should be prepared to help his clients experience meaningful success within an environment that normally produces mostly failure.

AS A FAMILY MEMBER

Numerous studies (Farber, 1959, 1960; Farber and Blackman, 1956; Farber and Jenne, 1963; Stubblefield, 1965) have indicated that the presence of one or more retarded members in the family has profound effects on family organization and development. Although many topics could be discussed, our attention is restricted to some of the problems of cultural-familial retardation.

The family of the cultural-familial retardate has been characterized as falling into one of two categories, the stable lower-class family or the poverty-stricken family (Robinson and Robinson, 1965). The stable lower-class family typically provides the retarded member with family cohesion, reasonable nutrition, health care, warmth, and personal acceptance. Usually, the parents have had little schooling and do not understand or value the upward mobility possible through education. Therefore, this type of family does not tend to provide the role models or pressures for high academic achievement.

The poverty-stricken family, in contrast, offers almost nothing to the developing retardate. Poor health care often starts before birth and continues through the child's development. The scarcity of food is usually evident, with the resulting deficits in nutrition. Over-crowded, uncomfortable, and unsanitary living quarters are the rule rather than the exception. Emotionally and intellectually, the family offers little more than it does physically. Changing role models through divorce or separation, little or no intellectual stimulation, and an environment of frustration and defeat typify this family.

Both situations offer interesting challenges to the counselor who attempts to work with both the retarded client and his family. The stable family is usually capable of longterm cooperation if they, themselves, can be provided direction, structure and support. The poverty-stricken family, on the other hand, appears not to have this capability of extended cooperation.

> Recommendation 2: When the family of a retarded client is fairly stable, they should be incorporated into the counseling process. When such stability does not exist, the chances of helping the client are minimal, unless extensive family counseling can be initiated, or the influence of the family upon the client can be weakened.

AS PEER-GROUP MEMBER

The problems of retardate personal and social adjustment can be examined also within the context of peer-group relationships. Research results suggest that the retarded child in the normal classroom tends to be rejected and is frequently a sociometric isolate, while the retardate in the special classroom is significantly superior in his development of healthy social adjustment. The reverse situation holds true for academic performance (Baldwin, 1958; Cassidy and Stanton, 1959; Ellenbogen, 1957).

Low intelligence may be a critical factor in peer-group rejection, but other variables can also be important. The retardate often has other identifying labels referring to national origin, color, or socioeconomic status; and it is often unclear whether the rejection stems from being retarded or being classified as a member of some other "odious" social category.

> Recommendation 3: The counselor should be aware of all the ways in which his retarded client deviates from local norms, in order to avoid focusing erroneously on retardation as the sole cause of peer-group rejection.

Peer-group adjustments within the school and the neighborhood do not necessarily conform to the same patterns. In a neighborhood sociometric study, Goldstein, Moss, and Jordan (1965) found that retarded children from regular classes tended to interact to a slightly higher degree with other neighborhood children than do the retarded children from special classes. However, *neither* group was overtly rejected by the other children in the neighborhood. It would seem that once the retarded youngster is removed from the academic environment, he is more likely to be judged on other personal and social dimensions and his chances are better for successful social integration.

> Recommendation 4: The counselor should help his retarded pupils to develop interests and activities outside of the school environment.

AS A WORKER

The end product of successful education in our culture is successful occupation (Wolfensberger, 1967a). The recent trend toward education and community placement of the retarded has been supported by a strong economic and moralistic ethos that remunerative employment should be the desired habilitation goal for the retarded as well as the normal. As a result of this ethos, the junior and senior high school curricula for the retarded have begun to reflect a vocational as well as a general education orientation. Cooperative agreements have been worked out between the school and other agencies to provide prevocational course work and training opportunities (Kolstoe and Frey, 1965).

Many retarded adults fail to achieve successful vocational adjustment because of personal and social deficiencies, rather than a lack of job-skills. Some of the most common problem areas include difficulty in making decisions, inability to tolerate long periods of nonreinforcement, lack of appropriate training, failure to observe safety requirements, unwillingness to risk failure, lack of initiative, cooperation, and cheerfulness, and inappropriate social behavior (Wolfensberger, 1967a).

> Recommendation 5: In helping retarded adolescents and adults achieve vocational success, the counselor should pay close attention to the personal and social demands of his client's work environment.

In summary, it would appear that the counselor who decides to work with mentally retarded clients will face some problems more frequently than he would tend to encounter while working with his nonretarded clients. Does this imply a need for counseling techniques that are uniquely applicable to the mentally retarded? The answer to this question seems to be a qualified "no."

COUNSELING THE MENTALLY RETARDED

Although the history of counseling and psychotherapy for the mentally retarded has been sparse and sporadic, the past fifteen years have shown a moderate burst of activities in this area. Comprehensive reviews of the literature on counseling retarded clients can be found in articles by Neham (1951), Sternlicht (1966), and Bialer (1967). The literature on counseling parents of the mentally retarded is reviewed by Wolfensberger (1967b) and sampled in two books of readings by Noland (1970) and by Wolfensberger and Kurtz (1969).

Examination of this literature reveals that much attention has been paid to the question of which techniques work for counseling the mentally retarded, whereas much less attention has been paid to the problem of developing a comprehensive theoretical foundation for such counseling. This is not surprising when we consider that a comprehensive theory of counseling in general is still a topic of moderate controversy. Although most theorists would agree that counseling is a learning process that evolves from the relationship between a counselor and one or more clients, there is precious little agreement concerning the precise nature of this learning process and its implications for counseling goals and techniques (Berenson and Carkhuff, 1967).

Given this state of theoretical uncertainty in the general field of counseling, it would surely be presumptuous to propose a comprehensive theoretical model for counseling the mentally retarded. This does not preclude, however, a theoretical and empirical exploration of some of the variables that have been investigated in various attempts to provide counseling services to the retarded. We shall examine these variables under three rubrics: (1) counselor variables, (2) client variables, and (3) process or technique variables.

Counselor Variables

The counselor's ability to provide his client with a central core of "facilitative conditions" seems to be a highly desirable, although not totally sufficient, agent of client behavioral change. The well-known conditions of (1) accurate empathy, (2) respect, positive regard, and nonpossessive warmth, (3) genuineness and self-congruence, and (4) concreteness or specificity have received considerable attention in terms of theory, practice, and research (e.g. Rogers, 1957; Rogers et al., 1967; Truax and Carkhuff, 1964, 1967; Carkhuff and Berenson, 1967; and Carkhuff, 1969a, b). These therapeutic ingredients also have emerged from the literature on counseling the retarded. In fact, one recent study investigated the facilitative conditions of counselors serving a mentally retarded client population (Browning, 1969; Browning and Butler, 1970).

Even though this "facilitative core" is very important, it does not describe adequately the full range of characteristics and qualifications that would be found in the idealized counselor of the mentally retarded. A list of additional qualifications is described by Wolfensberger (1967b).

First, the counselor of the mentally retarded must possess a certain body of knowledge above and beyond a competency in counseling principles and techniques in general. Specifically, he must know about the broad medical, social, educational, and habilitational aspects of mental retardation and must also be aware of the various programs and community resources that are available to the mentally retarded client and his family.

Second, the counselor of the mentally retarded must possess certain attitudes about mental retardation and its treatment. He must be free from stereotypes about retardation, such as the often-held belief that all forms of retardation are inherited and invariably associated with other deviancies like mental illness or delinquency. Also, he must possess genuinely positive attitudes toward the mentally retarded and their families.

> Recommendation 6: In addition to being generally facilitative, the counselor who works with retarded clients should become intimately acquainted with the broad field of mental retardation on both intellectual and experiential levels.

Third, and perhaps most important, the counselor must appreciate the necessity of environmental manipulation in his attempt to provide assistance to retarded clients. Farber (1968) has presented a convincing argument that the mentally retarded, as a group, constitute part of America's "surplus population." The term "surplus" is construed in an organizational sense, meaning that there are more people than slots in "the machinery of social organization," and that the goal of this machinery is *efficiency*. But the retarded are not always able to perform satisfactorily when the norm for evaluation is an external criterion of efficiency. Environmental props are often needed. Their importance is documented well by Edgerton (1967) who found, in a carefully executed follow-up study, that successful adult adjustment for the retarded was usually dependent upon the existence of a "benefactor" who assumed a role, often covertly, of the retarded person's advocate.

> Recommendation 7: Since many problems of the mentally retarded result from society's demands for competence, the counselor should help his retarded clients manipulate their environments to either meet or reduce these demands.

To summarize, if a counselor possesses the understanding of and attitudes toward the mentally retarded that have just been described, is able to provide a minimal level of the core facilitative conditions, is tuned in to the environmental needs of his clients as well as their psychological needs, and is patient in terms of his expectations for progress, his mentally retarded clients will have a better-than-ever chance of being significantly helped during the counseling process.

Client Variables

Most people who have been labeled as mildly retarded feel greatly ashamed of this label. The most pervasive psychological defenses against the stigma of mental retardation, according to an intensive follow-up study by Edgerton (1967), are denial and passing. The mildly retarded individual is consumed with the dual life-task of blaming others for his predicament and discovering ways of disguising his deficits from the awareness of others. The motivational strength of these two defenses is understandable when one considers that the stigma of mental retardation is all-pervasive and has no redeeming qualities within the context of contemporary American society. The label states without equivocation that its bearer is inherently stupid.

Understanding these defenses should help the counselor when he encounters resistance from the mentally retarded clients. Since the very offer to provide assistance may imply to the potentially retarded client a reinforcement of his stigma, many retarded clients are initially reluctant to engage in counseling activities. It is easier to blame others for their incompetence than to be forced to come to grips with one's own.

Regardless of whether or not the counselor encounters strong initial resistance, he will undoubtedly be faced many times with various manifestations of these two defenses. And it may be that his most important role will be to help the client to further develop and refine these defenses, for to strip them away may leave a festering wound for which there is no available balm.

Recommendation 8: When a retarded client exhibits the defenses of passing and denial, his counselor should help him to utilize these defenses adaptively, rather than attempting to dissolve them.

The importance of client insight is a second issue of some concern when we consider the potential sources of gain for counseling progress with the mentally retarded. Since the very possibility of acquiring insight seems to presuppose skill in the subtle use of language, and since the mentally retarded are, almost by definition, relatively deficient in this skill, any approach to counseling which relied heavily on insight as an agent of change would immediately stack the odds against the mentally retarded client. It is not clear, however, that insight is a necessary agent of change, even within the context of traditional verbal counseling with the nonretarded client (Hobbs, 1962). If insight is, indeed, not essential, the counselor is then freed from regarding the retarded client's relative lack of verbal skills as a sign that such clients are really unsuitable for counseling.

Recommendation 9: Don't assume that client insight is a necessary prerequisite of therapeutic change within *any* form of counseling, including those that are highly verbally oriented.

A third topic in the area of client characteristics involves some issues concerning differential diagnosis. Although mental retardation is presently defined in terms of current behavior, there are many known causes that have been shown to be associated with the occurrence of retardation in an individual (Heber, 1961). These causes can be grouped into three broad categories: Physiological, environmental, and psychological. Regardless of causality, the mentally retarded individual is likely to develop problems in adjustment that will make him a potential client for counseling. The question which arises is whether or not differences in causality imply differences in treatment.

Opinion on this matter has been far from unanimous. Lindsley (1964) argues strongly against the principle that "like causes call for like treatment," e.g. that physiologically caused retardation should be treated medically and that psychologically caused retardation should be treated psychologically. He argues instead that mental retardation, regardless of cause, can be treated with behavior modification techniques based on operant conditioning.

Sternlicht (1964) has argued in an apparently opposite fashion. He states that the goals and techniques of counseling can and should vary as a function of the etiology of the retardation. Psychologically induced retardation should be treated with the goal of "curing" the retardation ("cure" in the sense that raising the IQ is an appropriate goal) whereas physiologically induced retardation should be treated with more limited goals of adjustment. When cause of the retardation is primarily environmental, then modification of the environment should become a primary form of treatment. Sternlicht's model obviously presupposes that differential diagnosis of mental retardation in terms of causality is a feasible enterprise. There are many problems concerning differential diagnosis, however, which still remain unresolved (Halpern, 1970).

It is possible to reconcile theoretically the positions of Lindsley and Sternlicht if one distinguishes between the effectiveness and efficiency of treatment. It is probably true that all behavioral aspects of mental retardation, regardless of cause, can be treated more or less effectively with the techniques of behavior modification. It is questionable, however, whether behavior modification or any other single technique will prove to be the most efficient procedure for resolving *all* problems of *all* retarded clients.

> Recommendation 10: Counselors should not rely *exclusively* on *any* single counseling technique with retarded clients. Until methods of differential diagnosis are refined, however, counselors should not attempt to select techniques on the basis of etiology of retardation. Other criteria for selection should be employed, such as counselor skills, client skills, and client problem areas.

Technique Variables

A wide variety of counseling techniques have been utilized with mentally retarded clients. Most of the literature reporting this work has been of three varieties: individual case studies, descriptions of counseling programs, or studies attempting to evaluate the *outcomes* of counseling the mentally retarded. A recently completed project by Ayer and Butler (1969) is an interesting and extensive effort to examine the counseling process with mentally retarded clients utilizing verbally oriented techniques. Two types of research are conspicuously missing from the literature: studies that compare the relative effectiveness of two or more different techniques, and studies that focus attention on the variables within the process that are related to specific outcomes. With regard to the latter, it is not uncommon to finish reading an elaborate study that shows significant and positive outcomes but to find, nevertheless, that the description of the process has been so meager that the reader is simply incapable of determining which elements of the process may have been responsible for bringing about the reported results.

In spite of the shortcomings in the literature, it is still possible to discern that a wide variety of counseling techniques have been attempted with mentally retarded clients and have met, apparently, with a fair measure of success. These techniques can be grouped into six broad categories: (1) individual verbal counseling, (2) play techniques, (3) group counseling, (4) role playing, (5) behavior modification, and (6) special techniques such as art or music therapy. Such a grouping is arbitrary and somewhat less than exhaustive, but it does capture and organize a large proportion of the available literature.

Verbal Counseling

Typical examples of the reports on individual verbal counseling with mentally retarded clients can be found in articles by Ackerman and Menninger (1936), Cooley (1945), Friedman (1961), Glass (1957), and Sion (1953). Since verbal skills are not normally among the strengths of the mentally retarded it is interesting to speculate as to why this traditional form of counseling has indeed been found to be effective with some retarded clients. One possible explanation is that aspects of the relationship other than introspection were the primary agents of client change. Possible sources of gain might include the learning of new and relevant information via simplified instruction or the opportunity to model one's behavior after an admired and well functioning adult. Another possible explanation, following Sternlicht's argument, is that the retarded clients who have been helped most by traditional verbal counseling are those who possessed strong verbal skills and whose retardation was largely psychogenic in origin. This position is somewhat supported by the fact that many of the case studies report a raise in IQ as one of their achieved outcomes. Whatever the ultimate explanation may be, it does appear that traditional verbal counseling can be of some value to some retarded clients. It is relatively time consuming, however, and may be far from the most efficient technique available.

> Recommendation 11: Individual verbal counseling can be an appropriate technique with retarded clients under any of the following conditions: (1) the client's problems can be handled appropriately by counselor instruction; (2) the client is competent and productive within the format of a verbally oriented relationship; (3) both counselor and client have the time and resources for maintaining a long-term relationship.

Play Techniques

Play techniques offer certain counseling opportunities that are not available within the traditional verbal counseling relationship, especially when the clients are of elementary or junior high school age. From a diagnostic perspective, the counselor can learn much about his client's behavioral strengths and weaknesses by engaging him in selected play activities and then observing his interactions with both his playmates and the play materials. In this fashion, the client's play becomes a primary channel of communication, thereby placing a lesser importance upon the retarded client's relative deficit in verbal skills. Since a child's "work" is his play, the counselor also enhances the likelihood of establishing an effective relationship with his client by allowing him to communicate in a manner that is more natural and less stressful.

The therapeutic aspects of play seem to be at least two-fold. If one believes in the value of emotional catharsis, play certainly allows the client an opportunity to let off steam. In addition, play provides the client an opportunity to experience success in an activity to which he attaches great importance. Furthermore, the client's experiencing of success can to a large extent be controlled by the counselor's manipulation of the dimension of structure. As Leland and Smith (1965) point out, structure, and therefore the possibility of success, can be controlled both in terms of the counselor's instructions and the complexity of the play materials. To the extent that structure is minimized, it becomes more and more difficult to fail at a given task and therefore more and more likely that the client will experience success. On the other hand, to the extent that the environment is structured, it comes closer and closer to approximating the world outside the counseling room. The counselor's task is to lead his client along the path of success with increasing structure until he is capable enough and confident enough to function fairly well within his own everyday environment.

Recommendation 12: Play techniques are appropriate for younger clients with minimal verbal skills. The play situation can be utilized both diagnostically and therapeutically. In the latter case, the structuring of both materials and instructions should be designed to maximize the opportunities for the client to experience success in his activities.

Group Counseling

After reviewing the relatively large literature that can be found on group counseling with the mentally retarded—more than fifty journal articles and project reports have been written in this area—Sternlicht (1966) suggests the hypothesis that the outcomes of the group counseling are more likely to be successful if the techniques used are more directive than nondirective and more nonverbal than verbal. If this is true, once again we are reminded of the need for counselors to extend their horizons beyond the parameters of traditional verbal counseling.

The main advantage of group counseling for mentally retarded clients is that the group can be structured in a variety of ways, all of which are geared to reduce the social or interpersonal deficits which lie at the core of the syndrome we call mental retardation. Examples of some creative group techniques with retarded clients can be found in articles by Cotzin (1948), Fisher and Wolfson (1953), Kaufman (1963), and Sternlicht (1965a, 1965b).

> Recommendation 13: Since impairment in adaptive behavior is the primary deficit of the mentally retarded, group techniques are particularly useful with retarded clients in that one of the most appropriate goals of group counseling is to enhance the clients' social adaptation. The group should be structured directively by the counselor, and the procedures should be oriented more towards activity than discussion.

Role Playing

One technique that can be readily employed within the context of group counseling is role playing or sociodrama. It is interesting to note that among the studies reported on group counseling with noninstitutionalized retarded clients, the clear majority have included the utilization of role-playing techniques (Pilkey, Goldman and Kleinman, 1961; McDaniel, 1960; Hormuth, 1955; Arnholter, 1955; Gootzeit, Lombardo, and Milner, 1960; and Lavalli and Levine, 1954).

The potential value of role playing as a counseling technique seems to be describable in terms of three broad functions: (1)

it provides the counselor an opportunity to diagnose, in simulations of real-life situations, his clients' strengths and weaknesses in the area of interpersonal relationships; (2) it enables clients to become more sensitive to their own social behaviors through a carefully structured examination of the roles that are enacted; and (3) it provides clients the opportunity to practice, in a simlated and sheltered environment, some possible solutions to their interpersonal problems.

From a utilitarian perspective, role playing also appears to be highly valuable in that it can be used in a wide variety of settings, including classrooms, sheltered workshops, and recreational clubs, as well as specially constituted counseling groups. Furthermore, the technique seems to be quite viable for a large variety of client problems, both personal and social in nature.

> Recommendation 14: Role playing is an especially promising technique with retarded clients, in either group or individual settings. It can be used in many contexts, both diagnostically and therapeutically. Whenever possible, this approach should be utilized.

Behavior Modification

The techniques of behavior modification are also being widely adopted in the care of the mentally retarded. Although these techniques have been derived from both classical and operant conditioning models, the majority of the work in mental retardation has involved procedures based on operant conditioning.

Perhaps the strongest argument to be made for the use of behavior modification by the counselor is that the principles are relatively easy to learn, and they can be utilized very appropriately in natural environments. Pinpointing behaviors to be changed, developing strategies with respect to these behaviors, charting rates of relevant behavior, and engineering the kinds and schedules of reinforcement are skills that can be taught in a relatively short period of time. There is little doubt concerning the initial effectiveness of these procedures, although generalization and maintenance of learned behaviors has been more difficult to achieve than the acquisition or extinction of specific behaviors within highly controlled environments. Although some have argued that behavior modification should be the *only* counseling approach used with mentally retarded clients (Gardner and Stamm, 1971), the position being adopted in this paper is that behavior modification should be regarded as one very important approach among a number of alternatives. An example of the utilization of behavior modification techniques in a classroom for the mentally retarded can be found in a recent study by Broden, Hall, Dunlap and Clark (1970). Gardner's recent book (1971) also contains a large section on the utilization of behavior modification techniques with the mentally retarded.

> Recommendation 15: The techniques of behavior modification tend to focus both counselor and client on specific, behaviorally defined problems. Feedback is regularly provided, so that progress can be monitored and evaluated. The interventions can be designed in both simulated and natural environments. With so many advantages, this technique is recommended very highly and should be adopted whenever possible.

Special Techniques

Finally, in our arbitrary classification of techniques, we come to a group of innovative procedures which have been labelled "special techniques." These techniques tend to focus on the therapeutic utilization of the creative arts and have been thoroughly reviewed by Bialer (1967). To the extent that these techniques are intrinsically interesting, involve modeling behaviors, and utilize nonverbal channels of communication, they share some of the advantages for use with retarded clients that have already been discussed.

> Recommendation 16: For the counselor who has talents in the creative arts, some techniques have been developed for utilizing these media therapeutically with retarded clients. These techniques provide the counselor with an alternative for relating to clients through an interesting and pleasurable activity.

SUMMARY AND CONCLUSIONS

Earlier in this chapter, the question was raised: "Are counseling techniques for the mentally retarded different from counseling techniques in general?" An answer of "no" was suggested. It seems clear that the counseling techniques that have been used with retarded clients are the same techniques with which we are all familiar. This is hardly surprising when we consider that mild mental retardation does not designate a discrete medical or behavioral syndrome, but rather is a label that administrators and professionals have found convenient to use and, not infrequently misuse. Given that this label exists, however, it is essential that the counselor understand its meaning, both as a descriptor and as a cause of retarded behavior ("cause" in the sense of self-fulfilling prophecy). Through such an understanding, the relative strengths of various counseling techniques with mildly retarded clients can be properly evaluated.

During the course of the review, sixteen recommendations were offered concerning ways of improving counseling services to mildly retarded clients. These recommendations were based upon both a review of appropriate literature and the author's personal experiences in counseling and teaching the mentally retarded. The recommendations were organized into four basic areas: (1) the roles of mildly retarded people in society, (2) counselor variables, (3) client variables, and (4) counseling techniques that can be used. The counseling techniques were grouped into six categories, and although each approach was seen as being valid under some circumstances, role playing and behavior modification emerged as the most promising and highly recommended techniques.

The most potent idea in the field of mental retardation today is the concept of normalization. Generally speaking, this means that services for the retarded should be structured in such a way as to maximize the possibility of a normal life-style. Many existing services, such as segregated educational classes and residential care in archaic institutions, are not consistent with the objective. If the counselor will work toward normalization with mildly retarded clients, utilizing the considerations that have been described and argued above, there is every reason to expect that his efforts will be met with a satisfying degree of success.

REFERENCES

Ackerman, N., and Menninger, K.: Treatment techniques for mental retardation in a school for personality disorders in children. *American Journal of Orthopsychiatry, 6*:294-313, 1936.

Arnholter, E.: Social drama for retarded adolescents. *Exceptional Children,* *21*:132-134, 1955.

Ayer, J., and Butler, A.: *Client-Counselor Communication and Interaction in Counseling With the Mentally Retarded.* Final Report R.D. 1798-P., 1969.

Baldwin, W. K.: The social position of the educable mentally retarded child in the regular grades in the public school. *Exceptional Children, 25:* 106-108, 1958.

Beier, D.: Behavioral disturbances in the mentally retarded. In Stevens, H. A., and Heber, R. (Eds.): *Mental Retardation: A Review of Research.* Chicago, University of Chicago Press, 1964.

Berenson, B., and Carkhuff, R. (Eds.): *Sources of Gain in Counseling and Psychotherapy.* New York, Holt, Rinehart, and Winston, Inc., 1967.

Bialer, I.: Psychotherapy and other adjustment techniques with the mentally retarded. In Baumeister, A., and Hawkins, W. (Eds.): *Mental Retardation: Selected Problems in Appraisal and Treatment.* Chicago, Aldine, 1967, pp. 138-180.

Brison, D. W.: Definition and classification. In Baumeister, A. (Ed.): *Mental Retardation.* Chicago, Aldine, 1967.

Broden, M.; Hall, R.; Dunlap, A.; and Clark, R.: Effects of teacher attention and a token reinforcement system in a junior high school special education class. *Exceptional Children, 36*:341-350, 1970.

Browning, P.: An Analysis of Counselor, Client, and Situational Conditions in Counseling the Mentally Retarded. Unpublished doctoral dissertation, University of Wisconsin, 1969.

Browning, P., and Butler, A. J.: Process research in counseling the retarded. In Prehm, H. J. (Ed.): *Rehabilitation Research in Mental Retardation.* Rehabilitation Research and Training Center in Mental Retardation, University of Oregon, Monograph No. 2, 1970, pp. 35-47.

Carkhuff, R., and Berenson, B.: *Beyond Counseling and Therapy.* New York, Holt, Rinehart, and Winston, Inc., 1967.

Carkhuff, R. R.: *Helping and Human Relations: Selection and Training.* New York, Holt, Rinehart, and Winston, Inc., 1969a.

Carkhuff, R. R.: *Helping and Human Relations: Practice and Research.* New York, Holt, Rinehart, and Winston, Inc., 1969b.

Cassidy, V. M., and Stanton, J. E.: An investigation of factors involved in the educational placement of mentally retarded children: A study of differences between children in special and regular classes in Ohio. U. S. Office of Education Cooperative Research Program, Project No. 043, Ohio State University, 1959.

Cooley, J.: The relative amenability of dull and bright children to child guidance. *Smith College Studies in Social Work, 16*:26-43, 1945.

Cotzin, M.: Group therapy with mental defective problem boys. *American Journal of Mental Deficiency, 52*:268-283, 1948.

Edgerton, R.: *The Cloak of Competence*. Berkeley, University of California Press, 1967.

Ellenbogon, M. L.: A comparative study of some aspects of academic and social adjustment to two groups of mentally retarded children in special classes and in regular grades. Unpublished Doctor's Dissertation, Evanston, Ill., Northwestern University, 1957.

Farber, B.: Effects of a severely mentally retarded child on family integration. *Monographs of Social Research in Child Development, 24*, 1959.

Farber, B.: Family organization and crisis: Maintenance of integration in families with a severely mentally retarded child. *Monographs of Social Research in Child Development, 25*, 1960.

Farber, B.: *Mental Retardation: Its Social Context and Social Consequences*. Boston, Houghton Mifflin Company, 1968.

Farber, B., and Blackman, L. S.: Marital role tensions and number and sex of children. *American Sociological Review, 21*:596-601, 1956.

Farber, B., and Jenne, W. C.: Family organization and parent-child communication: Parents and siblings of a retarded child. *Monographs of Social Research in Child Development, 28*, No. 7, 1963.

Fisher, L., and Wolfson, I.: Group therapy with defectives. *American Journal of Mental Deficiency, 57*:463-476, 1953.

Friedman, E.: Individual therapy with a "defective delinquent." *Journal of Clinical Psychology, 17*:229-232, 1961.

Gardner, W., and Stamm, J.: Counseling the mentally retarded: A behavioral approach. *Rehabilitation Counseling Bulletin, 15*:46-57, 1971.

Gardner, W. I.: *Behavior Modification in Mental Retardation*. Chicago, Aldine Publishing Company, 1971.

Glass, H.: Psychotherapy with the mentally retarded: A case history. *Training School Bulletin, 54*:32-34, 1957.

Goldstein, H.; Moss, J.; and Jordan, L.: The efficiency of special class training on the development of mentally retarded children. (Urbana: Institute for Research on Exceptional Children, University of Illinois, 1965), (USOE Cooperative Research Project No. 619).

Gootzeit, J.; Lombardo, A.; and Milner, S.: Situational diagnosis and therapy. *American Journal of Mental Deficiency, 64*:921-925, 1960.

Halpern, A.: Some issues concerning the differential diagnosis of mental retardation and emotional disturbance. *American Journal of Mental Deficiency, 74*:796-800, 1970.

Heber, R.: *A Manual on Terminology and Classification in Mental Retardation*. American Association on Mental Deficiency, 1961.

Hobbs, N.: Sources of gain in psychotherapy. *American Psychologist, 17*: 18-34, 1962.

Hormuth, R.: The utilization of group approaches in aiding mentally retarded adults adjust to community living. *Group Psychotherapy, 8*:233-241, 1955.

Kaufman, M.: Group psychotherapy in preparation for the return of mental defectives from institution to community. *Mental Retardation, 1:*276-280, 1963.

Kolstoe, O., and Frey, R.: *A High School Work-Study Program for Mentally Subnormal Students.* Carbondale, Southern Illinois University Press, 1965.

Lavalli, A., and Levine, M.: Social and guidance needs of mentally handicapped adolescents as revealed through sociodrama. *American Journal of Mental Deficiency,* 58:544-552, 1954.

Leland, H., and Smith, D.: *Play Therapy with Mentally Subnormal Children.* New York, Grune and Stratton, 1965.

Lindsley, O.: Direct measurement and prosthesis of retarded behavior. *Journal of Education, 147:*62-81, 1964.

McDaniel, J.: Group action in the rehabilitation of the mentally retarded. *Group Psychotherapy, 13:*5-13, 1960.

Meyerowitz, J. H., and Farber, B.: Family background of educable mentally retarded children. In Farber, B. (Ed.): *Kinship and Family Organization.* New York, Wiley, 1966.

Neham, S.: Psychology in relation to mental deficiency. *American Journal of Mental Deficiency,* 55:557-572, 1951.

Noland, R. L.: *Counseling Parents of the Mentally Retarded.* Springfield, Ill., Charles C Thomas, 1970.

Pilkey, L.; Goldman, M.; and Kleinman, B.: Psychodrama and empathic ability in the mentally retarded. *American Journal of Mental Deficiency,* 65:595-605, 1961.

Robinson, H. B., and Robinson, N. M.: *The Mentally Retarded Child: A Psychological Approach.* New York, McGraw-Hill, 1965.

Rogers, C.: The necessary and sufficient conditions of therapeutic personality change. *Journal of Consulting Psychology, 21:*95-103, 1957.

Rogers, C. (Ed.): *The Therapeutic Relationship and Its Impact: A Study of Psychotherapy with Schizophrenics.* Madison, Wis., The University of Wisconsin Press, 1967.

Sion, A.: Casework with an adolescent boy of moron intelligence. *American Journal of Mental Deficiency,* 57:709-718, 1953.

Sternlicht, M.: A theoretical model for the psychological treatment of mental retardation. *American Journal of Mental Deficiency,* 68:618-622, 1964.

Sternlicht, M.: Establishing an initial relationship in group psychotherapy with delinquent retarded male adolescents. *American Journal of Mental Deficiency,* 69:39-41, 1965 (a).

Sternlicht, M.: Psychotherapeutic procedures with the retarded. In Ellis, N. (Ed.): *International Review of Research in Mental Retardation,* New York, Academic Press, 1966, vol. 2, pp. 279-354.

Sternlicht, M.: Psychotherapeutic techniques useful with the mentally retarded: A review and critique. *Psychiatric Quarterly,* 39:84-90, 1965 (b).

Stubblefield, H.: Religion, parents and mental retardation. *Mental Retardation, 3:*8-11, 1965.

Truax, C., and Carkhuff, R.: Significant developments in psychotherapy research. In Abt, L., and Reiss, B. (Eds.): *Progress in Clinical Psychology.* New York, Grune and Stratton, 1964, pp. 124-155.

Truax, C., and Carkhuff, R.: *Toward Effective Counseling and Psychotherapy: Training and Practice.* Chicago, Aldine Publishing Company, 1967.

Wolfensberger, W.: Vocational preparation and occupation. In Baumeister, A. (Ed.): *Mental Retardation.* Chicago, Aldine Publishing Company, 1967 (a).

Wolfensberger, W.: Counseling the parents of the retarded. In Baumeister, A., and Hawkins, W. (Eds.): *Mental Retardation: Selected Problems in Appraisal and Treatment.* Chicago, Aldine Publishing Company, 1967, pp. 329-400 (b).

Wolfensberger, W., and Kurtz, R. (Eds.): *Management of the Family of the Mentally Retarded.* Follett Educational Corporation, 1969.

Chapter 14

BEHAVIORAL COUNSELING WITH THE MENTALLY RETARDED

John Stamm

R EHABILITATION PROGRAMS for the retarded are designed to enhance the emotional, social, and vocational growth of individuals in a population presenting a wide range of personal limitations. The general objective is to assist the handicapped person to adapt to a variety of new and changing experiences and
circumstances as they are encountered in the home, at work, and
in the community (Heber, 1963). The purpose of this response
to the peculiar needs of the retarded is essentially to reshape
modes of adaptation through influencing behavior in the direction of increased adaptability. To achieve this objective, a variety of rehabilitation techniques are employed.

Counseling and psychotherapy have prevailed in practice and
have always been maintained theoretically as an integral, heavily
emphasized component in the rehabilitation process with the retarded (e.g. Ayers and Duguay, 1969; Sternlicht, 1966; Yepsen,
1958). Within the past five years, however, the effectiveness and
efficiency of traditional counseling and psychotherapy with the
mentally retarded has been questioned repeatedly (e.g. Gardner,
1967; Gardner and Stamm, 1971). Traditional counseling and
psychotherapy, as used here, refers to predominantly verbally-
oriented procedures conducted most frequently in an office or
clinic, the purpose of which is to change the personality structure of the client. Consideration of whether the best results are
in fact obtainable from a psychotherapeutic approach has been
stimulated in a large measure by the articulation of another behavior therapy that has taken root in areas where changing behavior (as opposed to depositional constructs which constitute
"personality") is a primary goal, namely, behavior therapy. As
a systematic approach that has been carefully and precisely de-

lineated in terms of both theory and practice, behavior therapy has challenged verbally-oriented counseling and psychotherapy and as a preferred method in the rehabilitation of the retarded to the extent that a new area of controversy has emerged within the literature.

The degree to which psychotherapy has been seriously questioned as an efficient and effective treatment is reflected in the central question of a journal article printed in *Mental Retardation* and entitled "Why Not Psychotherapy?" This question was raised by Halpern (1968) in response to the position taken by Gardner (1967) that on the basis of conceptual clarity and operational utility the use of traditional (i.e. verbally-oriented) counseling and psychotherapy with the retarded should be discontinued and replaced with behavior therapy techniques. Finding Gardner's supporting arguments unconvincing, Halpern recommended an exploration of a variety of rehabilitation technique in order that an answer to the following question might be found: Which technique works best, under what circumstances, and with whom? This point is well taken and of the highest priority for research activity, theoretical discussion, and professional practice.

The practice of counseling and psychotherapy, however, does not facilitate the clinical measurement necessary for empirical assessment of the relative effectiveness of rehabilitation therapies. Moreover, it is doubtful whether counseling psychotherapeutic practices and their attendant research paradigms will be sufficiently refined to permit this type of needed research for quite some time. This will be fully elaborated upon throughout the following discussion, which presents a theoretical estimation of the relative value of the two approaches as rehabilitation tools for the retarded.

More specifically, it is the purpose of the present chapter to explore, from the vantage point of behavior counseling, some of the theoretical issues underlying the assertion by Gardner (1967) and Gardner and Stamm (1971) that better results are obtainable with behavior therapy techniques, in spite of their relative recent use in rehabilitation of the retarded, than by traditional counseling and psychotherapy. In light of the general goal of rehabilitation, the following question is examined: What significant differences in the concepts and practices of the two approaches begin to explain the advantages of the one over the other and shed light on the position that as far as general effectiveness and efficiency is concerned, behavior therapy holds greater potential for rehabilitation practices with the retarded?

In this effort, the major focus is upon behavior therapy—its method, possibilities, and advantages as contrasted with the inherent limitations of psychotherapy. Accordingly, attention is directed to: (1) a comparison of general concepts; (2) a comparison of conceptual and operational utility, with an emphasis on logic, analysis, evaluation and implementation; and (3) a summary of the relative merits of behavior therapy, with an emphasis on three relevant factors variously considered in sections one and two.

DEFINITION AND EXPLANATION OF
PRINCIPAL CONCEPTS

Behavior therapy is designed to change behavior through the systematic application of learning principles, whereas psychotherapy effects behavior change through personality adjustment. What are the general concepts that distinguish the two approaches and begin to suggest the particular relevance of behavior therapy for use with the retarded?

Behavior therapy refers to the systematic and deliberate application of principles and techniques derived from learning theory and related research. As defined by Wolpe (1969, p. 7), behavior therapy is "the use of experimentally established principles of learning for the purpose of changing unadaptive behavior. Unadaptive habits are weakened and eliminated; adaptive habits are initiated and strengthened."

Frequently the terms "behavior modification," "social learning," and "operant conditioning" are used interchangeably with the word behavior therapy. Insofar as all of these concepts have a common foundation, namely, applied behavior science, they are synonymous in usage. The basic tenet of a behavioral science approach is that behavior becomes more effective and efficient through a change in the environmental circumstances of which it is a function. Its major focus is upon influencing an individual to function more efficiently through the manipulation of events controlling his behavior. As stated by Fordyce et al. (1971), from a behavior therapy perspective, "rehabilitation is concerned with increasing the effectiveness of social and vocational performance by improving the rate, precision, and reliability of whatever behaviors are essential to these activities" (p. 29). The therapist, or behavior change agent, is usually a behavioral psychologist. Having been professionally trained in learning theory and applied behavior change techniques, he works directly with clients in the various environments in which behavior is unadaptive. Verbal-oriented techniques are minimized.

In proposing a definition of psychotherapy Bialer (1967) observed that "in synthesizing the views of experts toward that end . . . a simple definition . . . or even a complex one that will meet everyone's criteria . . . is well nigh impossible." However, he went on to state that "it is generally agreed that it refers broadly to effecting behavioral or personality changes through planned psychological, as opposed to medical means" (p. 138). Further, "the chief medium through which the psychological treatment is effected is a close and oftentimes emotional relationship between the subject . . . and the therapist" (p. 139).

The best known and most frequently used psychological treatment is a verbal-based, one-to-one, or in some instances, small group encounters between therapist and client(s). The purpose of this emotive or expressive therapy is to achieve behavior change by facilitating a more adequate personality adjustment.

Personality growth and adjustment implies movement toward maturity, competence, and self-actualization, which in turn requires some measure of achievement of insight, resolution of conflicts, self-acceptance, management of problems, and ego strength. Moreover, Yepsen (1958) reported that promotion of insight is emphasized in the current literature as a major counseling goal for the retarded. In gaining insight, a person becomes aware of where he is in relation to the environments of time, place, and social relations. Increased insight, self-awareness, understanding, and ego functioning become a verbal modification process between two people in which the therapist or counselor seeks to directly change the verbal and, indirectly, the nonverbal behavior of the client. In clinical practice, the therapist is a professionally-trained person, usually a psychiatrist, clinical psychologist, psychiatric social worker, or rehabilitation counselor.

CONCEPTUAL AND OPERATIONAL UTILITY

Inherent in behavior therapy are possibilities for a more refined development of rehabilitation practices with the retarded in the direction of general utility and efficiency. What are the conceptual and operational differences that reveal these potentialities? Obviously, the primary differences dividing the techniques are not found at the level of general purpose; rather, they lie at the level of logic, and generate differences in practice, analysis, evaluation and implementation.

Differences in Logic

From a common sense view, it would seem that behavior therapy's more direct line of influence on unadaptive behaviors via the environments in which they occur would effect more immediate and observable changes. Whereas the behavioral science approach focuses on what an individual does (i.e. behaviors) and the environmental events of which behavior is a function, in traditionally-oriented rehabilitation programs, particularly when psychotherapy and verbal counseling are core processes, emphasis is on intra-individual personality factors. In psychotherapeutic practices, feelings such as anxiety, alienation and self-doubt are seen as barriers to client success, and particular attention is given to the relationship between unadaptive behaviors and the environments in which they occur rather than a person-to-person relationship maintained on a predominately verbal basis. Thus, while psychotherapy and counseling practices tend to be carried out in isolation from the realities of the home, work environment or school, behavior-based therapy takes place in the environment(s) in which behaviors are seen as unadaptive. Behavioral science procedures, moreover, require the behavior change agent to be actively involved with the client on more than a passive verbal basis and in many different environments.

Differences in Analysis, Evaluation, and Implementation

Apart from common sense differences, the practical value of the two approaches is affected by the degree to which they permit the analysis and evaluation of behavior change techniques and facilitate their implementation.

As noted earlier, psychotherapy does not readily lend itself to empirical evaluation. A major requirement in the resolution of this problem is for psychotherapists and counselors to provide precise, i.e. operational and technological, definitions of their functions. Much of what is said and written about psychotherapy and counseling is obscured by mystical vocabulary which thwarts operational definition and hinders communication. Thorsen (1969) has asked some important questions which emphasize this point: "What are the referents (the actual behaviors of clients) of terms such as constructive growth, therapeutic reinforcement, experimental syndrome, and autonomous, genuine and congruently-related activities?" Moreover, one could ask what is meant by "greater insight," "better self-awareness," "therapist-directed insight," or "normal therapy."

Failure to provide unambiguous definitions and descriptions of terms and procedures has made it nearly impossible to glean any useful information necessary for accurate assessment of psychotherapeutic effectiveness and efficiency from most published reports. As observed by Island (1969):

> The nature of the "treatment" is often insufficiently outlined in the reported experiments. Authors and editors, rather than limiting treatment descriptions to a few sentences or labels, should insist on accurate, extensive and detailed treatment descriptions, including observation schedules and check lists of activities (pp. 245-246).

Failure to operationalize terms and concepts has frequently led to the erroneous assumption that one therapeutic treatment equals another and that the procedures and effects are similar across treatment populations. A prime example of this problem is a study by Cooley (1945) in which the relative effectiveness of practices labeled "child guidance," "psychotherapy," and "psychiatric treatment" were used with sixteen retarded and twenty-five bright children. The author reported that "the methods of treatment were so diverse as to elude classification" (p. 38). More-over, "the outcome of therapy *appeared* (italics ours) to be equally successful with the dull group" (p. 38) as it was with the bright. It was concluded that "because the problems listed at referral can be regarded as only symptomatic of the child's *real difficulty*, and symptoms cannot be regarded as an adequate mea-sure of the child's *emotional maladjustment* (italics ours) treat-ment effects were at best nonspecific" (p. 36).

A behavioral science approach to the analysis and change of unadaptive behavior provides several ways of avoiding the prob-lems inherent in traditional counseling and psychotherapy prac-tices through a functionally integrated analytical approach to conceptualization of behavioral development and treatment. There is conceptual parsimony insofar as a minimum number of theoretical statements, which are operationally defined and facilitate empirical verification, are used to account for the de-velopment of both adaptive and unadaptive behaviors. To achieve this, the practice of behavioral therapy is predicated on analytical applications of

> sometimes tentative principles of behavior to the improvement of specific behaviors, and simultaneously evaluating whether or not any changes noted are indeed attributable to the process of applica-tion—and if so, to what part of the process. In short, analytical be-havioral application is a self-examining, self-evaluating discovery-oriented procedure for studying behavior (Baer, Wolf and Risley, 1968, p. 91).

The behavioral emphasis is extremely important. The thera-pist or counselor using behavior therapy must empirically and pragmatically answer the question: How can I help the client *do* something more, or less, frequently and more efficiently? The treatment focus is the client's behavior, i.e. what he can be in-fluenced to do rather than say, unless, of course, a verbal re-sponse is the desired behavior to be changed. "Accordingly, a cli-ent's verbal description of his own nonverbal behavior would not be accepted as a measure of his actual behavior unless it were independently substantiated" (Baer, Wolf and Risley, 1968, p. 93).

This is in direct contrast to much of the traditional rehabilitation counseling and psychotherapy, in which most of the treatment remains at a verbal level. This practice rests on the tenuous assumption, which is eschewed in behavior therapy, that changed verbal behavior will change actual overt behavior. To illustrate:

> If psychotherapy results in changes in verbal behavior from "I do not like to work and will not cooperate with my supervisor" to "I like to work and will cooperate with my supervisor because I can get along better if I do so," it is assumed that there will be a change in work and work-related behaviors. The verbal behavior will gain control over and give direction to other overt (nonverbal) behaviors in other settings (Gardner and Stamm, 1971, p. 47).

Closely related to the behavioral emphasis, is the emphasis on pragmatics. That is, the model requires that unadaptive behaviors be analyzed into functionally-related hierarchies and dealt with clinically one at a time. Thus, instead of dealing with undifferentiated entities such as "greater self-understanding," or "better identity as a worker," their behavioral referents are determined. Once determined, they are dealt with successively until an appropriate adaptive level is reached. As Bijou (1966) observed, instead of trying to change and/or reorganize part of, or a whole, personality, or a hypothetical (i.e. no direct behavioral referents) dimension of personality, it is much more advantageous to deal with specific (i.e. less global) behaviors which are more easily managed clinically.

Behavioral specification facilitates clinical measurement necessary for empirical evaluation of the relative effectiveness of rehabilitation therapies. Samler (1966), commenting on the shortcomings of psychotherapy in this area, observed that "the nature of the counselor-client interaction is by no means clear, and the reasons for client change, when change occurs at all, are not really known" (p. 1). This state of affairs reflects the absence of a therapeutic model which incorporates effective measurement parameters. Conceptualization of human behavior (i.e. personality) in abstract terms tends to preclude the efficient development of "sound generalizations and firm principles through the arduous labor of digging, of systematic observation and data gathering," as Samler has further remarked. "We have not yet done this with respect to human personality" (Samler, 1966, p. 1).

The behavioral therapy model is also analytic. That is, to achieve a rehabilitation objective, the therapist or counselor must carefully analyze the events and conditions of which the retardate's unadaptive behavior is a function. A functional analysis of behavior, from a clinical perspective, obtains when the treatment agent can pinpoint and control (i.e. differentially influence) behaviors in question. Failure to achieve control, therefore, indicates that, analytically and functionally, therapy is not successful. If a functional analysis is achieved, behavioral therapy then lends itself to technological description.

Technological description "means simply that the techniques making a particular behavioral application are completely identified and described" (Baer, Wolf and Risley, 1968, p. 95). Descriptions of treatment such as "child guidance," "psychiatric treatment," and "psychotherapy," as well as descriptors such as social reinforcement and reality therapy, are not technological descriptions of treatment; neither is insight interpretation of the client's dreams. Technological description is achieved when any reasonably well-trained therapist can, in the treatment procedure, engage in the same behaviors, manipulate similar classes of variables, and achieve the same or similar results as the original therapist. For example, the following description of a therapy practice would be technological, and the procedure replicable. The client was given token reinforcers in the form of check marks on a card, on a fixed-interval twenty minute schedule, contingent upon continuous, active involvement with his job and product production. Tokens were redeemed for a variety of manipulative objects (razors, magazines, newspapers, books) at the end of each day.

If one is to empirically determine what treatment procedures are the most effective, under what conditions this obtains, and what behavioral repertoires of the subject differentially interact with both procedures and conditions, then a new research paradigm must be used in rehabilitation therapy. For the most part, research in counseling and psychotherapy has evaded applied behavioral analysis procedures (i.e. well controlled and systematic observation and manipulation of behavior) (Thorsen, 1969). The results have been deleterious in that descriptive studies abound which do not report the controlled systematic observation of individual behavior. Such studies merely describe loosely such things as group means and correlations of test responses on questionnaires.

Clearly, a different research paradigm needs to be employed in order to assess the effects of counseling and psychotherapy. The most promising paradigm and one that is both conceptually and operationally an integral part of the behavior therapy model, is predicated on Skinner's (1953) empirical case study (cf. Ulrich, Stachnik and Morby, 1966, 1970). This paradigm is built around the controlled, systematic observation and manipulation of specific behaviors of a single client. Island (1969) has observed that such research would "focus primary attention on the behavior of individuals, baseline, treatment and followup performance, and . . . move away from the increasingly limited value of designs requiring large N's concerned only with mean differences" (p. 247). Conceptually, then, therapy practices in the rehabilitation of the retarded would transfer a body of technology into a discipline rather than a "bag of tricks."

RELATIVE MERITS OF BEHAVIOR THERAPY

Having underlined the significant differences in the principal concepts and practices of the two approaches, we may proceed to examine in more detail three factors which suggest that behavior therapy may be a more appropriate alternative with the retarded than verbal-based, one-to-one counseling and psychotherapy. These factors are: (1) the nature of retardation and the requirements of psychotherapy; (2) the nature of psychotherapy and the lack of definitive information on its effectiveness; and (3) the parsimony of the behavior therapy model for rehabilitation practice and research.

Requirements of Psychotherapy

Mental retardation is defined chiefly in terms of language impairment. The language development of mildly (IQ = 65-80) and moderately (IQ = 50-65) retarded persons may be characterized as stereotyped as opposed to functionally differentiated and complex. In other words, the retarded do not reach a functionally adequate linguistic or conceptual level. In exploring the functional role language plays in controlling the behavior of the retarded, Luria (1963) observed that a verbal "signal system" activated by present experiences permits previous experiences to generalize to the present, but that retarded individuals do not use language effectively and efficiently in mediating learning experiences.

Results of verbal learning research with the retarded also document a language deficit at all levels of retardation (e.g. Griffith and Spitz in Ellis, 1958; Borokowsky and Johnson, 1968; Penny, Seim, and Peters, 1968; Prehm, 1966). In reviewing this literature, Gardner and Stamm (1971) concluded:

> This research indicates that the retarded when confronted with . . . verbal learning tasks, do not spontaneously generate effective verbal mediators, nor when provided, use them appropriately in associating stimulus and response items. This suggests that their intraverbal behaviors (thinking or verbal associations) are relatively ineffective. That is, appropriate associations are absent or distorted. To the degree that this is true, the acquisition of "insight" (e.g., verbal understanding or description of co-relationships between behavioral histories and contemporaneous events), which is deemed crucial in psychotherapy, is limited, and the possible control of verbal behavior over classes of nonverbal behavior is greatly reduced. More studies are needed that systematically investigate the degree to which verbal response classes of the retarded may be differentially conditioned and the degree to which these response classes, acquired independently of a discriminative association over nonverbal behavior, may in turn exercise control over nonverbal behavior (p. 49).

A study was conducted by Dubros (1966) in which he attempted to modify the unadaptive verbal and motor behavior of retarded subjects through systematic shaping of language behavior. This was achieved by reinforcing positively with praise a class of verbal responses supporting appropriate social norms which were emitted during therapy sessions. These included, for example, statements indicating the necessity to be friendly toward others so one will have friends. It was assumed that the

newly acquired and strengthened verbal behaviors would function as discriminative stimuli to control behavior outside the
therapy environment. Two case studies were reported (CA 12
and 13, IQ 75 and 81 respectively) in which problems of inferiority, low self-esteem and social aggressiveness were dealt with.
The results, depicted in part in behavioral graphs, are at best
equivocal. First, the data clearly indicate major changes in the
clients' behavior during the baseline (pre-treatment) period.
Second, the author reported clinical observations indicating that
the discriminative function of the verbal behavior was not
maintained outside the therapy situation. It was suggested that
the clients needed additional help in behaving appropriately outside the therapy situation.

Brodsky (1967) reported a study whose purpose was to evaluate changes in nonverbal behavior resulting from changes in
verbal behavior, and changes in verbal behavior produced by
changes in nonverbal behavior. Two mildly retarded young
adults (CA 17 and 25) were given direct social reinforcement
for appropriate verbal and nonverbal social behavior in playground and clinical settings. In the playground situation, the
subjects were reinforced for social contact (i.e. cooperative
play) with their peers. In the clinical setting, subjects were reinforced for interacting socially with highly social mongoloids,
and for appropriate social response to a list of fifteen questions.
Baseline (i.e. pre-treatment) data indicated that both subjects
had low rates of both verbal and nonverbal social behavior. Results failed to support the assumed positive relationship between
changes in verbal and nonverbal behavior, i.e. that reinforcement for social behavior (as opposed to pro-social statements)
in a clinical setting leads to higher rates of pro-social behavior
on the playground. Modification of social statements had little
effect on pro-social behavior.

Considering the importance placed on language in verbal-
based counseling and psychotherapy, with its attendant emphasis
on verbally mediated conceptual behavior such as insight, self-
understanding and self-awareness, together with the inability to
directly change a retardate's nonverbal behavior by changing
verbal behavior, traditional psychotherapy may not be the treat-

ment of choice with most retarded. There is no reason to believe that this conclusion would be any different for individuals whose retarded behavior is "psychogenic" in origin (e.g. Halpern, 1968). Psychogenic retardation reflects a functional language disability also, rendering the traditional goals of counseling and psychotherapy difficult to achieve.

Lack of Empirical Data

It has been correctly observed that it would seem reasonable to "look at the literature . . . focused directly upon the process of psychotherapy with the . . . retarded . . . to arrive at an empirical estimate of its effectiveness . . ." (Halpern, 1968, p. 49). However, the extant literature on this specific subject, when closely reviewed, provides little, if any, definitive information on whether psychotherapy with the retarded is effective and, if so, what variables account for the success (e.g. Chidester, 1934; Cooley, 1945; Heiser, 1954; Sion, 1953; Wegman, 1943).

Reported studies frequently do not fully delineate the treatment used. In reference to studies by Cooley (1945) and Heiser (1954), for example, treatments were described by Cooley as "psychotherapy," "child guidance," and "psychiatric treatment" and, by Heiser, as "warm, sympathetic interest by the therapist which helped the patient gain rational insight into the present situation and possible future." The results of these therapeutic efforts are equally vague: Heiser reported that "therapist attention improved the client's ego development" (p. 22), while Cooley (1945) reported that the treatment effects were indeterminate "because the problems as listed at referral can be regarded as only symptomatic of the child's real difficulty, and symptoms cannot be regarded as an adequate measure of the child's emotional maladjustment . . ." (p. 36). Other reports of psychotherapy with the retarded are equally vague. As Sternlicht (1966) observed in concluding his review of individual and group psychotherapy procedures with the retarded, "Therapeutic work in this field . . . lacks a sufficient theoretical and empirical basis. . . . A major shortcoming is efficient research dealing with outcomes . . . the review of research . . . pointed out the need for greater clarification of terms" (p. 349).

This, in part, is a function of the fact that counselors and clinicians have, "for too long, settled for apparent insight as the criterion for success, with little or no concern for the behavior of the patient outside of, or following therapy. Perhaps most significant, the complexity of abstractions, and their vague implications for therapeutic treatment takes the form of crude judgments based on the modification of hypothetical dynamics (Carkhuff and Berenson, 1967, p. 87).

SUMMARY

Thus, having only vague descriptions of psychotherapy techniques, along with indeterminate results, it is difficult, if not impossible, to delineate what "processes" produce what behavioral changes, under what conditions, with what types of clients. Given that there is little or no research which unambiguously delineates what constitutes effective counseling and psychotherapy procedures with the retarded, and that the basic language deficit of the retarded makes a verbal-based rehabilitation therapy a dubious procedure, a behavior therapy approach appears to be a more viable treatment of choice. It is predicated on a behavioral science model which requires a systematic evaluation of specific treatment practices. Thus, a more direct assessment of the relative effectiveness and efficiency of rehabilitation therapy can be achieved. In addition, therapy is not isolated to a clinical hour but extended into environments where unadaptive behavior occurs, thus facilitating the generalization and maintenance of adaptive behavior outside the therapy environment.

REFERENCES

Ayers, E., and Duguay, R.: Critical variables in counseling the mentally retarded. *Rehabilitation Literature, 30:*2, 42-45, 50, 1969.

Baer, D. M.; Wolf, M.; and Risley, T. R.: Some current dimensions of applied behavior analysis. *Journal of Applied Behavior Analysis, 1:*91-97, 1968.

Bialer, I.: Psychotherapy and other adjustment techniques with the mentally retarded. In Baumeister, A. A. (Ed.): *Mental Retardation: Appraisal, Education and Rehabilitation.* Chicago, Aldine, 1967.

Bijou, S. W.: Implications of behavioral science for counseling and guidance. In Krumboltz, J. D. (Ed.): *Revolution in Counseling.* Boston, Houghton Mifflin, 1966.

Borokowsky, J. S., and Johnson, L. O.: Mediation and the paired-associate learning of normals and retardates. *American Journal of Mental Deficiency*, 72:610-613, 1968.

Brodsky, G.: The relation between verbal and nonverbal behavior change. *Behavior Research and Therapy*, 5:183-191, 1967.

Carkhuff, R. R., and Berenson, B. G.: *Beyond Counseling and Therapy.* New York, Holt, Rinehart and Winston, 1967.

Chidester, L.: Therapeutic results with mentally retarded children. *American Journal of Orthopsychiatry*, 4:464-472, 1934.

Cooley, J. M.: The relative ameriability of dull and bright children to child guidance. *Smith College Studies in Social Work, 16:26-43*, 1945.

Dubros, S. G.: Behavior therapy with high-level, institutionalized retarded children. *Exceptional Children, 34:229-233*, 1966.

Fordyce, W. E.; Sand, P. L.; Frieschman, R. B.; and Foliver, K. S., Jr.: Behavior systems analyzed. *Journal of Rehabilitation*, March-April:29-31, 1971.

Gardner, J. M.: The behavior modification model. *Mental Retardation, 6:* 51-53, 1968.

Gardner, W. I.: What should be the psychologist's role? *Mental Retardation, 5:29-31*, 1967.

Gardner, W. I., and Stamm, J. M.: Counseling the mentally retarded: A behavioral approach. *Rehabilitation Counseling Bulletin, 15:46-57*, 1971.

Griffith, B. C., and Spitz, H. H.: Some relationships between abstraction and word meaning in retarded adolescents. *American Journal of Mental Deficiency, 63:247-251*, 1958.

Halpern, A. S.: Why not psychotherapy? *Mental Retardation, 6:48-50*, 1968.

Heber, R. (Ed.): *Vocational Rehabilitation of the Mentally Retarded.* Proceedings of a conference sponsored by the University of Wisconsin, Madison and supported by the Vocational Rehabilitation Administration of the U. S. Department of Health, Education, and Welfare, 1963. Rehabilitation Service Series No. 65-16.

Heiser, K. F.: Psychotherapy in a residential school for the mentally retarded. *Training School Bulletin, 50:211-218*, 1954.

Island, D. D.: Counseling students with special problems. *Review of Educational Research, 39:263-281*, 1969.

Luria, A. R.: Dynamic approach to the mental development of the abnormal child. In N. R. Ellis (Ed.), *Handbook of Mental Deficiency.* New York: McGraw-Hill Book Co., 1963, pp. 353-387.

Penny, K. R.; Seim, R.; and Peters, R.: The mediational deficiency of mentally retarded children: I. The establishment of the retardate's mediational deficiency. *American Journal of Mental Deficiency, 77:626-630*, 1968.

Prehm, II. J.: Verbal learning research in mental retardation. *American Journal of Mental Deficiency, 71*:42-47, 1966.

Samler, J.: The counselor in our time. In Wright, G. N. (Ed.): *Madison Lectures on Vocational Rehabilitation.* Madison, University of Wisconsin, 1966.

Sion, A.: Casework with an adolescent boy of moron intelligence. *American Journal of Mental Deficiency, 57*:709-718, 1953.

Skinner, B. F.: *Science and Human Behavior.* New York, Free Press, 1953.

Sternlicht, M.: Psychotherapeutic procedures with the retarded. In Ellis, N. R. (Ed.): *International Review of Research in Mental Retardation,* New York, Academic Press, 1966, vol. 2.

Thorsen, C. E.: Relevance and research in counseling. *Review of Educational Research, 39*:263-281, 1969.

Ulrich, R. E.; Stachnick, T.; and Mobry, J.: *Control of Human Behavior,* New York, Scott-Forsman, 1970, vol. II.

Wegman, B. S.: Intelligence as a factor in the treatment of problem children. *Smith College Studies in Social Work, 14*:244-245, 1943.

Wolpe, J.: *The Practice of Behavior Therapy.* New York, Pergamon Press, 1969.

Yepsen, L. N.: Counseling the mentally retarded. In DiMichael, S. G. (Ed.): *Vocational Rehabilitation of the Mentally Retarded.* U. S. Department of Health, Education and Welfare, Office of Vocational Rehabilitation, U. S. Government Printing Office, 1958.

Chapter 15

OUTCOME STUDIES ON COUNSELING WITH THE RETARDED: A METHODOLOGICAL CRITIQUE

PHILIP L. BROWNING
MERLE KEESEY

MOST RESEARCH IN COUNSELING and/or psychotherapy can be characterized as process or outcome research. This latter type of study has dominated research efforts in counseling the retarded. These outcome studies raise the general research question: "Is counseling effective with the retarded?" Investigators are interested in changes in the retarded client's behavior and/or personality that are the result of counseling intervention.

Attempts have been made, naturally, to interpret the reported findings of these studies within the context of the efficacy of specific treatment approaches with the mentally retarded. However, to interpret the findings without evaluating the research methodology is to ignore a crucial aspect of the validity of these results. While research problems encountered by these studies have been recognized (Cowen and Trippe, 1963; Robinson and Robinson, 1965; Sternlicht, 1966, and Bialer, 1967) only limited attention has been devoted to research design.

The intent of this chapter was to investigate the methodological validity of a select number of experimental-control group studies in counseling the retarded. More specifically, the purpose was: (1) to critically and systematically analyze the research designs employed in the studies, and (2) discuss within the context of counseling outcome investigations, eight potential "confounding" variables which may account for research findings.

PROCEDURES
Sample

The three criteria used in the selection of the studies reviewed were: (1) they pertained to counseling and psychotherapy with the retarded, (2) the research was experimental, and (3) a control group(s) was included in the research design. An annotated bibliography (Butler, 1970) comprised of 129 articles on counseling and psychotherapy with the mentally retarded was used as the single source for obtaining the studies incorporated in this paper. The bibliography contained a total of seven studies which met the three criteria and thus constituted the sample (Mehlman, 1953; O'Conner and Yonge, 1955; Wilcox and Guthrie, 1957; Albini and Dinitz, 1957; Snyder and Sechrest, 1959; Gorlow, Butler and Einig, 1963; and Humes, Adamczyk and Myco, 1969).

These studies are relatively heterogeneous in terms of counseling approach, retarded age and IQ, and quality of research design. Even though they were not randomly selected, the authors are of the opinion that these seven studies are representative of the population of experimental-control group investigations dealing with the efficacy of psychotherapeutic techniques with the retarded.

Methodology

Campbell and Stanley (1963) have identified eight types of potential confounding variables in experimental studies. These sources of "internal invalidity" have been considered appropriate for evaluating the adequacy of research designs employed in outcome studies on counseling and psychotherapy (Goldstein, Heller and Sechrest, 1966), and were used in this paper for critiquing the research designs of the seven studies.

Each of the seven studies were individually rated according to how well they controlled for eight sources of internal invalidity, i.e. history, maturation, test reaction, instrumentation, statistical regression, selection, mortality, and interaction between selection and maturation. In essence, these are sources of variance which, if left uncontrolled, could account for the results obtained in the study. The nature of each of these potential sources of outcome variance will be covered in the discussion section.

The rating values were based on the following code signs: + (adequately controlled); − (inadequately controlled); and ? (the control is marginal or questionable). The two authors independently evaluated each study on each criterion using the sign values. The sign data was then compared to determine areas of agreement and disagreement. Extended discussion occurred where there was disagreement between the two raters until a consensus was reached as to the appropriate sign value. The ? code sign was primarily used when the article was lacking in information needed in order to make a judgment.

RESULTS

The results of this critical comparative analysis of experimental-control group studies on counseling the mentally retarded are reported in Table 15-I. The reader will note considerable diversity between the seven studies regarding the quality of the research design. For example, in study #1 a research design was utilized which failed to control for seven of the eight sources of variance; whereas, the design employed in study #7 controlled for all eight of the potentially confounding variables. The actual sources of internal invalidity also varied among the studies. For example, the research design used in study #4 con-

TABLE 15-I

AN ANALYSIS OF INTERNAL INVALIDITY SOURCES FOR SEVEN
STUDIES ON COUNSELING THE RETARDED

Studies*	History	Maturation	Test Reaction	Instrumentation	Statistical Regression	Selection	Mortality	Interaction	
1	−	−	−	−	−	−	+	−	7†
2	−	+	+	−	+	+	−	+	3
3	?	+	+	−	+	+	+	+	2
4	+	+	+	+	+	−	+	−	2
5	−	+	?	?	+	+	+	+	1
6	+	?	+	+	+	?	+	?	0
7	+	+	+	+	+	+	+	+	0
	3‡	1	1	3	1	2	1	2	

* The authors felt that the identification of the studies would be of no additional use for the purpose of this paper.

† The research design employed in study #1 inadequately controlled for seven of the eight sources of internal invalidity.

‡ Three of the seven studies inadequately controlled for *history* as a source of internal invalidity.

trolled for history but not selection; whereas, the design employed in study #5 controlled for selection but not history.

In summary, six of the seven studies yielded results which could be attributed to variables other than counseling. Consequently, it is impossible to empirically demonstrate from them the efficacy of counseling with the mentally retarded.

DISCUSSION

The remainder of this section is devoted to discussing eight types of confounding variables which can serve as plausible explanations for the research results if they are not controlled for in the design of the study.

History

The first of the possible rival hypotheses or confounding sources to be discussed is *history*. History refers to *events* which are external to the treatment (e.g. pay raise, break in routine), occur during the time period of the treatment, and which may give rise to changes in experimental outcomes. The longer the interval between observations before and after treatment, the more history becomes a plausible rival explanation for recorded change in outcome measures. Studies in counseling have been particularly prone to this source of internal invalidity, especially when they have failed to employ a "true" control group in the design.

The ideal research design to control for this confounding variable is one in which the control Ss have the identical experiences the experimental Ss have throughout the experimental process—except for the treatment influence. As an example, institutional Ss who are provided counseling may simply experience a pleasant break in institutional routine living. Thus, in order to evaluate possible change due to this extra-counseling experience rather than the defined treatment variable, the control group should also receive activities which include pleasant breaks in routine.

Three of the seven studies utilized an "ignored" control group in the design of their study and thus failed to adequately control for history. By contrast, the investigators of another study employed as their control groups a placebo and a no-treatment or "ignored" group. The Ss in the placebo group were told that they had been especially selected for participation in a study and were asked to attend some meetings. During the meetings, an attempt was made to provide them the feeling that someone was interested in them and that they were involved in something that was different from their usual institutional routine. In addition, they were permitted to talk about the same things which were discussed in the experimental or therapy groups. With the design of this study, which adequately controlled for history, the significant changes in the experimental Ss's behavior could not be ascribed to novel experiences in routine schedules.

In summary, to adequately control for *history*, a control group should have identical experiences during the course of the experiment except for the occurrence of the critical variable, i.e. counseling or psychotherapy. The investigator can best be assured of eliminating history as a rival hypothesis by: (1) randomly selecting and assigning Ss to the experimental and control groups, and (2) employing at least one "true" control group in the design of the study.

Maturation

The second factor to be considered regarding the validity of an experimental finding is *maturation*. This term refers to those events specific to the individual that may occur over time and are not related to external events. More specifically, changes in behavior over time may be ascribed to internal psychological or biological processes, such as growing older or more tired or bored. Goldstein et al. (1966) have noted that research on psychotherapy with adolescents may provide an example of maturational processes operating as an alternative hypothesis to psychotherapeutic effect. Adolescence is a period in which the individual may be extremely sensitive and lacking in self-confidence. Any therapy experience instituted at this time may have effects attributed to it that would have occurred "naturally" as the subjects approached adulthood.

The study, which failed to control for this source of internal invalidity, used retarded youngsters aged between seven and fifteen years. The experimental *Ss* had behavioral problems; where-as, the comparison *Ss* were free of maladjusted behaviors. In this case, the investigator's design did not justify canceling out maturation as a plausible rival hypothesis to explain changes in behavior for the therapy groups.

Goldstein et al. (1966), indicate that if a control group is to have any meaning at all, opportunities for change must be equal for both treated and untreated groups. In reference to con-trolling maturation as a potential confounding variable, experi-mental and control groups must be equated on *Ss* variables, e.g. age, behavioral problems, etc. This can best be accomplished by randomly selecting *Ss* from the "same" population and then randomly assigning them to the experimental and control groups.

Test Reactivity

A third alternative explanation as the possible cause of change which must be controlled for in experimentation is the effect of *testing*. When subjects take tests, the effect of the tests them-selves may be a stimulus to behavior change. This may vary from a simple practice effect on a pretest to a situation where the test is a stimulus to wider psychological change. Measures differ as to their reactivity, i.e. their potential for instigating change. Atti-tude scales are particularly prone to this criticism.

In one of the studies, the investigators used an adaptation of an acceptance-rejection attitude scale given verbally to each sub-ject. Had there been any changes in the retarded boys' attitudes toward their parents noted on this scale, it could have been at-tributed to the effect of testing rather than to the therapeutic process. By contrast, the authors of another study made use of relatively unobtrusive, non-reactive measures of behavior, there-by controlling for the effect of *testing*. Routine housing reports on each individual submitted by the ward charge every four months was one source of information on the *Ss's* behavior. This housing report covered thirty-one items under "Conduct Characteristics" and thirty-six items under "Personal Characteris-tics." The other source was a record of more serious violations of conduct which were submitted to a behavior court who decid-

ed on disciplinary measures. These investigators were primarily
interested in behavioral adjustment to institutional routine. It
would be more difficult to design non-reactive measures of changes in self-attitudes or basic changes in personality.

It is preferable to use nonobtrusive (or non-reactive) measures when studying behavior (Webb, Campbell, Scartz and
Sechrest, 1966). If this is not possible or feasible, two alternatives are available: (1) a control group can be pre and post-
tested to estimate the effects of testing, or (2) pretesting can be
eliminated for both groups on the assumption that random assignment to control and experimental groups has resulted in
groups equal on relevant variables.

Instrumentation

Another factor which must be controlled for is called *instrumentation*. This term refers to changes in the measuring instrument which might account for a difference in behavior over
the course of the experiment. When human observers are used
to record behavior, they may become more expert or less vigilant
as time progresses. Another common situation which may arise
is that the observers may become aware of the nature of the experiment, i.e. who is assigned to the experimental and control
groups. Other research has clearly shown the effects of experi-
menter bias on outcomes. While the first two problems can be
controlled for by the use of a control group, observer knowledge
of the nature of the experiment cannot.

In one of the studies, change after therapy was measured by
a behavioral rating form which was filled out by matrons and attendants who were with the Ss throughout the duration of the
study. It was presumed by the investigators that the raters knew
which Ss were receiving therapy and which were not. In this
case, it is not possible to rule out instrumentation as an alternative hypothesis to psychotherapy as being an agent of change.

When behavioral ratings are used as a measure of change, and
these measures are collected unobtrusively, many of the objections against those studies employing *reactive* measures do not
hold. This is not to say, however, that there must be a tradeoff

between testing as a source of internal invalidity and *instrumentation.* Samples of behavior can be taken by trained observers who are not involved in the lives of the *S*s and do not know which subjects are under which experimental condition. If this is done then a study cannot be faulted on *testing* or *instrumentation.*

Statistical Regression

At the risk of simplifying too much, *statistical regression* can be explained by referring to "chance." A subject's score on a test is composed of a theoretical "true" score plus an error or chance factor. If the *S* scores extremely low on a test, the probability is that whatever chance factors were operating that contributed to his low score will not occur again in that particular combination on a subsequent testing and the probability is that his score will go up slightly. The same effect occurs on the other end of the continuum. This effect is not due to test-retest practice effect or any effect of the treatment. When subjects are selected because of their low scores on some instrument, given an experimental treatment, and take the test again, their scores may go up, but not because of treatment effect.

Although there were no significant results in this series of studies which could be attributed to the statistical regression phenomenon, there is an example of a failure to control for this effect in an initial experimental design. The authors of this study selected subjects because of their high incidence of negative behaviors. These experimental subjects were observed before and after therapy. Because of the lack of an equivalent control group, any differences that might have been observed could have been attributed to the effect of statistical regression.

In order to best control for this potential confounding variable, the investigator should attempt to have equivalent groups, i.e. experimental and control. Regression effects should then occur in all groups.

Selection

The sixth factor contributing to the internal invalidity of experiments is *selection.* Biases can result from the differential selection of subjects for comparison groups. As was stated earlier, the major assumption underlying the use of a control group is that the two groups are alike as possible on all variables relevant to the study in question, and proceed to stay the same except that the experimental group has some kind of treatment and the control group(s) does not.

A glaring example of selection bias was the study which was comprised of non-equivalent groups. In this case, the experimental Ss were identified as having behavioral problems whereas the control Ss were considered to be free of maladjusted behaviors. One of the studies which did control for *selection* proceeded by matching Ss in triplet on the basis of the number of negative comments on their last housing report. They were then randomly assigned to one of three conditions.

Some investigators have attempted to obtain equal groups by using the matching procedure alone; however, it is impossible to match on all relevant variables. Consequently, more researchers are coming to be in agreement with Campbell and Stanley (1963) that the only way to have equivalent groups is to randomly assign a sufficient number of subjects to conditions.

Mortality

This source of variance is a common problem affecting research that requires an extended period of time for completion. The term refers to the differential loss of Ss from experimental and control groups. As a factor influencing internal validity of an experiment, it is unlike most of the others in that it is almost impossible to control.

One study began with 150 Ss which were divided into twelve therapy and three control groups. Before the study terminated, thirty-six Ss were dropped, twenty-three from the therapy groups and thirteen from the control groups. This experiment essentially lost one half of its control group before the completion of the study. In another investigation, forty-five Ss finished the study which began with fifty-four Ss divided into three equal groups. The dropout rate was comparable over the three groups. It is possible that this mortality might have affected the results, but the number was equal by groups and not excessive.

As Goldstein et al. (1966) indicate, "In psychotherapy evaluations, mortality during the course of an experiment may be a serious problem and may operate either to enhance or detract from estimates of the effectiveness of the treatment" (p. 22). A final resort is for the investigator to compare the input characteristics of dropouts from both groups. This information can possibly provide some estimate of the impact of mortality.

Interaction Between Selection and Maturation

The final source of internal invalidity to explain experimental control group differences is the occurrence of an *interaction* between *selection* and *maturation*. This kind of interaction may occur when experimental and control groups do not have pre-experimental sampling equivalence. This may be because the subjects were not assigned randomly to the experimental or control groups. In this situation, selection may result in groups who are likely to react differently to the effects of maturation.

The best example of a failure to eliminate this rival hypothesis was a study in which thirty-seven behaviorally disturbed *Ss*, seven to fifteen years of age, received treatment, whereas, thirty-six *Ss* rated free from behavioral problems were selected as a comparison group. It is quite likely that the experimental group, because of the selection process, was more likely to show effects of *maturation* and this interaction could have been mistaken for the effect of the therapeutic treatment.

SUMMARY

Most research investigations on counseling and psychotherapy with the mentally retarded can be characterized as outcome studies. However, there are relatively few of these experimental studies which include control groups as a part of the research design.

The seven studies included in the sample were considered representative of the population of experimental-control group investigations on counseling the retarded. Each study was critically analyzed in terms of eight potential sources of internal invalidity. Only one of the seven studies had an adequate enough research design to control for each of these confounding sources.

Consequently, one could not safely attribute change in retarded clients due to counseling for six of the seven studies. Finally, the nature of each source of internal invalidity was discussed.

REFERENCES

Albini, J. L., and Dinitz, S.: Psychotherapy with disturbed and defective children: An evaluation of changes in behavior and attitudes. *American Journal of Mental Deficiency, 69*:560-567, 1965.

Bialer, I.: Psychotherapy and other adjustment techniques. In Baumeister, A. A. (Ed.): *Mental Retardation: Appraisal, Education, Rehabilitation.* Chicago, Aldine Publishing Company, 1967, pp. 138-180.

Butler, A.: Annotated bibliography on counseling the mentally retarded (Unpublished), Department of Studies in Behavioral Disabilities, University of Wisconsin, Madison, 1970.

Campbell, D. T., and Stanley, J. C.: *Experimental and Quasi-experimental Designs for Research.* Chicago, Rand McNally and Company, 1963.

Cowen, E. L., and Trippe, M. J.: Psychotherapy and play techniques with the exceptional child and youth. In Cruickshank, W. M. (Ed.): *Psychology of Exceptional Children and Youth.* Englewood Cliffs, N. J., Prentice-Hall, Inc., 1963, pp. 526-591.

Goldstein, A. P.; Heller, K.; and Sechrest, L. B.: *Psychotherapy and Psychology of Behavior Change.* New York, John Wiley and Sons, Inc., 1966.

Gorlow, L.; Butler, A.; Einig, K. G.; and Smith, J. A.: An appraisal of self-attitudes and behavior following group psychotherapy with retarded young adults. *American Journal of Mental Deficiency, 67*:893-898, 1963.

Humes, C.; Adamczyk, J.; and Myco, R.: A school study of group counseling with educable retarded adolescents. *American Journal of Mental Deficiency, 74*(2):191-195, 1969.

Mehlman, B.: Group play therapy with mentally retarded children. *Journal of Abnormal and Social Psychology, 48*:53-60, 1953.

O'Conner, N., and Yonge, K. A.: Methods of evaluating the group psychotherapy of unstable defective delinquents. *Journal of Genetic Psychology, 87*:191-201, 1955.

Robinson, H. B., and Robinson, N. M.: *The Mentally Retarded Child: A Psychological Approach.* New York, McGraw-Hill Book Company, 1965.

Snyder, R., and Sechrest, L.: An experimental study of directive group therapy with defective delinquents. *American Journal of Mental Deficiency, 64*:117-123, 1959.

Sternlicht, M.: Psychotherapy procedures with the mentally retarded. In

Ellis, N. R. (Ed.): *International Review of Research in Mental Retardation.* New York, Academic Press, 1966, pp. 279-354.

Webb, E.; Campbell, D. T.; Schwartz, R. J.; and Sechrest, L.: *Resourceful Measurement: Cooperation-free, Non-reactive Measures in Social Science.* Chicago, Rand-McNally, 1966.

Wilcox, G. T., and Guthrie, G. M.: Changes in adjustment of institutionalized female defectives following group psychotherapy. *Journal of Clinical Psychology, 13:*9-13, 1957.

Appendix A

BASIC READINGS ON MENTAL RETARDATION

Baumeister, A. A. (Ed.): *Mental Retardation: Appraisal, Education, and Rehabilitation.* Chicago, Illinois, Aldine Publishing Company, 1967.

Clarke, A. M., and Clarke, A. B. (Eds.): *Mental Deficiency: The Changing Outlook.* New York, The Free Press, 1965.

Dybwad, G.: *Challenges in Mental Retardation.* New York, Columbia University Press, 1964.

Ellis, N. R. (Ed.): *Handbook of Mental Deficiency: Psychological Theory and Practice.* New York, McGraw-Hill Book Company, 1963.

Ellis, N. R. (Ed.): *International Review of Research in Mental Retardation.* New York, Academic Press, 1966, vol. 1.

Ellis, N. R. (Ed.): *International Review of Research in Mental Retardation.* New York, Academic Press, 1966, vol. 2.

Ellis, N. R. (Ed.): *International Review of Research in Mental Retardation.* New York, Academic Press, 1968, vol. 3.

Ellis, N. R. (Ed.): *International Review of Research in Mental Retardation.* New York, Academic Press, 1970, vol. 4.

Ellis, N. R. (Ed.): *International Review of Research in Mental Retardation.* New York, Academic Press, 1971, vol. 5.

Ellis, N. R. (Ed.): *International Review of Research in Mental Retardation.* New York, Academic Press, 1973, vol. 6.

Flanigan, P. J.; Baker, G. R.; and LaFollette, L. G.: *An Orientation to Mental Retardation: A Programmed Text.* Springfield, Ill., Charles C Thomas, 1970.

Farber, B.: *Mental Retardation: Its Social Context and Social Consequences.* Boston, Houghton Mifflin Company, 1968.

Grossman, H. J. (Ed.): *Manual on Terminology and Classification in Mental Retardation,* 1973 revision. American Association on Mental Deficiency, Special Publication Series, No. 2, 1973.

Heber, R. (Ed.): *A Manual on Terminology and Classification in Mental Retardation,* 2nd ed. American Association on Mental Deficiency, Monograph Supplement to the *American Journal of Mental Deficiency,* 1961.

Hutt, M. L., and Gibby, R. G.: *The Mentally Retarded Child: Development, Education and Treatment.* Boston, Allyn and Bacon, Inc., 1965.

Jordon, T. E.: *The Mentally Retarded.* Columbus, Ohio, Charles E. Merrill Books, Inc., 1961.

McGovern, K. B., and Browning, P. B. (Eds.): *Mental Retardation and the Future.* University of Oregon, Rehabilitation Research and Training Center in Mental Retardation, Monograph No. 5, 1972.

Masland, R. L.; Sarason, S. B.; and Gladwin, T.: *Mental Subnormality: Bio-*

logical, Psychological, and Cultural Factors. New York, Basic Books, Inc., 1958.

Philips, I. (Ed.): *Prevention and Treatment of Mental Retardation.* New York, Basic Books, Inc., 1966.

Prehm, H. J.; Hamerlynck, L. A.; and Crosson, J. E. (Eds.): *Behavioral Research in Mental Retardation,* 2nd ed. University of Oregon, Rehabilitation Research and Training Center in Mental Retardation, Monograph No. 1, 1970.

Robinson, H. B., and Robinson, N. M.: *The Mentally Retarded Child: A Psychological Approach.* New York, McGraw-Hill Book Company, 1965.

Rothstein, J. H. (Ed.): *Mental Retardation: Readings and Resources,* 2nd ed. New York, Holt, Rinehart and Winston, Inc., 1971.

Sarason, S. B.: *Psychological Problems in Mental Deficiency,* 3rd ed. New York, Harper, 1959.

Smith, R. M.: *An Introduction to Mental Retardation.* New York, McGraw-Hill Book Company, 1971.

Stevens, H. A., and Heber, R. (Eds.): *Mental Retardation: A Review of Research.* Chicago, The University of Chicago Press, 1964.

BASIC READINGS ON REHABILITATION AND MENTAL RETARDATION

Ayers, G. E.: *Selected References on the Education and Vocational Rehabilitation of Mentally Retarded Adolescents and Adults.* Mankato, Minnesota, Mankato State College, Rehabilitation Counselor Education Program, 1967.

Ayers, G. E. (Ed.): *New Directions in Habilitating the Mentally Retarded.* Elwyn, Pennsylvania, Elwyn Institute Print Shop. Proceedings of the Vocational Rehabilitation Subsection Meetings held at the American Association on Mental Deficiency Conference, Denver, Colorado, May 15-20, 1967.

Ayers, G. E. (Ed.): *Program Developments in Mental Retardation and Vocational Rehabilitation.* Proceedings of the Vocational Rehabilitation Subdivision Meetings held at the American Association on Mental Deficiency Conference, Boston, Massachusetts, April 30-May 4, 1968.

Berard, W. R., and Halpern, A. S.: *Abstracts of Federally Sponsored Work-Study Programs for the Mentally Retarded.* Rehabilitation Research and Training Center in Mental Retardation, The University of Texas, Monograph No. 3, 1970.

Cobb, H. V. et al.: *The Predictive Assessment of the Adult Retarded for Social and Vocational Adjustment: A Review of Research, Part I Annotated Bibliography.* Research Project RD-1624-P, Rehabilitation Services Administration, Social and Rehabilitation Service, U. S. Department of Health, Education, and Welfare, 1966.

Cobb, H. V.: *The Predictive Assessment of the Adult Retarded for Social and Vocational Adjustment: A Review of Research, Part II Analysis of the Literature.* Research Project RD-1624-P, Final Report, Rehabilitation Services Administration, Social and Rehabilitation Service, U. S. Department of Health, Education, and Welfare, 1969.

Cobb, H. V.: *The Forecast of Fulfillment: A Review of Research on Predictive Assessment of the Adult Retarded for Social and Vocational Adjustment.* New York, Teachers College Press, Teachers College, Columbia University, 1972.

Cohen, J. S.: Vocational rehabilitation of the mentally retarded: The sheltered workshop. *Mental Retardation Abstracts,* 3(2):163-169, 1966.

Cohen, M. (Ed.): *International Research Seminar on Vocational Rehabilitation of the Mentally Retarded.* Washington, D. C., American Association on Mental Deficiency, Special Publication Series, No. 1, 1972.

Daniels, L. K. (Ed.): *Vocational Rehabilitation of the Mentally Retarded: A Book of Readings.* Springfield, Ill., Charles C Thomas, 1972.

DiMichael, S. G. (Ed.): *Vocational Rehabilitation of the Mentally Retarded.* Washington, D. C., U. S. Government Printing Office, Superintendent of Documents, Rehabilitation Service Series No. 123, 1950.

DiMichael, S. G. (Ed.): *New Vocational Pathways for the Mentally Retarded.* American Rehabilitation Counseling Association, Division of American Personnel and Guidance Division, 1966.

Fraenkel, W. H.: *The Mentally Retarded and Their Vocational Rehabilitation: A Resource Handbook.* New York, National Association for Retarded Children, Inc., 1961.

Galazan, M. M.: Vocational rehabilitation and mental retardation. In Philips (Ed.): *Prevention and Treatment of Mental Retardation.* New York, Basic Books, Inc., 1966, pp. 294-307.

Gardner, W. I.: *Behavior Modification and Mental Retardation: A Behavior Modification Approach to the Education and Rehabilitation of the Mentally Retarded.* Chicago, Illinois, Aldine Publishers, 1971.

Gold, M. W.: Research on the vocational rehabilitation of the retarded: The present, the future. In Ellis, N. R. (Ed.): *International Review of Research in Mental Retardation.* New York, Academic Press, 1973.

Goldstein, H.: Social and occupational adjustment. In Stevens, H. A., and Heber, R. F. (Eds.): *Mental Retardation: A Review of Research.* Chicago, The University of Chicago Press, 1964, pp. 214-258.

Gootzeit, J. M.: *A Handbook on Personal Adjustment Training for Workshops Serving the Mentally Retarded.* New York, National Association for Retarded Children, 1964.

Gunzberg, H. C.: Vocational and social rehabilitation of the subnormal. In Clarke, A. M., and Clarke, A. B. (Eds.): *Mental Deficiency: The Changing Outlook.* New York, The Free Press, 1965, pp. 385-416.

Heber, R. F.; Flanigan, P. J.; and Ryak, W. S. (Eds.): *Changing Concepts in Mental Retardation: Pre-Vocational Evaluation of the Mentally Retarded.* Madison, Wisconsin, The University of Wisconsin, Rehabilitation Research and Training Center in Mental Retardation, 1969, Monograph No. II.

Heber, R. F. (Ed.): *Special Problems in Vocational Rehabilitation of the Mentally Retarded.* Rehabilitation Service Series No. 65-16, Vocational Rehabilitation Administration (now the Rehabilitation Services Administration), U. S. Department of Health, Education, and Welfare, 1963.

Hensley, G., and Buck, D. P. (Eds.): *Exploring Rehabilitation-Special Education Relationships.* University East Campus, Boulder, Colorado, Western Interstate Commission for Higher Education, May, 1968.

Jaffe, J. (Ed.): *Challenges in Vocational Rehabilitation and Mental Retardation.* Proceedings of the Vocational Rehabilitation Subdivision Meetings held at the American Association on Mental Deficiency Annual Meeting, Washington, D. C., May 25-30, 1970, February, 1971.

Jageman, L., and Clevenger, L. J.: The sheltered workshop for trainable mentally retarded: A selected bibliography in outline form. *Mental Retardation Abstracts, 9*(2):1-9, 1972.

Kolstoe, O. P., and Frey, R. M.: *A High School Work-Study Program for Mentally Subnormal Students.* Carbondale, Illinois, Southern Illinois University Press, 1967.

Mackie, R. P.; Williams, H. M.; Dabelstein, D. H.; and Heber, R. I. (Eds.): *Preparation of Mentally Retarded Youth for Gainful Employment.* Washington, D. C., U. S. Department Printing Office, Superintendent of Documents, Rehabilitation Service Series No. 507, 1961.

Morgenstern, M., and Michal-Smith, H.: *Psychology in the Vocational Rehabilitation of the Mentally Retarded.* Springfield, Ill., Charles C Thomas, 1972.

Peterson, R. O., and Jones, E. M.: *Guide to Jobs for the Mentally Retarded,* revised edition. Pittsburgh, Penn., American Institute for Research, 1964.

Prehm, H. J. (Ed.): *Rehabilitation Research in Mental Retardation.* Eugene, Oregon: University of Oregon, Rehabilitation Research and Training Center in Mental Retardation, Monograph No. II, July, 1970.

"Rehabilitation of the mentally retarded: Special report." *Journal of Rehabilitation,* November-December:21-48, 1962.

Stahlecker, L. V.: *Occupational Information for the Mentally Retarded.* Springfield, Ill., Charles C Thomas, 1967.

Vocational rehabilitation for the mentally retarded. In Heath, E. J.: *The Mentally Retarded Student and Guidance* (Guidance and the Exceptional Student: Series V). Boston, Houghton Mifflin Company, 1970, pp. 33-51.

Windle, C.: Prognosis of mental subnormals. Monograph supplement to *American Journal of Mental Deficiency, 66*:5, 1962.

Wolfensberger, W.: Vocational preparation and occupation. In Baumeister, A. A. (Ed.): *Mental Retardation: Appraisal, Education, Rehabilitation.* Chicago, Aldine Publishing Company, 1967, pp. 232-273.

Younie, W. J. (Ed.): *Guidelines for Establishing School-Work Study Programs for Educable-Mentally Retarded Youth.* Richmond, Va., Special Education Service, State Department of Education, Volume 48, No. 10, June, 1966.

Zaetz, J. L.: *Organization of Sheltered Workshop Programs for the Mentally Retarded Adult.* Springfield, Ill., Charles C Thomas, 1971.

BASIC READINGS ON COUNSELING AND MENTAL RETARDATION

Ayer, M. J., and Butler, A. J.: *Client-Counseling Communication and Interaction in Counseling with the Mentally Retarded.* Madison, Wis., Department of Studies in Behavioral Disabilities, University of Wisconsin, 1969.

Bialer, I.: Psychotherapy and adjustment techniques with the mentally retarded. In Baumeister, A. A. (Ed.): *Mental Retardation: Appraisal, Education, Rehabilitation.* Chicago, Aldine Publishing Company, 1967, pp. 138-180.

Catalog of Audio-Visual Aids for Counselor Training in Mental Retardation and Emotional Disability. Devon, Penn., The Devereux Foundation Press, October, 1967.

Cowen, E. L., and Trippe, M. J.: Psychotherapy and play techniques with the exceptional child and youth. In Cruickshank, W. M. (Ed.): *Psychology of Exceptional Children and Youth.* Englewood Cliffs, N. J., Prentice-Hall, Inc., 1963, pp. 526-591.

Gardner, W. I.: Use of behavior therapy with the mentally retarded. In Menolascino, F. J. (Ed.): *Psychiatric Approaches of Mental Retardation.* New York, Basic Books, 1970, pp. 250-275.

Gunzburg, H. C.: Psychotherapy with the feebleminded. In Clarke, A. M., and Clarke, A. B. (Eds.): *Mental Deficiency: The Changing Outlook.* New York, The Free Press, 1965, pp. 417-446.

Heath, E. J.: *The Mentally Retarded Student and Guidance* (Guidance and the Exceptional Student Monograph Series No. V). Boston, Houghton Mifflin Company, 1970.

Leland, H., and Smith, D. E.: *Play Therapy with Mental Subnormal Children.* New York, Grune and Stratton, 1965.

Noland, R. L. (Ed.): *Counseling Parents of the Mentally Retarded.* Springfield, Ill., Charles C Thomas, 1970.

Ricker, L. H.; Pinkard, C. M.; Gilmore, A. S.; and Williams, C. F.: *A Comparison of Three Approaches to Group Counseling Involving Motion Pictures with Mentally Retarded Young Adults.* Tampa, Fla., MacDonald Training Center Foundation, Inc., Research and Education Division, 1967.

Robinson, H. B., and Robinson, N. M.: Psychotherapy with retarded children. In Robinson, H. B., and Robinson, N. M.: *The Mentally Retarded Child: A Psychological Approach*. New York, McGraw-Hill Book Company, 1965, pp. 479-505.

Sarason, S. B.: Psychotherapy. In Sarason, S. B.: *Psychological Problems in Mental Deficiency*. New York, Harper and Brothers, 1959, pp. 263-330.

Stacey, C. L., and DeMartino, M. F. (Eds.): *Counseling and Psychotherapy with the Mentally Retarded*. Glencoe, Ill., The Free Press, 1957.

Sternlicht, M.: Psychotherapeutic procedures with the retarded. In Ellis, N. (Ed.): *International Review of Research in Mental Retardation*. New York, Academic Press, 1966, vol. 2, pp. 279-354.

Szurek, S. A., and Philips, I.: Mental retardation and psychotherapy. In Philips, I. (Ed.): *Prevention and Treatment of Mental Retardation*. New York, Basic Books, Inc., 1966, pp. 221-246.

The mentally retarded child. In Gowan, J. C.; Demos, G. D.; and Kokaska, C. J. (Eds.): *The Guidance of the Exceptional Child: A Book of Readings*, 2nd ed. New York, David McKay Company, Inc., 1972, pp. 199-306.

Wolfensberger, W.: Counseling the parents of the retarded. In Baumeister, A. A. (Ed.): *Mental Retardation: Appraisal, Education, Rehabilitation*. Chicago, Aldine Publishing Company, 1967.

Appendix B

REHABILITATION RESEARCH AND DEMONSTRATION PROJECTS IN MENTAL RETARDATION

Since 1954, the Rehabilitation Research and Demonstration program of the Social and Rehabilitation Service has sponsored approximately 2,300 projects, of which 188 have dealt with mental retardation. The program was authorized by Section 4(a)(1) of the 1954 Amendments to the Vocational Rehabilitation Act, and is administered by the Rehabilitation Research Branch of the Division of Research and Demonstrations.

The disability category pertaining to mental retardation reprinted here was excerpted from *Research 1971*, an annotated list of all research projects sponsored by SRS since the beginning of the program. *Research* is published annually by the Research Utilization Branch. At the end of the mental retardation category is a list of Selected Demonstrations which conform to prototypes derived from successful demonstrations previously supported by the Social and Rehabilitation Service. After providing a means of putting into operation improved methods in many different parts of the country, these demonstrations were dropped from the Research and Demonstration program, their innovative services having become part of the ongoing State vocational rehabilitation programs.

SRS projects completed before July 1, 1970, retain their original numbers, but those still active on that date or funded later have been assigned new numbers by the Division of Project Grants Administration.

The letters "RD" preceding each *old number* indicate that the project is part of the Rehabilitation Research and Demonstration program. The number is followed, in parenthesis, by the fiscal year in which the project was activated and the anticipated duration. All old numbers after RD-750 are followed by a letter designating the SRS Study Section that monitored the project— General (G), Medical (M), or Psycho-Social (P).

Note: Reprinted from *Programs for the Handicapped*, Secretary's Committee on Mental Retardation, U. S. Department of Health, Education, and Welfare, Washington, D. C. 20201, February 29, 1972.

The new numbering system consists of (1) a two-digit numerical program identifier code; (2) the capital letter "P" as a constant in all cases: (3) a five-digit sequential numerical control to identify each grant; (4) a number corresponding to the SRS Region in which the grantee institution is located; and (5) a number to relate the transaction to a particular year in the project period.

Completed projects are designated by an asterisk after the number, followed by the grantee's name and address and the name of the project director. Key words in the annotation are italicized.

Upon completion of each project, a final report is prepared by the grantee, giving the results of the investigation or demonstration. Copies of recent final reports and other publications produced under projects can often be obtained by writing directly to the grantee. Furthermore, most SRS final reports published from the beginning of the program through 1970 are now available from the National Technical Information Service, Springfield, Virginia 22151. Remittance should accompany orders. Prices currently effective range from $3 to $6 for hard copy and $.95 for microfiche copy. Other possible sources for SRS reports are the Departmental Library, Department of Health, Education, and Welfare, Washington, D. C. 20201, and the San Francisco State College Library, San Francisco, California 94132. *Do not write to the Social and Rehabilitation Service for final reports,* as it does not stock them.

Detailed information about the Research and Demonstration program can be obtained by writing to the Chief, Division of Research and Demonstrations, Social and Rehabilitation Service, Department of Health, Education, and Welfare, Washington, D. C. 20201. Copies of *SRS Research* can be obtained by writing the editor of *Research,* Research Utilization Branch, Office of Research and Demonstrations, Social and Rehabilitation Service, Department of Health, Education, and Welfare, Washington, D. C. 20201.

PROJECTS

RD-20 (55-5).* Working for Maturity: Specialized Rehabilitation Training for Mentally Retarded Young Adults. Association for the Help of Retarded Children, N. Y. C. Chapter, 380 Second Avenue, New York, New York 10010; Max Dubrow, Ph.D.

To demonstrate that special sheltered *workshop training* can rehabilitate mentally retarded *young adults* previously considered unemployable. See also RD-211.

RD-50 (56-3).* Habilitation of Mentally Retarded Youth. MacDonald Training Center Foundation, 4424 Tampa Bay Boulevard, Tampa, Florida 33607; Robert Ferguson.

To evaluate the potential for vocational rehabilitation of mentally retarded *youths* with muscular, orthopedic, and emotional impairments, through *workshop and other types of training.*

RD-222 (58-1).* Development of a System of Job Activity Elements for the Mentally Retarded. American Institute for Research, 410 Amberson Avenue, Pittsburgh, Pennsylvania 15232; R. O. Peterson, Ph.D.

To develop a system for *analyzing activity elements of jobs* available to the mentally retarded as a basis for their vocational training and rehabilitation.

Special report, *Guide to Jobs for the Mentally Retarded— Handbook and Job Requirements Profile.*

RD-330 (59-3).* Adjustment of the Retarded. Connecticut Association for Retarded Children, 29 Pearl Street, Hartford, Connecticut 06457; Ann Switzer.

To investigate certain job factors, personal characteristics, and educational experiences of *adult* retardates discharged from institutional and community facilities in relation to their *vocational and social adjustment.*

Special report, *Operation Connecticut.*

RD-383 (59-4).* Employer, Parent and Trainee Attitudes Toward the Rehabilitation of the Mentally Retarded. The Woods Schools, Langhorne, Pennsylvania 19047; Mrs. Dorly D. Wang.

To study employer, parent, and trainee *attitudes* affecting the employability of the mentally retarded (IQ 50-69).

RD-404 (59-4).* An Evaluation Study and Demonstration Work Experience for the Mentally Retarded During their Last Year in Public School. Jewish Vocational Service, 207 East Buffalo Street, Milwaukee, Wisconsin 53202; Michael M. Galazan.

To demonstrate and evaluate a *cooperative* program of *academic school* work and concurrent *work experience* in the vocational rehabilitation of mentally retarded *high school youth* during their senior year.

RD-417 (59-4).* The Vocational Rehabilitation of Retarded, Brain-injured Youth in a Rural Regional Center. The George Everett Partridge Memorial Foundation, P. O. Box 67, Springfield, Virginia 22150; Marvin Patterson, Ph.D.

To demonstrate the feasibility of *on-the-job training* in a *rural residential center* followed by vocational placement and appropriate followup services, contrasting the training methods for brain injured to those used with non-brain injured mentally retarded.

RD-419 (60-3).* Predicting Vocational Capacity of Retarded Young Adults. MacDonald Training Center Foundation, 4424 Tampa Bay Boulevard, Tampa, Florida 33614; C. M. Pinkard, Jr., Ph.D.

To develop, validate, and standardize a *scale* to *assess the training potential* of mentally retarded *youth*.

RD-425 (59-4).* Evaluating and Developing Vocational Potential of Institutionalized Retarded Adolescents. Edward R. Johnstone Training and Research Center, Bordentown, New Jersey 08505; Joseph J. Parnicky, Ph.D.

To develop techniques for *predicting students' performance* at various levels in an evaluation, training, and vocational placement program for mentally retarded *youth* in a *State institution*.

RD-451 (60-3).* Study of the Effects of Special Training Procedures Upon the Efficiency with which Mentally Retarded People will Learn Vocational Skills. University of Colorado, Boulder, Colorado 80304; M. P. Smith, Ph.D.

To study the effects of *special training procedures* upon the efficiency with which mentally retarded youth will learn vocational skills.

RD-470 (60-3).* Halfway House for Mentally Retarded Men. Illinois Department of Mental Health, 2449 West Washington Boulevard, Springfield, Illinois 62707; Arthur A. Wolonstein, M.D.

To demonstrate the effectiveness of a transitional home *halfway house* providing personal and vocational adjustment training in the vocational rehabilitation of mentally retarded *men*.

RD-517 (60-1).* Planning Study for Vocational Rehabilitation of the Mentally Retarded in Kansas Neurological Institute. Kansas Neurological Institute, 3107 West 21st Street, Topeka, Kansas 66614; C. C. Vickery, M.D.

To assess the vocational rehabilitation *services needed in a newly established State facility* for the mentally retarded and to determine the feasibility of a *coordinated statewide program* for the retarded.

RD-537 (60-1).* Development of a State-wide Program for the Vocational Rehabilitation of the Mentally Retarded. Vocational Rehabilitation Division, Information Office, 1427 Lee Street East, Charleston, West Virginia 25301; D. P. Rogers, Ph.D.

To plan an intensive *statewide* vocational rehabilitation *program* for the mentally retarded based upon a thorough *analysis of needs*, assessment of existing services, and development of new resources.

RD-568 (60-5).* Development of Optimum Vocational Potential of Young Mentally Retarded Adults in a Sheltered Workshop Program. Association for the Help of Retarded Children, New York City Chapter, 380 Second Avenue, New York, New York 14301; Max Dubrow, Ph.D.

To develop more effective *techniques for evaluating and training young* mentally retarded *adults* to attain optimum sheltered or competitive vocational potential.

RD-581 (60-1).* Rehabilitation and Research in Retardation. Southern Methodist University, Dallas, Texas 75222; Barry Holton.

To conduct a *conference* of investigators engaged in OVR research and demonstration projects in the field of mental retardation to advance research methods and develop additional research opportunities.

RD-603 (61-3).* Personality and Ability in the Lower Intellectual Range: A Study of Assessment Methods. University of Washington, Public Opinion Laboratory, Seattle, Washington 98105; J. B. Taylor, Ph.D.

To investigate the influence of a number of social, vocational, familial, and personal variables on the *work adjustment* and rehabilitation potential of the mentally retarded.

RD-655 (61-1).* A Connecticut Community Revisited: A Study of the Social Adjustment of a Group of Mentally Deficient Adults in 1948 and 1960. Connecticut College, New London, Connecticut 06320; R. J. Kennedy, Ph.D.

To study the personal, social, and economic *adjustment* of selected *noninstitutionalized* mentally retarded *adults*.

RD-681 (61-3).* Retarded Youth: Their School-Rehabilitation Needs. Minneapolis Public Schools, 807 Northeast Broadway, Minneapolis, Minnesota 55413; E. D. Deno, Ph.D.

To develop facilities and techniques for giving *vocational evaluation, training, and on-job experience* to educable mentally retarded youth during the last year of *high school*.

RD-730 (61-1).* A Guide for Functional Teachings of Mentally Retarded Children. University of Colorado, Boulder, Colorado 80304; Maurice P. Smith, Ph.D.

To study, record, analyze, and report methods which have

been used successfully in the *vocational training* of lower level mentally retarded people.

RD-836-P (62-3).* Vocational Rehabilitation for Mentally Retarded Pupil-Clients. Georgia Division of Vocational Rehabilitation, 629 State Office Building, Atlanta, Georgia 30334; John S. Prickett, Jr.

A demonstration to assist secondary schools of Georgia in meeting the vocational needs of mentally retarded *adolescents* through *coordination* of rehabilitation, educational, and local *community resources*.

RD-842-G (62-3).* Special Class Curriculum and Environment and Vocational Rehabilitation of Mentally Retarded Young Adults. University of Alabama, University, Alabama 35501; Jasper Harvey, Ph.D.

To develop and evaluate, through *followup, vocational training* procedures for mentally retarded *youths* within several rehabilitation facilities in cooperation with local school systems and other educational and rehabilitation resources.

RD-861-P (61-1).* The Mentally Retarded and Their Vocational Rehabilitation: A Resource Handbook. National Association for Retarded Children, 386 Park Avenue, South, New York, New York 10016; William A. Fraenkel, Ph.D.

To assist in making available selected technical *material* for use in the *vocational rehabilitation* of the mentally retarded.

RD-902-P (62-3).* Independent Living Rehabilitation Program for Seriously Handicapped Mentally Retarded Adults. Commercial edition. *The Retarded Adult in the Community*. Aid Retarded Children, 1362 9th Avenue, San Francisco, California 94122; Elias Katz, Ph.D.

To demonstrate a program of services to *adult* mentally retarded, necessary to achieve greater competence in *independent living;* work and personal adjustment training are included.

RD-957-P (62-3).* Out of the Shadows: A Program of Evaluation and Prevocational Training for Mentally Retarded

Young Adult Females. West Virginia Division of Vocational Rehabilitation, State Board of Vocational Education, Charleston, West Virginia 25122; William R. Phelps.

A *statewide* demonstration for the vocational rehabilitation of the mentally retarded, consisting of a *residential training* program followed by maximum utilization of *coordinated public and private resources.*

RD-981-P (63-3).* The Kent Occupational Education and Training Center. Kent County Board of Education, 316-318 Ottawa Avenue, N. W., Grand Rapids, Michigan 49502; R. J. Van Hattum, Ph.D.

To demonstrate the feasibility and value of combining many *small school districts* within a community into a cooperative centralized program to meet the needs of high school educable retardates.

RD-987-P (62-3).* The Occupational Success of the Retarded: Critical Factors, Predictive Tests and Remedial Techniques. Laradon Hall Society, East 51st Avenue, and Lincoln Street, Denver, Colorado 80216; Lewis E. Kitts.

To analyze mental levels of retarded *young adults* and on this basis construct a *test battery* for *prediction of employability;* to develop training procedures to remedy vocational defects.

RD-989-P (63-2).* A Comparison of Three Approaches to Group Counseling Involving Motion Pictures with Mentally Retarded Young Adults. MacDonald Training Center Foundation, 4424 Tampa Bay Boulevard, Tampa, Florida 33607; C. M. Pinkard, Jr., Ph.D.

To evaluate a *motion picture training* technique for promoting social development in mentally retarded *young adults.*
Film. *Training for Tomorrow.*

RD-991-P (62-1).* Mid-Life Attainment of the Mentally Retarded: A Longitudinal Study. University of Nebraska, Lincoln, Nebraska 68508; Warren R. Baller, Ph.D.

To *followup* retardates tested twenty-five or more years previously and determine experience associated with good or poor *adjustment in midlife.*

RD-993-P (63-3).* Automation in Vocational Training of the Mentally Retarded. The Devereux Foundation, Devon, Pennsylvania 19333; Henry Platt, Ph.D. and Louis Kukoda.

To develop and evaluate the effectiveness of *automated instruction* as a method of vocational training with *mentally retarded* or *emotionally disturbed adolescents.*

RD-1036-G (62-3).* Employment of the Mentally Retarded in a Competitive Industrial Setting. Human Resources Foundation, Albertson, New York 11507; Leonard S. Blackman, Ph.D.

To develop and test methods of *training* the mentally retarded for effective *employment in a competitive industrial setting.* See also RD-2599.

RD-1059-P (62-3).* Personality Measurement with Mentally Retarded and Other Subcultural Adults: A Personality Test for Persons of Limited Reading Skills. Alabama Institute for Deaf and Blind, P. O. Box 268, Talladega, Alabama 35106; Herbert W. Eber, Ph.D.

To develop a *personality test* for mentally retarded and for normally intelligent but illiterate or poorly educated *adults.*

RD-1067-P (63-3).* Increasing Parental Contribution to Work Adjustment for the Retarded. United Association for Retarded Children, 207 East Buffalo Street, Milwaukee, Wisconsin 53202; George Prentice.

To develop methods of increasing *parental participation* and effectiveness in *vocational training* of retarded adolescents and *young adults.*

RD-1075-P (63-3).* The Efficacy of a Prevocational Curriculum and Services Designed to Rehabilitate Slow Learners Who Are School Drop Outs, Delinquency, and Unemployment Prone. Champaign Community Schools, 703 South New Street, Champaign, Illinois 61822; Merle B. Karnes, Ph.D.

To test the effectiveness of a *prevocational curriculum and progressive work experience for slow learners* (IQ 75-90) in preventing school dropouts, delinquency, and unemployment.

RD-1158-P (63-2).* The Successful Retardate. Department of Education, Commonwealth of Puerto Rico, Hato Rey, Puerto Rico 00919; C. Albizu-Miranda, Ph.D.

To study vocationally successful mentally retarded persons in order to identify various *psychological processes related to success.*
Special report, *List of Occupations Requiring No More Than a Below-Average Intelligence.*

RD-1189-P (63-4).* A Cooperative Vocational Pattern for In-School Mentally Retarded Youth. Occupational Center of Essex County, 391 Lakeside Avenue, Orange, New Jersey 07050; Arthur Bierman.

To demonstrate the effectiveness of a comprehensive vocational rehabilitation program for mentally retarded *high school youth* in which a *public school, State* vocational rehabilitation agency, and *sheltered workshop* provide *coordinated services.*

RD-1200-P (63-1).* Planning Grant for Demonstration Project to Demonstrate Comprehensive Community-Based Services for the Retarded. Parents and Friends of Mentally Retarded Children of Bridgeport, 415 Knowlton Street, Bridgeport, Connecticut 06608; Maurice Mezoff.

To plan a demonstration which will utilize *total community resources* in order to provide a program of comprehensive rehabilitation services to all mentally retarded. See also RD-1435.

RD-1221-P (64-3).* Standardization of the Vocational Interest and Sophistication. Assessment (VISA): A Reading-Free Test for Retardates. Edward R. Johnstone Training and Research Center, Bordentown, New Jersey 08505; Joseph J. Parnicky, Ph.D.

To determine the reliability and validity of a *vocational interest and sophistication assessment scale* (VISA) developed by the Center.

Special report, *Vocational Interest and Sophistication Assessment: Manual.*

RD-1222-P (64-3).* A Study of the Johnstone Community House for Educable Young Men. Edward R. Johnstone Training and Research Center, Bordentown, New Jersey 08505; Joseph J. Parnicky, Ph.D.

To develop a *halfway house* program for the retarded for transition from institutional life to increased independence and responsibility.

RD-1275-P (64-4).* A Transitional Program for Institutionalized Adult Retarded. Elwyn Institute, Elwyn, Pennsylvania 19063; Gerald R. Clark, M.D.

A demonstration and evaluation of *comprehensive* diagnostic, training, placement, and adjustment *services,* beginning *within the institution* and continuing *extramurally,* to prepare retardates for *independent community living.*
Special report, *Guide to the Community.* 3 volumes.

RD-1290-P (64-2).* Mental Retardation: A Programmed Manual for Volunteer Workers. MacDonald Training Center Foundation, 4424 Tampa Bay Boulevard, Tampa, Florida 33607; Alden S. Gilmore and Thomas A. Rich, Ph.D.

To develop and test *programmed training materials* for use in orientation and *instruction of volunteers* working with the retarded.

RD-1319-G (64-1).* The Utilization and Design of Physical Facilities for the Rehabilitation of Mentally Retarded. Parsons State Hospital and Training Center, 2601 Gabriel Street, Parsons, Kansas 67357; Howard V. Bair, M.D.

To determine the most effective use of *staff and facilities in a multidisciplinary* rehabilitation *center* for the retarded.

RD-1331-G (64-5).* A Structured Community Approach to Complete Services for the Retarded. Jewish Vocational Service, 207 East Buffalo Street, Milwaukee, Wisconsin 53202; Mrs. Patricia J. Bertrand.

To demonstrate an *organized community approach* to complete rehabilitation services for the mentally retarded.

RD-1385-P (64-3).* Satellite Workshops on Extensions of a Central Vocational Rehabilitation Program. Association for the Help of Retarded Children, New York City Chapter, 320 West 13th Street, New York, New York 10014; Max Dubrow, Ph.D.

To demonstrate *satellite sheltered workshops* around an existing facility to provide employment for mentally retarded.

RD-1388-P (64-3).* Social Inference Training of Retarded Adolescents at the Prevocational Level, University of Kansas Medical Center, 39th and Rainbow, Kansas City, Kansas 66103; Dr. Ethel Leach and Mrs. Barbara Edmonson.

To develop a method of *testing and training the social insight* of mentally retarded *youth,* increasing their awareness of relevant social cues and appropriate responses, in order to extend their social adjustability in vocational and community living.

Special report, *Social Perceptual Training for Community Living: Pre-Vocational Units for Retarded Youth.*

RD-1391-P (64-1).* The Influence of Occupational Information Counseling on the Realism of Occupational Aspirations of Mentally Retarded High School Boys. College of Education, University of Nevada, Reno, Nevada 89507; George A. Jeffs, Ed.D.

Effectiveness of *occupational counseling* upon mentally retarded *high school boys'* level of occupational *aspirations* and realism of occupational *goals.*

RD-1394-P (64-3).* An Assessment of Vocational Realism of High School and Post-High School Educable Mentally Retarded Adolescents. Exceptional Children's Foundation, 2225 West Adams Boulevard, Los Angeles, California 90018; Molly C. Gorelick, Ed.D.

To measure the degree of *realism of vocational plans* of mentally retarded *adolescents* in their last year of *school* and to determine what training and guidance procedures facilitate vocational realism.

RD-1435-G (64-5).* On the Pursuit of Change: Experiences of a Parents' Association During a Five Year Development Period. Monographs 1-6. (1) Day Camping and Leisure Time Recreation Activities for the Mentally Retarded; (2) Experiences of Former Special Class Students and an Educational Work/Experience Program for Secondary School Educable Mentally Retarded Students; (3) Residential Programming and Residential Centers for the Mentally Retarded: The Experience in Bridgeport; (4) The Evolution of a Sheltered Workshop for the Retarded; (5) Administrative and Sociological Factors in Organizing Change: Toward New Services for the Retarded; (6) Process of Change: Goals, Obstacles, and Results in Generating New Services for the Retarded. Parents and Friends of Mentally Retarded Children of Bridgeport, 4695 Main Street, Bridgeport, Connecticut 06606; Louis H. Orzack.

To demonstrate the development of *comprehensive community services* to provide a spectrum of opportunity for the retarded. See also RD-1200.
Special report, *Follow-up Study on Clients Seen by the Kennedy Center Diagnostic Clinic.*

RD-1465-P (64-5).* Training Mental Retardates with Severe Defects for a Productive Occupation. Laradon Hall Society, East 51st Avenue and Lincoln Street, Denver, Colorado 80216; F. William Happ, Ph.D.

An investigation of *prevocational* and vocational methods of rehabilitating individuals with severe mental retardation for eventual *employment* in the *community* or in a *sheltered workshop.*

RD-1500-G (64-1).* A Study of the Relation of Parental Attitudes to the Progress of Retarded Children in a Regional Center. University of Hartford, P. O. Box 1948, Hartford, Connecticut 06117; David D. Komisar, Ph.D.

To plan a study of the relation of *parental attitudes to progress of retarded children* in a regional center. See also RD-1816.

RD-1535-G (64-1).* Service Needs of the Mentally Retarded in San Francisco. San Francisco Coordinating Council on Mental Retardation, 1600 Scott Street, San Francisco, California 94115; Mary Duran.

To plan a *comprehensive community organizational approach* to providing a continuum of care for the mentally retarded. See also 12-55260-5.

RD-1550-G (65-2).* Planning Workshops for the Retarded in Ohio. Ohio Association for Retarded Children, 131 East State Street, Columbus, Ohio 43215; Bernard F. Niehm.

To prepare guidelines for *statewide* and *local workshop services* for *retarded* youth and adults in Ohio.
Special report, *Ohio Workshop Planning Institute on Sheltered Workshops Under the Fair Labor Standards Act.*

RD-1556-G (65-3).* The Relationship Between Organizational Factors and the Acceptance of New Rehabilitation Programs in Mental Retardation. University of Wisconsin, Madison, Wisconsin 53706; Michael T. Aiken.

To study the *relationship and process* in welfare agencies between *organizational factors* and acceptance of new *programs* on mental retardation.

RD-1561-G (65-3).* Coordination of Workshops for the Mentally Retarded in a Metropolitan and Suburban Area. Exceptional Children's Foundation, 2225 West Adams Boulevard, Los Angeles, California 90018; Robert D. Shushan.

To demonstrate the role of a system of *coordinated (satellite) workshops* for the mentally retarded in a *metropolitan* and *suburban* area.

RD-1588-P (65-1).* To develop Work Evaluation and Work Training Techniques Designed to Facilitate the Entry of Mildly Mentally Retarded into Service Occupations. Institute for Crippled and Disabled, 400 First Avenue, New York, New York 10010; Salvatore G. DiMichael.

To plan a *training* program to facilitate the entry of the mildly *mentally retarded* into *service occupations.*

RD-1589-P (65-3).* Depersonalization Stops Here! A Placement-Oriented Special Work Adjustment Program for Mentally Retarded Adolescents and Young Adults with a History of School Drop-out. Federation of the Handicapped, 211 West 14th Street, New York, New York 10011; Milton Cohen.

To demonstrate the effectiveness of a *placement oriented work adjustment* program for *adolescents* with a history of *school dropout.*

RD-1602-P (65-1).* Vocational Rehabilitation of Physically Handicapped and/or Mentally Handicapped Youth Being Served by a Special Youth Opportunity Center. Lane County Youth Study Board, 1901 Garden Avenue, Eugene, Oregon 97403; Edgar W. Brewer.

To provide comprehensive vocational rehabilitation services to *physically or mentally* handicapped *youths.*

RD-1604-G (65-3).* Out-Plant Supervised Janitorial Service Employing the Mentally Retarded. Services, Inc., 10241 Main Street, Bellevue, Washington 98004; Albert Jacobson.

To demonstrate the feasibility of *supervised janitorial work* for the mentally retarded.

RD-1606-P (64-4).* Factors Contributing to Successful and Non-Successful Community Adjustment of Discharged Retardates. Pineland Hospital and Training Center, Box C, Pownal, Maryland 04069; Peter W. Bowman, M.D.

An analytical and descriptive study of discharged *mental retardates* to determine the *predictive elements* in their lives most closely associated with their *success or failure in community adjustment.*

RD-1607-P (65-1).* Personality and Learning in the Retardate. Department of Institutions and Agencies, Division of Mental Retardation, State Colony at Woodbine, Woodbine, New Jersey 08270; J. C. Brengelmann, M.D. and H. F. Schultz, Ed.M.

To demonstrate that significant *relationships* exist between *personality* and learning in the retardate.

RD-1635-G (64-1).* Study of the Feasibility of an Inter-District Program for Trainable Retarded Adolescents. Educational Research and Development Council of Twin Cities Metropolitan Area, University of Minnesota, Minneapolis, Minnesota 55455; Donald E. Davis, Ph.D.

To plan an *interdistrict* program of *educational* and *community services* to *adolescent trainable retardates.* See also RD-1810.

RD-1637-G (64-1).* A Planning Grant to Develop Methods in Implementing the Role of a DVR in Federal Employment of the Mentally Retarded Under Civil Service Regulations. D. C. Department of Vocational Rehabilitation, 1331 H Street, N. W., Washington, D. C. 20005; Leslie B. Cole.

A planning grant to develop methods and techniques in implementing the *role of the DVR* in the *Federal employment* of the mentally retarded under Civil Service Regulations. See also RD-1799.

RD-1660-G (65-2).* Coordination of a University Program in the Rehabilitation of the Mentally Retarded. Medical College of Alabama, 1919 Seventh Avenue South, Birmingham, Alabama 35233; H. P. Bentley, Jr., M.D.

To determine the role of the *university* in rehabilitation of *mentally retarded* individuals.

RD-1689-G (65-1).* A New York World's Fair Mental Retardation Workshop Exhibit. Joseph P. Kennedy, Jr. Foundation, 1411 K Street N. W., Washington, D. C. 20005; John M. Throne, Ph.D.

To plan a *Mental Retardation Workshop Exhibit* for the New York World's Fair.

RD-1699-G (65-3).* A Program for Institutionalized Mentally Retarded Adults. Arkansas Rehabilitation Service, 211 Broadway, Little Rock, Arkansas 72201; Robert L. Parson.

To develop effective *methods and techniques* for rehabilitating *older institutionalized mentally retarded adults.*

RD-1769-G (65-1).* Mental Retardation—Blueprint for Action. Welfare Federation of Cleveland, 1001 Huron Road, Cleveland, Ohio 44155; Rilma Buckman, Ph.D.

A planning project to develop a "blueprint for action" in the field of *mental retardation* for Cuyahoga, Geauga, and Lake Counties. See also 12-55200-5.

RD-1799-G (65-2).* State DVR Role in Implementing the Federal Program for Employment of Mental Retardates. Department of Vocational Rehabilitation, 1331 H Street, N. W., Washington, D. C. 20005; Leslie B. Cole.

To demonstrate the role of a vocational rehabilitation agency in developing and implementing a program for *employment of the mentally retarded in Federal agencies.* See also RD-1637.
Film. *Jobs Well Done.*

RD-1810-G (66-5).* Cooperative School-Rehabilitation Centers. Educational Research and Development Council of Twin Cities Metropolitan Area, University of Minnesota, Minneapolis, Minnesota 55455; Donald E. Davis, Ed.D.

To demonstrate the effectiveness of a comprehensive *interdistrict,* school-based, *vocational rehabilitation program for* trainable *mentally retarded requiring intensive services.* See also RD-1635.

RD-1816-P (65-3).* Retardates in Residence: A Study of Institutions. University of Hartford, P. O. Box 1948, Hartford, Connecticut 06101; David D. Komisar, Ph.D.

To determine the effects of differential *daily living experiences* on retarded persons living in residential centers. See also RD-1500.

RD-1853-G (66-3).* The Planning and Implementation of Comprehensive Services for the Mentally Retarded in Los Angeles

County. Mental Retardation Service Board of Los Angeles County, 1313 West Eighth Street, Los Angeles, California 90017; M. M. Mooring.

To demonstrate techniques of *coordinating rehabilitation services for the retarded* in a large metropolitan area through a legally constituted joint public authority.

RD-1919-P (66-3).* Influence of Low Socio-Economic Class and Parent Participation on the Adaptation of Retarded Adults to a Vocational Rehabilitation Program. Association for Help of Retarded Children, New York City Chapter, 200 Park Avenue South, New York, New York 10003; Max Dubrow, Ph.D.

To study various *differences between low socio-economic and middle-class retardates;* develop training and treatment *programs to meet needs of low socio-economic group;* study various aspects of *parent involvement* in rehabilitation of young adult retardates.

RD-1928-G (65-1).* This Isn't Kindness. National Association for Retarded Children, 2709 Avenue E East, Arlington, Texas 76010; John Becker.

To produce a *film* depicting the capabilities of rehabilitated mentally retarded persons in industry to *increase employment opportunities.*
Film: *Selling a Guy Named Larry.*

12-55260-5.* Community Organization Action Plan for the Mentally Retarded. San Francisco Coordinating Council on Mental Retardation, 948 Market Street, San Francisco, California 94102; Lillian Creisler.

To demonstrate, through the *community organization process,* ways of (1) developing and expanding new *services needed by the mentally retarded and their families,* (2) coordinate expansion of existing services, and (3) changing attitudes and values which negate maximum use of available services. See also RD-1535.

RD-1930-G (65-1).* The Hope and the Promise. Film. National Rehabilitation Association, 1522 K Street N. W., Washington, D. C. 20005; E. B. Whitten.

To produce a *film* on the techniques of *selective placement* of the handicapped.

RD-1944-P (66-3).* The Fairfax Plan: A Work-Study Program for the Mildly Retarded. Fairfax County School Board, 10700 Page Avenue, Fairfax, Virginia 22030; Bernard J. Cameron.

To establish, evaluate, and maintain an intensive program of *educational and vocational* training geared specifically to the habilitation of *mildly mentally retarded youth.*

RD-2031-G (65-2).* New Work Opportunities for the Mentally Retarded. National Association of Sheltered Workshops and Homebound Programs, 1029 Vermont Avenue N. W., Washington, D. C. 20005; Antonio C. Suazo.

To demonstrate the feasibility of training the *mentally retarded* in workshops for *new work opportunities in candle making* and related industries.

RD-2039-P (66-1).* You're It. Film. MacDonald Training Center Foundation, 4424 Tampa Bay Boulevard, Tampa, Florida 33614; Alden S. Gilmore and Thomas A. Rich.

To produce a *film* to illustrate effective techniques of *recreational leadership* with the *mentally retarded* for use with *volunteer workers* and others.

12-55200-5. Greater Cleveland Mental Retardation Development Project. Welfare Federation of Cleveland, 1001 Huron Road, Cleveland, Ohio 44115; Rilma O. Buckman, Ph.D.

To demonstrate ways of providing a *continuum of vocational rehabilitation services* for the *mentally retarded,* drawing on all resources of the community. See also RD-1769.

RD-2057-G (66-3).* Social Adjustment Center for Mentally Retarded Adults. South Carolina Habilitation Center, Ladson, South Carolina 29456; Erbert F. Cicenia, Ed.D.

To demonstrate the efficacy of a *social adjustment residential center* in *preventing institutionalization of mentally retarded adults* who require security, supervision, guidance, and training not presently available in the community.

RD-2125-P (66-1).* Task Training Methods for the Severely Mentally Retarded. Springfield Goodwill Industries, 285 Dorset Street, Springfield, Maryland 01008; Alvin J. Gagnon.

A project to demonstrate the efficacy of preparing the severely retarded for *vocational adjustment* by applying techniques derived from *learning theory.*

12-55244-4. Industrial Training Resources in Rehabilitation Programs for Retardates. Work Experience Center, 8200 Exchange Way, St. Louis, Missouri 63144; Patricia B. Lacks, Ph.D.

To explore various methods for utilizing *industrial training resources* in the rehabilitation of mentally retarded individuals.

RD-2209-G (67-3).* Demonstration Project to Determine the Feasibility of Producing and Distributing Digests of Written Materials on Recreation for the Handicapped. Southern Illinois University, Carbondale, Illinois 62901; William H. Freeberg, D. Rec.

To establish a series of critical *digests of existing programs and written materials* devoted to *recreation* for the handicapped.

RD-2245-P (67-1).* Films for Vocational Rehabilitation Counselors. MacDonald Training Center Foundation, 4424 Tampa Bay Boulevard, Tampa, Florida 33614; L. H. Ricker, Ph.D.

To produce a series of six *films* for training rehabilitation counselors and others working with the mentally retarded.

RD-2286-P (67-2).* Techniques Facilitating Discrimination Learning. Catholic University, Psychology Department, Washington, D. C. 20017; R. A. Wunderlich, Ph.D.

To investigate and develop techniques to facilitate learning by normal and retarded children *under adverse conditions* of contiguity.

RD-2294-P (66-1).* Peer Knowledge and Subsequent Adjustment of Mentally Retarded Youth. University of Oregon, College of Education, Eugene, Oregon 97403; John E. deJung, Ed.D.

To investigate the relationship of *inter-person awareness* by institutionalized higher level retardates upon their subsequent *social and vocational adjustment.*

RD-2304-P (66-1).* A Preliminary Investigation of Personal-Social Interaction in Job Opportunities Available to the Retarded. University of Georgia, Athens, Georgia 30601; A. L. Shotick, Ph.D.

A pilot investigation of the *personal-social interactions* in various job opportunities available to mentally retarded youth.

RD-2346-P (67-3).* Inter-Generational Relationship in the Vocational Rehabilitation of Mentally Retarded. Federation Employment and Guidance Service, 215 Park Avenue, South, New York, New York 10003; Roland Baxt.

To establish a demonstration *multidimensional vocational rehabilitation program for mentally retarded adults* with opportunities for *inter-generational relationships* with older disabled persons and to assess the impact of the program on their rehabilitation.

RD-2382-P (67-1).* The Development of Reasoning, Moral Judgment, and Moral Conduct in Retardates and Normals. Temple University, Philadelphia, Pennsylvania 19122; Will Beth Stephens, Ph.D.

A project to study *reasoning, moral judgment,* and *moral conduct* in retardates and to compare retardates' performance with that of normal individuals. See also 15-55121-2.

RD-2425-G (67-1).* A National Follow-up of Mental Retardates Employed by the Federal Government. Department of Vocational Rehabilitation, 1331 H Street N. W., Washington, D. C. 20005; Leslie B. Cole.

To conduct a *followup study* of the initial two thousand *mental retardates* employed by the Federal Government.

RD-2471-G (68-1).* Training of Program Supervisors of Mentally Retarded Workers. Rhode Island Association for Retarded Children, 333 Grotto Avenue, Providence, Rhode Island 02906; George J. Hickey.

To demonstrate *increased work opportunities* for the *mentally retarded by training industrial work supervisors* to work with them.

RD-2568-P (68-3).* Assessing the Work Personalities of Mentally Retarded Adults. University of Minnesota, Minneapolis, Minnesota 55455; Lloyd H. Lofquist, Ph.D.

To investigate the *work personality of mentally retarded* individuals in terms of vocational abilities and vocational needs.

15-55114-3.* Cognitive and Attitudinal-Motivational Factors in Performance of Retarded. The Catholic University of America, Washington, D. C. 20017; Norman A. Milgram, Ph.D.

A research-demonstration of *cognitive and attitudinal factors* which directly contribute to the response of *mentally retarded adolescents* and *adults* to rehabilitation and training efforts.

RD-2599-P (68-2).* Skill Analysis as a Technique for Predicting Vocational Success of the Mentally Retarded. Human Resources Center, Albertson, New York 11507; Henry Viscardi, Jr., LL.D.

To develop and validate instruments *predictive* of *training success* and *employment* of retardates in specific *clerical and industrial occupations.* See also RD-1036.

RD-2625-P (68-1).* Decision Criteria in Endogenous Mentally Retarded Adults. The Regents of the University of Michigan, 2008 Administration Building, Ann Arbor, Michigan 48104; Wilson P. Tanner, Jr.

To develop *techniques* for studying the limits of *decision criteria* of *retardates* and the nature of their *response criteria.*

12-55008-3.* New Approaches to Competitive Employment for the Mentally Retarded. Flame of Hope, Inc., 592-A Washington Street, Wellesley, Maryland 02181; Stephen E. Blum.

To assist *sheltered workshops* for the *mentally retarded* in development, design, production, promotion, and marketing of salable items that can be produced in quantity and sold nationally.

RD-2690-G (68-1).* Employment of Mentally Retarded in Competitive Industry. Human Resources Center, Albertson, New York 11507; Henry Viscardi, Jr., LL.D.

To produce a *film* showing progress in rehabilitating the *educable mentally retarded* at Human Resources Center.

RD-2753-P (68-1).* A Comparison of the Doman-Delacato Method and Behavior Modification Method Upon the Coordination of Mongoloids. Teaching Research Division, Oregon State System of Higher Education, Monmouth, Oregon 97361; Gerald E. Gage, Ed.D.

A pilot project to apply the *Doman-Delacato method* of patterned therapeutic exercises to *mongoloids* to determine if it improves their *motor coordination.*

15-55273-2. Return to the Community of the Mentally Ill. San Mateo County Hall of Justice and Records, Redwood City, California 94063; H. Richard Lamb, M.D.

To determine the extent to which an *alternative program* can be developed in a community to *supplant long-term hospitalization* of the *chronic* and *severely mentally ill* in the State hospital. See also RD-2054.

RD-2878-P (68-1).* Conference on Residential Care. University of Hartford, 200 Bloomfield Avenue, West Hartford, Connecticut 04117; Dr. Michael Klaber.

A conference on residential services and programs for the *retarded* to *disseminate* pertinent research *findings* among an assembled group of experts in the field of mental retardation.

12-55178-2. Improving Standards for Services to the Retarded in Residential Centers. Joint Commission on Accreditation of Hospitals, 645 North Michigan Avenue, Chicago, Illinois 60611; John D. Porterfield, M.D.

The further development and implementation of standards of service to the retarded in public and private residential centers and the formation of a categorical council under the Joint Commission on Accreditation of Hospitals for *accreditation of residential centers for the retarded.*

15-55212-2. Problem Solving and Development of Social and Work Skills in the Mentally Retarded. University of Wisconsin, 750 University Avenue, Madison, Wisconsin 53706; Alfred J. Butler, Ph.D.

To develop and refine a *theory of problem-solving* which will focus on factors *contributing to the development of work and social skills* in retarded persons.

12-55213-2. Comparative Efforts in Community Organization: A Study of Five Interorganizational Comparative Projects. University of Wisconsin, Madison, Wisconsin 53706; Jerald Hage, Ph.D.

A comparative study of five large *community organization* projects serving the *retarded.*

15-55298-2. Measurement and Remediation of Social Competency Deficits. University of Oregon, Eugene, Oregon 97403; John E. de Jung, Ed.D.

To study requisites of adequate *social behavior* within populations of *retarded* and low income adolescents; to develop an experimental social competency curriculum for junior high school students; and to modify and *validate the Test of Social Inference* on these populations.

15-55121-2. The Reasoning, Moral Judgment, and Moral Conduct of Retardates—Phase Two. Temple University, Broad and Montgomery Streets, Philadelphia, Pennsylvania 19122; Will Beth Stephens, Ph.D.

To assess the development of *moral reasoning, moral judgment, and moral conduct* among mental *retardates.* See also RD-2382.

RD-3705-P (69-1).* Restructuring the Role of the Consumer Representative in the Change Process to Improve Services for the Mentally Retarded. California Council for Retarded Children, 1107 Ninth Street, Room 1020, Sacramento, California 95814; H. David Sokoloff.

A pilot study to analyze and structure a *change process* that will lead to improvement *in the services available to the retarded.*

RD-11-P (62-1).* These Are Not Children: A Play About Opportunities for the Mentally Retarded. Plays for the Living, Family Services Association of America, 44 East 23rd Street, New York, New York 10010; Clare M. Tousley.

To develop an educational and informative *theatrical production* demonstrating the effectiveness of the rehabilitation process in the vocational rehabilitation of the mentally retarded. See also RD-2309.

22-55092-1. Conference on Vocational Rehabilitation of the Retarded. American Association on Mental Deficiency, 5201 Connecticut Avenue N. W., Washington, D. C. 20015; George Soloyanis, Ph.D.

To provide a forum for the *international* exchange of current research results bearing on the vocational rehabilitation of the *retarded.*

22-55100-1.* Conference on the Mentally Retarded in the Caribbean Area: Needs, Resources, and Approaches. Jamaica Association for Mentally Handicapped Children, 6 Norman Road, Kingston 10, Jamaica; Marigold J. Thorburn, M.B.

To arrange and conduct a Caribbean area conference on *mental retardation.*

15-55215-1. A Programmed Work Environment for the Retarded and Emotionally Disturbed Adults for Training and Maintaining Productive Work Activity. Jewish Vocational Service of Milwaukee, 207 E. Buffalo Street, Milwaukee, Wisconsin 53202; Chandler C. Screven, Ph.D.

To demonstrate specific applications of *operant conditioning* techniques and *programmed instruction* methods in meeting the needs of a work training and rehabilitation facility.

SELECTED DEMONSTRATIONS

Occupational Training Centers for the Mentally Retarded

RD-202 (58.4).* C-BARC Occupational Center. Caddo-Bossier Association for Mentally Retarded Children, 351 Jordan Street, Shreveport, Louisiana 71101; Fortson Almand, Sr.

RD-204 (58-3).* Vocational Training of Mentally Handicapped Adolescents. Southern Illinois University, Carbondale, Illinois 62901; O. P. Kolstoe, Ph.D.

RD-205 (58-4).* Work-Training Center. Aid Retarded Children, 1362 Ninth Avenue, San Francisco, California 94103; Elias Katz, Ph.D.

RD-211 (58-5).* A Demonstration Project to Establish a Sheltered Workshop for Severely Retarded Adults to Duplicate O.V.R. Special Project Number 11. Philadelphia Association for Retarded Children, 1440 North Broad Street, Philadelphia, Pennsylvania 19121; Edward R. Goldman. See also RD-20.

RD-232 (58-3).* Occupational Training Center. Aid for Retarded Children Association of Jefferson County, Occupational Training Center, 4244 Third Avenue South, Birmingham, Alabama 35222; Carl Monroe, Jr.

RD-237 (58-3).* Occupational Training Center and Sheltered Workshop. Orange Grove School, 1002 East Main Street, Chattanooga, Tennessee 37408; N. R. Hafemeister, Ed.D.

RD-254 (58-4).* Developing Employability in Mentally Retarded Adults. The Sheltered Workshop Foundation of Lucas County, 1155 Larc Lane, Toledo, Ohio 43614; Mrs. Josina Lott.

RD-258 (58-4).* The South Texas Rehabilitation Center. The Rio Grande Association for the Mentally Retarded, P. O. Box 533, Edinburg, Texas 78539; Arthur E. Brown.

RD-268 (58-3).* George Mason Occupational Center. Arlington County School Board, 1426 North Quincy Street, Arlington, Virginia 22207; Edward F. Rose.

RD-274 (58-3).* Rehabilitation Training Center and Sheltered Workshop for Mentally Retarded Young Adults. Project, Inc., 401 South Edwin Street, St. Louis, Missouri 63103; Thomas W. Phillips.

RD-278 (59-4).* Work-Citizenship Preparation of Mentally Retarded Adults. Goodwill Industries of Greater Kansas City, 1817 Campbell Street, Kansas City, Missouri 64108; Herbert T. Gragert.

RD-308 (58-5).* Development of Occupational Evaluation and Training Center for the Mentally Retarded. Goodwill Industries of Tacoma, 2356 Tacoma Avenue South, Tacoma, Washington 98402; James E. Gentry.

RD-357 (59-3).* Laradon Hall Occupational Center. Laradon Hall Society, East 51st Avenue and Lincoln Street, Denver, Colorado 80216; Alfred H. Gallagher.

RD-373 (59-3).* Bridge Building: Occupational Training Center for the Mentally Retarded. Maryland Association for Retarded Children, Baltimore Chapter, 2538 Greenmount Avenue, Baltimore, Maryland 21218; Mrs. Helen Nussear.

RD-436 (60-4).* Delaware County Occupational Center. Delaware County Council for Retarded Children, 2000 West 7th Street, Muncie, Indiana 47302; Mrs. Mary Alice Cooper.

RD-444 (60-5).* Occupational Training Center for Mentally Retarded Adults. Rhode Island Association for Retarded Children, Greater Providence, Rhode Island 02909; Otis Clay Oliver, Jr.

RD-461 (60-3).* Occupational Training Center for the Mentally Retarded. Chatham Association for Retarded Children, P. O. Box 3911, Savannah, Georgia 31404; Julius Hornstein.

RD-480 (60-4).* Occupational Training Center for Mentally Retarded. Occupational Training Center for the Mentally Retarded, 84th and Adams, Lincoln, Nebraska 68507; Delwyn C. Lindholm.

RD-484 (60-3).* The Vocational Adjustment Center. Vocational Adjustment Center, 27 Damrell Street, Boston, Massachusetts 02127; Diwakar S. Salvi.

RD-489 (60-5).* Concepts for Working: Specialized Training for Mentally Retarded Young Adults. San Antonio Council for Retarded Children, P. O. Box 10210, 227 West Drexel Street, San Antonio, Texas 78210; R. L. Merz, Jr.

RD-531 (60-4).* The Atlanta Occupational Center for Mentally Retarded. Atlanta Chapter for Retarded Children, 1100 Sylvan Road S. W., Atlanta, Georgia 30310; Norman L. Meyers.

RD-606 (61-3).* Vocational Unit of Good Samaritan Training Center. Harrison County Association for Retarded Children, P. O. Box 597, Gulfport, Mississippi 39502; Novella Tandy.

RD-621 (61-4).* Occupational Training Center and Sheltered Workshop for Mentally Retarded. Hinds County Association for Retarded Children, 1044 Voorhees Street, Jackson, Mississippi 39209; Henry Eaton.

RD-663 (61-2).* Hawaii Work Training Program for the Adult Mentally Retarded. Hawaii Vocational Rehabilitation Division, P. O. Box 339, Honolulu, Hawaii 96809; Harold Ajirogi.

RD-678 (61-4).* Occupational Training Center for the Mentally Retarded. Richmond Goodwill Industries, 9 South 14th Street, Richmond, Virginia 23219; Mrs. Jean P. Seward.

RD-698 (62-3).* Development of a Program of Rehabilitation for Mentally Retarded Young Adults in a Rural Setting. Morrilton Public Schools Training Center for the Mentally Retarded, Morrilton, Arkansas 72110; Terry A. Humble.

RD-719 (61-4).* An Occupational Center for Retarded Children. South Dakota Association for Retarded Children, James Valley Chapter, 620 North Kittridge Street, Mitchell, South Dakota 57301; Charles F. Pagel.

RD-735 (61-4).* Lake Region Sheltered Workshop. Lake Region Sheltered Workshop, 201 North Whitford, Fergus Falls, Minnesota 56537; Norman Doeden.

RD-743 (61-2).* An Analysis of the Occupational Training Project for the Retarded. Whitten Village, Clinton, South Carolina 29325; B. O. Whitten.

RD-773-G (61-4).* Sheltered Workshop and Training Program for the Mentally Retarded. Cabell County Sheltered Workshop, 701 Jackson Avenue, Huntington, West Virginia 25704; Alex Darbes, Ph.D.

RD-854-G (62-3).* Sioux City Work Evaluation and Training Project for the Mentally Retarded. Wall Street Mission, 312 South Wall Street, Sioux City, Iowa 51104; John P. Hantla, Jr.

RD-875-G (62-3).* Occupational Training Center for the Mentally Retarded. Palm Beach County Association for Retarded Children, P. O. Box 1148, Lake Worth, Florida 33461; Mrs. Delores S. Benedict.

RD-956-G (62-3).* Volunteer State Vocational Centers. Tennessee Association for Retarded Children, 210 Whitley Building, 1701 21st Avenue South, Nashville, Tennessee 37212; Hale C. Donaldson, M.A.

RD-977-G (62-3).* Worcester Area Occupational Training Center for the Mentally Retarded. Worcester Area Association for Retarded Children, 162 Chandler Street, Worcester, Massachusetts 01609; Edwin A. Hastbacka.

RD-980-G (63-3).* Occupational Training Center for the Mentally Retarded. Hope for Retarded Children, Inc., 888 Delmas Avenue, San Jose, California 95125; Mrs. Patricia Hobbs.

RD-1122-G (63-3).* . . . And . . . Someday, Perhaps, My Chance

Will Come. Vocational Training Center, 1044 Tenth Street, North, Fargo, North Dakota 58102; Warren M. Abbott.

RD-1203-G (63-3).* Opportunity Training Center, Inc. Opportunity Training Center, 101 Chestnut Street, Grand Forks, North Dakota 58201; Roy E. Kimbrell.

RD-1204-G (64-3).* Occupational Training Center for the Mentally Retarded. Lee County Association for Retarded Children, 2570 Hanson Street, Fort Myers, Florida 33901; Kenneth Sanne.

RD-1207-G (63-3).* An Occupational Training Center for the Mentally Handicapped. Lt. Joseph P. Kennedy, Jr. School, 123rd and Wolf Road, Palos Park, Illinois 60464; Melvin Greenstein.

RD-1257-G (64-3).* Vermont Occupational Training Center for the Mentally Retarded. The Vermont National and Savings Bank Building, 381 Main Street, Bennington, Vermont 05201; Milton G. Moore.

RD-1345-G (64-3).* Program Outline: Lewiston-Auburn Occupational Training Center. Committee for the Intellectually Handicapped, Central School-Special Education Department, Academy Street, Auburn, Maine 04210; Arthur Bennett.

RD-1546-G (65-3).* Occupational Training and Evaluation Center for the Mentally Retarded. Benevolent and Protective Order of Elks, Lodge #242, Lockwood Boulevard, Charleston, South Carolina 29401; John F. Nimmich.

RD-1547-G (65-3).* The Sheltered Workshop and Occupational Training Center. Council for Retarded Children of Jefferson County, 809 East Washington Street, Louisville, Kentucky 40202; Jesse T. Richardson, Jr.

RD-1695-G (65-3).* Northern Kentucky Goodwill Industries Occupational Training Center for the Mentally Retarded. Northern Kentucky Goodwill Industries, 228 Court Street, Covington, Kentucky 41011; John C. Wilson, Ph.D.

RD-1824-G (65-3).* A Demonstration of Evaluation, Training, Personal Adjustment and Vocational Placement of Adolescent Mentally Retarded. Christ Child Extension School for Retarded Youth, 2064 Summit Avenue, St. Paul, Minnesota 55105; Sister Anna Marie.

RD-2101-G (66-3).* Work Adjustment Training for Mentally Retarded Young People in a Community Setting. Caruth Memorial Rehabilitation Center, 7850 Brook Hollow Road, Dallas, Texas 75235; Raymond L. Dabney.

SELECTED DEMONSTRATIONS

Coordinated Program of Vocational Rehabilitation and Special Education Services for the Mentally Retarded

RD-1285-P (64-3).* Cooperative Efforts of Schools and Rehabilitation Services for the Mentally Retarded. Bourbon County Schools, Administration Office, Paris, Kentucky 40361; George W. Stewart.

RD-1498-P (64-3).* Rehabilitation Services for Educable Retarded Students. Eugene School District #4, 275 East Seventh Avenue, Eugene, Oregon 97401; Lloyd H. Gillett, Ph.D.

RD-1509-P (64-3).* Demonstration Project Concerning Training and Vocational Placement for Educable Mentally Retarded Pupils. Vigo County School Corporation, 1101 South 13th Street, Terre Haute, Indiana 47802; William J. Hamrick.

RD-1522-P (64-3).* Vocational Rehabilitation and Special Education for the Mentally Retarded in Harlan County, Kentucky. Bureau of Rehabilitation Services, Box 879, Harlan, Kentucky 40831; John M. Burkhart.

RD-1523-P (64-3).* Vocational Rehabilitation and Special Education for the Mentally Retarded in Rockcastle County, Kentucky. Bureau of Rehabilitation Services, Box 879, Harlan, Kentucky 40831; John M. Burkhart.

RD-1524-P (64-3).* An Organized Coordinated Program of Vocational Rehabilitation and Special Education for the Mentally Retarded. Bureau of Rehabilitation Services, Mayo State Vocational School, Paintsville, Kentucky 41240; Basil T. Mullins.

RD-1548-P (64-3).* A Selected Demonstration for the Vocational Training of Mentally Retarded Youth. University of Kansas Medical Center, 39th and Rainbow, Kansas City, Kansas 66103; Norris G. Haring, Ed.D.

RD-1638-P (64-3).* A Coordinated Program of Vocational Rehabilitation and Special Education Services for the Mentally Retarded. Massachusetts Rehabilitation Commission, 296 Boylston Street, Boston, Massachusetts 02116; Dorothy M. Singer, Ed.D.

RD-1631-P (65-3).* Coordinated Program of Special Education and Vocational Rehabilitation Services for the Mentally Retarded. Division of Vocational Rehabilitation, Department of Public Instruction, State Capitol Building, Pierre, South Dakota 57501; R. Chadwick Hoffbeck.

RD-1640-P (64-3).* Coordinated Program of Vocational Rehabilitation and Special Education Services for the Mentally Retarded. State Board of Vocational Education, Vocational Rehabilitation Division, State Capitol Building, Charleston, West Virginia 25305; Cornelius L. Williams.

RD-1649-P (65-3).* Coordinated Program of Special Education and Vocational Rehabilitation Services for the Mentally Retarded. Richland County School District No. 1, 1331 Marion Street, Columbia, South Carolina 29201; Mrs. Sarah Trusdale.

RD-1656-P (64-3).* A Handout of Silence. State Board of Vocational Education, Vocational Rehabilitation Division, State Capitol Building, Charleston, West Virginia 25305; Carl G. Anderson.

RD-1665-P (64-3).* Help Along the Way: Coordinated Program of Vocational Rehabilitation and Special Education Services for the Mentally Retarded. State Board of Vocational Education, Vocational Rehabilitation Division, State Capitol Building, Charleston, West Virginia 25305; Thorold S. Funk.

RD-1668-P (65-3).* A Review of the Educable Mentally Retarded Work-Study Program in the Chattanooga Public Schools, 1964-67. Chattanooga Public Schools, 1161 West 40th Street, Chattanooga, Tennessee 37407; Oscar Allen.

RD-1674-P (65-3).* A Coordinated Program of Special Education and Vocational Rehabilitation Services for the Mentally Retarded. Connecticut State Department of Education, Box 2219, Hartford, Connecticut 06115; Kenneth Jacobs.

RD-1676-P (65-3).* Education and Habilitation for the Adolescent Mentally Retarded: A Team Approach. Services for Exceptional Children, Division of Instruction, State Department of Education, 118 State Office Building, Atlanta, Georgia 30334; Richard M. Bartlett.

RD-1681-P (65-3).* A Coordinated Program for Vocational Rehabilitation Services for the Mentally Retarded. School District No. 1, Child Service Center, 220 N. E. Beech Street, Portland, Oregon 97212; Edgar A. Taylor, Jr.

RD-1682-P (65-3).* Coordinated Program for Vocational Rehabilitation and Special Education Services for the Mentally Retarded. Board of Education, Memphis City Schools, 2597 Avery, Memphis, Tennessee 38112; Harold W. Perry.

RD-1743-P (65-3).* A Cooperative Education/Rehabilitation Work-Study Program for Educable Mentally Retarded: The Essex Plan. Board of Education, 21 Winans Street, East Orange, New Jersey 07050; Patricia F. Lewis.

RD-1744-P (65-3).* A Coordinated Program of Vocational Rehabilitation and Special Education Services for the Mentally Retarded. Southern Gloucester County Regional High, Blackwoodtown Road, Franklinville, New Jersey 08322; Pierre S. Heimrath.

RD-1749-P (65-3).* A Coordinated Program of Vocational Rehabilitation and Special Education Services for the Mentally

Retarded. Office of Rehabilitation Services, 1200 University Club Building, 136 East South Temple, Salt Lake City, Utah 84111; Vaughn L. Hall.

RD-1761-P (65-3).* On-the-Job Training Program: Educable Mentally Retarded. Pocatello School District No. 25, 3115 Pole Line Road, Pocatello, Idaho 83201; Charles Sanford.

RD-1917-P (65-3).* Cooperative Program of Vocational Rehabilitation and Special Education in the Winston-Salem/Forsyth County Public School System. Division of Vocational Rehabilitation, Department of Public Instruction, Raleigh, North Carolina 27603; Harold J. Pope.

RD-1931-P (66-3).* A Human Development Program for Educable Retarded Youth. West Springfield Public Schools, 130 Park Street, West Springfield, Massachusetts 01105; Chris Grammaticas.

RD-2068-P (66-3).* A Coordinated Program of the Department of Vocational Rehabilitation and Public Schools for Mentally Retarded Students in Basic Academic Track. Department of Vocational Rehabilitation, 1331 H Street N. W., Washington, D. C. 20005; David O. Songer.

RD-2097-P (66-1).* Special Education of Mentally Retarded Youth. Idaho State Department of Education, State House, Boise, Idaho 83702; Reid Bishop.

SELECTED DEMONSTRATIONS

A Work Experience Program for the Mentally Retarded in Their Last Year in School

RD-1525-G (64-3).* Work Experience Center: Habilitation of the Retarded. Jewish Employment and Vocational Service, 1727 Locust Street, St. Louis, Missouri 63103; Samuel Bernstein.

RD-1528-G (64-3).* Coordinated Program for Mentally Retarded in the Denver Public Schools and the Colorado Department of Rehabilitation. Denver Public Schools and Colorado Department of Rehabilitation, 705 State Services Building, 1525 Sherman Street, Denver, Colorado 80203; Richard Heberlein.

RD-1675-G (65-3).* A Work Experience Program for the Mentally Retarded in Their Last Year in School. Opportunity Center, P. O. Box 254, 3030 Bowers Street, Wilmington, Delaware 19899; John D. Zimmerman.

RD-1736-G (65-3).* A Work Experience Program for the Mentally Retarded in Their Last Year in School. Goodwill Industries of Oregon, 512 S. E. Mill Street, Portland, Oregon 97214; William Wiegers.

RD-1759-G (65-3).* Work Adjustment Center: A Bridge Between School and Work. Greater Portland Association for Retarded Children, 1777 West Broadway, South Portland, Maine 04106; J. Philip Chandler.

RD-1762-G (65-3).* Work Experience Program. Omaha Public Schools, 3902 Davenport Street, Omaha, Nebraska 68131; Don Warner.

RD-1830-G (66-3).* A Cooperative Work Experience Program for Mentally Retarded Adolescents. Crossroads Rehabilitation Center, 3242 Sutherland Avenue, Indianapolis, Indiana 46205; Shelley C. Stone, Ph.D.

RD-2058-G (66-3).* A Work Experience Program for the Mentally Retarded in Their Last Year in School. Vocational Guidance and Rehabilitation Service, 2239 East 55th Street, Cleveland, Ohio 44103; John L. Campbell.

COUNSELING AND PSYCHOTHERAPY WITH THE MENTALLY RETARDED: A SELECTED ANNOTATED BIBLIOGRAPHY

ALFRED J. BUTLER

Abel, T. M.: Resistances and difficulties in psychotherapeutic counseling of mental retardates. *Journal of Clinical Psychology Monograph Supplement*, 9:9-11, 1953.

Note: The preparation of this paper was supported, in part, by RD 1798-P, Social Rehabilitation Services, Department of Health, Education, and Welfare, Washington, D. C. 20201.

Many professional persons reject the idea of doing therapy with the mentally retarded. However, "if one can enjoy the individuals one works with, have some simple goals, flexible techniques, then the therapeutic results with mental retardates may be not less effective and not more difficult to bring about than they are with more intelligent individuals; in fact, they may be often more adequate and surprisingly easy to elicit." Three examples are cited to illustrate approaches found helpful with particular mentally defective problem children.

Ackerman, N. W., and Menninger, C. E.: Treatment techniques for mental retardation in a school for personality disorders in children. *American Journal of Orthopsychiatry,* 6:294-313, 1936.

A report and discussion of therapeutic attitudes and methods applied to management of retarded children at Southard School. A departure from the conservative medical approach to mental retardation is encouraged: ". . . we set out to treat not retardation alone, but the whole child." Emphasis is on functional retardation and associated disturbances. Program areas discussed are: medical therapy, milieu therapy, psychotherapy, training in acceptance of reality, occupational therapy, recreational therapy, special functions, and academic education. A case study is presented.

Albini, J. L., and Dinitz, S.: Psychotherapy with disturbed and defective children: An evaluation of changes in behavior and attitudes. *American Journal of Mental Deficiency,* 69(4):560-567, 1965.

Changes in attitudes and behaviors were evaluated in seventy-three institutionalized mental retardates involved in a psychotherapy study. Ss had an age range from seven to fifteen and an IQ range from forty to seventy-eight. They were divided into two groups. The experimental group was comprised of thirty-seven boys with a history of "behavior disturbance: (frequent fighting and arguments, stealing, lying, temper tantrums, setting fires, and destroying property) while the comparison group consisted of thirty-six "non-disturbed" boys. The psychotherapy program was oriented towards the identification, comprehension, and working through of problems. Certain principles were observed: complete verbal permissiveness was encouraged, strong emotional support was provided, the child was supported in setting realistic goals for his future and was encouraged to discriminate between thought and overt action. Both individual and group therapy were given; Ss received fifty-eight half-hour sessions. Ss were evaluated with a classroom behavior checklist, a pupil evaluation schedule, and a scale which assessed acceptance-rejection attitudes. Analysis of the data suggested that short-term psychotherapy resulted in very limited improvement. Of the six measures used, only two showed a nonsignificant trend toward improvement. These two measures were concerned with "negative classroom behaviors and teacher ratings of the S's habits and attitudes toward learning." Possible factors contributing to these results were discussed.

Appel, E., and Martin, C.: Group counseling for social adjustment. *American Journal of Mental Deficiency*, 62:517-520, 1957.

Discussed the formation of Community Living Groups to help alleviate what the authors felt the most serious handicap to the retardate's successful re-integration into the normal community—his social inadequacy. The Living Groups were essentially discussion groups functioning within a friendly relaxed atmosphere and focusing on areas of conflict and friction for the retardates. Subjective estimation of results indicated overall beneficial results of the groups, particularly in developing more self-confidence, poise and self-pride in the participant.

Arje, F. B., and Berryman, D. L.: New help for the severely retarded and emotionally disturbed child. *Journal of Rehabilitation*, 32(1):14-15, 1966.

Educational rhythmics is discussed as a useful therapeutic modality. It is felt that this technique is proving effective in stimulating the interest of the disabled child, developing a sense of physical harmony and internal equilibrium.

Astrachan, M.: Group psychotherapy with mentally retarded female adolescents and adults. *American Journal of Mental Deficiency, 60*:152-156, 1955.

Results from the use of group psychotherapy with thirty-one female patients are described. The sessions are described in terms of the following: role of the therapist, kind of communication, number of group interactions, formalism, content, ratio of patient to therapist and group composition. The author notes that the most conspicuous change was a reduction in the patients' feelings of isolation, shame and fear. . . . The patients used group therapy to explore the significance of their mental retardation. It, therefore, seems that discussion group psychotherapy has a place among the treatment resources for institutionalized mental defectives diagnosed as familial or undifferentiated.

Axline, V.: Mental deficiency—symptom or disease? *Journal of Consulting Psychology, 13*:313-327, 1945.

The records of fifteen children were studied to see how they reacted to play therapy, how their parents reacted to them, and what effect therapy had on their behavior and IQ. The question is raised as to what extent did emotional tensions, frustrations, conflicts and deficiencies hamper some children in realizing their potential.

Ayers, C. E., and Duguay, A. R.: Critical variables in counseling the mentally retarded. *Rehabilitation Literature, 30*(2):42-44, 50, 1969.

The emotional problems, level of intellectual functioning, personality characteristics (motivation, self-concept and temperament), communication factors, learning ability, parental influences, and environmental factors are critical variables that necessitate consideration in counseling the mentally retarded. Regardless of the particular theoretical counseling technique of mode or therapy employed, all of these variables directly and indirectly influence the overall adjustment of the retarded. Hence, it is imperative that counselors become aware of them if they are to help the mentally retarded develop to their fullest physical, mental, social, educational and vocational potential.

Ayer, J. M., and Butler, A. J.: Client-counselor communication and interaction in counseling with the mentally retarded. The University of Wisconsin, Final Report R. D. 1798-P, January, 1969. Sponsored by The Social and Rehabilitation Service, Department of Health, Education, and Welfare, Washington, D. C., and The Joseph P. Kennedy Jr. Foundation.

A three-year investigation on the counseling process with the mentally retarded. The six individual studies resulting from this project and included in the final report are: (1) Content Analysis of Counselor and Client Responses in Counseling with the Mentally Retarded; (2) Dimensions of Counselor Relationship and Depth of Client Intrapersonal Exploration as Measures of Process in Counseling the Mentally Retarded; (3) Four Process Variables in Counseling with Mental Retardates; (4) The Relationships Between Language Abilities and Content of the Counseling Process; (5) The Relationship Between Personality Dimensions and Changes of Content in the Counseling Process; and (6) Verbal Expressivity as a Client Variable in Counseling the Mentally Retarded.

Baumanis, D.: Both sides of the coin: The retarded child and his family. *Canada's Mental Health*, XVIII:23-28, May-August 1970.

Concerns a social worker and counselor viewing an institution for retarded children in Canada. Case history of a young boy and how the family handled him at home before placing him in an institution. Conflicting opinion of a psychiatrist, who felt that if the family would have submitted to more counseling there would not have been a reason for institutionalization. Counselor felt the parents should be helped to make plans beneficial to the child.

Baumgartner, B. B., and Lynch, K. D.: *Administering Classes for the Retarded: What Kinds of Principals and Supervisors Are Needed?* New York, The John Day Company, 1967.

Guidance and counseling are discussed in Chapter 9. Suggests guidance for the parent and child so that they become more realistic in accepting the limitations to gainful employment. Asserts that employers recognize a difference in counseled and not counseled retarded employees. Suggests that job counseling begin when the teenager is ready for a job. Stresses the importance of the counselor's work with the family and the need for communication between counselor, teacher, and employer. Discusses community agencies and hiring the retarded.

Bennis, J.: The use of music therapy in the special education classroom. *Journal of Music Therapy*, 6(1):15-18, 1969.

The use of music therapy with the mentally retarded, physically handicapped, emotionally disturbed, and deaf is discussed. The goal of music therapy is to establish rapport with the child which will aid in his return to a group situation.

Blackhurst, A. E.: Sociodrama for the adolescent mentally retarded. *Training School Bulletin*, 63(3):136-142, 1966.

Points out the need for increased emphasis on training the adolescent mentally retarded for social adjustment. A rationale, based on Lewin's field theory, is proposed for the application of the technique of sociodrama. Sociodrama is described and suggestions are made for its implementation in the classroom.

Bozarth, J. D., and Roberts, R. R.: Effectiveness of counselor-trainees with mentally retarded sheltered workshop clients. *Training School Bulletin*, 67(2):119-122, 1970.

Investigated the effectiveness of counseling vs. attentive non-counseling treatment for twenty-three male and twenty female mentally retarded clients in a sheltered workshop setting. Results based on the pre and post ratings by work supervisors on fifteen criterion variables suggest that counseling was not an effective means of improving the performance of this mentally retarded population. There was some indication that attention treatment of the type in the project tended to be detrimental for these kinds of clients.

Bradley, B. H.; Maurer, R.; and Hundziak, M.: A study of the effectiveness of milieu therapy and language training for the mentally retarded. *Exceptional Children,* 33(3):143-150, 1966.

Attempted to evaluate the effectiveness of milieu therapy and specific language training based on the analysis of profiles obtained with the Illinois Test of Psycholinguistic Abilities (ITPA) for a period of seven months. Thirty institutionalized mentally retarded children ranging in CA from 7.3 to 18.3 were paired on total raw scores from the ITPA and divided into two general types of language difficulties on the basis of the neurophysiological theory of Gellner. The teaching was based on the highest performance area or strengths of the child. The program was evaluated by pre- and post-test scores on the ITPA, as well as eight other psychological and educational tests. The results indicate significantly higher scores for the experimental group on total raw scores of the ITPA, as well as on six subtests.

Browning, P. L.: An analysis of counselor, client, and situational conditions in counseling the mentally retarded. *Dissertation Abstracts,* 30(11-12A):5227, 1969.

Browning, P. L., and Butler, A. J.: Process Research in Counseling the Retarded. In Prehm, H. J. (Ed.): *Rehabilitation Research in Mental Retardation.* University of Oregon, Rehabilitation Research and Training Center in Mental Retardation, Monograph No. 2, 1970, pp. 35-47.

Discusses the efficacy of counseling with the client population in general and the mentally retarded in particular. Presents outcome and process research as the two major strategies for investigating counseling and psychotherapy. Indicates only sparse attention given to process research in counseling with retarded clients. Finally, discusses the "blueprint" of an actual process study which is one of several such investigations generated from a three-year research project entitled, "Client-Counselor Communication and Interaction in Counseling with the Mentally Retarded."

Burton, A.: Psychotherapy with the mentally retarded. *American Journal of Mental Deficiency*, 58:486-489, 1954.

A discussion of the historical influences upon the prevailing negative attitudes surrounding the efficacy of psychotherapy for the mentally retarded. The use of psychotherapy, especially group therapy, for this group of individuals is encouraged and the incorporation of ancillary medical personnel (nurses, psychiatric ward attendants, etc.) into the group therapy team is advised by the author.

Carlson, B. W., and Ginglend, D. R.: *Play Activities for the Retarded Child*. Nashville, Tennessee, Abingdon Press, 1961.

Presents games, crafts, and musical activities. All the activities are divided according to the five key areas of development—mental health, social, physical, language, and intellectual. The complexity of the activities ranges from the simplest ones to the more complex. All the activities are based on sound psychological principles.

Chandler, C. A.; Norman, V. B.; and Bahn, A. B.: The mentally deficient in out-patient psychiatric clinics. *American Journal of Mental Deficiency*, 67:218-226, 1962.

Data on psychiatric out-patient services for the mentally retarded are presented.

Chase, M. W.: The practical application of psychotherapy in an institution for the mentally deficient. *American Journal of Mental Deficiency*, 58:337-341, 1953.

The results of the use of psychotherapy at an institution for the mentally deficient in the State of Washington are described. Three typical cases are discussed. In general, results of psychotherapy have been found gratifying in this institution.

Chess, S.: Psychiatric treatment of the mentally retarded with behavior problems. *American Journal of Orthopsychiatry*, 32 (5):863-869, 1962.

Three years of experimentation with psychotherapy within a clinic for mentally retarded children are reviewed. Of twenty-nine cases started in therapy, nineteen remained to receive from six to thirty-nine sessions. The best results were obtained with those youngsters with mental retardation and secondary behavior disorder. Psychotherapy should be made available to retarded children, but goals must be individualized and pertinent to the knowledge that, except for pseudo-retardates, continued functioning on a retarded level is to be expected.

Chidester, L.: Therapeutic results with mentally retarded children. *American Journal of Orthopsychiatry*, 4:464-472, 1934.

A report of three different cases of mental deficiency with the various treatments accorded each and their effects upon the patient's IQ scores. IQ increases were recorded after treatment for all three patients. The author offers these cases as "examples of mental retardation which are subject to treatment or amelioration."

Chidester, L., and Menninger, K. A.: The application of psychoanalytic methods to the study of mental retardation. *American Journal of Orthopsychiatry*, 6:316-325, 1936.

A case study of a boy who tested mentally retarded but revealed little organic pathology at clinical examination. A fixation in emotional development was suspected and psychoanalytic methods were employed over a period of approximately four years. Authors conclude that defenses which inhibited intellectual development were broken down by the treatment. An IQ increase of twenty-eight points was recorded.

Cogan, F.; Monson, L.; and Bruggeman, W.: Concurrent group and individual treatment of the mentally retarded. *Corrective Psychiatry and Journal of Social Therapy*, 12(5):404-409, 1966.

The application of the treatment approach (simultaneous casework and groupwork) by social workers on the same population is noted as being effective in developing stronger self-images, reducing behavior problems and increasing the understanding of role expectations in a group of institutionalized mentally retarded, especially those retarded being prepared to return to community living.

Cooley, J. M.: The relative amenability of dull and bright children to child guidance. *Smith College Studies in Social Work, 16*:26-43, 1945.

Case records of twenty-five children with IQ below eighty-five were matched with an equal number of records of children with IQ of 115 and above. Therapy with the duller children was at least as effective as that with the more intelligent. The duller children required fewer hours of treatment, possibly having simpler problems. Dull children tended to present problems which were more externalized.

Cotzin, M.: Group therapy with mental defective problem boys. *American Journal of Mental Deficiency, 52*:268-283, 1948.

Group psychotherapy was used with nine boys whose chronological ages ranged from 11-6 to 14-11 and whose IQ's ranged from fifty to seventy-nine. The length of time each had been in residence at the Southbury Training School varied from two years, one month to six years, one month. Brief descriptions of each case are given as well as descriptions of the therapeutic sessions. The general results, according to the author, are entirely encouraging and they indicate the usefulness of the method with mental defectives.

Council for Exceptional Children: *Counseling and Psychotherapy with Handicapped Exceptional Children. Bibliography Series.* Sponsoring Agency: Department of Health, Education and Welfare, Washington, D. C., pp. 11-69.

A bibliography of forty-one abstracts concerned with psychotherapy and counseling of mentally retarded, aurally and visually handicapped. Included are subject and author index and information on using the bibliography.

Craft, M.: Psychotherapy for the young male sex offender. *Journal of Mental Subnormality, 11*(21):58-61, 1965.

A Midlands psychiatric practice which catered to "dull" adolescents differentiated three types of young male sex offenders: (1) the isolated offense, requiring reassurance and sex education; (2) the unstable adolescent, often requiring placement in a residential setting with good prognosis; and (3) the persistent sex offender, for whom all available resources must be used to aid community, group and specific reconditioning processes to change the line of sexual desire. Two accounts were given of a psychotherapeutic method based on learning theory. Emphasis was on out-patient psychotherapy and adjustment within the home and community setting of young male sex offenders.

Crowley, F. J.: Psychotherapy for the mentally retarded: A survey and projective consideration. *Training School Bulletin,* 62(1):5-11, 1965.

Psychotherapy may be a significant tool in helping the mentally retarded. All too often a diagnosis of mental retardation brings with it a negative therapeutic orientation. The mentally defective is given custodial care at his worst, vocational training at his best. Few psychologists and psychiatrists see a positive role for psychotherapy with the retarded. But within the theoretical realm, there is an emerging tendency to view the human organism as a total unity. This holistic approach would seem to indicate an aspect of the retardate's personality open to the restructuring growth of psychotherapy. Little research has been done with this area. The slight amount existing shows contradictory results. Without more empirical testing, a valuable tool for working with the retardate may go unused, condemned by an insufficiently tested hypothesis.

Davis, D. A.: Counseling the mentally retarded. *Vocational Guidance Quarterly,* 7:184-188, 1959.

An essay pointing out the importance of social training and character development in the education of the mentally retarded. Special attention and training with the objective of social and occupational adjustment in adult life rather than formal academic schedules are recommended. Group therapy "in a warm, friendly and democratic atmosphere" is recommended to ameliorate social attitudes, beliefs, and modes of conduct. The author urges attention to the self concept of the retardate who is being counseled.

Denton, L. R.: Psychotherapy with mentally retarded children. *Bulletin of the Maritime Psychological Association,* 8:20-27, 1959.

Twenty mentally retarded children with a mean IQ of 60.6 were given weekly individual therapy. The mean therapeutic hours per case was twenty-four. Therapeutic success was rated on a scale of A, B, C, or D, using criteria of: freedom from original symptoms leading to commitment, and adjustment to institutional life. High ratings of A were given to eight cases, B ratings to eight, and C ratings to four. From the results of this and other experiments the author is optimistic about the value of psychotherapy in cases of mild mental retardation.

DePalma, N.: Group psychotherapy with high grade imbeciles and low grade morons. *Delaware Medical Journal,* 28:200-203, 1956.

Discusses the effects of group psychotherapy with five groups of institutionalized retardates. Emphasizes the limitations encountered with group therapy, yet concludes that a measure of success can be claimed in its ability to serve as a screening device for separating quasi-chronic from more prospective individuals.

Dewing, D.: Use of occupational therapy in the socialization of severely retarded children. *American Journal of Mental Deficiency,* 57:43-49, 1952.

Describes an institutional occupational therapy program aimed primarily at improving the adjustment of severely retarded children to their social environment. Three brief case histories illustrate the kinds of problems encountered and the therapist's approach to each.

DiMichael, S. G.: Vocational diagnosis and counseling of the retarded in sheltered workshops. *American Journal of Mental Deficiency, 64:652-657,* 1960.

Evaluates some features of the sheltered workshop on the basis of a study of progress reports from eleven major projects receiving support from Vocational Rehabilitation. Cites the need for improving the professional competence of workshop personnel. Suggests improving the quality rather than the length of the vocational diagnosis or "basic evaluation." Suggests greater efforts be made to coordinate the efforts of the school and workshop. Discusses the "schizophrenia of the IQ" or the practice of decrying emphasis on IQ while still using it. Supports the trends toward the use of carefully selected work samples, the devising of rating scales, and, in the case of standardized manual ability tests, the lengthening of time of the tests and the developing of norms for a typical workshop population. Discusses group counseling as a "new approach" in the workshop and distinguishes between educational (most frequent) and psychological (less frequent) group counseling aims. Individual counseling occurs as needed in the workshop situation.

DiMichael, S. G., and Terwilleger, B. B.: Counselors' activities in the vocational rehabilitation of the mentally retarded. *Journal of Clinical Psychology,* 9:99-109, 1953.

Introduces a symposium instigated by the federal office of Vocational Rehabilitation on counseling the mentally retarded and their parents. Illustrates the community nature of such work by describing the varied contacts of counselors for a sample of cases seen at eleven state vocational rehabilitation centers.

Dubros, S. G.: Behavior therapy with high level, institutionalized, retarded adolescents. *Exceptional Children, 33*(4):229-233, 1966.

The thesis is that instrumental, nonverbal behavior can be modified by a deliberate, repetitive, and systematic conditioning of verbal behavior according to experimentally established principles of learning. Verbal aggression or obnoxiousness, when extinguished during therapy, will lead to the extinction of overt, motor aggression, since what a person does is reinforcing what he says. Two therapy cases are presented in support of this thesis.

Duhrssen, A.: The problem of intelligence in psychotherapy. *Nervenarzt, 35:*22-28, 1964.

It was proposed that intelligence, reflected in the ability to relearn, is essential to psychotherapy with the mentally retarded. The concept of intelligence is linked with achievement; therefore, a certain ability of the patient to relearn is necessary for psychotherapeutical effectiveness. Also damaging influences of the development of early childhood concern especially the ability to retain impression and the perception of detail. These disturbances result when a child is given inadequate care and attention necessary for psychic development.

Part of psychotherapy is concerned with relearning, in other words, the individual must unlearn inappropriate responses and acquire new responses appropriate to the reality of his problems. These skills are found more often in intelligent persons than in those with limited intelligence. It was concluded that it would be beneficial if a subtest could be built into the standard intelligence test which would examine an individual's specific ability to relearn. The performance of such items would be of value in attempting to program for psychically ill persons.

Duncan, J., and Gazda, G.: Significant content of group counseling sessions with culturally deprived ninth grade students. *Personnel and Guidance Journal, 46*(1):11-16, 1967.

Presents examples of the problems that were verbalized during group counseling sessions with four groups (thirty-six students) of culturally deprived white ninth grade boys and girls. There was a general lack of identification with school, a pattern of using inappropriate means to gain acceptance and recognition, a philosophy of life geared toward immediate material gratification, and parental models that do not result in positive parental identification. It is suggested that group counseling may aid these students.

Elkstein, R., and Wallerstein, J.: Observations on the psycho-therapy of borderline and psychotic children. *Psychoanalytic Study of the Child,* 11:303-311, 1956.

Technical difficulties and techniques of psychotherapy of the mentally retarded are discussed.

Ferry, C.: Aspect psychologique—orientation professionnelle psychotherapie. (Psychological aspect—professional orientation psychotherapy.) *Sauvegarde de l'Enfance,* 20(1):210-215, 1965.

The psychologist in a medico-pedagogical institution is concerned with numerous diversified aspects of diagnosis, classification, education, and evaluation. Diagnostic techniques include laboratory examinations, projective tests, observations, conferences, research, reports, and consultations with other technicians. Additional duties involve parent conferences and counseling, placement of children in classes, vocational guidance, method comparison and evaluation, and psychotherapy.

Fine, M. J.: Counseling with the educable mentally retarded. *Training School Bulletin,* 66(3):105-110, 1969.

Proposes that counseling services are needed by the educable mentally retarded child in the schools, and that a number of unresolved issues exist in this field. Related studies, issues, and considerations are reviewed and a pilot study that utilized a group client-centered approach is reported.

Fine, R. H., and Dawson, J. C.: A therapy program for the mildly retarded adolescent. *American Journal of Mental Deficiency,* 69(1):29-30, 1964.

A comprehensive patient-care and psychiatric treatment program was developed for institutionalized mildly retarded adolescents and young adult women. The fifty-six Ss involved in the development of this program represented a heterogeneity of diagnostic classes with a mixture of syndromes and different degrees of behavioral disturbances. They had a CA range from fifteen to thirty. A representative patient used in this program would be characterized as a mildly retarded adolescent girl who was "behaviorally disturbed and hyperactive with a severe character disorder of borderline psychosis."

A special fifty-six-bed cottage was selected to house the patients involved in this program. It was designed to provide a warm, home-like atmosphere. Sleeping quarters were divided into two, four, and six bedrooms. The ward physician was a psychiatric resident and the nursing staff consisted of fifteen women for three eight-hour shifts. In addition, a full-time psychiatric social worker, a clinical psychologist, a recreational therapist, and an occupational therapist were provided for this program.

An open-door policy was maintained and patients were given the privileges and responsibilities of a permissive setting. School, recreational, socialization, and formal psychiatric treatment programs were provided. The focus of the program was to "provide a group experience for the patient as preparation for successful living outside of the hospital." Therapy was primarily concerned with the future goal of each girl in her new role in the community.

During the first eighteen-month period of the program thirty-seven patients were returned to the community, during the following twelve-month period fifteen more patients left the hospital. This was a much higher discharge rate for this group as compared with a comparable group of patients, not involved in the special program—without the program very few girls were leaving the hospital.

Fisher, L. A., and Wolfson, I. W.: Group therapy with defectives. *American Journal of Mental Deficiency*, 57:463-476, 1953.

Group techniques (of Slavson Activity-Interview type) employed with two groups of young female patients. Eight of the twelve Ss showed improved attitudes and behavior after the group experience. Analysis of group processes showed a shift from ego centered behavior to an ingroup centered interest. No increase in psychometric was noted but a more alert—"more conducive to learning"—attitude seemed to develop. Authors caution that the worker must forget the child is defective and respond to him as to any other child with problems. Authors believe that the results give support to the idea that retarded children can respond to psychotherapy.

Freeman, M.: Drawing as a psychotherapeutic intermedium. *American Journal of Mental Deficiency, 41*:182-187, 1936.

Several cases are cited as examples of using spontaneous drawings as a line of communication between the high-grade mentally defective patient and the therapist.

Furrer, B.: Therapeutic possibilities of music with severely feeble-minded children in remedial schools. *Heilpadagogische Werkblatter, 33*(3):119-126, 1964.

Children are grouped homogeneously as "torpid" and needing stimulation or "erethic" and needing calming down. The series of activities in one session is described in minute detail for these two types of mental defectives. Music therapy is believed to be an effective adjunct in modifying behavior of the feeble-minded.

Garfield, M. M.: Client verbal resistance as a function of counselor's technique with mentally retarded. *Dissertation Abstracts, 32*(5-6A):3026, 1971.

Geller, M.: Group psychotherapy with girls institutionalized for mental deficiency: A study of psychotherapeutic process and effects. *Dissertation Abstracts,* 1258-1259, 1953.

Glass, H. L.: Psychotherapy with the mentally retarded: A case history. *Training School Bulletin, 54*:32-35, 1957.

"Psychotherapy with the mentally retarded and mentally deficient is in need of considerable study. Before hypotheses and theories can be drawn up for experimental examination facts must be collected which require being put in order. The case history of Jerry has been offered in an over-simplified manner primarily to illustrate certain of the phenomena of therapy. The first of these was the straight-forward acting out of the aggressive impulse toward the therapist. Second, there was the nearly complete absence in the entire therapy series of interpretations, clarifications of feelings, and other intellectualized verbal exchanges, and third, there was the absence of a superimposed theory of treatment. The question of what constitutes the basic nature of psychotherapy is still unanswered. It is hoped that a systematic collection of successes and failures may one day provide that answer."

Glassman, L. A.: Dull normal intelligence and psychotherapy. *Smith College Studies in Social Work,* 13:275-298, 1943.

A study comparing the results of psychotherapy upon a group of dull normal (IQ 80-90) and a group of above average (IQ 110-136) children. The findings result in a conclusion that "dull normal children are as good prospects for psychotherapy as children of superior intelligence." The author also states that "community resources are no more needed in treating dull children than in treating bright children."

Gondor, E. L., and Levbarg, M.: Techniques and expressive therapy integrated into the treatment of mentally retarded children. *American Journal of Mental Deficiency,* 63:60-63, 1958.

The art and play room in the team approach as well as the use of art in diagnosis and expressive therapy are described.

Gootzeit, J. M.; Lombardo, A. J.; and Milner, S.: Situational diagnosis and therapy. *American Journal of Mental Deficiency,* 64:921-925, 1960.

Two case histories involving situational therapy (bringing about therapeutic effects through social relations and environmental changes) as applied by the AHRC Sheltered Workshop at White Plains, N. Y., are presented. Situational therapy is discussed and further exploration of this area is urged by the authors.

Gorlow, L.; Butler, A.; Einig, K.; and Smith, J.: An appraisal of self attitudes and behavior following group psychotherapy with retarded young adults. *American Journal of Mental Deficiency,* 67:893-898, 1963.

"The study tested the hypothesis that group psychotherapy with young institutionalized, female retardates would occasion greater self-acceptance and more positive institutional behavior. Samples were drawn randomly from a defined subpopulation of the Laurelton State School and resulted in an experimental (group therapy) population of thirty-eight and a control group of thirty-one. After twelve weeks of thrice-weekly hour therapy sessions, differences in self-attitudes and behavior were sought between the experimental and control groups. No differences were observed. The data offered some suggestions for assessment of motivation for treatment. That is, erratic attendance in group therapy is associated with less conforming behavior and more extreme positive and negative attitudes toward the self.

Gowan, J. C., and Demos, G. D.: *The Guidance of Exceptional Children, A Book of Readings.* New York, David McKay Co., Inc., 1965.

A compilation of sixty-two readings, the book considers the guidance of all types of exceptional children. An overview section presents papers dealing with self-concept, social rehabilitaion, behavior modification and the guidance counselor. Articles dealing with mentally retarded are concerned with counseling, pre-vocational evaluation, vocational planning, curriculum tutorial counseling and parent group meetings.

Gunzburg, H. C.: The role of the psychologist in the Mental Deficiency Hospital. *International Journal of Social Psychiatry,* *1*:31-36, 1956.

Shows how the psychologist is well-equipped to help educate, train, and rehabilitate the mentally deficient individual for living in his society.

Gunzburg, H. C.: Therapy and social training for the feeble-minded youth. *British Journal of Medical Psychology,* 30:42-48, 1957.

Seven years of experience with a psychologically-oriented, individualized treatment program for feeble-minded male youth is described. There is emphasis on both habit training and individual needs and counseling. The results of the program are not yet clear, but a preliminary assessment is grounds for optimism that rehabilitation will be substantial in a large majority of the cases.

Halpern, A. S.: The role of client verbal expressivity in counseling the mentally retarded. *Dissertation Abstracts, 28*(3-A): 940, 1968.

Hartman, W. D.: A psychotherapeutic approach toward mentally retarded children. *Japanese Journal of Child Psychiatry, 6*(2):98-104, 1965.

The success of therapy with mentally retarded children is primarily influenced by a clear understanding of the goals to be employed. It was suggested that too often those charged with the treatment of the retarded are driven by needs similar to the parents, i.e. denial of the reality of limited intelligence along with acceptance of the assets and liabilities of the individual. A review of the literature concerning mental illness in the mentally retarded was included and a conclusion drawn that mental disease may be more common among them than among the normal population, due to their limited intellectual capacity to cope with frustrations. In order to combat the problem of mental illness in the retarded it was held essential that a treatment program impart a framework for developing and improving ego structure. Specific suggestions were given for such a program. Included were psychotherapeutic techniques employed in various clinics and hospitals in the United States.

Heath, E. J.: The mentally retarded student and guidance. In Stone, S. C., and Shertyer, B. (Eds.): *Guidance and the Exceptional Student: Guidance Monograph Series No. V.* Boston, Houghton Mifflin Company, 1970.

One of eleven monographs on guidance and the exceptional student. The five chapters for this monograph are given the following titles: (1) Philosophy of Education and Guidance for the Mentally Retarded; (2) Assessment and Evaluation of Mental Retardation; (3) Vocational Rehabilitation for the Mentally Retarded; (4) Vocational Counseling, Planning, and Placement of the Mentally Retarded; and (5) Needed—A Revolutionary Approach in Rehabilitation.

Heber, R. (Ed.): *Special Problems in Vocational Rehabilitation of the Mentally Retarded.* Rehabilitation Services Series No. 65-16, U. S. Department of Health, Education, and Welfare, Vocational Rehabilitation Administration: U. S. Government Printing Office, Washington, D. C., 1964.

Counseling of the mentally retarded along with his family and others in the community is discussed in chapter four. Considers the retardate's need for counseling at various times of stress including: the search for employment; the early stages of employment; at times of necessary job changes; at times of failure on the job; and at times of social or personal crises. Discusses the social-vocational outlook of the mildly, moderately, and severely retarded. Suggests that the counselor's role must be that of champion and spokesman; that he should assure the employer that he will be available when needed; and that many services and resources should be made available to the client.

Heiser, K. F.: Psychotherapy for the mentally retarded child. *Training School Bulletin, 48*:111-119, 1951.

The two chief psychological factors interfering with intellectual potential are lack of cultural or intellectual stimulation and mental or emotional illness or disorder in childhood. Three cases illustrate how therapy may help solve an emotional problem and thus release talents, overcome early familial handicaps, and even assist in a case of childhood schizophrenia.

Heiser, K. F.: Psychotherapy in a residential school for mentally retarded children. *Training School Bulletin, 50*:211-218, 1954.

A progress report on a year's therapy with fourteen children gives changes in behavior, personally and socially, changes in IQ where of interest, and an evaluation of therapeutic efforts.

Hellinger, E.: Counseling and guidance in the vocational adjustment and placement of mentally retarded institutionalized girls. *Dissertation Abstracts, 29A*(3):813, 1968.

Hellner, A. D.: Group therapy with mental defectives. *Mental Health of London, 14*:97-99, 1955.

Discussion and art sessions over approximately a two-year period (forty-four one-hour sessions) were held for thirty-three female retardates. Response to therapy was judged by the therapist on the basis of his observations. Response was rated 42 percent very good to good; 49 percent slight to poor; and 9 percent negative.

Henker, B. A., and Whalen, C. K.: Pyramid therapy in a hospital for the retarded. *Proceedings of the 77th Annual Convention of the American Psychological Association, 4*(Pt. 2):779-780, 1969.

A therapeutic pyramid was created in an institutional setting: professional therapists taught retarded patients to use modeling-reinforcement techniques to train younger retardates. Each retarded "tutor" applied these techniques with two younger patients, thus broadening the base of the pyramid. Results of a test of elementary social behaviors, administered before and after the investigation, showed that youngsters trained by the retarded tutors gained significantly over children who participated in play sessions with these tutors. Not only can moderately retarded patients learn to apply these techniques effectively, but they themselves develop new and complex patterns of social functioning.

Himelstein, P.: Vocational guidance for the mentally handicapped. *Education, 83*:275-278, 1963.

"Unfortunately, the additional years of education coupled with new and challenging techniques for teaching the educable mentally handicapped (EMH), have not been paralleled by the development of a guidance program that is tailored to the unique characteristics of EMH pupils and to the roles in which they will function as adults." The author attributes this to the pessimistic assumptions held in the past that retardates have poor social and occupational prognosis and are not suitable candidates for counseling or psychotherapy. Ways in which the counseling procedure will possibly have to be modified for EMH clients are discussed.

Hitchcock, A. A.: Vocational training and job adjustment of the mentally deficient. *American Journal of Mental Deficiency,* 59:100-106, 1954.

Provides guidelines for the counselor in dealing with mentally retarded individuals in the area of job placement. Very specific discussion of the responsibilities of the counselor in planning, training, placement, and adjustment.

Hormuth, R.: The utilization of group approaches in aiding mentally retarded adults adjust to community living. *Group Psychotherapy,* 8:233-241, 1955.

The selective use of the various group techniques of group therapy, psychodrama, sociodrama, etc., on the basis of a classification of types of individuals has not been prevalent in the area of their application in the field of mental retardation. Too often specialists have tried to make their own approach meet all of the needs of the mentally retarded. Most of the mentally retarded have many unmet needs which are basic to life in the community. Special approaches should be applied only after the basic needs have been met. This paper describes a specific program, the Association for the Help of Retarded Children, which operates within this framework.

Howell, J. E.: Casework with retarded children in an institutional setting. *American Journal of Mental Deficiency,* 61:592-594, 1957.

The author points out "that casework has a specific and important place in working with retarded children but that to be successful it must be done with the child, the parents, the community, and as an integral part of the total therapy of the training school. Casework helps to prevent a deficiency from becoming a handicap."

Humes, C. W., Jr.: Group counseling with educable mentally retarded adolescents in a public school setting: A description of the process and a quantitative assessment of its effectiveness. *Dissertation Abstracts,* 29(4-A):11-5-11-6, 1968.

Joseph, H., and Heimlich, E. P.: The therapeutic use of music with "treatment resistant" children. *American Journal of Mental Deficiency,* 64:41-49, 1959.

"The methodology, theory and clinical experiences of music therapy at Edenwald School have been presented. The therapeutic results with a group of children have been described. 'Music therapy' as a specific psychotherapeutic discipline is effective as an adjunct to other forms of treatment or as a substitute when others have failed. Further study over a long-range period is necessary to evaluate techniques and further to objectify data."

Kadis, A. L.: *The Use of Fingerpainting in Psychotherapy with Mentally Retarded Children.* Paper presented at a panel on Psychotherapy with Mental Defectives, 75th Annual Meeting of the American Association on Mental Deficiency, May 25, 1951.

Discusses the use of fingerpainting in therapy as a means for setting up communication, providing a means for social contacts, and exploration and mastery of the mentally retarded child's world. Stresses fingerpainting in initial phases of therapy in preparation for the needs and capacities of the M. R. child.

Kaldeck, R.: Group psychotherapy with mentally defective adolescents and adults. *International Journal of Group Psychotherapy,* 8:185-192, 1959.

"A large percentage of mental defectives are incapacitated more by their emotional difficulties than by their intellectual deficit." This implies the importance of psychotherapy for them even though only a very limited degree of insight can be achieved by them. Group psychotherapy in an institution for mental defectives has been shown to be helpful in enabling them to express their often conflicting feelings, to relieve their tension and to improve their interpersonal relationships. Experience has shown that the desirable approach in group psychotherapy with mental defectives needs to be dynamically oriented and permissive and to include some repressive-inspirational features.

Katz, G. H.: Re-educational therapy. *The Nervous Child,* 2:37-43, 1942.

The feebleminded is described as an individual with limited intelligence, thus a "crippled ego," due to continual and repeated failure to progress along normal avenues. It claims that rearing these children in their natural homes often increases the possibility of behavior problems. To alleviate this situation, the child should be "re-educated" away from the family in a special boarding school. Re-educative factors and methods used in this special school are discussed. Heavy emphasis is placed upon psychotherapy and spontaneous play activities.

Kaufman, M. E.: Group psychotherapy in preparation for the return of mental defectives from institution to community. *Mental Retardation,* 1(5):276-280, 1963.

Describes the technique of group psychotherapy used specifically to prepare long-term residents of an institution for mental defectives for community life. Problems of developing appropriate social and emotional attitudes necessary for successful placement are discussed. After one year of therapy, 75 percent of the group had been successful in placement for three years or longer.

Knight, D.; Ludwig, A. J.; Strazzulla, M.; and Pope, L.: The role of varied therapies in the rehabilitation of the retarded child. *American Journal of Mental Deficiency,* 61:508-515, 1957.

The role of occupational therapy, music, speech, and remedial reading is described in the treatment of a single child who presented the problems of retardation and hyperactivity.

Kolburne, L. L.: A transformation through psychotherapy and special education. *Psychiatric Quarterly,* 27:165-187, 1953.

Five years of psychotherapy and education transformed an apparently mentally deficient boy of thirteen into a successfully balanced individual.

Kraak, B.: Nichdirective Gruppentherapie mit Heimkinern (Non directive group therapy with institutionalized children). *Zeitschrift fur Experimentelle und Angerioandte Psychologie,* 8:595-622, 1961.

Twenty institutionalized retarded children were treated with non-directive psychotherapy and compared with matched controls after six months.

Kriegmen, G., and Hilgard, J. R.: Intelligence level and psychotherapy with problem children. *American Journal of Orthopsychiatry, 14:*251-265, 1944.

Twenty-nine children were administered psychotherapy for a minimum of twenty sessions over a period of at least seven months. The parents were also seen. Each child was examined before and after on the Stanford-Binet. Findings listed by the authors were: (1) Accuracy, cooperation, and interval between termination and retest are of little significance in variation of IQ, (2) Children age ten or less show greatest therapeutic success, (3) Children with IQ 110 or above show greatest therapeutic success, (4) A significant relationship between IQ level and symptom improvement for children above eight years of age, (5) Therapeutic success is related to the number of times child and parents are seen. The findings are interpreted by the authors to indicate psychotherapy may increase IQ ratings in certain cases. Influences of emotional disturbances upon intellectual behavior and ability to perform on intelligence tests is discussed. Data was seen as supporting theory that therapeutic success tends to be greater with the anxious, guilty child who inhibits his hostile impulses. Prognosis was seen as enhanced if parents are amenable to treatment.

Landau, M. E.: Group psychotherapy with deaf retardates. *International Journal of Group Psychotherapy, 18*(3):345-351, 1968.

Seven deaf training center residents were selected on the basis of age (19-60 yr.), IQ (scores over fifty on the Leiter International Performance Scale and Goodenough Draw-a-Man), and sign language proficiency (manual communication). They met weekly for one hour with a member of the psychology staff from the institution and a sign-language translator from the community. The purpose was to improve social responsiveness and ability to interact. Three phases are described: nondirective, quasidirective, and problem oriented. The five female and two male *Ss* not only had a positive therapeutic experience as a result of the year's sessions, but demonstrated to the staff the unique problems of this type of institutionalized population.

Lavalli, A., and Levine, M.: Social and guidance needs of mentally handicapped adolescents as revealed through sociodramas. *American Journal of Mental Deficiency*, 58:544-552, 1954.

A report of the use of sociodrama as a technique for recognizing and ventilating the personal and social problems of mentally retarded adolescents. Excerpts from several sociodramas are presented.

Leland, H.; Walker, J.; and Taboada, A. N.: Group play therapy with a group of post-nursery male retardates. *American Journal of Mental Deficiency*, 63:848-851, 1959.

A study to determine whether group play therapy would be efficacious with mentally retarded post-nursery children where other therapeutic techniques have failed. Eight boys between the ages of four years six months and nine years six months, all behavior problems, were given the Vineland Scale and the WISC before and after the experimental program of about ninety hours of group play therapy in a little over a month. The authors report that "there is good evidence to say that the experience did activate some of the intellectual potential which could not be tapped before the experiment." It appears that the group play therapy did not produce major alterations in the level of social maturation.

Leland, H., and Smith, D. E.: *Play Therapy with Mentally Subnormal Children*. New York, Grune and Stratton, 1965.

Demonstrates that the abnormal behaviors of the mentally

subnormal children occur out of an attempt to relieve their tensions. This attempt can be relieved by the therapist's reward which allows the children to have their own choice of activities, and his punishment which makes them avoid producing deviant behaviors in order to be permitted to continue their activities.

Lenard, H. M.: Supportive placement for the mentally retarded. *Journal of Rehabilitation*, 26(5):16-17, 1960.

Addresses the problem of the retardates: their inability to maintain themselves on the job due largely to defective social interaction with co-workers. Discusses the retardates' need for relatedness, interaction, reciprocity, and hence, acceptance; and the unfortunate stereotyping and prejudice often encountered. Describes the effectiveness of group counseling, role playing techniques, and supportive placement (two clients in the same work environment) used to improve the social interaction of the retarded.

Lodato, F. J., and Sokoloff, M. A.: Group counseling for slow learners. *Journal of Counseling Psychology*, 10:95-96, September, 1963.

A pilot study conducted on a group of junior high school students who were classified as slow learners with IQ's ranging from seventy-seven to ninety who were given group counseling. Results after six months showed significant gains in area of self-confidence and appropriateness of expressions of non-verbal aggression. The language patterns remained limited and characterized by poor articulation. The need for self-respect seemed a very important factor in an educational setting.

Long, W. J.: An exploratory study of the use of role playing with severely retarded children. *American Journal of Mental Deficiency*, 63:784-791, 1959.

Such children in an experimental day school seemed to enjoy the sessions, but much practice is needed by this kind of child before it can be effectively used in training.

Lott, G. M.: Psychotherapy of the mentally retarded. *Journal of the American Medical Association, 196*(3):229-232, 1966.

The advantages and disadvantages of psychotherapy with some types of mental retardates are discussed with reference to six cases of disturbed but socially adequate slow learners. An individualized approach is needed for the different types of emotional problems. It was noted that the mentally retarded are less able to deal with emotional problems than are people of normal intelligence. More psychotherapy has been attempted recently due to diagnostic difficulties on standard tests. Caution in therapy was exercised when defenses of the patient were weak, but in one case better results were achieved when less caution was used; as therapy continued, regressive behavior was replaced by a more mature adjustment. In another case, therapy was supportive and led to increased insight in a patient with a dependency-independence conflict accompanied by neurotic guilt. Adjustment to the community and to her parents was the result of therapy in a case involving emotional and neurotic problems. A mistaken diagnosis of mental retardation was cleared in therapy where rebellious negativism had been obscured by defective performance. Analytic therapy can benefit many, especially the more capable persons having primary or secondary emotional problems, or brain injury. Exploratory and supportive therapy can be an aid to those suffering from aphasia, deafness, and speech problems. An approach involving character building and planned education may be of greater help than psychotherapy in some cases of personality development. Early diagnosis and therapy may prevent further complications and lead to greater happiness.

McDaniel, J.: Group action in the rehabilitation of the mentally retarded. *Group Psychotherapy, 13*:5-13, 1960.

A report on the use of group action methods employed to manipulate a therapy group of young adult retardates with the objective of "making group relationships more meaningful. . . ." Sociometric techniques were used to measure initial and terminal group structure. The author concluded that "some increase in group cohesion has taken place as revealed by changes in sociometric structure as a result of manipulation and reorganizing activities." None of the reported changes were statistically significant. No control group.

Maisner, E. A.: Contributions of play therapy techniques to total rehabilitative design in an institution for highgrade mentally deficient and borderline children. *American Journal of Mental Deficiency, 55:235-250,* 1950.

Reviews an intensive type of treatment in addition to normal play therapy techniques. Special personality re-educative process deals with acceptance and rapport, clarification and desensitization, diagnosis and interpretation, and termination of the re-educative process.

Mann, P. H.: The effect of group counseling on educable mentally retarded boys' concepts of themselves in school. *Dissertation Abstracts, 28(9-A):*3467, 1968.

Mann, P. H.; Beaber, J. O., and Jacobson, M. D.: The effect of group counseling on educable mentally retarded boys' self concepts. *Exceptional Children, 35:359-366,* 1969.

The effect of group counseling on the self concepts of young educable mentally handicapped boys were studied, along with the variables of anxiety, deportment and achievement in reading and arithmetic as rated by teachers, attendance, IQ and age. Results indicate that those who receive group counseling tended to exhibit greater improvement in self concept, more reduction in anxiety, and better grades in deportment and the academic subjects of reading and arithmetic, than those who did not receive the counseling. No significant difference was found between experimental and control groups in attendance. Age and IQ were not found to be significant factors in the counseled group.

Mannoni, M.: Problems poses par la psychotherapie des debiles. (Problems posed by the psychotherapy of the retarded.) *Sauvegarde de l'Enfance, 20(1):*100-108, 1965.

The psychoanalytic aspect of mental retardation was defined and clarified. No single cure was proposed, but a way of approaching the problem was discussed. Emphasis was placed upon the relationship of the mentally retarded child and his family, especially the mother-child relationship. What is said about the child in the family was viewed as very important. The psycho-analyst seeks to find the words associated with anguish or a deficiency of the body. An undesirable relationship between the child and his environment was cited as a reason for a child's seeking self-expression through his illness or taking refuge in his weakness. The mother is the best source of understanding for the analyst. She often does not want the child to develop normally, but to remain dependent. Breaking the pathogenic relationship of mother and child may permit development of an autonomous self. Case histories are cited to illustrate that the family's attitude toward a mentally retarded child may indicate the best way to treat a particular case.

Marra, J.; Moore, A.; and Young, M. A.: Job training for the mentally retarded. *Journal of Rehabilitation,* 23(1):10-12, 29-30, 1957.

Describes a vocational rehabilitation program in Hartford for the mentally retarded which provides prevocational appraisal, personal adjustment, and on-the-job training for retarded adults between sixteen and thirty-five years of age with an IQ of fifty to seventy-five. Both group and individual counseling are discussed. Group sessions were taped and found to lessen the anxiety previously exhibited in the individual sessions. Discusses significant contribution of the occupational therapist's findings about each patient's interests and abilities.

Mehlman, B.: Group play therapy with mentally retarded children. *Journal of Abnormal Social Psychology,* 48:53-60, 1953.

"Thirty-two institutionalized, endogeneous, mentally retarded children, divided into three individually matched groups, were used in an investigation into the personal and intellectual changes, and the interrelationships between such changes, evoked as the result of an experience in nondirective, group play therapy."

Menzel, M. J.: Psychotherapeutic techniques among the mentally deficient. *American Journal of Mental Deficiency,* 56:796-802, 1952.

A description of the use of occupational therapy as a psychotherapeutic technique with an institution for the mentally deficient. A case study is presented.

Michal-Smith, H.: Rehabilitation of the mentally retarded blind: Past, present and future. *Rehabilitation Literature,* 30(7):194-198, July 1969.

A brief historical overview of the changing role of counseling, particularly vocational counseling, of the MR blind. Stresses that rehabilitation is not a salvage operation, but a developmental process from birth through life. The MR blind need as much help in vocational training as any other group.

Michal-Smith, H.; Gottsegen, M.; and Gottsegen, G. A.: A group technique for mental retardates. *International Journal of Group Psychotherapy,* 5:84-90, 1955.

The authors applied group therapy techniques to mentally retarded adolescents, using (1) motoric group activity, and (2) oral language training. Favorable results are reported as regards the reintegration of the body-self and social development. Justifications for group therapy for retardates are presented.

Morris, C.; Christopher, L. L.; Nellis, B.; and Stromber, C. C.: The development of an intermediary psychotherapeutic program in an institution for the mentally retarded. *American Journal of Mental Deficiency,* 63:604-610, 1959.

The authors report that "the systematic and controlled use of the concepts of modern psychotherapy has apparently enabled the staff at the Austin State School to effect very definite changes among themselves, via the medium of a modified type of staff therapy-group under experienced leadership; and these interpersonal changes have had both direct and indirect influences on the total program. These changes have helped to streamline the admission and discharge of students, to lay out more effective and more realistic programs for their habilitation, to humanize the institution, to raise staff morale, to guarantee more appropriate overall management of the children committed there, and thus all in all to approach being the kind of progressive and modern training school that the state desires."

Mousner, E. A.: Contributions of play therapy techniques to the total rehabilitative design in an institution for high-grade mentally deficient and borderline children. *American Journal of Mental Deficiency,* 55:235-250, 1950.

A discussion of the problems involved with mentally deficient/emotionally handicapped children. Description of play room materials. Contributions of the play therapy project suggest possible use of described methods as an adjuvant to rehabilitation in an institution.

Muehlberger, C. E.: Counseling educable retardates at the early secondary level: A methodological approach. *Child Study Center Bulletin, State University College, New York, Buffalo,* 4(3):53-63, 1968.

Discusses the educable mentally retarded child who at puberty experiences behavioral and attitudinal difficulties related to social maturity, emotional stability, and realistic occupational goals and values. Because of the child's limited intellectual abilities, a number of counseling techniques must be utilized in helping him achieve a satisfactory adjustment. Problems related to the achievement of social maturity and emotional stability are discussed. Case studies are presented and a discussion of methodology utilized in ameliorating the atypical conditions under study. Problems related to occupational goals are handled most effectively through group counseling techniques. A discussion of methodology helpful in instilling realistic occupational goals and values within the child is portrayed.

Muhlefelder, W. J.: Mental retardation and the anatomy of existential therapy. *Pennsylvania Psychiatric Quarterly,* 9(2):25-32, 1969.

Mundy, L.: Therapy with physically and mentally handicapped children in a mental deficiency hospital. *Journal of Clinical Psychology*, 13:3-9, 1957.

Play therapy was effective with imbecile children as measured by IQ changes. Children seen for several interviews to assess the relative weight of psychiatric factors in the retardation often became treatment cases but most of these cases were not retested by the therapist. One group of fifteen cases was matched with ten control cases as closely as possible on age, initial 1937 Binet IQ, age at institutionalization, degree of disturbance, and retest interval. The treated group showed very significant gains in IQ after about nine to thirteen months of treatment. Similar results were found on eight severely physically handicapped children whose change in Drever-Collins Performance Test IQ between tests given on hospitalization and prior to the treatment was compared with change from prior to after treatment. The social improvements noted in the treated children are described.

Neham, S.: Psychotherapy in relation to mental deficiency. *American Journal of Mental Deficiency*, 55:557-572, 1951.

An overview of psychotherapy with the mentally deficient. Various psychotherapeutic techniques utilized in therapy with the mentally deficient are presented; their limitations and successes are discussed. The author urges further development of projective techniques for use with the mentally defective to aid in a more accurate differential diagnosis of mental deficiency. More accurate definition of terms used in defining mental deficiency is encouraged.

Ney, G.: Community transitional adjustment program for mentally retarded (HIP). *Project News of the Parson's State Hospital and Training Center*, 2(4):5, 1966.

The primary goal of the Hospital Improvement Program's individual counseling program is the development of responsibility and independent functioning in the vocational, social, and personal realms. Forty vocational division students are currently participating in a group counseling program. A vocational coordinator counsels those employed in the community; the project counselor works with those considered for employment or those with unsuccessful job experience. The group sessions emphasize independent problem solving.

Niehm, B. F.: A study of counseling, personal adjustment and parent education services in Ohio workshops for the mentally retarded. *Dissertation Abstracts, 30*(1-A):136-137, 1969.

Nitzberg, J.: Training and counseling retarded adults. *Canada's Mental Health, 14*(5-6):14-20, 1966.

O'Connor, N., and Yonge, K. A.: Methods of evaluating the group psychotherapy of unstable defective delinquents. *Journal of Genetic Psychology, 87*:89-101, 1955.

A study of attitudinal and intellectual change following group psychotherapy is described and compared with two control groups. The *Ss* are adolescent defective delinquents. Significant differences between treated and control groups are reported. Emphasis is placed on method.

Pancratz, L. D., and Buchan, G.: Exploring psychodramatic techniques with defective delinquents. *Group Psychotherapy, 18* (3):136-141, 1965.

"The authors have demonstrated that psychodrama is a tool that can be used with defective delinquents. The method of treatment on the ward was expanded by its use. However, it is difficult at this stage of the investigation to substantiate the degree of therapeutic gain." Further, other questions are raised by this particular study, including the appropriateness of the group which was actually used, the overall change in behavior and attitudes which could be effected through psychodrama as well as the question, "Will retarded persons unfamiliar with traditional therapy be less likely to perform as well?"

Pankratz, L. D., and Buchan, L. G.: Techniques of "warm-up" in psychodrama with the retarded. *Mental Retardation, 4*(5): 12-15, 1966.

Describes methods of "warm-up" for actionally exploring the problem areas of institutionalized mentally retarded patients.

Peckham, R. A.: Problems in job adjustment of the mentally retarded. *American Journal of Mental Deficiency, 56*:448-453,
1951.

A study conducted, where each counselor in eight districts was
instructed to select a group of ten recent cases and define prominent client problems that occurred immediately following initial
placement on the job and methods by which prominent job adjustment problems were solved. Job adjustment problems were
solved principally by the use of the following three basic methods of process: (1) employer-counselor conferences; (2) family-
counselor conferences; and (3) counselor-client conferences.

Peins, M.: Client-centered communication therapy for mentally
retarded delinquents. *Journal of Speech and Hearing Disorders, 32*(2):154-161, 1967.

A communication therapy program for ten institutionalized,
mentally retarded, and borderline retarded delinquent adolescents is described. These cases were deficient in all areas of oral
communication. "Communicative speech responses" form the
nucleus of therapy sessions and acted as the corrective medium.
No emphasis was placed on conventional drills or exercises. Lessons were designed to emphasize meaningful speech responses
within a framework of realistic communicative experiences. The
purpose of the program was to give these cases optimum communicative effectiveness.

Prall, R. C., and Heiser, K. F.: Psychotherapy with retarded children of different etiologies. *Training School Bulletin, 50*:
211-213, 1954.

A summary of progress of the psychotherapy program at the
Vineland Training School. The author concludes that therapy
was beneficial although there are "several special problems which
require careful attention in the institutional setting." Some of
these problems discussed are: attitudes and expectations of parents, attitudes and expectations of cottage parents, the institutional pattern or hierarchy of authority and goals, and the
status of social case work.

Psychotherapy with the mentally retarded. *Mental Retardation Abstracts, 1*(4):535-538, 1964.

The references included in this annotated bibliography on psychotherapy with the mentally retarded were based on the reported literature during the ten-year period of 1954 to 1964. The thirty-eight citations included both American and foreign publications.

Rank, B.: Adaptation of the psychoanalytic technique for the treatment of young children with atypical development. *American Journal of Orthopsychiatry, 19*:130-139, 1949.

Young children whose development has been arrested at a primitive, infantile level and who have generally been considered psychotic or feebleminded are the subjects of this study. It is claimed that these children in reality suffered gross emotional deprivation as a result of a special family constellation in which a narcissistic immature mother was not able to offer the infant in his early stages an environment with an emotional climate favorable for the formation and differentiation of the self and the establishment of the reality principle. The scattered, fragmented personality of such children and their retreat and withdrawal are understood as an escape from a dangerous world. Treatment must start with restitution through acceptance of the child on whatever level of emotional development he may be, regardless of chronological age.

Ringelheim, D., and Polatsek, I.: Group therapy with a male defective group: A preliminary study. *American Journal of Mental Deficiency, 60*:157-162, 1955.

The results of a pilot study on the use of group therapy with a male defective group are presented. The observational data obtained from the therapy sessions are discussed.

Rose, G. W.: A content analysis of counseling with the mentally retarded. *Dissertation Abstracts, 31*(9-10A):4473, 1971.

Rosen, H. G., and Rosen, S.: Group therapy as an instrument to develop a concept of self-worth in the adolescent and young adult mentally retarded. *Mental Retardation, 7*(5):52-55, 1969.

This paper discusses group treatment approach to assist retardates in their effort to learn to cope with community life. The group therapy is part of a larger program where the "trainees" learn about the world of work in a workshop and receive training for more independent community living in units in public housing project where they reside. It was noted that the mildly and moderately retarded trainees made excellent use of the group process and appeared to use it successfully in their effort to grow and to manage. Further efforts and follow-up evaluations will be necessary to determine the value of the program.

Rudolf, G. de M.: An experiment in group therapy with mental defectives. *International Journal of Social Psychiatry, 1*(1): 49-53, 1955.

Demonstrates how group therapy in five cases of mental deficiency did some positive good.

Rusalem, H., and Darer, H.: Vocational counseling of the slow learner. *National Association of Women Deans and Counselors Journal*, 23:110-116, 1960.

A guidance experiment in a N.Y.C. high school is reported. *Ss* were "slow learners" (median IQ approximately eighty). The experimental group received modified curriculum, modified teaching methods, group vocational guidance, individual counseling, and consultation with teachers. Results suggest that "vocational guidance is a valuable ingredient in the total educational program for slow learners in the secondary schools." Several suggestions for school vocational guidance programs are offered.

Sakurai, Y., et al.: Study on therapeutic group activity of mentally retarded adolescents. *Journal of Mental Health, 15*:21-28, 96-97, 1967.

Assesses the effectiveness of therapy on attitudes and consciousness of retardates in a day care center as compared to the effectiveness of vocationally trained retardates. Differences are observed, and it is suggested that both processes have much to offer the retardate.

Sarason, S. B.: Individual psychotherapy with mentally defective individuals. *American Journal of Mental Deficiency,* 56:803-805, 1952.

A listing and discussion of problems in the area of psychotherapy with mentally defective individuals. Many questions posed which can be answered only through additional research.

Schacter, F. F.; Meyer, L. R.; and Loanes, E.: Childhood schizophrenia and mental retardation: Differential diagnosis before and after 1 year of psychotherapy. *American Journal of Orthopsychiatry,* 32:584-594, 1962.

Twelve schizophrenic, six mentally retarded, and eleven normal preschool boys were evaluated before and after therapy.

Schaefer-Simmern, H., and Sarason, S. B.: Therapeutic implications of artistic activity. *American Journal of Mental Deficiency,* 49:185-196, 1944.

An experiment in creative therapy with a thirty-year-old mentally retarded woman. A lawful development of inherent "gestalt-formation" in the visual arts is assumed and followed throughout the discussion of the case. Authors conclude that the process influenced the personality of the patient, resulting in improvement.

Scheer, R. M., and Sharpe, W. M.: Group work as a treatment. *Mental Retardation,* 3(3):23-25, 1965.

A social group work approach was discussed as a method of treating social-emotional problems of the institutionalized mental retardate. The core of the program is to learn, observe, imitate, experiment and test reality within the confines of a specially-selected small group. Through making decisions, handling conflicts, assuming leadership and planning activities, the program helps the individuals help themselves toward social readjustment. Values inherent in the program include: (1) promotion of personality development in the individual, (2) modification of behavior toward more socially-acceptable goals, (3) allowance of democratic group experience and teaching of social responsibility, (4) exposition of the individual to many life experiences he might otherwise miss, (5) fostering of self-esteem and self-reliance, (6) helping members gain respect for individual differences, and (7) teaching of social-adaptive skills.

Schlanger, B. B.: Speech therapy results with mentally retarded children in special classes. *The Training School Bulletin, 50:* 179-186, 1953.

Describes experimental program of group therapy used to improve speech problems of a group of retarded children in special classes. Base behavior, tests used, and results are included. Most useful part may be the description of the method which stresses emphasis on the individual rather than the problem. The goal was improved social adequacy.

Schler, E. W.; Hall, R. C.; Gordon, M.; and Evans, J.: A nonsurgical approach to the treatment of mentally retarded children who are brain injured. *Pennsylvania Psychiatric Quarterly, 3*(4):18-25, 1963.

Six brain-injured children, each mentally retarded and physically handicapped to varying degrees, were placed in a treatment program employing a slightly modified version of treatment methods used by workers at the Rehabilitation Center, Philadelphia, Pennsylvania. After three to ten months in the program, each S was felt to have made sufficient progress to warrant the continued experimental use of the program for at least another year.

Selwa, B. I.: Preliminary considerations in psychotherapy with retarded children. *Journal of School Psychology, 9*(1):12-15, 1971.

Psychotherapy for the retarded child with emotional problems may be the responsibility of the school psychologist. Because the literature dealing with the most profitable techniques and procedures is sparse, an overview of the special needs and characteristics of retarded children has been made. The child brings a language deficit, emotional attitudes related to retardedness, and social experiences to the therapeutic situation. Group and individual therapy are discussed with suggestions for successful implementation.

Sheer, R. M., and Sharpe, W. M.: Group work as a treatment. *Mental Retardation, 3*(3):23-25, 1965.

The institutional retardate is plagued by many social-emotional problems. Frequently the area of interpersonal relationships and group interaction is overlooked or minimized in therapeutic efforts. This paper attempts to look at what the social group worker in particular and the institution in general can do to foster social-adaptive skills. The social group work program serves to help patients help themselves and others toward social readjustment through decision making, handling conflicts, assuming leadership, and planning activities.

Simmons, J. Q.: Emotional problems in mental retardation: Utilization of psychiatric services. *Pediatric Clinics of North America, 15*(4):957-968, 1968.

Psychiatric services are essential in the treatment of emotional problems of the mentally retarded and their parents, but they are not performed independently of the professional team. Several case histories are presented. In general, traditional psychotherapeutic techniques were used; however, operant conditioning techniques also have wide application and can be used regardless of the degree of retardation.

Sion, A.: Casework with an adolescent boy of moron intelligence. *American Journal of Mental Deficiency, 57*:709-718, 1953.

An example of casework with an adolescent boy of moron intelligence is given. Information concerning the various interviews held with the boy is described fully.

Slivkin, S. E., and Bernstein, N. R.: Goal-directed group psychotherapy for retarded adolescents. *American Journal of Psychotherapy, 22*(1):35-45, 1968.

Short-term group psychotherapy offers many possibilities in the care of mentally retarded adolescents. The therapist responded in an uninhibited manner to the hyperactivity and affect hunger of the boys while constantly encouraging them to verbalize their feelings. His behavior and comments were brief, dramatic, and sincere. This spontaneity of interaction was crucial to the relationship and it fulfilled the affective needs of the group. The approach warrants further applications to other groups of retarded individuals by psychiatrists in training schools as well as in the community.

Smith, M. H.; Gottsegen, M. G.; and Gottsegen, G.: A group therapy technique for mental retardates. *International Journal of Group Psychotherapy*, 5:84-90, 1955.

Group therapy of a specialized nature is beneficial in preparation of retardates for adjustment into society without undue frustration. The program is set up to meet their needs which are: (1) stimulation and socialization, (2) development of ego strength, (3) strengthening of self concept, and (4) integration of phantasy and reality orientation. The retarded are capable of group therapy following a specialized technique consisting of a two step therapeutic process; motoric group therapy and oral language therapy.

Snyder, R., and Sechrest, L.: An experimental study of directive group therapy with defective delinquents. *American Journal of Mental Deficiency*, 54:117-123, 1959.

"This research presents the results of an investigation of the application of group therapy procedures to institutionalized, chronically delinquent defective males. Departing from most procedures which have been followed in the past the therapy was directive and didactic in nature. Two therapy groups, two placebo groups, and one no-treatment group were followed over a thirteen-week period. At the end of thirteen weeks of treatment the inmates receiving therapy were superior to both placebo and no-treatment Ss in their institutional adjustment as represented by significantly more positive comments on routine housing reports and fewer appearances in behavior courts for more serious violations. The writers believe that the results are attributable to the more structured, directive nature of therapy and to the nature of the measurements which were definitely and closely related to the institutional program as a whole."

Soper, R. L.: Occupational therapy, its contribution to the training of mental deficient patients at the Newark State School. *American Journal of Mental Deficiency,* 51:296-300, 1946.

Author discusses opportunities, programs, facilities and available personnel that run Newark School. Development of students treated individually, ward personnel being trained in techniques, and principles of occupational therapy are discussed.

Stacey, C. L., and DeMartino, M. F. (Eds.): *Counseling and Psychotherapy with the Mentally Retarded.* Glencoe, Ill., The Free Press, 1957.

A collection of forty-nine articles related to counseling and psychotherapy with the mentally retarded are divided into nine chapters as follows: (1) Introduction, (2) Counseling and Psychotherapy, (3) Psychoanalytic Methods, (4) Group Therapy, (5) Play Therapy, (6) Psychodrama, (7) Speech Therapy, (8) Vocational-Occupational-Industrial Therapy, and (9) Counseling with Parents. Chapter 10 is devoted to observations concerning psychotherapeutic techniques with the mentally retarded.

Stafford, R. L., and Meyer, R. J.: Diagnosis and counseling for the mentally retarded child. *Clinical Pediatrics,* 7(3):153-155, 1968.

The emotional, behavioral, and educational aspects of the mentally retarded should be subject to constant evaluation by health care teams which should consist of teachers, doctors, psychologists, and social workers and is important to successful management of the mentally retarded. The usefulness of psychotherapy should be considered in each individual case. The assessment of parental attitudes and anxieties is also important. Regularly scheduled interviews with the parents should chart the progress and adjustment of the mentally retarded child in school, community, and the home.

Stafford, R. L., and Meyer, R. J.: Diagnosis and counseling of the mentally retarded: Implications for school health. *Journal of School Health,* 38(3):151-155, 1968.

Discusses diagnosis and counseling as one continuous and interacting process. Rehabilitation depends upon assessment of the child's entire environment and a teamwork approach of the family and health professionals.

Sternlicht, M.: The inapplicability for mental defectives of the client-centered approach. *Journal of Client-Centered Counseling,* 1:11-12, 1963.

Rogers feels that non-directive therapy is not indicated for mental defectives and that it would be rare for an individual of borderline intelligence or below to be selected for psychotherapy. Author states that experiences at Willowbrook State School confirm Roger's view in that psychotherapy, both individual and group, with moderately and severely retarded youngsters proved ineffective. The client-centered approach was abandoned at Willowbrook although elements of it are still included in the more directive approach now employed. ". . . an eclectic approach incorporating directive therapy with non-directive reflection is probably most useful." Author takes issue with Roger's earlier assertions and states that much therapeutic success has been achieved both at Willowbrook and in CRMD community classes.

Sternlicht, M.: A theoretical model for the psychological treatment of mental retardation. *American Journal of Mental Deficiency,* 68(5):618-622, 1964.

Such techniques include projective techniques, finger-painting, music therapy, dance therapy, relationship therapy, supportive therapy, directive counseling, social casework, play therapy, psychodrama, group therapy, and counseling of relatives.

Sternlicht, M., and Wexler, H. K.: Cathartic tension reduction in the retarded: An experimental demonstration. *American Journal of Mental Deficiency,* 70(4):609-611, 1966.

A miniature tension-producing and tension-reducing experimental situation with ninety educable retarded adolescents was constructed, with associative cognitive cathartic activity as the experimental variable. The results indicate that educable retardates can employ cathartic techniques.

Sternlicht, M.: Treatment approaches to delinquent retardates. *International Journal of Group Psychotherapy,* 16(1):91-98, 1966.

At Willowbrook State School, "groups were closed, attendance was compulsory, and sessions were held weekly and lasted ninety minutes. The number of patients ranged from ten to fourteen, the age range was from fourteen to twenty, and the IQ range from thirty-seven to seventy. Two of the groups were seen for a total of one year each, the other for fifteen months. Among the traditional techniques used were play therapy, finger-painting, and socio- and psychodrama in pantomime. The "novel nonverbal methods consisted of 'silence-insult' technique and the use of dramatizations, mirrors, and balloons." It is concluded that "activity and other nonverbal techniques are the method of choice in the group psychotherapeutic treatment of delinquent adolescent retardates."

Sternlicht, M.: Innovations in therapeutic and environmental manipulative techniques with the mentally retarded. Paper presented as part of a symposium—Approaches to Expanding Services for the Retarded. New York, New York, American Psychological Association, September 1966, 6 p., mimeo.

Recent innovations in psychotherapeutic approaches and environmental manipulative techniques that are being utilized with mentally retarded individuals are discussed. A new application of milieu therapy is a procedure known as "Remotivation." The goal of this technique is to encourage and guide patients in meaningful relationships with adults, peers, and their general environment. This is done by having small groups meet for half-hour sessions five days a week. An aide-leader is used to stimulate conversation and group activity. Other environmental manipulations include recreational activities that are designed to facilitate socialization experiences, and programs geared toward community placements. Psychotherapeutic techniques now being employed with retardates include music therapy, nonverbal therapeutic procedures, "insult" techniques, hypotherapeutic techniques, and various play therapy procedures. Workers in the field of mental retardation are encouraged to use their imaginations in developing new methods of aiding the retardate to realize and fulfill his potential. Suggestions included having the rooms with sides and ceiling completely mirrored so that the retardate may view himself as others do and more constructive arts and crafts.

Sternlicht, M.: Establishing an initial relationship in group psychotherapy with delinquent retarded male adolescents. *American Journal of Mental Deficiency,* 69(1):39-41, 1964.

The problem of establishing a meaningful relationship with delinquent adolescent retardates was discussed. The author conducted group psychotherapy with four different groups of eight to thirteen patients per group. These male adolescents had a CA range from fourteen to eighteen and an IQ range from thirty-eight to sixty-eight. All patients were considered to be severe behavior problems.

Rapport was established with the groups by asking each group for its "strongest" member. Next fighting matches were held between these individuals who thought they were the strongest in the group. The victor then Indian-wrestled with the therapist. The therapist always saw to it that he won, and this appeared to impress the group, resulting in awe and admiration for the therapist. While the effects of Indian-wrestling were still present, the therapist established a working relationship with the patients with little difficulty.

In addition to facilitating the development of a working relationship, the therapist's own authority appeared to be enhanced. It appeared to permit an "authority-dependency transference" to develop rapidly and it also resulted in patients becoming emotionally aware that they could obtain certain valuable knowledge from the therapist.

Strang, R.: The counselor's contribution to the guidance of the gifted, the under-achiever, and the retarded. *Personnel and Guidance Journal, 34:*494-497, 1956.

The counselor has seven responsibilities for the exceptional children: to identify them, to help teachers provide needed experiences, to assist in helping these students make the most of themselves, to hold interviews with the students and their parents, to open up community resources and educational opportunities for them, to call case conferences when needed to explore baffling problems and to further the development of the students, and to advise administrators and curriculum committees about changes in school programs which will benefit these students.

Straughan, J. H.; Potter, W. K., Jr.; and Hamilton, S. H.: The behavioral treatment of an elective mute. *Journal of Child Psychology and Psychiatry, 6(2):*125-130, 1965.

A fourteen-year-old educable mentally retarded boy who was an elective mute was treated with behavioral techniques. The boy remained silent except with intimate friends, was unusually timid and shy, and was mute in school since the age of six and was doing unsatisfactory academic work. Neurological examination was normal and IQ ranged from fifty-two to sixty-five. Treatment was divided into preliminary observation, systemic observation, treatment and post-treatment observation. The problem appeared to be essentially a social and verbal non-responsiveness directed largely towards his teacher. His behavior was then recorded for twenty-one days, twenty minutes a day. Reinforcement was used so that appropriate responses turned on a light that was connected to an automatic counter placed in front of the class. Treatment lasted for eighteen days with twenty minutes a day of reinforcement. The class was treated to a party when the counter registered a certain number. After treatment, he was observed for nine days, thirty minutes a day. Frequency of talking, talking in response to his instructor, and peer vocal approaches to him all improved with treatment to a

0.001 level of significance. This achievement continued to improve during the post-treatment period.

Stubblebine, J. M.: Group psychotherapy with some epileptic mentally deficient adults. *American Journal of Mental Deficiency, 61*:725-730, 1957.

"Six epileptic anti-social male patients in a chronic ward of a hospital for the mentally deficient were in group psychotherapy twice weekly for about six months. Four of the patients became better socialized during this period while two were unchanged. These four old and new in hospital seemed to profit from the greater than average time spent with them in a group setting while searching for some measure of mutual understanding.

Stubblebine, J. M., and Roadruck, R. D.: Treatment program for mentally deficient adolescents. *American Journal of Mental Deficiency, 60*:551-556, 1956.

A program of treatment for mentally deficient male adolescents is described. Weekly group sessions of all personnel on the ward were held. "Demonstrated to our satisfaction is that a milieu conducive to emotional growth of disturbed retarded adolescents can be created using the lay staff of psychiatric technicians. We feel that the maturation of patients was directly proportional to the earnestness and effectiveness with which the adults about them obtained some measure of personal insight. Insofar as each staff member was able to face his own feelings with regard to life requirements and satisfactions, he seemed able to appreciate the problems of the patients. Although time consuming, the many conferences were an essential substrata for cooperation and good communication, and the team approach was the preferred method of operation. Time spent with the patients by sympathetic, supportive adults was the keystone of the treatment program. . . . Individual and group psychotherapy with such patients can be successful and rewarding for both patient and therapist.

Subotnik, L., and Callahan, R. J.: A pilot study in short-term play therapy with institutionalized educable mentally retarded boys. *American Journal of Mental Deficiency*, 63:730-735, 1959.

"Eight institutionalized, educable mentally retarded boys, eight to twelve years old, nominated for treatment by teachers and cottage parents, were given a short-term series of individual play therapy sessions. Several quickly administered tests—Children's Anxiety Pictures, Auditory Memory for Digits, Vocabulary Draw a Person, and Bender Gestalt—were obtained from the subjects (1) eight weeks before therapy, (2) immediately before therapy, (3) after eight weeks of therapy, and (4) after eight weeks follow-up. Improvement during the therapy period and during the therapy plus follow-up period were compared with improvement during the eight weeks without treatment. Results on all tests were negative. In addition, Behavior Ratings on six categories of behavior by teachers and cottage parents were obtained at the beginning and end of therapy, but differences during this period also proved non-significant. The obtained data serve to point up some methodological problems inherent in evaluating psychotherapy."

Tavris, E.: Some notes on group psychotherapy for severe mental defectives. *Delaware Medical Journal*, 33:301-307, 1961.

An experimental study with a group of nearly inarticulate individuals attempts to learn whether therapy can be effective without verbal insight, free associations and interpretations, which are the "sine qua non" of traditional psychotherapy.

Tawardas, S. M.: Spontaneity training at the Dora Institute, Alexandria, Egypt. *Group Psychotherapy*, 9:164-167, 1956.

Mildly retarded boys and girls received spontaneity training by means of group psychotherapy and psychodrama.

Thorne, F. C.: Counseling and psychotherapy with mental defectives. *American Journal of Mental Deficiency*, 52:263-271, 1948.

"Contrary to established attitudes in the child guidance movement, counseling and psychotherapy with mental defectives is both possible and profitable. This paper reports the results of the systematic application of a comprehensive guidance program at the Brandon State School during a two-year period. Methods of administration are described and an evaluation has been made of the methods of counseling and psychotherapy which have been found to be effective with mental defectives. An analysis of the results indicates that marked improvement occurred both in the general morale of the whole institution and in the individual welfare of the children. It is concluded that counseling with mental defectives is practical and that the magnitude of the problem renders it desirable that an extensive program of research be undertaken to exploit the possibilities of a new philosophy of case handling."

Thorne, F. C., and Dolan, K. M.: The role of counseling in a placement program for mentally retarded females. *Journal of Clinical Psychology Monograph Supplement,* 9:110-113, 1953.

"This paper has reported on the development and accomplishments of a state sponsored guidance and training program for female mental defectives. The Rutland Colony House operated by the Brandon (Vt.) State School was founded in 1925 and to date has trained more than one hundred girls for community living. The philosophy behind the operation of the colony house is explained with special emphasis on the program of counseling and guidance which in our opinion has been largely responsible for its success. It is concluded that counseling and guidance with mental defectives requires a systematic and extensive use of directive methods intended to resolve every detail of adjustment which can be dealt with."

Thorne, F. C.: Tutorial counseling with mental defectives. *Journal of Clinical Psychology,* 16:73-79, 1960.

"The same principles of learning apply to mental defectives as to normals with the exception that much more attention must be given to creating conditions conducive to learning and then to provide much longer practice periods than are ordinarily provided." The rationale and technique of methods of tutorial education and counseling of mental defectives is outlined. The case studies reported suggest that the intellectual functioning of mental defectives may be improved if they can be taught to act in a given situation as would a more intelligent person.

Trajan, B., and Benson, F.: Report on the pilot study at Pacific Colony. *American Journal of Mental Deficiency,* 57:453-462, 1953.

A description of a concentrated and individualized program "to demonstrate what can be done in the way of successful community placement of high grade morons and borderline mental defectives who are primarily personality problems." The leave of absence program was liberalized and patients were given therapeutic measures such as psychotherapy, psychiatric case work procedures, scholastic and vocational education, and rehabilitation therapies in preparation for leaves of absence. Findings were indicative of success.

Vail, D.: Mental deficiency: Response to milieu therapy. *American Journal of Psychiatry, 113:*170-173, 1956.

The experiences of mentally retarded adolescents and young adults in milieu therapy are described.

Vail, D.: An unsuccessful experiment in group therapy. *American Journal of Mental Deficiency,* 60:144-151, 1955.

An unsuccessful experiment in group therapy with institutionalized adolescent mentally defective boys is described. "The meaning and dynamics of the process of therapeutic failure" are treated. The principal technical weakness of therapy in this instance appears to have been in insufficient divergence from standard, classical nondirective techniques. This concerned specifically insufficient control by the therapist of the group membership and composition, and inadequate attention to oral needs of the patients.

Wanderer, Z. W., and Sternlicht, M.: Alternative guidance: A psychotherapeutic approach to mental deficiency. *International Mental Health Research Newsletter, 6*(3):12-15, 1964.

Describes a two-year study wherein thirty-eight patients ranging in age from nine to fifty-four years were seen by members of the psychology department for individual therapy. A most important finding was the appearance of a method of psychotherapy called "Alternative Guidance," wherein the therapist assumed the role of a source of data, a provider of alternative suggestions for the client to consider.

Weedy, R. H., and Billy, J. J.: Counseling and psychotherapy for the mentally retarded: A survey of opinions and practices. *Mental Retardation, 4*(6):20-23, 1966.

The study comes to various conclusions which deal with the counseling of retarded patients: (1) eclectic approaches seem most promising, (2) individual therapy is most effective, (3) attempts to see the retardates point of view is most rewarding to the client, and (4) much more time and research can be spent upon helping the retardate perceive himself in relationship to his environment.

Weigle, V.: Functional music, a therapeutic tool in working with the mentally retarded. *American Journal of Mental Deficiency, 63*:672-678, 1959.

" 'Functional music' is music used not for any aesthetic value, but for its effectiveness in reaching practical therapeutic goals outside of music itself. The place of the music therapist in work with the mentally retarded is gradually being recognized by the several disciplines working in this field." The program at the Flower and Fifth Avenue Hospital's Clinic for the Mentally Retarded is discussed.

White, W. F., and Allan, W. R.: Psychodramatic effects of music as a psychotherapeutic agent. *Journal of Music Therapy, 3* (2): 69-71, 1966.

"When Negro male adolescents diagnosed as mentally retarded participated in psychodramatics structured with music mediation or in the chorale of a therapeutic music program, indications of marked modifications in self-concepts were noted. Significant differences between pretest and post-test W-A-Y scores were found in five categories. In general, results of the study have confirmed the hypothesis that music participation and the stimulus figure of the same race and sex may help to bring about, in educable mentally retarded Negroes, more positive and healthy concepts of self."

Wiest, G.: Psychotherapy with the mentally retarded. *American Journal of Mental Deficiency,* 59:640-644, 1955.

The problems and possibilities for use of psychotherapy with the mentally retarded are discussed.

Wilcox, G. T., and Guthrie, G. M.: Changes in the adjustment of institutionalized female defectives following group psychotherapy. *Journal of Clinical Psychology,* 13:9-13, 1957.

Ninety-seven girls were divided into twelve therapy groups whose members had previously been classified as aggressive, as passive, and of mixed passive and aggressive girls. "Change after therapy was measured by a behavioral rating form which was filled out by matrons and attendants who were continually with the girls for the duration of the study. The same rating form was filled out before and after therapy. . . . There was a significant difference . . . in the number of girls showing improvement in the combined experimental as compared to the combined control groups. No significant differences were found between groups of different types or between therapists." The interrater reliability of the rating form was .55. The therapists were graduate students. *Ss* varied in age from fifteen to forty-three; in length of institutionalization from one to twenty-seven years.

Woodward, K. F.; Jaffe, N.; and Brown, D.: Psychiatric program for very young retarded children. *American Journal of Diseases of Children,* 108(3):221-229, 1964.

A psychiatrically-oriented nursery school program for twenty-six preschool children, ranging in age from twenty-three months to four and one-half years, with retarded functioning was outlined. A review of twenty-three major references with published research regarding psychogenic factors in retarded functioning and the authors' experiences with thirty-four previous similar cases led them to regard the first three months in the program as a "clinical trial." Functions of members of the therapeutic team and the coordination provided as a feature of the program was reviewed.

Description of the types of cases and the constitution of their families indicated that all children selected were behind their age group in at least two of the following areas: (1) motor development, (2) speech development, (3) toilet training, (4) self care, and (5) use of materials and equipment, even though retarded functioning was the only basis for selection. Ranked progress for the ten cases with minimal or questionable brain damage was indicated in anecdotal reports. In the group which showed no demonstrable organicity, children showed varying degrees of emotional disturbance which appeared to fall into four categories: (1) neurotic patterns, (2) neurotic patterns with schizoid or autistic features, (3) autistic patterns, and (4) probably psychotic patterns where marked negativism was the outstanding feature.

Of those identified as not clearly psychotic, a high percentage showed considerable improvement, reaching a point where they tested (Binet, Vineland) within the normal range. Explorations effected in the study led the authors to conclude: (1) retarded functioning without demonstrable organic basis in the early years need not be regarded with pessimism; and (2) that psychogenic factors play a major role in the developmental lag. Early therapeutic treatment was recommended.

Woody, R. H., and Billy, J. T.: Counseling and psychotherapy for the mentally retarded: A survey of opinions and practices. *Mental Retardation,* 4(6):20-23, 1966.

A questionnaire regarding counseling and psychotherapy for the mentally retarded was mailed to each doctoral level Fellow in the Section of Psychology of the American Association on Mental Deficiency. From the total group of 113 *S*s, ninety-four (83.2 percent) responded. The results reveal: (1) the percentage of the *S*s' experience spent in providing clinical services to retardates, (2) a ranking of the espoused theoretical approaches used by the *S*s, (3) rankings of various modes of therapy, (4) opinions regarding the value of counseling and psychotherapy according to level of intelligence and in selected problem areas, (5) the frequency of current use of counseling and psychotherapy in selected problem areas of retardation, and (6) rankings of factors that limit the use of counseling and psychotherapy with retardates.

Yanki, K. A., and O'Connor, N.: Measurable effects of group psychotherapy with defective delinquents. *Journal of Mental Science, 100*:944-952, 1954.

Seven mildly retarded psychopathic youths underwent psychotherapy for six months.

Yepsen, L.: Counseling the mentally retarded. *American Journal of Mental Deficiency, 57*:205-213, 1952.

Discusses the aim of counseling as development of an adjustable individual and the limitations of counseling. Gives important questions a counselor must answer and some common practices. States that similar procedures can be used in counseling mentally retarded but that goals must be more immediate.

Yonge, K. A., and O'Connor, N.: Measurable effects of group psychotherapy with defective delinquents. *Journal of Mental Science, 100*:944-952, 1954.

A group of seven institutionalized retarded adolescents with psychopathic character traits were treated experimentally over a six-month period with a view to assessing the therapeutic value of group discussion methods. The experimental group showed significant improvement in attitudes, workshop behavior, and diligence.

Zook, L., and Unkovic, C.: Areas of concern for the counselor in a diagnostic clinic for mentally retarded children. *Mental Retardation, 6*(3):19-24, 1968.

Discuss the dilemma of the counselor in: (1) providing a specific and realistic assessment of the extent of the child's retardation so that optimum training progress may be achieved, and (2) conveying empathetic encouragement and hope to aid parental acceptance. Approaches to information conveyance and collection, to aid the counselor as mediator of the parent-child relationship, are discussed.

Appendix C

SELECT FILMS ON MENTAL RETARDATION: AN ANNOTATION* CARE OF THE YOUNG RETARDED CHILD

This film will be of interest to individuals concerned with early child development. "Care of the Young Retarded Child" illustrates the importance of an adequate understanding on the part of parents and those working with the retarded regarding the normal progression of the motor-perceptual developmental phases of early childhood. A lack of awareness of the "signs" indicating retardation or other childhood diseases has caused many parents to become frustrated when their child has failed to learn or develop at a normal pace. In such cases, a progression of unpleasant failure experiences has often followed for the child. This film provides an overview of the basic principles of child development, diagnosis, training, and care of retarded children with varying levels of adaptive behavior. In addition, many of the day-to-day problems facing parents of the retarded are displayed. A flyer providing information for discussion leaders is included with the film. (16mm, Color, 18 min.)

International Film Bureau, Inc.
332 South Michigan Avenue
Chicago, Illinois 60604

Kinsmen NIMR Building
(York University)
4700 Keele Street
Downsview, Toronto, Canada

Association-Industrial Films
333 Adelaide Street
West, Third Floor
Toronto, Canada

---

* Taken from McGovern, K. B., and Brummer, E. R.: Films in Mental Retardation: A Select Annotated Bibliography. Rehabilitation Research and Training Center in Mental Retardation, University of Oregon, Working Paper No. 68, March, 1973.

DANNY AND NICKY

This two-part film portrays the life styles of two mongoloid children, Danny, age 9 and Nicky, age 14. Nicky has been placed in an institution for the retarded, whereas Danny lives at home and attends a special education class. Throughout the fifty-minute film, the assets and limitations of the two environmental settings are contrasted. For example, Nicky is observed interacting with peers in a large shabby recreation room at the institution, while being supervised by custodial aides. In comparison, Danny is shown receiving individualized attention at home from his parents and siblings. Particularly dramatic is the contrast between the responsiveness of the two boys, underscoring the implications of environmental effects upon behavior. (16mm, Color, 56 min.)

Association-Industrial Films
333 Adelaide Street, West, Third Floor
Toronto, Canada

Contemporary/McGraw-Hill
828 Custer Avenue
Evanston, Illinois 60202

Contemporary/McGraw-Hill
330 West 42nd Street
New York, New York 10036

Contemporary/McGraw-Hill
1714 Stockton Street
San Francisco, California

Kinsmen NIMR Building
(York Univ.) 4700 Keele Street
Downsview, Toronto, Canada

Special Education Instructional Materials Center
Clinical Services Building
University of Oregon
Eugene, Oregon 97403

HANDLE WITH CARE

"Handle With Care" depicts the varied services received by selected mentally retarded persons in the greater Los Angeles area, often with the initial help of one particular agency. The emphasis is on implementation of the "fixed-point-of-referral" concept.

Other points made by the film are: the importance of early identification and treatment; the unique contributions to the habilitation process made by various professionals; and, the importance of the integration of these contributions.

The film was produced in the early 1960's and is dated in some respects. The important points it communicates are still relevant, however. (16mm, B&W, 28 min.)

National Association for Retarded Children
420 Lexington Avenue
New York, New York 10017

Association-Industrial Films
333 Adelaide Street, West, Third Floor
Toronto, Canada

INTRODUCING THE MENTALLY RETARDED

Views of the etiology and prognosis of mental retardation prevalent ten to fifteen years ago are reflected in this film. It is a disease extremely difficult to control or prevent and the mentally retarded *cannot* develop socially adaptive behaviors.

The opening scene shows pilots and stewardesses getting off a plane while the narrator informs us that the mentally retarded throughout the nation will never be able to achieve sociological status as pilot or stewardess. The problems that face the retarded throughout their lives are also stressed. The medical aspects of mental retardation are emphasized.

Today, the approach to mental retardation emphasizes that the retarded *can* learn through appropriate methodology. Consequently, this film could probably be used best as an illustration of a certain "era" in the history of mental retardation. It could

provide a contrast between how the retarded were dealt with ten years ago and the methodologies currently being used, such as precision teaching, token economy systems, and operant conditioning. Using the film in this context would illustrate the progress being made in the area of mental retardation. (16mm, B&W, 15 min.)

Division of Mental Health
Jefferson City, Missouri 65701

Psychological Cinema Register
Audio-Visual Aids Library
Pennsylvania State University
University Park, Pennsylvania

MENTAL RETARDATION

Part 1

Part 1 presents an overview of types of mental retardation, current research and research accomplishments, and the importance of early diagnosis and adequate community facilities in the treatment of mental retardation. A thread heavily woven throughout the presentation is that of hope and humanitarianism.

There are two very interesting and useful segments of this film. The first deals with a comprehensive evaluation and formulation of plans for treatment of a mentally retarded child. Several important points are made here, e.g. the importance of early diagnosis and the contributions made by different disciplines. The discussion of on-going research and the impact of research on treatment is also well done.

An unfortunate aspect of the film, however, is that while the narrator is saying that the mentally retarded are "more like us than unlike us," stress is placed upon the severe end of the continuum of retardation. There is relatively little mention of the 85 percent of diagnosed retardates at the upper end of the continuum.

Because of the severity of the physical anomalies presented,

audiences should be selected and/or screened prior to showing the film. (16mm, Color, 30 min.)

Part 2

The major focus of Part 2 is the movement toward keeping retarded children at home and includes a discussion of the community facilities and agencies necessary to accomplish the goals of this movement.

Using the child who was diagnosed in Part 1 as a focus, the provision of public school training classes, day care centers, vocational training and placement, etc. included in this second section provides a fairly complete overview. The presentation of special education, vocational training in the schools, sheltered workshops, and other types of vocational preparation is enhanced by the use of real-life settings for filming.

Bureau of Audio-Visual Instruction
University of Wisconsin
P. O. Box 2093
1327 University Avenue
Madison, Wisconsin 53701

Special Education Instructional Materials Center
Clinical Services Building
University of Oregon
Eugene, Oregon 97403

Pennsylvania State University
Audio-Visual Services
University Park, Pennsylvania 16802

OUT OF THE SHADOWS

This film demonstrates an intensive training program for severely retarded children in an institution. When the children enter the institution most of them require constant nursing care. After a year in the program, which is based on a well-organized reinforcement system, they are toilet-trained, able to feed themselves properly, and able to travel institution grounds alone.

Parents, special educators, institution personnel, etc., who view this film will be given two major messages: reinforcement therapy is effective; and there is hope for the more severely retarded child. (16mm, Color, 17 min.)

Bureau of Visual Instruction
6 Bailey Hall
The University of Kansas
Lawrence, Kansas 66044

SOMEBODY WAITING

This very exciting film illustrates how staff members at Sonoma State Hospital in Napa, California made a variety of therapeutic improvements at a cottage for severely retarded, multiply handicapped children. The narration of the film, which includes voices of several staff members, demonstrates how these severely disabled children were being habilitated prior to implementation of a new program. The apathy of the residents was matched by the apathy of the staff. During the film, the staff members illustrate several creative changes. For example, a physical therapist taught the staff how to use some important principles; the children were exposed to live rabbits and roosters; members of the community were encouraged to interact with the severely disabled children. By altering the ward's activities and staff attitudes, an alternative, refreshing form of milieu therapy is provided for an almost forgotten population of disabled children.

Since this film is likely to cause a variety of emotional reactions among the viewers, it should be closely monitored. (16mm, Color, 25 min.)

Extension Media Center
University of California
Berkeley, California 94720

Special Education Instructional Materials Center
Clinical Services Building
University of Oregon
Eugene, Oregon 97403

THE NATURE OF MENTAL RETARDATION

This first film in a series of 5 portrays basic concepts, definitions, and classifications related to the term, "mental retardation." It begins by contrasting the varying rates of development of young retarded and nonretarded children and illustrates the fact that retarded children have a more arduous time adjusting to their environment. The remainder of the film outlines the categories of retardation, including brain infection, toxic agents, physical damage, disorders of metabolism, brain tumors, prenatal disease or damage, postnatal disease, and social or environmental causes. Individuals manifesting mental retardation associated with conditions such as microcephaly and hydrocephaly are also presented.

The film stresses that a perfect correlation between the various causes of retardation and potential adaptive behavior does not exist. The importance of thoroughly assessing behavioral, emotional, and cognitive assets and limitations is emphasized. Through a coordinated comprehensive rehabilitation plan, the family, teacher, physician, and counselor can provide the individual classified as retarded with sensible social, educational, and vocational learning experiences. (16mm, Color, 25 min.)

National Medical Audiovisual Center
(Annex) Station K
Atlanta, Georgia 30324

The Special Education Instructional Materials Center
1115 Louisiana Street
Lawrence, Kansas 66044

Bureau of Visual Instruction
6 Bailey Hall
The University of Kansas
Lawrence, Kansas 66044

THEY CALL ME NAMES

The effects of the stereotype that has developed in reference to the retarded are displayed in this film, leading to a fresh

awareness of the cruelty of stigmatization. During part of the presentation, children tell their own stories about how it feels to be retarded and what it means to be stereotyped.

"They Call Me Names" also portrays people's reactions to the retarded child as another aspect of the effect of the stereotype. Reactions of fear and/or apprehension have been the source of many misguided decisions and ideas. For example, such feelings have often caused parents to institutionalize a child who could have been kept at home.

The error of evaluating a person on the basis of IQ alone is discussed. It is emphasized that evaluation must consider the total person, including his level of adaptive behavior.

Excerpts from the Special Olympics held for the retarded are presented, meant as evidence that, when provided with appropriate education and respect for their self-image on the part of society, individuals classified as retarded can achieve levels of maturation that approximate that of normals. (16mm, Color, 16 min.)

Educational Films for the Exceptional
8519 Ceylon Avenue
Pico Rivera, California 90660

The Learning Garden
1081 Westwood Blvd.
Suite 213
Los Angeles, California 90024

TO SOLVE A HUMAN PUZZLE

To demonstrate progress in the area of mental retardation, interviews are conducted with recipients of the Kennedy awards for research, service, etc., in the area. Several approaches to prevention, education, and habilitation of the mentally retarded are presented around the central theme of the film, new hope for the mentally retarded.

In a particularly moving segment of the film, a group of parents discuss the dynamics involved in their own acceptance of their retarded child. Helping professionals who work with these

parents might well benefit from this discussion of the dynamics of adjustment.

Since the film was produced, several of the movements cited as radical have become routine. It is interesting to note the dramatic advances in the field of mental retardation in a relatively short period of time. (16mm, B&W, 18 min.)

National Association for Retarded Children
420 Lexington Avenue
New York, New York 10017

WHO ARE THE WINNERS?

This film is based on the Milwaukee Project, a study of a preventive approach to cultural familial retardation. The project, a research program designed by Dr. Rick Heber and staff, has implications for those concerned with the mentally retarded and with the relationship between poverty and mental retardation.

Through this program, infants who have a high probability of becoming retarded are placed into an extensive training program for a long-term period. In addition, their mothers are given vocational, social, and educational training opportunities.

The viewer witnesses the contrasting behaviors presented by the children who were in the extensive learning program and those who were placed in a no-treatment control group. Although the long range effects of this program are still unknown, the film and the findings upon which it is based, suggest that a large percentage of cultural familial retardation can be prevented through an enriched early learning program. (16mm, Color, 20 min.)

University Extension
University of Wisconsin
Bureau of Audio-Visual Instruction
P. O. Box 2093
Madison, Wisconsin 53703

WHO WILL TIE MY SHOES?

The nature of this film requires that it be followed by appropriate discussion. "Who Will Tie My Shoes?" opens with a state-

ment to the effect that the public is apathetic about the role of the mentally retarded in society. It then proceeds to tell the story of the retarded persons in the institutions of New York City. Viewers learn that for many retarded individuals the waiting list is over a year; for some, it is as long as four years. Then viewers are confronted with a sensitivity group composed of retarded persons. During the group process, the members give emotional responses to questions regarding what it means to be retarded; how this affects them today; how it affected them when they were children. Another group therapy scene is presented, in which parents respond to the question of what it means to have a retarded child.

The film has several shortcomings. Some of the content is out-of-date. For example, the narrator talks about cultural or sociological brain damage. Nevertheless, the film retains its value, except for use as an introduction to mental retardation. (16mm, B&W, 60 min.)

Association-Sterling Films
8165 Directors Row
Dallas, Texas 75247

Mr. Charles Nelson
CCM Films
866 Third Avenue
New York, New York 10022

SELECT FILMS ON REHABILITATION AND COUNSELING WITH THE MENTALLY RETARDED: AN ANNOTATION*

Assessment

Five methods used in the vocational evaluation of rehabilitation clients are described and demonstrated in "Assessment." These methods are: psychological testing; work samples; situational assessment; job analysis; and job tryout. Advantages and disadvantages of each approach are discussed.

---

* Taken from McGovern, K. B., and Brummer, E. R.: Films in Mental Retardation: A Select Annotated Bibliography. Rehabilitation Research and Training Center in Mental Retardation, University of Oregon, Working Paper No. 68, March, 1973.

"Assessment" would be informative and interesting for rehabilitation counselors and work evaluators, especially. (16mm, Color, 26 min.)

Materials Development Center
Rehabilitation and Manpower Services
University of Wisconsin-Stout
Menomonie, Wisconsin 54751

COUNSELING THE MENTALLY RETARDED (FIVE PARTS)

This series of films was developed at the University of Kansas and was based on the proceedings of a conference on special problems in the vocational rehabilitation of the mentally retarded. It is one of the few resources in the field which is directly relevant to all phases of the vocational rehabilitation process with this group. The five films can be used separately or sequentially.

Besides being useful for pre-service or in-service training of rehabilitation counselors, the films could be used very productively with a number of other groups. Teachers, parents, social workers, all others who are concerned with the adjustment of the retarded and with his ability to work as a key aspect of that adjustment, would find these films informative. Four of the five films are described below; the first film in the series entitled, "The Nature of Mental Retardation" is described in the previous section.

National Medical Audiovisual Center
(Annex) Station K
Atlanta, Georgia 30324

The Special Education Instructional Materials Center
1115 Louisiana Street
Lawrence, Kansas 66044

Bureau of Visual Instruction
6 Bailey Hall
The University of Kansas
Lawrence, Kansas 66044

PART II: EVALUATING THE RETARDED CLIENT

The importance of the individualized evaluation of the client throughout the rehabilitation process is emphasized in this film. Of particular value in arriving at a valid assessment of the client are (1) multidisciplinary evaluations, and (2) viewing the client in his own lifespace, outside of the counselor's office. The psychologist, physician, vocational evaluator, psychiatrist, all have valuable data to be integrated by the rehabilitation counselor into a complete picture of the assets and limitations of his client. Since adaptive behavior is at least as important in the client's adjustment as intellectual competence, and since adaptive behavior can be taught, it is imperative that as much of the client's behavior as possible be observed by the counselor.

Evaluation of the client is only one aspect of the evaluation process. The other component is the evaluation of community resources and programs. Only by assessing both components, can progress toward rehabilitation be made. (16mm, Color, 20 min.)

PART III: TRAINING RESOURCES AND TECHNIQUES FOR THE RETARDED CLIENT

In this reel of the series, the counselor is presented as an intermediary and expediter of community resources. Again, the integration of several professional disciplines into the rehabilitation process is stressed.

The training resource of the sheltered workshop and the training technique of a token economy system are given special emphasis. Four guidelines for training programs are given: realism, reward, recognition, and responsibility. The goals of training for the mentally retarded are: occupational responsibility, self-esteem, and community integration. (16mm, Color, 20 min.)

PART IV: COUNSELING THE RETARDED CLIENT AND HIS FAMILY

The mentally retarded person has the same emotional and psychological needs as any other person, but is usually frustrated in his attempts to satisfy these needs. The film suggests that by helping to rearrange his client's values, the counselor can help to have his client's needs met.

The importance of the family in the adjustment of the retardate is stressed. Without attention to possible problems in the home, or to lack of support for the client's independence, the counselor may be short-circuiting his own efforts toward facilitating the success of the client.

Helping the mentally retarded client to learn to behave like other people is a major purpose of counseling. It is also clear that behavior in one situation may not be appropriate to another situation and the counselor may have to help in the transition. Such transitions are likely to be necessary at four "crisis points" in the life of the client. The importance of maintaining contact is thus underscored. (16mm, Color, 20 min.)

PART V: POST-PLACEMENT COUNSELING

In this reel of the series, teachers, counselors, parents, and employers talk about the adjustment problems of mental retardates. Total life adjustment is the focus, including the crucial hours before 9:00 a.m. and after 5:00 p.m.

Examples of retardates' difficulties with day-to-day stresses of life are presented. The lack of leisure time activities, inadequate preparation for sexual relationships, community misconceptions and negative attitudes are all problems which are discussed.

This is the most aesthetic film of the series. (16mm, Color, 25 min.)

GRADUATION

"Graduation" follows a group of mentally retarded young persons into the community after their graduation from a high school special class. While their need for special services continues, the necessary resources are frequently not available. The dearth of sheltered workshops, activity centers, and recreational programs is illustrated with the aid of statistics drawn from the follow-up study on which the film is based.

The film would lend itself to fund-raising as well as to training activities. (16mm, Color, 20 min.)

The Stanfield House
900 Euclid Avenue
Santa Monica, California 90403

GROOMING FOR MEN

Designed for use directly with mentally retarded persons, the film's purpose is to communicate the importance of good grooming and personal hygiene in both social and job settings. Using a cartoon character named Albert, the film covers proper body care and selection and care of clothing.

"Grooming for Men" would be especially useful in a group discussion situation, possibly augmented by role-playing. (16mm, Color, 30 min.)

Materials Development Center
Rehabilitation and Manpower Services
University of Wisconsin-Stout
Menomonie, Wisconsin 54751

HORIZONS FOR THE MENTALLY RETARDED

This film shows job analysis, as part of a meaningful training program, can open up many important jobs for the retarded. It was produced at the Albertson Training Center on Long Island, New York, and is narrated by the Center's director, Henry Viscardi. Viscardi maintains that the most important step in expanding job opportunities for the retarded is job analysis, both within the workshop and in the community. When jobs are broken down into their component parts within the workshop, the result is a wider variety of tasks that can be learned effectively by persons with intellectual limitations. Task analysis in industry will accomplish the same goals. This means that many jobs are available to the retarded other than sorting nuts and bolts or sewing bean bags. Job analyses have shown that there are a large number of jobs, e.g. keypunching, computer coding, console operating, sautering, for example, that can be mastered by retarded individuals.

This film would be appropriate not only for rehabilitationists interested in the area of workshops for the retarded, but to employers who are reluctant to hire the retarded. (16mm, Color, 20 min.)

Abilities, Inc.
Human Resources School
Albertson, New York 11507

A LIGHT FOR JOHN

The film dramatizes a day in the life of a thirty-five-year-old mentally retarded man who lives with his elderly mother. She narrates the film, describing John's activities, his problems, and her attitude toward them. The feeling dimensions beyond her words are emphatically shown in the film: loneliness, apathy, resignation, interdependency.

The film is dated in some respects; e.g. the cars and clothing are out-of-style and the quality of sound is not good. Despite these factors, however, the film does an adequate, at times articulate, job of presenting the situation of mentally retarded man who has not received special services. The fact that relatively few films deal with the adult retardate in the community increases the value of "A Light for John." (16mm, B&W, 22 min.)

Division of Cinema
University of Southern California
University Park
Los Angeles, California 90007

OPERANT CONDITIONING: A TOKEN ECONOMY

Produced at Camarillo State Hospital under the direction of Raymond McBurney, M.D. and Jacqueline Montgomery, Ph.D., this film describes a token economy system employed by the hospital staff with their population of retarded residents. Evidence is presented to illustrate the utility of this type of treatment system for retarded persons living within an institutional environment. The description focuses on a three-level token economy system through which retarded residents learn adaptive behavior. After acquiring skills and behaviors defined for the first level, the residents are confronted with progressively higher levels of competency demanded by levels B and C. The behaviors appropriate to each level are clarified, and the types of reinforcers built into each level are illustrated and explained. A major goal of the program is to teach the client a set of behaviors that will increase his likelihood of functioning effectively in the outside world.

In summary, this film provides a non-technical overview of the

principles related to a token system, including the roles of various staff members. This film can be well used with rehabilitation and mental health personnel interested in behavioral approaches. (16mm, Color, 15 min.)

Jacqueline Montgomery, Ph.D.
Box A, Division 4
Camarillo, California 93010

TEACHING THE MENTALLY RETARDED: A POSITIVE APPROACH

The "positive approach" used in this film is behavior modification. By following the progress of profoundly retarded children who are taught by this approach, several points are dramatically made.

Beginning with the first scene in which profoundly retarded children are shown performing stereotypic behaviors, the film proceeds to counter many of the usual objections to behavior modification. That is, the custodial care, failure, and hopelessness depicted in this scene provide a vivid background for the progress which is shown later.

Several of the basic tenets of such an approach are presented in non-technical terms. For example, the importance of immediacy and precision in providing reinforcement, of breaking tasks down into simple components, and of the contiguity of primary and secondary rewards are presented through a series of episodes showing an attendant working with a profoundly retarded boy. The method is presented as simple and practical, with dramatic implications for opening the world to the retarded.

The film is not designed to make its audience into skilled behavioral technicians. Instead, it realistically and powerfully presents a very viable approach to the habilitation of the mentally retarded. (16mm, B&W, 25 min.)

National Medical Audiovisual Center
(Annex) Station K
Atlanta, Georgia 30324

THERE WAS A DOOR

This dated, British film's theme of non-institutional treatment of the retarded centers around the problems of one family faced with the decision of whether to commit their nineteen-year-old son.

The largest portion of the film, in terms of time and number of words, deals with the mentally retarded as "poor unfortunates." Several stereotypes are perpetuated; e.g. they are adults with the minds of children, they have a preference for routine work, some "even" learn to think. There is only perfunctory attention paid to community treatment implemented through activity centers and sheltered workshops. The need for and advantages of such facilities is underplayed.

One possible way in which "There Was a Door" might be used with a group interested in the habilitation of the mentally retarded would be as a contrast with where we are in philosophy and treatment today. (16mm, B&W, 30 min.)

Audio-Visual Center
Film Rental Services
University of Kansas
746 Massachusetts Street
Lawrence, Kansas 66044

Psychological Cinema Register
Audio-Visual Aids Library
Pennsylvania State University
University Park, Pennsylvania 16802

TO LIGHTEN THE SHADOWS

Recreational activities for the mentally retarded is the focus of this film. Children with mental retardation are portrayed participating in normal camping activities such as boating, fishing, crafts, and singing. The fact that these campers have special needs is presented, along with the fact that they are very much like other children. (16mm, B&W, 20 min.)

International Film Bureau, Inc.
332 South Michigan Avenue
Chicago, Illinois 60604

TRAINING FOR TOMORROW

This film focuses on the job evaluation and job training program carried out at the MacDonald Training Center in Tampa, Florida, illustrating the types of jobs that an individual classified as retarded can adequately perform. Retarded adolescents and adults are shown performing farming tasks, working with power tools, repairing soft drink boxes, learning basic carpentry skills, and operating a printing press. Individuals are also shown building television antennas, and operating recreational equipment at a local carnival.

The film is narrated, in part, by a retarded young adult. He explains that many individuals classified as retarded can satisfactorily perform a variety of work tasks. (16mm, Color, 14 min.)

MacDonald Training Center Foundation, Inc.
4424 Tampa Bay Boulevard
Tampa, Florida 33614

YOU'RE IT

This film points out the importance of and availability of recreational activities for retarded children and adolescents. Regarding importance, Stan Musial explains how a sequentially planned physical fitness program can contribute to the development of the basic physical skills, strengths, and endurance that will help the retarded participate in recreational activities and cope with future jobs. Also, the value of arts and crafts within the context of both vocational and avocational goals is discussed. The Boy Scout program is presented as an example of the availability of recreational activities open to the mentally retarded.

"You're It" treats this topic somewhat superficially, but it could be used as a stimulus for discussion focusing on the leisure-time activities of the retarded, an area too often overlooked by rehabilitationists.

MacDonald Training Center Foundation, Inc.
4424 Tampa Bay Boulevard
Tampa, Florida 33614

AUTHOR INDEX

SUBJECT INDEX*

A

Adaptive behavior, in retardation
  classification, 14-17
  definition, 13
  measurement problems, 14, 16
  relationship to intelligence, 16-17
  scale for measurement, 14
Agencies/programs (*see* Government)
Assessment (*see* Evaluation; Tests)

B

Behavior / modification / analysis / pro-
    gramming, 21-38, 153-176, 290-305
  acquisition of task behavior, 158-159
  conditioned reinforcers, 30
  counseling/therapy, behavioral, 283-
    284, 290-305
  data collection, 168-170
  discriminative stimuli, 26, 32
  evaluation/assessment, behavioral,
    157-158, 165, 296-299
  operants, 25-26
  prevocational model, behavioral, 111-
    114
  program operations/phases, behavior-
    al, 164-168
    contract workshop, 165
    evaluation and pre-training, 165
    follow-up, 166
    in-placement training, 165-166
    prevocational programming, 165
  reinforcers, 25, 162-164
  research, vocational, 112-113, 170-
    174
  retarded behavior, explanations for,
    26-34
    critical timing, 33-34

reinforcement history, 28-31
response deficiency, 26-28
stimulus deficiency, 31-33
system, 25-26
task analysis, 157-158
training objectives, behavioral, 155-
  157
transenvironmental programming,
  111-112, 155-168
Bibliographies (annotated), on retardation, 324-430
  counseling and psychotherapy, 358-
    412 (Appendix B)
  film, 413-430 (Appendix C)
  rehabilitation research and demon-
    stration projects, 324-358 (Ap-
    pendix B)

C

Classification systems, in retardation
  adaptive behavior, 14, 16-17
  education, 14
  etiology, 17-18, 21-24
  intelligence, 14-15
  legal-administrative, 14
  psychiatric, 14
Counseling/psychotherapy
  behavior counseling/therapy, 283-
    284, 290-303
  bibliography, annotated, 358-412
    (Appendix B)
  client characteristics, rehabilitated
    (*see* Rehabilitation)
  client variables, 276-279
  definition, 293
  efficacy, 290-291, 308-309
  film, 413-430 (Appendix C)

---

* The subject index does not include the bibliographic materials contained in
Appendices A, B, and C, pp. 318-430.

441